Barry Spector's book is a strikingly imaginative rumination on our society, reaching back into Greek mythology to illuminate the world today. It is a fascinating blend of literature, history and myth, and while we have had many critiques of contemporary America, his is unique in the way it draws upon the Greek gods to examine, with devastating accuracy, our present deities of war and greed. This is truly an original work.

HOWARD ZINN, AUTHOR OF *A PEOPLE'S HISTORY OF THE UNITED STATES*

Our world lives, loves, suffers and triumphs by myth, often unseen and unconsidered. In the tradition of Carl Jung and Joseph Campbell, Barry Spector makes myths come alive; he helps us in the desperately important task of re-imagining our way.

JACK KORNFIELD, AUTHOR OF *A PATH WITH HEART*

Barry Spector's Madness At The Gates of The City *explores how Euripides'* Bacchae, *written to warn his late fifth-century Athenian compatriots of the internal destructive forces threatening their beloved city, might help us look more honestly at the false innocence that sustains our illusions about the American dream and prevents our acknowledging its dark underside. Yet, the book ends with a beautifully voiced "story that could be true": we could lift these repressive blinders, we could learn to hear and heed an archetypal cry for initiation into a way of being in the world that honors the life-giving energies the Greeks called by the name Dionysos.*

CHRISTINE DOWNING, AUTHOR OF *THE GODDESS*

Spector uses the ancient mythical confrontation of the puritanical and dictatorial King Pentheus of Thebes with his cousin, the god Dionysus — who shows up at the gates of the city with the liberating blessings of madness as a stranger who is no stranger at all — as the paradigm for a devastating psychoanalytical critique of contemporary America's attitudes towards the imagined outsider. The power of myth is that it is eternal, and Spector not only offers much to contemplate about today's society, but also new perspectives upon an ancient classic, Euripides' tragedy of the Bacchants.

CARL RUCK, PROFESSOR OF CLASSICS, BOSTON UNIVERSITY, CO-AUTHOR OF *THE ROAD TO ELEUSIS: UNVEILING THE SECRET OF THE MYSTERIES* AND *PERSEPHONE'S QUEST: ENTHEOGENS AND THE ORIGINS OF RELIGION*

In this disturbing and evocative book, Barry Spector offers us a trenchant commentary on the ignorance, pathos and shadows residing in the American addiction to innocence. Mythologically wise and instructive, the author gives us keys to the hidden kingdom, and the potential to participate in an emerging new and creative story as we once again join forces with the genius inherent in myth and the guidance and warnings that it holds. This is a work that should be read by anyone who wants to make a difference. To respond and become proactive in the mythic tasks that are now upon us, our basic human nature is challenged by Spector to deepen, discover, evolve. We must become mything links.

JEAN HOUSTON, AUTHOR OF *A MYTHIC LIFE*

ISBN 13: 978-1-58790-173-7
ISBN 10: 1-58790-173-0
Library of Congress Control Number: 2009936499

Spector, Barry.
Madness at the Gates of the City : the Myth of American Innocence / Barry Spector.
p. cm.
ISBN 978-1-58790-173-7
Includes bibliographical references and index.
1. United States–Civilization. 2. History–United States. 3. Mythology, Greek. 4. Mythology,
United States. 5. Mythology, Classical. 6. National characteristics, American. 7. Social
psychology–United States. 8. Popular culture –United States –Psychological aspects. I. Title.

E169.1 .S7145 2010
973—dc22
2009936499

Printed in the USA by Regent Press
2747 Regent Street
Berkeley, CA 94705
www.regentpress.net

MADNESS

at the

GATES OF THE CITY

THE MYTH OF
AMERICAN INNOCENCE

∽

BARRY SPECTOR

REGENT PRESS
BERKELEY, CALIFORNIA

Thanks and all praises

FOR INSPIRATION FROM THE FIRST GENERATION: Carl Jung, Joseph Campbell, Marija Gimbutas.

FOR WISDOM FROM THE SECOND GENERATION: Robert Johnson, James Hillman, Robert Bly, Marion Woodman, Christine Downing, Howard Zinn, Noam Chomsky, Milton Woolf.

FOR MENTORING FROM THE THIRD GENERATION: Michael Meade, Malidoma Somé, Jack Kornfield, Luis Rodriguez, Martin Prechtel, Doug Von Koss, Marsh McCall, Cathleen Rountree, William Brater, Thomas Chance, Michael Smith, Rose Bank.

FOR SUPPORT FROM FRIENDS: Larry Robinson, Cynthia Kishi, Dan and Dale Zola, George Viney, Gershon Reiter, Janis Dolnick, Maurice Wren, Alan Cohen, Alexa Singer, Marc Telles, Alan and Laura Hawkins, Geoff and Patria Brown, Paul Feder, Paul Robins, Freyja Anderson, Barbara and Gerry Hiken, Barbara Clark, Zann Erick, Robert Badame, Doug Ballon, John Carlson, Greg Kimura, Conni Piesinger, Marc Deprey, Michael Stone, Dyane Sherwood, Hank and Maggie Skewis, Bob Jenne, Judith Lynne, Betty Clinton, Carol Fitzgerald, Bill Denham, Adrian Bozzolo, Damon Miller, Robin Mankey, Marcia Rayene, Ralph Bartholemew, Mark Weinman, Leah Aronow, Lana Brewer, Jon Spector, Richard Blau, Jesse Moore, Jo Burrows, Melinda Jean, Marty Pulvers, Antonio Sacre, Victoria Lee, Tom Muthig, Judy Kasle, Jane Kos, Jessie Moore, Carolyn Power, Joe and Joan Sutton, Joe Shakarchi, Leona Tockey, Laura Gans, Alan Ptashek, Ward Ashman, Wendolyn Bird, Locke and Chandrama Anderson, Richard Bale,

Santiago Escruceria, Charlie and Linda Bloom, Carolyn Baker, Shepherd Bliss, John Gunty, Wil and Meghan Nolan, Hari Meyers, Richard Naegele and the men of Gualala and Mendocino, especially the young men.

FOR LOVE FROM THE NEXT GENERATION: Max, Alex, Emily, and those who will come after us.

AND DEDICATION OF THIS BOOK TO MAYA: my editor, mentor, poet, priestess, storyteller, co-creator, sounding board, partner and love of my life, who patiently tolerates my harangues and pontifications and brings my insights down to earth. If I have created something of value, it is all due to her.

CONTENTS

feminine. The American hero. The redemption hero. The paradox of the outsider. Boy psychology. American shadow myths. The twin towers. Mythic views of the twin towers. Revenge and the woman in the burkha. Nature bats last.

PART THREE: WAKING FROM THE AMERICAN DREAM

FOREWORD

When political, economic and religious leaders no longer offer any solutions to the massive crises that confront us, it's time to re-imagine who we are as individuals and as a nation. *Madness at the Gates of the City: The Myth of American Innocence* shows how America regularly re-enacts old patterns that cause us to subvert our goals, miss the deeper meaning in events and, perhaps, fail to prevent our headlong slide into cultural collapse. But by looking at our history, politics and popular culture through the lenses of Greek mythology, indigenous wisdom and archetypal psychology, Barry Spector discovers new hope in very old ways of thinking.

To the Greeks, Dionysus was the god of paradox and extremes, of passion and masks, of ecstatic joy and vengeance, of tragic drama and of madness. But that was long ago. Or was it? After two millennia of Christianity and five hundred years of scientific rationalism, Dionysus and his modern substitutes persist in our imagination as images of "the Other." He is everything that America has cast into the shadows: woman, race, nature and the body.

European settlers brought a legacy of puritanical intolerance to the New World. They developed literature, theology and political rhetoric that gradually coalesced into a mythology of divinely inspired new beginnings, heroic destiny and good intentions — the myth of American innocence. However, these stories covered over a legacy of racism and violent imperialism. Fear of the dark, Dionysian strangers at our doors — first Indians, then witches, then slaves and their descendants, then communists — both stimulated our anxieties and held them in check. Nearly four hundred years later, these mythic narratives have not lost their hold upon us. Now the fear of terrorism helps to define us as "not them."

The Other provides a unique window into American history, and especially our current political madness. This irrepressible aspect of both soul and society may re-emerge at any moment, bringing either mass chaos or longed-for healing. The choice is up to us, because Dionysus is part of us.

Madness at the Gates of the City should appeal to anyone interested in myth, Classics, history, progressive politics or psychology. It will provide much new insight for people searching for new ways to understand how we behave in the world and what we might become.

ROBERT A. JOHNSON, AUTHOR OF *WE* AND *INNER WORK*

Be good to us, you girl-crazy goat!

We the poets begin and end our singing through you.

And it's impossible without you.

Without you, we cannot remember our sacred songs!

HOMERIC HYMN TO DIONYSUS, SEVENTH CENTURY B.C.

PART ONE

THE MYTH OF DIONYSUS

INTRODUCTION

I have lived on the lip of insanity, wanting to know reasons,
knocking on a door. It opens. I've been knocking from the inside!

"Living on the lip of insanity" is Jelaluddin Rumi's thirteenth-century description of a state of mind, a desperate longing for meaning, when old explanations no longer make sense and all the signposts of convention and morality have been obliterated.

It also describes the madness of American public life in our time of diminished imagination. We have constructed walls, both physical and emotional, to protect against the terror outside. Inside, while we distract ourselves with consumerism and fundamentalism, the anxiety drains our vitality. If we accidentally lift the veil of denial, we view the madness on *this* side of the wall. Shocked by the implications, we quickly drop it.

Long before 9/11 our noblest intentions were corrupted into their opposites. The America that once symbolized to the entire world a place of opportunity, where people could overcome the past and begin anew, evolved into a symbol of willful ignorance and exclusion and a purveyor of innocent violence and violent innocence. Americans came to believe in a story that all capacity for goodness resides *here*, within the walls, while absolute evil stalks us from out *there*.

Introduction means "leading inward." This book invites you inside our mythic walls and asks you to examine your own ideas of freedom, community and individualism. When we acknowledge that we've dug ourselves into a hole, we must first stop digging and then realize how we have colluded with stories that no longer work. Only then we can begin — initiate — something new, drop our innocence, create new myths and rejoin the human and natural communities.

Myths are the stories we tell ourselves about ourselves. They organize and justify existence and speak to our unresolved conflicts, needs and fantasies. The world's oldest stories appear in our dreams, our relationships — and our politics. Caught in these mythic patterns, we are likely to encounter grimly predictable results, but only when we live our lives unconscious of them. Indeed, awareness of our myths is critical to imagining new — or extremely old — solutions to our terrible contemporary problems. To knock down the walls of our mental incarceration, we need to start asking ourselves what myths do *all* Americans share? What myths are our leaders enacting for us all?

As the post-modern world lurches toward the disasters and bereavements that signal the end of an age, we turn to myth to comprehend the elemental forces that move through our lives, to know who we are, to understand which stories inform our consciousness. For much too long, we've been telling ourselves stories that hatred is inevitable and that violence is the only way to resolve disputes. We've been telling them for so long and so insistently that they have become our myths.

Desperate to stay on this side of the "lip of insanity," we have become actors in stories that have played out countless times. *The myths are not in us; we are in the myths.* Indeed, we each live at the intersections of several myths. But the most profound myths don't provide answers; they provoke the imagination, inviting us to plunge deeper into life. The characters in myths may change, but myths themselves never die. "They are only sleeping at the bottom of our minds," wrote poet Stanley Kunitz, "waiting for our call."[1]

Despite the passage of time, Greek myths still remain vital because each generation, and at each stage of life — adolescence, productive adulthood, elderhood — we can perceive new meanings. We gain insight when we consider myths from the perspectives of different characters. No single version can completely encapsulate a myth. Myths are always multiple in meaning, reflecting our own multiple "selves." Yet one thing is certain: these

fundamental themes can still move us as deeply as they affected ancient
Greeks.

GREEK MYTH

Why should we care about ancient Greece? The reasons have changed often
over the 500 years since Europe rediscovered Plato and the Parthenon.
Renaissance artists, after 1,500 years of Church restriction, learned of people
like themselves who had valued the individual and praised the beauty of
the human body. Eighteenth century revolutionaries studied Greek ideas
of democracy, which influenced social change movements everywhere.
Romantic artists and poets employed images from the old stories that
conveyed relational and feminine values. Nineteenth century researchers
used the Greek foundations of rational thought to replace old religious
dogmas with individualism and science as modernity's highest ideals.

The Renaissance, however, also saw decades of savage religious wars and
thousands of witch burnings. Eighteenth century colonialism ravaged tribal
culture, and nineteenth century imperialism raped the Earth itself. In the
twentieth century, humanity endured *world* wars, unspeakable genocides,
nuclear devastation, environmental decline and frenzies of conspicuous
yet unsatisfying consumption. Glorification of the individual brought
narcissism, loneliness and *alienation* — the condition of the outsider,
estranged from both society and his own body.

Careless inattention to democracy resulted in the tyranny of
corporations and religious fundamentalists, a state of constant fear
and perpetual war. Science birthed the most powerful god of our age,
materialism, which mocks our creative and spiritual lives. Reduced to the
category of environmental rapists, we joke nervously about spending our
children's inheritance. Still, despite the dissatisfaction and complaints that
life was better in the "old days," few of us have any sense of just *how much* we
have lost, how deeply diminished our lives actually are. We literally cannot
imagine it. Who can remember how much they have forgotten? Meanwhile,
attempting to address our spiritual vacuum, religious institutions merely
leave us malnourished.

We fear — *perhaps we wish* — that we are at the edge of catastrophe ("to turn downward"). We veil our anxieties but know we must ultimately face a vast, ancestral grief that edges closer with each headline.

Yet underneath the masks of believer, consumer, alcoholic or normal neurotic lives something older — an *indigenous soul*.* Searching for it, millions have sampled Asian spirituality and discovered contemplative practices that ground their lives in authentic values. Others, however, found that forms that evolved on ground not of their ancestors are too alien. Now, when we look to Greek myth, it is because we seek nourishment in modes of meaning that fit our own consciousness. The American soul may well need the images that Europe created before Christianity.

The Greek deities were the dream-creations of *poets*, not of priests; and other poets kept their stories alive by re-imagining them. Even if we aren't Greek, as psychologist James Hillman writes, these stories "...work in our psyches whether we like it or not...unless we understand that these tales depict the basic motifs of the Western psyche, we remain unaware of... our psychological dynamics.[2] Here is the danger of not knowing our myths: if we remain unaware — or *innocent* — of trauma, we continuously re-enact it.

Women in the 1970s were the first in our time to re-imagine Greek images. Athena, Aphrodite, Persephone and Artemis are some of the guiding deities of feminism. Still older goddesses (Demeter and Gaia) are the Earth Mothers who inspire environmentalism. Behind them all stands *Mnemosyne,* memory herself, mother of the Muses who serve her by rendering her essence — history — into art. The memory of more natural ways has never completely left our indigenous bones. The ancients knew that it was only Memory, giving birth to art, who could defeat Time.

Men, however, have been privileged to assume masculine images of God, which, sadly, are the models for tyrannical rule at every level of organization. Men must confront the entire history of patriarchy and understand how divine figures like Zeus and Apollo — and Christ — were constructed to oppress women. But they are much more than symbols of male control. They model the human psyche's astonishing diversity. Though dormant, they can still feed us. However, they demand attention, respect and active, collective *participation* in the difficult process of renewal. The psyche has infinite depth, and it can be transformed. *Psyche*, or soul, was also the Greek

* "Indigenous soul" is copyright Martín Prechtel.

word for butterfly, the beautiful creature that grew miraculously from a caterpillar. If psyches can transform, then so can nations.

This book uses an old myth to look at America. Euripides' play *The Bacchae* was first presented in 406 B.C.E., near the end of the long Peloponnesian War that destroyed Greek democracy. Highly controversial then, it still has surprising appeal to modern readers, with its startling parallels to the events of 9/11.

In this play, the god Dionysus drives the women of Thebes mad, leading them beyond its walls in ecstatic celebration. King Pentheus imprisons Dionysus, but the god escapes, causing an earthquake that destroys the palace. Pentheus responds by threatening to call out his army. By analogy, we are like Pentheus at this point halfway through the play. Several years after 9/11, America stands arrogant and alone, projecting our darkness onto dark-skinned people, denying the presence of an immense force that grows more destructive because we never heed its warnings.

Throughout the book, I will be stressing the power of imagination, which Albert Einstein declared is more important than knowledge, which J.K. Rowling says "…enables us to empathize with humans whose experiences we have never shared."[3] We must learn to stretch our imagination backward — past our more recent Judeo-Christian mythologies of misogyny and violent redemption — before we can stretch it forward.

We need to comprehend our myth of innocence, to understand the American stories we have inhabited — fully, painfully — before we can re-imagine them or tell new ones. More than any people in history, we suffer from a queasy rootlessness at the foundation of our identity. Its source is the bedrock of unexpressed grief for the incomprehensibly massive suffering that Europeans have inflicted on this continent.

While bombarding us with images of happy kitchens, pristine coastlines and family reunions, TV commercials actually give us peeks at the despair we struggle to veil. What is it we long for, and why do we feel so manipulated?

"Nostalgia" (Greek: "return") refers not to another time, but to another *place*. Even after four centuries of white (and black) residence on this land, we tread uncomfortably — and disrespectfully — upon it. We remain exiles, uninvited guests longing to be welcomed, to call it home. It will be lengthy and painful, but the way through is by re-awakening our indigenous souls. Learning *who* we are, below the easy identifications with nation, ethnicity and brand names, will lead us to love *where* we are. Myth implies that our troubles have happened before, and that there is still time to change, to awaken from this dream of innocence and return home.

Why emphasize politics in a book on mythology? Or why dwell on mythological themes in a book on history? Does it help to view history through a mythological lens? Can we find deeper meaning in the tragedy of 9/11? Indeed, haven't our conventional economic, political, psychological and theological explanations for this madness failed us? What does the madness itself want from us?

Mythology connects psychology and history, inviting them both to deeper truths. As a student of myth, I am a generalist, working — like Dionysus — at the boundaries. With apologies to academics in Classics, History, Psychology, Literature, Religion, Sociology, Anthropology, Economics, American Studies and Popular Culture, I prefer to seek out the mythic patterns that underlie events and ideas in all these areas.

I hope to convince the reader to *think* mythologically, to muse on the archetypal images that can help us understand our situation. Knowing the stories that arise in the mind (as dream and poetry) and in the nation (as myth) will help us penetrate the unique narratives that make up "America." This book traces several themes through history, always with one eye on the mythic issues. I will compare America to ancient Greece, but I will also consider even older perspectives, the bone-memory of so-called "primitive" people.

If we cannot imagine — and mourn — how much we have lost, then we lack the capacity to imagine real alternatives. We must unveil an immensely old double amnesia; we've *forgotten that we have forgotten* how to live in harmony. All this will be necessary before we can begin to tell new stories, to deepen the American Dream by first awakening from it.

Keep in mind this question of innocence. Why did commentators speak — very briefly — of losing our innocence on 9/11? Why do we continue to define ourselves this way? If America is innocent — despite 250 years of slavery, the native genocide, Hiroshima, Viet Nam, Guantanamo and Abu

Ghraib, despite our malicious intervention in literally dozens of countries — then every time we "lose" our innocence, aren't we compelled to rebuild it? Not everyone, of course, has slept through history: Novelist Walter Mosely writes, *"I have never met an African-American who was surprised by the attack on the World Trade Center."*[1]

Like actors in an annual religious drama, other forces are determined to help America lose that innocence. And the cycle continues. Who remains innocent in this world? What does our fascination with innocence force *others* to bear? How long can they bear it?

But I want to go deeper. "What is madness," asked another poet, Theodore Roethke, "but nobility of soul at odds with circumstance?" I want to pursue the myth of innocence to its core; perhaps there, only there, will we re-discover America's nobility. So this book has some very specific intentions:

1. To clarify the mythic themes in American history.
2. To encourage mythological thinking.
3. To support the re-emergence of initiation, authentic ritual, the oral tradition, deep memory and the imagination.
4. To confront readers with the hidden bedrock of their value systems.
5. To avoid muddling things with academic jargon.
6. To circle around these themes in a Hermetic, Dionysian, soulful, non-linear manner, showing more interest in surprising connections and brief liftings of the veil than in logical proof.
7. To re-imagine America's purpose in the world.

Call the world... "The vale of Soul-making."
JOHN KEATS

———

This never happened, but it always is.
SALLUSTIUS

———

I am in the world to change the world.
MURIEL RUKEYSER

———

Believe those who are seeking the truth. Doubt those who find it.
ANDRE GIDE

———

He who begins with facts will never arrive at essences.
JEAN-PAUL SARTRE

———

To be born is to be weighed down with strange gifts of the soul, with enigmas and an inextinguishable sense of exile.
BEN OKRI

01

THE CREATIVE IMAGINATION

RATHER THAN EXPLAINING myths ("explain" means to flatten and limit), we need to explore their impact on the psyche. It is a mystery; while many stories or mythic figures have no interest for us, others seem to choose us, and we must respond. Then, asks Christine Downing, "How does recognizing this god, this particular mode of sacred power, help me become aware of dark hidden urges and fears…(and) my hitherto unhonored strengths?"[1]

Mythologists are neither objective nor dispassionate, but *interested* (to "be between") in *complication* ("folding together.") We are drawn to an image or story because it is compelling and perhaps a little dangerous. We can't ignore its call to move out of our solitary awareness toward a "between" place. Its language — metaphor and paradox — confronts us with our own nature and invites us to identify the mythic patterns underlying our belief systems. This book approaches *The Bacchae* and its meaning for America by considering it through the lenses of archetypal psychology and mythopoetic, polytheistic, animistic or pagan thinking. I call this the *creative imagination*.

PURPOSE

Many traditional peoples assume that we enter life with a purpose. African teacher Malidoma Somé of the Dagara people believes that "Purpose is something that the individual has framed and articulated *prior to* coming into a community. This purpose is known to the village even before the individual's birth."[2]

Both the Biblical and scientific stories of our roots are linear, from low to high. But only modernity assumes that we have ascended from apes. Indigenous people assume that they are *descended* from gods. They typically think in terms of obligations to their ancestors and to their descendents, who will be obligated to them in turn.

This is no simplistic idealization of the "noble savage." Indeed, some traditional groups practice forms of patriarchal brutality. Others, however, still emphasize ecological and spiritual values over aggressive materialism. We must refrain from judging or patronizing; then we need to use what is valuable and relate it imaginatively to our own situation. We are searching for alternatives in the areas where modernity has failed, such as with the idea of purpose.

Plato wrote that in the afterworld each soul picks an incarnation best suited to its needs. Then it drinks from a spring called *Lethe* (Forgetfulness) and remembers nothing of what it has learned. Similarly, in Jewish tradition, it is said that when a soul is ready to be born, an angel places a finger over its lips, gesturing "Shhhh…," thereby forming the cleft found there, and the soul remembers nothing. West Africans say that souls form agreements with divine twins regarding their purpose in the next life. Heading toward birth, however, all souls embrace the "tree of forgetfulness" and again remember nothing.

These myths imply that life is an effort to fulfill forgotten obligations — a series of surprises, disappointments and initiations that shock the soul into remembering. The soul *returns* to the truth it once knew but forgot. The return is a process of "un-forgetting" (*a-lethe-ia* in Greek) that requires re-crossing that same river of forgetfulness. Truth is remembering. In a Mayan dialect, "remember" means "to feed."

From this perspective our inevitable family wounds don't necessarily limit us. *What limits us is our capacity to imagine.* Mental or physical symptoms ("to fall together with") appear when we have forgotten something essential. They arise, inevitably, from the underworld — or the body — where they have been exiled by the mind. Illness, then, indicates the need to establish a relationship with a particular deity. A troubled person is considered sacred, touched by a god, needing to serve that god. "All who survived the touch of the god became followers of the god," writes mythologist Michael Meade.[3]

No one denies genetics. Yet modernity assumes that everyone is born as a clean slate or blank page *(tabula rasa)*. In this view, "nurture" dominates nature; we are who we are mostly because of our environment. We could become Nobel laureates or mass murderers, depending on our childhoods, and we blame everything on our parents.

But indigenous people say that we are born with built-in stories. Our personal myths determine much of our life experience. In this imagination we *choose* the environment and parents that will inevitably taint us, but in just the appropriate way. The community, however, intuits one's purpose, and reminds her when she forgets. People are at *home* in this kind of world. "Life is suffering," said the Buddha. The real question, however, is whether we experience the particular wounds we were *meant* to suffer. Sadly, many Christians have taken this poetic idea and literalized it into the doctrine that we incarnate in order to be *punished.*

Carl Jung taught that most neurosis substitutes for *legitimate* suffering. Often, our personal problems only mask the real work we have come to do. We convert neurosis into *authentic* suffering through active participation, or soul-making. Paradoxically, our wounds point toward specific and unique gifts we owe to our communities and to our ancestors — gifts that only we can give. This is the essence of individuality. Tribal people expect everyone to accept the challenge, since the alternative — not bringing our irreplaceable gifts into incarnation — results in more suffering. Psychologist Marie-Louise Von Franz wrote, "Nothing in the human psyche is more destructive than unrealized, unconscious creative impulses."[4]

The word "passion" has evolved from its original meaning of suffering and, later, erotic love. These days, many speak of *having* a passion, meaning a strong enthusiasm, from biking to Opera. A recent *Food Network* program featured the words "passion" or "passionate" five times in one hour. But "passion" misses both the consequences of not following the muse, as well as the paradox of wound and purpose. *Vocation* ("a calling") comes closer, as in the *Gospel of Thomas:*

> *If you bring forth what is within you,*
> *What you bring forth will save you.*
> *If you do not bring forth what is within you,*
> *What you do not bring forth will destroy you.*[5]

Without knowing our wounds, we cannot bless others. The Greeks knew this; commentators on drama note that the tragic hero's character flaws are inseparable from his virtues.

"Passion" approaches cliché status, and so does "purpose." Recent best sellers limit it to a specifically Christian perspective.[6] Still, they are on to something. Millions now ask, as tribal people have always wondered, what is the meaning of *my* life? Why did *I* come here? What is the difference between fate and destiny? What do I owe to my ancestors and my descendants? The Indian poet Rabindranath Tagore lamented,

> *For years I have been stringing and re-stringing my instrument,*
> *while the song I have come to sing remains unsung.*

THE POLYTHEISTIC IMAGINATION

In a polytheistic society like Ancient Greece, religion reflected the understanding that the soul is inherently multiple. To Hillman, we need a polytheistic psychology that takes this into account. However, "...another God is not merely another point of view. The gods are not persons who each rule over a different area of human activity... they are ways the world reveals itself."[7] Personality is a drama in which 'I' participate but may not even be the main character.

Polytheistic thinking provides a framework for us to address the plural patterns of our existence. Unlike the familiar Judeo-Christian universe, the pagan gods are amoral and generally uninterested in human good or evil. "Nature and history do not agree with our conceptions of good and bad;" writes historian Will Durant, "they define good as that which survives and bad as that which goes under..."[8] The *soul of the world,* the collective unconscious, isn't interested in morality, but in *innocence versus experience.* Good answers should evoke more interesting questions. Novelist Ken Kesey wrote, "The need for mystery is greater than the need for an answer."[9]

Ignoring any of the gods means that some aspect of our consciousness is so much in the foreground that it has pushed other aspects out of awareness. In a sense, their mythology is our psychology, our human nature. However, if we say that the gods are merely inside us, we reduce and limit them. They are worlds of meaning in which we participate, reflecting natural forces in the world as well as within our psyches.

Metaphor leaps the chasm between thoughts and transmits multiple levels of meaning. Unlike fantasy, which is self-centered, imagination implies dialogue. Indeed, some languages lack the verb "to be." Speakers *must* communicate indirectly, tolerate ambiguity and endure the tension between opposites rather than settling for "either-or" resolution.

This moves us from contradiction through paradox into *mystery.* Only monotheistic thinking sees difference as a threat to be eliminated. But dreams can indicate that anything taken to its extreme becomes its opposite! Jung used the old Greek word *enantiodromia* to indicate this mystery. William Blake wrote, "Excess of sorrow laughs; excess of joy weeps," while Physicist Niels Bohr said that the opposite of a correct statement is a falsehood, but the opposite of a profound truth may be another profound truth.

Indeed, the creative process often requires artists to hold both sides of a dilemma simultaneously until something new emerges. Rather than concepts, *images* — sounds and pictures — signal the dissolution of boundaries that actually occurs in the imagination. So the polytheistic imagination can also be called the *creative* imagination.

Our imaginations are constantly at work, producing an incessant efflorescence of pictures and events, in both our night-dreams and our daydreams, thousands upon thousands of images, most seemingly unrelated to each other. Yet sometimes they coalesce into a meaningful narrative, a significant dream. In the same way, but over immense periods of time, entire societies evolve their myths. It is as if the images themselves want to be brought together into a *story*. Meade writes, "Every event, inner and outer, has hidden meaning waiting to be revealed. Yet it takes a story, a narrative shape to uncover the meanings that hide within the facts of matter."[10]

The imagination creates myth and is in turn held by myth. Cultures with living myths encourage infinite expressions of creativity. However, in societies like ours that lack living myths, cultural institutions actively suppress creativity.

The soul speaks in dream, poetry and myth. But we miss the meaning hiding in our wounds if we have no sense of the story trying to live through us. When the soul cannot be heard, it speaks through the *body* (the human body or the body politic), as illness or as "accidental" and self-destructive behavior.

Sadly, the creative imagination has long been almost entirely lost. With the rise of patriarchy it polarized into the *paranoid imagination* and the *predatory imagination*. The first is based on irrational fear, the second on an insatiable drive for control. Both express a narcissism that objectifies and negates other perspectives. They limit our perceptions and choices, and powerful elites use them to manipulate us.

LITERALISM

We must attempt to go past the literal to see through every theme and action toward deeper myths or images. For example, Dionysus is the god of the vine, of wine and of drunkenness. But in a deeper sense, we can see him as the god of communal ecstasy, or deeper still, of ecstasy itself. The metaphorical hell of alcoholism can express the unconscious search for that same ecstasy (consuming "spirits").

Certain animals look like superficially similar but poisonous ones to trick predators into avoiding them; they become "toxic mimics." This phrase describes our modern tendency to interpret things in the most literal fashion. In a world that devalues the spiritual many forget how to think mythologically and are drawn to its toxic mimic, addiction. When myths that bind us together in worlds of meaning die, the soul — and the soul of the culture — find substitutes. Contemporary religious, political and scientific ideologies are monotheistic, allowing no alternative viewpoints. Ideologies force us to think the same idea, while myth invites us to have our own ideas about the same thing.

The losses of meaningful stories and divine images have produced a "culture of celebrity." Instead of developing relationships with Aphrodite or Zeus, we adore each in a succession of actresses or politicians, who inevitably betray us by proving to be all too human. Ritual breaks down as mythologies collapse. Ritual conflict degenerates into literal violence. But we can ask, what (or whom) would an action or event serve if it were freed of its literal meaning? By revealing the symbolic patterns behind self-destructive behavior, or by ritually enacting our myths, we may be able to keep ourselves from acting them out literally.

Mythical thinking differs from *thinking mythologically*. When we reduce things from the symbolic to the literal, we are inside a myth and don't know it. Unconsciously enacting such a narrative (or several at once), we are in mythical thinking and repeat unsatisfying behavior without any positive change. We see others in one-dimensional images. By contrast, when we think mythologically, we search for the archetypal nature of an event. We perceive meaning on several levels simultaneously, aware that the literal, psychological and symbolic dimensions of reality complement and interpenetrate each other to make a greater whole.

There is no reason to assume that indigenous people cannot do this. Actually, it is *we* who have, by and large, lost this capacity. The curses of modernity — alienation, environmental collapse, totalitarianism, consumerism, addiction and world war — are the results. Literal, mythical thinking is the "toxic mimic" of thinking mythologically.

Mythical thinking reduces multi-layered mystery to the simplistic dualisms of monotheism: whatever isn't aligned with our god must necessarily follow his opposite. Here is a clue: if *your people* consider their story to be literally true and *other people's* stories are "myths," then you and your people are thinking mythically or literally. Other *mono*-words share the brittleness of one correct way: *monopoly, monogamy, monolithic, monarchy, monotonous*. If solutions to our great social and environmental crises emerge, they will originate outside of the *monoculture's* arrogantly *monocular* view, from people on the edges.

The life of mythology springs from the metaphoric vigor of its symbols, which bring together and reconcile two contraries into a greater whole. But if we concretize a symbol into a single vision, if we confuse a myth with historical truth, or if we allow dogma to determine the effect the symbol is supposed to have, the symbol dies. Since monotheism rejects ambiguity and diversity, it requires *belief,* which implies not merely a single set of truths but also the obligation to convert — or eliminate — others. It invites misogyny, aggression, hatred of the body and a single creation myth.

Pagan thinking appreciates diversity and encourages us to imagine. It welcomes all gods and all emotions, including humor. Hillman insists, "The Gods don't require my belief for their existence, nor do I require belief for my experience of their existence."[11] Likewise, astrologer Caroline Casey encourages us to *believe nothing... entertain possibilities.* The triumph of monotheism resulted in the transformation of difference into "otherness." But if we entertain possibilities, then strangers can become guests.

By transcending the literal or concrete, we avoid the mistake of scholars who saw hysteria in accounts of Dionysian cults rather than recognizing the god behind hysterical behavior. The former reduces the image to pathology, while the latter sees beyond the suffering to the soul's attempt to know itself. The former judges, while the latter, by identifying the framework of a story that isn't finished, invites creative renewal.

For tribal people, to explain is not a matter of presenting literal facts, but to tell a story, which is judged, writes David Abram, by "whether it *makes sense... to enliven the senses"* to multiple levels of meaning.[12] Similarly, when we reduce memory to "data storage," we forget how to make images and weave new meaning. The Baal Shem Tov, founder of Hassidism said, "In remembrance is the beginning of redemption." Truth, *aletheia, is* memory; and myth is truth precisely because it refuses to reduce the world to one single perspective.

Polytheism is no panacea. It too can become literalized, as in India's caste system. Marx was right: institutionalized religion inevitably supports injustice. Still, by offering multiple images, polytheism invites us to look deeper into ourselves than does monotheism.

SOUL-MAKING

A fundamental paradox: I must remain who I am in essence, even become more of who I am. Yet to do so, I must periodically change. Soul-making is not about transcending the ego or escaping the world, but plunging deeper into it to discover our purpose and the spirits we are called to serve. We entertain mythic images and follow their emotional trails. We don't look to them for answers, but for the invisible background that keeps us questioning.

Soul-making involves re-dreaming and re-framing our lives as "healing fictions." The patient isn't sick, but the story she tells may be. Facts can't change, but we can change their meaning through artful telling, so that we live not *from* our wounds, but *with* them. Not to simply blame parents, but to constantly recast events within a story infused with meaning. Not to form new belief systems which calcify into dogmas, but to "entertain possibilities." Soul-making is rooted in these possibilities, or *archetypes*, the universal patterns of the collective unconscious. Its endlessly complex and ambiguous images compose the basic contents of myths and dreams.

The multiple archetypes that appear in myth as divine images point us toward the impersonal and universal — what Jung called the Self — that lies behind all dualities. In stories, however, the gods can be spiteful, unpredictable, childish, incestuous and violent. They can fight amongst themselves or be humorously detached. They are unconcerned with good and evil or pious behavior. Mortals rarely approach this world. Certain gods may occasionally have affection for individual humans, but they expect little of us, other than to amuse and feed them.

Archetypes can force their way into our lives in astonishing and destructive ways. Such iconic figures as Adolf Hitler, Marilyn Monroe and David Koresh were all seized by archetypes. They *identified* with them rather than allowing these energies to flow through them. Instead of serving the archetype of the King, for example, one may believe that he *is* the King. He becomes inflated and entitled and assumes that conventional moral restraints don't apply to him. Other archetypal experiences include romantic love and religious conversion.

Perfect yet amoral, the gods reflect human nature, which — to Pagans — is neither good nor evil. If they want anything from mortals, it is not to transcend our nature but to penetrate further *in,* toward our — their — mysterious essence. The poet Hafiz wrote of a god who spoke only four words: "Come dance with me."

Doing soul-work, like doing art, we struggle to hold multiple meanings in consciousness simultaneously without reducing them to a single answer. Putting together both poles *(syn-thesis)* allows a third thing to arise that may resolve the dilemma. Developing relationships with images from the other world and serving them in the material world leads to insight.

Jung wrote, "Everything in the unconscious seeks outward manifestation."[13] The soul's natural expression is art and ritual, *enacting* dream and myth. If we are deaf to this language and don't live out our dreams, we may force our children to embody them. We may live out the dreams of others, or envy may compel us to crush those who do live their dreams. Our genocidal modern history is a catalogue of this loss of soul in the world. But sometimes this language does emerge in the voice of poets like Gary Snyder:

> *I hold the most archaic values on earth. They go back to the late Paleolithic: the fertility of the soil, the magic of animals, the power-vision in solitude, the terrifying initiation and rebirth, the love and ecstasy of the dance, the common work of the tribe.*[14]

A RECIPROCAL RELATIONSHIP

Modernity assumes that the universe consists of inanimate matter distinct from the human spirit; the "I" who relates to matter is dematerialized mind, split from the body. It sets up hierarchies beginning with mind *over* body and spirit *over* matter, leading inevitably to the deadly dichotomies of race and gender.

By contrast, consider this statement by a Native American elder: "The uncounted voices of nature that for…Whites are dumb, are full of life and power for us."[15] Tribal people speak of communities of beings bound by reciprocal ties and obligations, where humans are relatively insignificant. To such animists, the world is alive — *animated* — and intelligent. And the *soul* of the world, the *anima mundi,* expresses itself in endlessly repeating mythic cycles. In rejecting such a world, the Judeo-Christian-Islamic traditions led inevitably to our environmental crises. If the world is dead or lacking soul, then nature is merely a resource; at best a backdrop to human dramas, at worst a dump for our toxic byproducts.

But older traditions imply a *reciprocal relationship between the worlds.* The spirits need humans for their work as much as humans need them. What is broken in one world is repaired in the other. Each needs the other because each feeds the other; neither is complete without the other. The world of the ancestors and spirits — the "other world" — isn't a *better* place. Nor is it the *next* world, as Christian doctrine, steeped in linear time, describes it. It is right next to this one.

In Mayan tradition, the spirits require three things: beauty, eloquence, and *grief.* They *feed* on grief, and when they don't receive enough of it, they feed directly on humans. In later chapters, we will consider modern history from this perspective.

Jung proposed that both the personal and collective psyches are inherently self-regulating. If individuals or nations *forget their purpose,* the collective unconscious compensates for such distortion by insisting on some opposing point of view to restore balance. This can take a very long time to manifest. Clearly, however, the past forty years have witnessed the emergence of both modern feminism and the environmental awareness that may yet reverse the ravages of modernity.

MYTH

Myth derives from *mythos* ("story"), which the Greeks of the Classical period contrasted with *logos* (doctrine, theory, rationality). Eventually, Western culture emphasized *logos* over *mythos,* and myth acquired its common meaning as fictional, especially when contrasted with science and history. *Mythos* became *fabula* in Latin, the root of "fable."

Mythographer William Doty takes eighty pages to come to a

comprehensive definition of myth.[16] For our purposes, however, I prefer to keep things simple: myths are *stories we tell ourselves about ourselves*. They give us meaning, tell us who we are and reveal our moral, social and spiritual priorities, or how we make sense of experience. Myths are so self-evident that we rarely question them. Many are religious in nature, while some (let us call them "political myths") are deliberately created by power elites. Such extremely powerful narratives can obscure other stories. It is not important, however, whether these stories are literally true; what matters is how aware we are of the extent to which we *inhabit* them.

But some myths deal with the most fundamental themes of human existence, providing insight into the cosmic as well as the personal. These stories are infinite, always providing something new when we return to study them. At this level, mythology can be called a psychology of the cosmos.

Each of us — and each culture — is *a point in time and space where many myths intersect*. Soul-making means identifying and struggling with myths that attract us, especially those we are initially unaware of. It means coming to consciousness — remembering — the stories that run our lives. While some are so patently false that we must reject them, others must come more directly to the forefront. This allows us to develop ritual, practical relationships with the archetypal forces reflected in them. They ask us, as Rumi said, "to spill the spring waters of your real life."

A PAGAN TOOLBOX

A Pagan view of myth, literature or history keeps several tools handy:

1. Images refer to other images. "Family," "house," "city" or "realm" may refer to the ego or self, as in the Japanese poet Shikibu:

    > *Although the wind blows terribly here,*
    > *The moonlight also leaks between*
    > *The roofs planks of this ruined house.*

2. Boundaries between inner and outer, or between subject and object, are permeable. Phrases like "madness at the gates of the city" are

deliberately ambiguous: where — on which side of the gates — is the madness?

3. Therefore, all characters in a story (as in a dream) may symbolize and evoke aspects of *the reader or listener*. As above, so below. But we do not reduce them to psychological terms. These characters also reflect cosmic relationships, the essence of the *world* soul. As such, any element in a story can direct our attention toward the ultimate unity that lies behind the infinitely variable procession of images.

4. I acknowledge a huge debt to feminists who describe the social construction of gender. However, indigenous thinking universally asserts that to speak of the soul, the duality of male and female is necessary. Male figures in stories may represent masculine *energy* in actual men or women, and similarly, female characters may represent the feminine in men.

5. In stories, *death* symbolizes the demise of *part* of a psyche within a natural cycle of rebirth. It can be meaningful if suffering produces knowledge, as it often does in Greek Tragedy. It is meaningless, however, when it results in denial or retaliation, as it usually does under modernity's demythologized conditions. But death is not an end state; it moves from chaos and decay into fermentation and regeneration. Still, nothing new appears until the death of the old; the King dies to revitalize the realm. So along with "Who has died?" we always ask, "What is being *born*?"

6. Time is "flexible" in ritual space, or in the imaginal world of myth. One hour in a story could represent years in real time, and the reverse could also be true.

7. We use etymology and imaginative approaches to language in order to approach insight. For example, "forget" is the opposite of "remember." But the opposite of *re-member* (putting something back together) is to "dis-member," which is exactly what happens to Pentheus in *The Bacchae*. Often, looking to the original meanings of words can help us think metaphorically. We also need to see past uninspired translation. The Aramaic word spoken by Jesus and translated into Greek as *diabolos* and into English as "evil" actually means "unripe." What if we

used "unripe" instead of "evil?" "Unripe" persons are simply immature. Aren't communities responsible for helping them "ripen," rather than punishing or eradicating them? This is critical: if we can't imagine a *sym*-bolic ("throwing together") world, then we are left with a *dia*-bolic world.

Even "diabolic" (related to *dance*), originally implied communication between adversaries. Unimaginative language, says Hillman, "displaces the metaphorical drive from its appropriate display in poetry and rhetoric...into direct action. The *body* becomes the place for the soul's metaphors."[17] In other words, if we can't make images in art, music or beautiful speech we get *sick*.

8. We remember the function of oral traditions. Indigenous myths were told or sung from memory for hundreds of years before they were written down. People *worked* with them, with strong emotion, in safe, ritual containers.

9. We continually attempt to "see through." While monotheism speaks in absolutes — good/bad/sinful — psychology brings nuance: behavior is either more or less healthy. Addicts need treatment because they are ill *(Yet America's penal system has shifted from one of rehabilitation to one of punishment. To ask why a nation would force such cruelty upon its young is to open a historical question into a mythological one)*. On the mythic level, addiction becomes a twisted search for meaning.

    If we can avoid *"either/or"* thinking, we imagine souls moving, consciously or not, toward wholeness. *"Yes/but"* is an improvement, but we are after *"yes/and."* So I ask, *what is this behavior, ideology, addiction, etc, trying to say? What does the symptom want? What would this person — or nation — do if they understood themselves symbolically? What are they trying to become?*

10. Finally, we proudly admit to being *amateurs* (Latin: *amare*, "to love"); we love stories. We aren't scientists or theologians, but like Heinrich Zimmer, reckless *dilettantes* ("to take delight"). He writes:

> The moment we abandon this dilettante attitude toward the images...to feel certain about their proper interpretation...

we deprive ourselves of the quickening contact, the demonic
and inspiring assault...What characterizes the dilettante is his
delight in the always preliminary nature of his never-to-be-
culminated understanding...We can never exhaust the depths
— of that we may be certain...a cupped handful of the fresh
waters of life is sweeter than a whole reservoir of dogma...[18]

Thus armed with mythological thinking, and somewhat *dis*armed of
our modern tendency to literalize and divide reality into safe dualisms,
we begin our investigation of Dionysus, his stories, and his meaning in a
worldwide pop culture dominated by the American empire.

*The fullness of life and the violence of death both
are equally terrible in Dionysus.*
WALTER F. OTTO

———•———

The road of excess leads to the palace of wisdom.
WILLIAM BLAKE

———•———

Too much of a good thing…is just fine!
LIBERACE

02

WHO IS DIONYSUS?

DIONYSUS IS AN immensely rich, core image of European consciousness. His myths come down to us filtered through many historical periods. The Classical period of fifth-century B.C.E. Greece occurred two centuries after Homer and eight centuries after the Trojan War. "The Greeks" lived as far apart in time from their Mycenean ancestors as we do from the Middle Ages, and the Minoan civilization that preceded them was far older. Poets of all these periods sang of Dionysus, adding many conflicting and contradictory elements. They assembled their stories for 2,000 years, and the world has retold them for another 2,000 years. He is all of these stages and stories at once. There is no single "real" account of him. Our task is to delight in these contradictions and the mystery behind them.

There is no scholarly consensus on the "meaning" of Dionysus. More than any other divinity, he is a projection screen for our obsessions: god of madness (Walter Otto); spiritual intoxication (Jane Harrison); illusion and change (Simon Goldhill); transformation (Karen Armstrong); homicidal fury (Rene Giraud); gay men (Arthur Evans) and indestructible life (Carl Kerenyi). Dionysus symbolizes the revenge of instinct over order (Ginette

Paris). He is the suffering god upon whom all tragic heroes are based, an allegory of the human condition (Freidrich Nietzche). To Philip Slater, he exemplifies identification with the aggressor, while Riane Eisler sees only a figure that supplanted older female deities. Is it surprising that Dionysus is also the god of masks?

He is all this and more. To me, he represents the archetype of *the Other*, an aspect of nature — and *human* nature — that is both outside the boundaries of the known, familiar and acceptable, but also within, at its very core. He symbolizes the mystery behind the reconciliation of opposites; our rational minds can only define him by what he isn't — "not us." *Dio-Nysus* means, "god (theos) of Nysus," the mythical Mount Nysa. Many areas, from North Africa to Bulgaria, claimed to be Mt. Nysa. Dionysus, indeed, came from some "other" place. And yet, "As soon as he appears," writes J.P. Vernant, "the distinct categories and clear oppositions that give the world its coherence and rationality fade, merge, and pass..."[1]

Dionysus as the Other will be our primary image for understanding American myth and history. *The Bacchae* calls him *xenos* (stranger, foreigner), which is the root of "xenophobia." But *xenos* also means "guest" or "friend." Here is the paradox of the Other. The Greek language expressed the profound truth that the soul *needs* the other for its completion.

DIONYSUS' BIRTH AND LIFE

Zeus' mortal lover Semele became pregnant. Enraged with jealousy, his wife Hera appeared in disguise and advised Semele to request that Zeus prove his divinity by revealing his immortal form. Zeus knew that humans could not survive such visions, but he had promised to honor her request and could not refuse. Reluctantly, he obeyed, and his lightning destroyed Semele. Zeus sewed the fetus into his own thigh. The semi-divine Dionysus — with bull's horns and snakes on his head — was born from Zeus' body.

Zeus gave the infant to the nymphs of Mount Ida, who raised him disguised as a girl in order to hide him from Hera. But she saw through their ruse and drove him insane. The boy wandered the world until another goddess, Cybele, cured his madness. Later, he spread his new religion, conquering those who resisted. His motley followers included his drunken tutor Silenus, the lusty, goat-hoofed, horse-eared *satyrs* and the ecstatic, female *bacchants.*

He appeared on an island, asking for passage. Some sailors saw an opportunity to kidnap and ransom the beautiful youth. But Dionysus caused grapevines to grow up the ship's mast; ivy and wild beasts appeared on the deck. Realizing they'd angered a god, the terrified sailors leaped overboard, and Dionysus transformed them into dolphins.

The gods had a domestic dispute. Hephaestus imprisoned his mother Hera in a magical chair. Unable to release her, Zeus called upon Dionysus, who got Hephaestus drunk on wine, brought him back to Olympus and released her. Now reconciled with Hera, Dionysus was admitted to the Olympian pantheon. But the only god who had a mortal mother never quite fit in among those aristocrats.

These tales have a comic tone. But Dionysus also brought madness and even death to mortals who rejected him. After establishing his mysteries (from *mystes,* an initiate) among mortals and lightening their load with the gift of wine, Dionysus descended to the underworld and raised his mother's ghost up to heaven.

Although Greek religion admitted Dionysus to its pantheon quite late, he actually emerged out of an incomprehensibly ancient past. The Semele story is only one of several birth tales, the "official" version that minimizes his matrilineal heritage. Dionysus arose out of the ancient Minoan civilization of the third and second millennia B.C.E. — with cultural antecedents reaching back 4,000 years further. Some researchers claim that the inhabitants of "Old Europe" lived in relatively peaceful, matrilineal, non-hierarchical societies. The familiar term "matriarchy" is inaccurate, because this world wasn't patriarchy's mirror opposite; *matricentric* is a better term. Life revolved around feminine values. We could define the feminine as a receptive, nurturing pattern that holds things in relationship and reflects the feeling values of consciousness. The masculine is seen as dynamic and expansive. It reflects the questing, goal-defining, ordering, discriminating qualities of consciousness. Both exist to varying degrees in both biological men and women.

Concepts of time reflected the natural cycles observed everywhere, especially in women's biology. Everything grew, decayed, died — and was reborn. It was a world of cycles within cycles. Creation did not happen once; it happened in the present moment, and human events had meaning because they were located at specific places within such a storied universe. Humanity engaged with these larger cycles through their initiation rituals and annual ceremonies.

Alternately nurturing and destroying, the Great Goddess was the matrix connecting the unseen with the natural world. Her body — the earth — was sacred, a manifestation of cosmic spirit. Male gods, her sons or consorts, periodically died and were reunited with her. Representing a masculine stimulating principle without which nothing would grow and thrive, they affirmed and complemented the feminine, with neither dominating. In myth, the two united in the "sacred marriage" (*hieros gamos*) that reassured life's continuation. The Goddess' devotees considered sex a ritual act of participation in her mysteries.

The Goddess existed in various manifestations for over 5,000 years *before* Classical Greece. Eventually, however, patriarchal invaders destroyed her world, and the masculine and feminine principles fell out of balance. The masculine became dogmatic, pathologically inflated and obsessed with control, while the feminine became diminished, inarticulate and ineffective. Mythic *images* of the Goddess, however, lingered in the collective consciousness.

Another birth story told of Zeus and Persephone's child, Zagreus, who was torn apart and eaten by the Titans. The first grapevine arose from the spot where his blood hit the ground. Zeus recovered the boy's heart, ate it and re-sired the child — now called Dionysus — upon Semele. In this seventh-century B.C.E. version, humanity, born from the ashes of the Titans, contains divine elements to be cultivated and evil elements that must be purged. It is one of the earliest stories describing the mind/body split lying at the heart of Western civilization. The Orphics elaborated it over the centuries, anticipating later theologies that insisted on an immortal soul and its accursed body.

THE RELIGION OF DIONYSUS

Small groups of women *(thiasoi)* celebrated nature's cycles with drumming, music and dancing. In these rituals *(orgeia,* root of "orgy"), they attempted to reach ecstatic *(en-theos,* "enthusiasm") states of union with Dionysus. Sometimes they evoked him by tearing apart live animals and eating them raw. Perhaps these rites recalled ancient human sacrifice, but they also symbolized the symbolic dismemberment and rebirth of the worshiper's ego. Carl Kerenyi wrote that they celebrated the mystery of *zoe,* the "indestructibility of life amid destruction."[2] Their rituals embodied the relationship between death, transformation and the hope of regeneration, and the animal represented the god himself.

These *maenads* (from *mania,* "possession") sought a cathartic madness, a holy spell caused by — but also cured by — Dionysus. They provoked extreme emotions, but opposed the other, more destructive madness he caused. *They engaged in the first to avoid the second,* losing their minds to become sane.

Centuries later, Athens incorporated toned-down Dionysian rites into its religion. Among its major festivals were the *Anthesteria,* when he returned from the underworld, and the *Greater Dionysia,* celebrated with presentations of tragic drama. Solemnity and mourning combined with dancing, drunkenness, and inversion of sex roles. Wild processions with large phalluses recalled his mythic intrusions into the city — and the mind.

THE OPPOSITES

Philosopher Alan Watts wrote that western culture, whether it is Christian or technological, celebrates the unique illusion "that good may exist without evil, light without darkness, and pleasure without pain."[3] Nature, however, does not recognize such distinctions. Thus the ambivalence of Dionysus embodies the mysterious unity of the opposites.

Part mortal, he suffers and dies every fall, yet he resurrects in the spring. Baby Dionysus (progenitor of the Christ child) expresses the Divine Child archetype — the perpetual hope of renewal that follows destruction. As an Olympian, he is detached from Earth's changing processes, yet as god of vegetation he is intimately involved with them. His mortal remains were buried at Delphi, yet he mysteriously returns there annually. He blurs distinctions between man and god, renewal and decline, sacrament and pollution and savage and civilized. He is effeminate, yet he conquers foreign lands.

Usually drunk, he values pleasure and conviviality and expresses sexuality for its own sake, serving neither procreation nor power. To think of him *only* in those terms, however, is to trivialize him. He isn't pleasure, writes Camille Paglia, but "pleasure-pain, the gross continuum of nature... subordination of all living things to biological necessity."[4]

In some of his images in art he is bearded and quite masculine. Generally, however, he is pictured as androgynous; this indicates that he mediates our greatest polarity, masculine and feminine. Dionysus was the only male god worshipped primarily by women. Popular clichés associate him with a liberating, rebellious, communal sexuality. Some said he and Aphrodite sired Priapus, the god with the enormous phallus, and three daughters, the Charities or Graces. Others write that he simply embodies *Zoe,* the life force, pure libido, neither male nor female. And for all the sex around him, some said that he was faithful to his wife Ariadne.

Dionysus descended to the underworld, found Semele and brought her to Olympus. He did this, however, in typically untypical fashion. Not knowing the way, he *asked directions* of a human, Prosymnos, who first extracted a promise that Dionysus would submit to intercourse upon returning. Prosymnos then guided him to a bottomless pool, the entrance to Hades. There he found Semele, bribed Persephone for her freedom and brought her to Olympus. Returning, he discovered that Prosymnos had died. So Dionysus carved a phallus out of wood, sat on it, and completed the agreement in effigy.

Here, mediating another polarity, active and passive, he reveals that losing one's identity to something greater can be a blessing. It is Plato's "poetic madness" — passively receiving the inspiration that precedes active creativity. This means, writes Hillman, "allowing the other to enter and occupy whole areas of your soul, to submit, to be penetrated, but not possessed."[5]

This mode of spirituality is both ancient and widespread. All Greek initiation festivals included dancing. Indigenous worship everywhere was *bodily* celebration, a dance of the entire community.[6] In many African languages, the words for music and dance are identical. A Haitian proverb says, "White people go to church to speak about God. We dance in the temple and *become* God."

Dionysian worshipers dissolve their separate egos, merge with him and seek *irrational* knowledge, to think instinctively, sensuously and intuitively rather than through abstract logic. But there is always a price to be paid: such thinking could never produce an advanced, technological civilization.

Dionysus usually appears in his wild community of satyrs and maenads in the procession we recreate during Mardi Gras. He rides in a chariot or ship on wheels, arriving from the sea, symbol of the unconscious. This community in movement symbolizes his crossing of boundaries and triumphal entrance into a city (or psyche) when it consciously welcomes him. In other images, however, he is imprisoned in the palace of the mind, or *forces* entrance against resistance. Then, his arrival (*epidemia*, the "divine epidemic") leaves devastation in its wake.

MADNESS AND PARADOX

Hera drove Dionysus mad, other goddesses healed him, and he learned to both cause and heal insanity himself. He was both hailed as gift-giver and feared for his vengeance. Otto writes:

> ...dancers appear with young animals in their hands, tear
> them into pieces, and swing the bloody members through
> the air... the elemental forms of everything that is creative,
> everything that is destructive, have arisen, bringing with them
> infinite rapture and infinite terror...[7]

In psychological terms, this is what Freud called the *id*, "a chaos, a cauldron full of seething excitations."[8] A healthy ego kept the id in check. It was a Victorian view of Dionysus. But Freud also realized that any repressed force demands recognition.

Older, indigenous psychologies understand that birth and death are dual aspects of life. When we approach one extreme, we are close to the other. So tribal people expect, at life's most intense moments — birth, initiation, weddings and funerals — that the spirits of the dead and powers of the underworld will be present, and must be honored.

To modern minds, this is madness. But the Greeks knew they had to honor the irrational. A *mad god* exists, writes Otto, "only if there is a mad world which reveals itself through him."[9] Only the divine intelligence of such a god can hold its contradictions together.

The Natural and the Divine

There were strict boundaries between gods and mortals. Dionysus, however, shared aspects of both, dying and being reborn. There he sat, raving and intoxicated, tolerated more than accepted, a trailer-trash cousin among the embarrassed Ivy-Leaguers of Mount Olympus.

The ancient writer Plutarch claimed that Dionysus stood for "the whole wet element" in nature: not only wine, but the life-blood of animals, male semen and the juicy sap of plants that rises in the spring. He made grapevines bloom and ripen. Wine gushed from a spring when Dionysus married Ariadne. At Elis, priests sealed empty vessels in a room. Entering it the next day, they found the vessels filled with wine. Divine madness — music, poetry, dance and prophecy — arises from the earth in the plant that intoxicates. Like the god, the wine also reaches completion through a second birth of fermentation, bringing both joy and suffering. Dionysus grieved deeply upon the death of the youth Ampelos, shedding tears that became wine. "So," says Otto, "the joy of men flows forth from the tears of a god."[10]

Ivy was his other plant. Creeping over and under fences and walls, ineradicable, it suggests his ability to dissolve barriers and intrude upon us. Devotees also worshipped him as the pine tree, which, like the ivy, stays green in winter. His animal forms were the bull, panther and goat; and dances to him as the goat-god were the ritual roots of tragic drama.

DIONYSUS AND APOLLO

Dionysus and Apollo were half-brothers with a unique relationship. Apollo appealed to those who sought knowledge, moderation, purity, contemplation and harmony. His bow and arrows signified his distance from humans and his ability to heal, send sickness, or purify the guilty from afar. He loved clearly defined boundaries. Apollo demanded: *Know yourself.* Dionysus attracted those whose longing expressed itself through rhythm, sexuality and *ekstasis* (standing outside oneself). He ignored the gender and class distinctions that Apollo favored. Instead of security he offered *freedom.*

Musically, Apollo is Bach's formal order, while Dionysus is Coltrane's passionate improvisation. Apollo represents the *descending symbolic order* of values and masculine authority from Heaven to earthly representatives to parents to children. Dionysus represents an *ascending order* originating in the earth's depths and moving upward. One represents spirit and mind, the other soul and body.

Mass religion expresses patriarchy's descending order. Worshipers typically form *right angles,* horizontal lines of attention ending in vertical lines. Since God (and, by implication, political authority) is high above, building design directs minds and eyes upwards; hence the nearly universal stress on great height. Rigid liturgies emphasize predictability, prohibit improvisation and keep ritual's transformative — and revolutionary — potential under control.

By contrast, the ascending order implies "radical ritual" — invocation of spirits, with strong emotion and little concern for predictability. It takes the form of a *circle* that focuses on Earth (the abode of the ancestors) rather than Heaven. Architecture is irrelevant; participants meet outdoors whenever possible, always invoking deities related to that specific locality. However, they have no control over *which* deities arrive, how long they remain or how they communicate their intentions.

Another way to imagine this contrast is Marshall McLuhan's distinction between *percept* and *concept.* Concepts, like Apollo, are detached; they neutralize our direct participation in the world, distancing us by relying on the eye's passivity, assessing from safe distances. Percepts are involved, relying on the "secondary" senses (olfactory, tactile, acoustic.) We are "perceptive" when we penetrate to the core. However, each requires the other — what we might also call *soul and spirit* — for completion, since life will not be confined to a single mode of knowing. Spirit is transcendent and soul is immanent. Zen teacher John Tarrant writes:

> … where spirit is too dominant, we are greedy for pure
> things: clarity, certainty, and serenity… (but) soul in itself
> does not have enough of a center… If soul gives taste, touch,
> and habitation to the spirit, spirit's contribution is to make
> soul lighter, able to escape its swampy authenticity, to enjoy
> the world without being gravely wounded by it.[11]

Historians portray Greek civilization as extremely rational. But the Greeks themselves imagined a balance between the brothers, which they enshrined at Delphi, their religious center. Apollo relinquished it to Dionysus for three months each year.

The history of religion is an unstable relationship between these opposites, with rebellious impulses periodically threatening patriarchal control. Perhaps *all* history oscillates between Apollonian order and Dionysian energy. Cultural stability, however, requires a dynamic, ever-shifting balance. Too much sunshine dries us up, while excess moisture rots us and drives us crazy. Extreme order leads to stagnation, dogma and authoritarianism; too much reliance on the intuitive soul brings chaos, anarchy and collapse. Emphasizing one extreme, we eventually endure the other as a correction. When society literalizes Apollo's spiritual beauty into formal religion, correct behavior and rational science, then literalized — and potentially violent — Dionysian subcultures arise.

THE LOOSENER

Dionysus as alcohol is *Lusios,* "the Loosener — destroyer of the household." *Lusios* is related to *analysis,* which means setting free. A catalyst is a chemical agent that precipitates a process without itself being changed. Mythologically, however, "household" refers to both the outer realm and the ego's inner household. Sexual indulgence in his stories symbolizes the breakdown of *psychic* boundaries. Similarly, the destruction of Pentheus' palace is *Lusios* shaking the foundations of identity.

Why is this "loosening" so tempting? Why do we crave release? E.R. Dodds explained that Dionysus "...enables you for a short time to *stop being yourself...*"[12] He could lift the burden of individual responsibility from his devotees. In the process, their sense of being isolated egos dissolved.

DIONYSUS AND US

Dionysus the Loosener tempts our psyches in the same way that he tempted the Greeks. Modernity forces each individual to carry the weight of meaning that gods, kings and queens once symbolically held for their entire communities.

Americans in particular confuse *individuality* and *individualism.* Chapter Five shows how we push each new generation into life without meaningful rites of passage to become individualists who, not knowing themselves, lack individuality. Further chapters argue that American violence arises from an immensely long process that resulted in the loss of myth, ritual, initiation and consciousness of the underworld, where Dionysus resides.

One difference between the Greeks and us is that they retained vestiges of myth and ritual that welcomed Dionysus in ways that acknowledged their purpose in the world. They could *name* the gods, celebrate them and lead young persons into relationships with them.

Dionysus is an image of the suffering, dismembered soul. We see perfection in other gods, but we see ourselves in him. He reflects our diminished, modern condition. But in the ultimate mystery, he also represents our instinctual, embodied, integrated, original face. *"I'm looking for the face I had,"* wrote Yeats, *"before the world was made."* As such, he shows us the way back to wholeness and the ecstasy of being outside ourselves. But with no communally accepted and ritually precise methods of accepting his invitation, we encounter ecstasy's other face: violence and horror. Denying him, we force him upon others, because he must reside somewhere. There he recruits his followers from imprisoned or marginalized regions of the culture (and the psyche), those with nothing to lose.

He requires that we endure the tension of irreconcilable opposites —

ecstasy and violence, male and female, sacred and profane — and resist the temptation to choose. As soon as we locate him in one half of any of his polarities, we repress the other side, and it begins to plot vengeance. Each truth is a mask that conceals its opposite. He enters our lives when that opposite quality breaks out past the mask. Often, by that point, it is too late to appease him.

*If we are truthful, we shall admit that we do
not understand it... Tragedy was a religious
ceremony, enacted not so much on the boards as
in the souls of the spectators...scholars are...
unable to reconstruct it. Until they have done
so, Greek tragedy will be a page written in a
language to which we possess no dictionary.*[1]

O3

TRAGEDY, EURIPIDES, AND *THE BACCHAE* IN MORE DETAIL

THE SOCIAL MEANING OF TRAGEDY

Jose Ortega Y Gasset wrote the words on the opposite page in 1957. A half-century later, "dumbed-down" from television, Americans have even less capacity to comprehend tragedy. However, our survival may depend upon developing such skills.

We can only understand the experience of tragic drama — one that required the attendance of the entire male citizenry of Athens — by analogy. It combined Easter mass, Independence Day, the World Series, West Point graduation, Jazz opera, a mass encounter group and a presidential debate.

When Tragedy was born democracy was still new and fragile, and there was a living tension between the mythic discourse (the poets) and the conceptual discourses (philosophers and scientists). Restriction of citizenship to adult males created a second tension, but those citizens participated intensely in the affairs of the city, the *polis*. To be apolitical was to be barbaric, or strictly speaking, "non-Greek." A person who was only concerned with his personal life was called an *"idiot."* A third conflict was

between allegiance to *polis* and duty to family (*oikos*, root of "economy").
Many citizens understood that these issues reflected archetypal conflicts
within the psyche itself. Tragic drama attempted to illuminate and
acknowledge them rather than to resolve them.

A democracy that tyrannized a vast empire created a fourth moral
conflict. Within Athens, the small part of the population that was free and
male made decisions democratically. But Athens' prosperity was supported
by thousands of slaves as well as tribute from its conquered neighbors.
Maintaining its standard of living required that Athens be perpetually at
war, and all male citizens were expected to defend her. Audiences generally
excluded women and were composed mainly of soldiers, former soldiers
and future soldiers.

Dramatic and choral competition took place during the several days
of the Greater Dionysia. Young men re-enacted the advent of Dionysus
by carrying his statue from the countryside to the amphitheater, where it
stood throughout the festival. Priests performed sacrifices. The fact that
the actors all wore highly stylized masks (a tradition rooted in Dionysian
worship) heightened the sense of ritual. Tribute from the empire's allies
was displayed. Each of the ten tribes of the city had its own section in the
amphitheater, but the *epheboi* — the next generation of soldiers — sat in
the center near the political leaders. Indeed, writes classicist John Winkler,
the Dionysia was "a social event focused on those young warriors," the best
of whom were chosen to dance and recite the parts of the chorus.[2]

Originally, plays were presented only once, not as ongoing
entertainment. Most plots came from ancient myths that everyone knew,
so there was little curiosity about endings. Instead, viewers wondered how
playwrights would use the familiar characters to illuminate the tensions of
polis, polites (citizen) and *oikos*. They looked to their poets for moral and
religious teaching, writes Classicist James Hogan: "Since they had no sacred
texts…poets were free to spin new versions of myth, new variations on old
doctrine, and new characters from old stories."[3] The clash of contradictory
values often threw characters into such confusion that they went mad. Enter
Dionysus, in the form of sudden madness. The term *bakkheuein* ("to rave

madly," or "to be maddened by Dionysus") occurs in over half of the plays that have survived.

Although everyone was familiar with the stories, they did not sit dispassionately, isolated in the darkness, as we do; they crowded together in broad daylight. Confronted with irresolvable conflicts, they suffered like Dionysus himself, weeping openly in a purging *(katharsis)* of emotion.[4] Aristotle explained that this came through "pity and fear," but — and this is critical — W.B. Stanford translates *eleos* ("pity") as "compassionate grief."[5] At the end of the day, they were exhausted but revitalized, not because their differences had been resolved, nor because a victim had been sacrificed for their sins, but *because they had suffered together.*

On a typical day, three tragedies were followed by a comedy. Originally, *komodia* was song produced by the *komos*, a group of men who went about honoring Dionysus with raucous dancing and singing. It was a specifically male form of intoxication, as much prayer as drunkenness. Eventually it became ritualized into a form of theater that ended the day in a final affirmation of life.

Tragedy paradoxically validated the social order while simultaneously questioning it. Ceremonies glorified the state, yet many plays subverted its dominant values by dramatizing shocking transgressions without providing resolution. The *polis* could look at itself within the ritual container of the theater. Simon Goldhill concludes, "Tragedy takes the developing notions, vocabulary, and commitments of democracy and places them under rigorous, polemical, violent and *public* scrutiny."[6]

EURIPIDES

Euripides (485-406 B.C.E.) was the youngest of Athens' three great playwrights. Aeschylus and Sophocles used the ancient sagas to illustrate the clash of great moral concepts, and their stately language emphasized a certain abstract remoteness from ordinary experience. But Euripides, more concerned with psychological insight, cast his mythical characters as contemporary persons. By altering their motives, he contrasted Athens' ideals with its imperial values and sympathized with its victims, especially women. Although he won fewer prizes, modern critics consider him more influential than the older men. Sophocles understood, admitting that he portrayed people as they ought to be, while Euripides showed them as they actually were.

In earlier plays (*The Trojan Women*, *Iphigenia At Aulis* and *Medea*) Euripides had been concerned with themes such as the killing of the children and feminine vengeance. Twenty-five years later, his critical and unpopular views led to self-imposed exile, and *The Bacchae* was produced after his death. We may consider it to be his final opinion of Athens, even as he sets the play in the Thebes of a mythical past.

THE BACCHAE IN FURTHER DETAIL

The audience in 406 B.C.E was already familiar with many stories of Dionysus's invasion from Thrace in the north (or Phrygia in the east, or Crete in the south). But they had never seen *this* version before.

Disguised as one of his own priests, Dionysus returns to his birthplace of Thebes, leading the Bacchants, his female followers. He intends to refute the slander that Semele had lied about her union with Zeus — and to establish his religion. He has driven the Theban women into a frenzy. Led by Pentheus' mother Agave and his two aunts, they are celebrating his rites in the mountains. *Thebes is empty of women.*

Elderly king Cadmus abdicates in favor of his grandson Pentheus (the audience knew that Pentheus means "man of sorrow"), who staunchly refuses to recognize the truth. Cadmus has accepted the new religion, while Pentheus intends to crush this intruder. Dionysus calmly allows himself and his Bacchants to be captured, and then facilitates their escape. Pentheus, ignoring the evidence of magic all around him, again arrests Dionysus, who responds by causing a great earthquake that destroys the palace. Pentheus emerges, stunned yet unrepentant and further enraged. He orders the army to attack the Maenads in the mountains. This is the play's halfway point.

A messenger arrives from the mountains, telling of miracles. The women had suckled young wolves and caused milk and wine to flow from the earth! Men had attacked them, however, and the women had responded by routing them. Then they'd torn cattle apart with their bare hands, pillaged local villages, and stolen the children. The Maenads, *maddened by Dionysus for their earlier refusal to honor him,* are contrasted with the Bacchants, who willingly follow him. Although the disguised Dionysus — same age and of the same family — warns him twice more about the likely consequences of his actions, Pentheus remains resolved in his macho defiance, refusing to question his own motives.

The action reaches a point of no return, and his extreme attitude turns into its opposite. The divine Dionysus weaves a spell upon the mortal Pentheus, gradually and completely possessing him. He dresses the dazed king in women's clothing, inviting him to spy upon the women. Pentheus is overcome with voyeuristic desire, but when he arrives on the mountain, the women quickly discover him perched on a pine tree. In their mad delusion, they mistake him for a lion cub. Then, in one of literature's most horrifying scenes, the women, led by his own mother Agave, tear Pentheus to bits.

They return to Thebes carrying Pentheus' head, believing it a trophy of their hunt. Having collected the scattered body parts, Cadmus makes Agave realize what she's done. An extended scene of mourning follows, after which (in certain translations) the family restores the severed head to its body. Finally, Dionysus banishes the survivors of the royal family to exile. The House of Thebes has fallen.

The Bacchae's ambivalent ending forces us to re-examine our most cherished assumptions. H.S. Versnel writes, "Every reader gets the *Bacchae* he deserves. No two scholars agree on (its) meaning..."[7] The next three chapters will introduce three themes that connect *The Bacchae* to contemporary social issues. Dionysus has warned us. The collapse of the palace — or New York's twin towers — merely hints at future transformations. We have only begun to suffer together. Yet it is precisely that possibility, or opportunity, that may be our redemption.

Only the shallow know themselves.
OSCAR WILDE

———

The past isn't dead. It is not even past.
WILLIAM FAULKNER

———

Don't push me, cause I'm close to the edge.
RAPPER MELLE MEL

———

En-lakesh (You are the other me)
MAYAN INDIAN CHANT

———

What is the knocking?
What is the knocking at the door in the night?
It is somebody wants to do us harm.
No, no, it is the three strange angels.
Admit them, admit them.
D. H. LAWRENCE

———

I am pregnant with murder.
The pains are coming faster now,
and not all your anesthetics
nor even my own screams
can stop them.
ROBIN MORGAN

04

THE RETURN OF THE REPRESSED

INNOCENCE HAS TWO primary definitions. First, it means "not guilty." Rudolf Hoess, commandant at Auschwitz, protested that he hadn't *personally* murdered anyone. "Innocent" often precedes another word: "victim." Curiously, oppressors often convince themselves that *they* are the innocent victims. Another Nazi, Hans Fritzsche, claimed, "I became guilty of the death of five million people — innocently."

Second, to be innocent is to be uninjured, inexperienced or naïve. In American history and in the American character, innocence merges with ignorance. The *childlike* innocence of old folktale heroes is replaced by the *childish* quality of people who refuse to grow up, who live a pseudo-innocence, hiding parts of themselves from their own awareness. Repression, however, always comes with a price. Myth tells us that when those repressed parts return — and they always do — they are likely to be angry.

DIONYSUS AND PENTHEUS
Pentheus suffers a uniquely gruesome fate. He is viciously *torn apart* by a mob of insane women, led by his own aunts and mother. Is a god who

instigates such bloodbaths worthy of worship? Was Euripides attacking religion? I think he intended to move his audience at deeper levels. Twenty-five centuries later, the soul's needs haven't changed, even if our ability to *know* those concerns has atrophied.

As Semele's mortal son, Dionysus demands acceptance; he will be. As Zeus' immortal son, however, he is eternal. He always is. He shifts constantly, in and out of mortality, time and gender. Masked as his own priest, he praises his god — himself!

Dionysus is *always* dying in the fall, resurrecting in the spring, fermenting magic out of rotten fruit. And the Pentheuses of the world (and the psyche) are always denying him. By nature he is always suffering repression and both threatening and tantalizing us with otherness. Bursting into awareness, he comes from the unknown, with a violence that causes unbelievers to madly dismember their own children.

Dionysus has long been relegated to the margins of our personal and collective psyches. The more insightful Athenians knew this, and they probably approved, given the realities of their social order, as we will see. Psychological repression was the price they paid for relative stability. Euripides, however, was describing the long-term costs. There, in Dionysus' own sacred precinct, he confronted Athens, including all its leaders, with immensely disturbing questions.

The god is angry because he has been dishonored. The longer something has been repressed, the more insistent it is, the greater the resistance by centers of power (ruling elites) or of consciousness (the ego). This is why Dionysus has cast his spell on the women, why Pentheus fights him so absolutely, and why his destruction is so savage.

Like Pentheus, we can ignore the appearance of an archetype. But it never totally disappears. It returns, charged with more energy, but manifesting in a more primitive way. What was a human impulse can become monstrous. Repressed diversity ultimately reappears as psychopathology, as madness at the gates.

But Jung said that the soul is *teleological*, always moving toward integration. We carelessly leave the gates unlocked for the Mystery to enter and do its destructive — and perhaps reconstructive — work. Grandiosity and innocence evoke betrayal and alienation. Usually we respond with "inauthentic suffering" — bitterness, depression or addiction. Sometimes, however, we fall into humility and grief. This may lead to repentance, compassion and wisdom, which the Greeks personified as the goddess *Sophia*. She could only be approached through authentic suffering. Aeschylus wrote:

> *Sing sorrow, sorrow, but good win out in the end.*

We see this deeper motivation when Pentheus orders his henchmen to find Dionysus:

> *Go, someone, this instant,*
> *to the place where this prophet prophesies.*
> *Pry it up with crowbars, heave it over,*
> *upside down; demolish everything you see...*
> *That will provoke him more than anything.*

"Provoke" (from *vocare*, to call) is marvelously appropriate. At some level Pentheus can choose. He can *invoke* or *evoke* his own Dionysian nature, or he can innocently project it outwards, *provoking* its expression somewhere else.

At this point, consider two cautions. Like anything else, psychology can be literalized. Dionysus is no more "within" us than Jehovah is "up there." Containing him within Thebes is as unrealistic as locking him out. We use psychology because of our modern inability to think mythologically. Jung wrote, "Only an unprecedented impoverishment of symbolism could enable us to rediscover the gods as psychic factors...of the unconscious."[1]

Secondly, in speaking of being centered, or of *balancing* the Apollonian and the Dionysian, we find ourselves on Apollo's ground, and we are literalizing again. To be "centered" is to exclude much; Dionysus tells us that being un-centered, or "ec-centric" has equal value. Indeed, any attempt to "make sense" of Dionysus short of actually *experiencing* him is to take

Apollo's view of him. The moment we emphasize one god to the exclusion of the others, they feel jealous.

Provoking Dionysus moves the story into the confrontation scenes between Pentheus and the disguised god, who, despite having predicted Pentheus' death from the beginning, says

> *If I were you, I would offer him a sacrifice, not rage and kick against necessity...*
> *Friend, you can still save the situation.*

"If I were you," indeed. The two cousins represent mirror opposites within the psyche. Kerenyi writes that originally the "man of suffering" was the god himself: "The contradictory nature ...of a god who suffers and lets himself be killed...was embodied in a man who destroyed himself."[2] Pentheus, in his desperate machismo, speaks his last line before the spell is cast:

> *Bring my armor, someone.*
> *And you* (Dionysus) *stop talking.*

Now he has provoked the god, *called him out,* and declared his willingness to engage the mystery. Here a break in the poetic meter of the text occurs that emphasizes the significance of Pentheus' fateful statement. When Dionysus responds with: "*Ahhh...Wait! ...Would you like to see their revels...?*" he provokes Pentheus' unconscious sexual voyeurism. Dionysus, masked as a priest, will send Pentheus to his destruction masked as a Maenad. After loosening the gates of the city, he loosens the boundaries of Pentheus' sanity.

The repressed energies turn deadly. Pentheus might have humbled himself before this immense natural force that was willing to meet him halfway. The Loosener, who — if invited — would have helped his cousin drop his armor and relax, who would rather lie drunk among his maidens, now appears as the Lord of Death. And Pentheus, having zealously defended the city, is trapped, ironically, *outside* its walls. Before his death he briefly joins his cousin as an outsider, *the Other.* Dionysus had come to refute lies told by his two aunts. Now they and Pentheus' own mother destroy him. The three sisters, universal symbols of the Great Mother, reveal her deadly features instead of her nurturing face.

The murder scene probably evoked extreme grief among the older Greeks, who knew quite well that they'd lost much of their indigenous souls while building a rational civilization.

THE OTHER

Innocence defines itself in terms of the "Other." Splitting off aspects of ourselves inconsistent with our self-image, we know who we are because we are not them. Why? Because *they* dress, act and speak differently, and very commonly, *they* engage in violence, while we do not. They exist on the far side of the line that determines who we are, just as the world exists on the other side of the skin that determines who "I" am. In truth, however, writes Daniel Deardorff,

> Every insider carries an infernal Otherness buried deep within, and it is that hidden abyss, denied and handed off, which creates society's Other Within. Desperately wishing to remain a "real member of the flock" the insider projects this interior darkness onto (and even into) some convenient outsider.[3]

Historian Regina Schwartz traces "othering" to the foundation of our Judeo-Christian tradition. The Old Testament "encodes Western culture's central myth of collective identity." Large sections are essentially narratives that forge Hebrew identity by distinguishing them from their neighbors. This is "the most frequent and fundamental act of violence we commit."[4]

That the Hebrews wrote much of the Bible during the sixth century B.C.E. Babylonian exile suggests another origin of othering. If a people are indigenous to a place, they define themselves by who they *are,* but if they live on someone else's land — as Americans do — they define themselves by who they are *not.* Ironically, the Other threatens our sense of who we are, even though we've invented him.

The Other's characteristics live in our shadows, so he is always *lesser*. Major categories of otherness are race, class and gender. Boundaries, however, are never permanent. Serious crises or periods of social anxiety can force communities to redefine "us." Boundaries shift, and so does the image of the Other. As we will see in Chapter Seven, Americans in particular have always defined the Other as those (like Dionysus) who cannot control their impulses.

Otherness inspires fear of pollution, but it also fascinates us. What disgusts us may reveal what we unconsciously desire. Racists and homophobes are deeply, irrationally dependent upon the objects of their prejudice. Their hatred implies its opposite, an *inability to rid the mind of obsessions* with the Other. It leads to fictions of innocence and more. Intense and detailed fantasies about the Other reveal a soul — or a nation — attempting to know itself.

Power elites deliberately determine who is Other in order to restrict access to privilege and justify the social order and its prejudices. Eventually, "we" come to believe that the Other *deserves* low status. Oppression produces segregation — women in the household, poor people in ghettoes and prisons, barbarians outside the gates, the insane within the asylums — so "we" can minimize those occasions when the Other might remind us of who we actually are. Segregation merely reinforces the sense of otherness, since there is little opportunity for the close, un-biased contact that might disconfirm our projections.

However, our innate *wholeness* always threatens to return. Psychologically speaking, what is repressed never dies or goes away; it exists in a timeless realm. The repressed signifies the *preserved*. Freud wrote of the mental processes of the unconscious: "…time does not change them in any way and the idea of time cannot be applied to them." Even in the realm of physics, Einstein wrote that the distinction between past, present and future is only "a stubborn, persistent illusion."[5] Mythologically speaking, all residents of the underworld await the time when they will return to this world.

Othering takes two primary modes. The first is exclusionary, making the Other as unlike us as possible. The second is incorporative — colonizing and assimilating him, denying his own voice. Together, they create "good" and "bad" opposites like noble savage/barbarian and Madonna/whore.

Othering is inconsistent. Europeans projected opposing images upon Jews: "id" figures who would sexually pollute Christian blood; and stingy, "superego" bankers, unwilling to assimilate. Bigots see black people as *both* lazy and threatening. Richard Nixon warned of *both* "the forces of totalitarianism and anarchy…"[6] During the 1991 Supreme Court confirmation hearings for Judge Clarence Thomas, right-wing senators alternatively accused Anita Hill as being either a spurned woman — or a lesbian. Such discourse doesn't care whether the terms of othering are logical or not. Any demonizing narrative will do.

We unconsciously split the Other into *inner and outer.* The more we define self or community by impermeable boundaries, the more we are obsessed with the Other, both without and within the walls. We fear barbarism without, and decadence within. Having invented "outer Others" to define what they were not, the Hebrews also found evil within: military defeats, claimed the prophets, were due to God's wrath at corruption. Indeed, raising fear of the "outer Other" (now, terrorists) inevitably evokes the "inner Other" (illegal immigrants).

Both the paranoid and the predatory imaginations depend upon othering, as fear of infection or as desire to manipulate. Either we locate Paradise within, to be protected from the Other; or else it is elsewhere, an empty space (like the female body or the American wilderness) ripe for exploitation. By contrast, the polytheistic or creative imagination sees *xenos* as guest. It knows that it *needs* the Other for *completion,* understood as a dynamic balance of good and evil, rather than as the victory of good over evil. Its constant flow of imagery produces an overflowing of boundaries as trade, cooperation and ecological interrelatedness.

Sexuality and aggression aren't the only characteristics we project upon others. Those who cannot manifest their own creativity or nobility are likely to perceive those features in public personalities. We personify a grand, transcendent cause — the cosmos itself — as *the King.* This is the basis of hero worship and the cult of celebrity.

Romantic love, a more benign form of othering, spread through Europe in the same centuries — the late Middle Ages — that religion began to unravel. In the overwhelming experience of erotic love we reach religious states of awe and transcendence. As Ernest Becker wrote, when modern man lost his God he fixed his urge for the divine "onto *another person* in the form of a love object."[7]

But in fact this is a great opportunity. Both our longing and our prejudices represent unconscious searching for the Other who is our own deepest nature. Modernity pays grudging attention to this truth with terms like diversity and tolerance. Pagan thinking, however, understands the Other as separate only because of our inability to perceive our oneness with him/her. This realization can potentially crack our innocence and recover our wholeness — but only by passing through the painful realms of grief.

Old languages often gave high priority to hospitality. As I have noted, *xenophobia* stems from *xenos*: "stranger" or "guest," while "love of the guest" is *philos-xenos*. Similarly, since indigenous myths are bound up with specific landscapes, tribal people are unconcerned if their neighbors' myths differ from their own; such myths were obviously meant to make sense of a different experience.

Perhaps there is no more fundamental divide between modern and tribal culture than in this approach to the Other. Consider that Americans use the same word for strangers — aliens — as we do for non-human extra-terrestrials. Many indigenous people called themselves "the people," seemingly implying that others weren't "people." Then why were they often so hospitable? Where identity is conferred by culture rather than by race or politics, where trade binds people into forms of mutual obligation, they perceive strangers not as non-human, but as lacking social status. They attempt to incorporate them into a recognized status system so they can relate to them. Genuine communities — even if they rarely exist in the world anymore — would perceive the Other not as a threat, but as one who may have something to contribute. Hence the friendly, if naïve, receptions reported by most colonialists.

Whites, however, have commonly described tribal rituals as "grotesque" and "savage." The essence of the Western, male mind, writes Barbara Ehrenreich, has been its ability to "…resist the contagious rhythm of the drums, to wall itself up in a fortress of ego and rationality against the seductive wildness of the world."[8]

Othering is most pronounced in monotheistic thinking, which, like any value taken to its extreme, turns into its opposite. In the second century, Clement of Alexandria declared that the gods of *all other religions* were demons. In 2003, Gen. William G. Boykin said, "…my God was *bigger* than his. I knew that my God was a real God and his was an idol."[9] With such boasts, fundamentalists reveal a curious sort of *polytheism.* To make Allah into the Other, they must acknowledge Allah's existence as separate from Jehovah's. When Jehovah is "bigger" than another god, he is no longer the only god.

Denying the Other, we deny ourselves. Othering is at the core of alienation, prejudice and violence. The way out of this trap, however, is not to avoid our suffering through either addiction or spiritual austerities, but to go *further into it,* toward mythic images such as Dionysus. We risk madness and dismemberment, but there is much to be gained.

Suppressing the Feminine

What had Greek civilization repressed by Euripides' time? Why do his women exact such vengeance upon Pentheus? As Western culture and science emerged, men manipulated the material world according to their dreams of power and control. What they lost, however, was something equally valuable: knowledge of being part of the world, not its enemy.

According to Marija Gimbutas, a series of invasions from the northeast ("Indo-Europeans") and south (Semites, including Hebrews) occurred between 4,500 and 2,800 B.C.E. "Old Europe" succumbed to these more aggressive peoples, their male sky-gods and their dominator model of human relations. They brought war, authoritarian social structures and slavery. Patriarchy's dubious genius was *disconnection and compartmentalization.* It severed intellect from emotion and thought from action.

In these warrior societies "Woman" became Other. As the universal primary caregiver to infants, she became the "nonself" from which self is progressively distinguished. New myths justified new social orders, reducing the Great Mother to consort or bride. In some stories, she was raped; in others she was a monster from whose dead body culture emerged. Almost everywhere, patriarchy consolidated itself, and Sun gods vanquished Earth Goddesses. Joseph Campbell summarized the historic changes reflected in myth:

> In the older mother myths and rites the light and darker aspects of the mixed thing that is life had been honored equally and together, whereas in the later, male-oriented, patriarchal myths, all that is good and noble was attributed to the new, heroic master gods, leaving to the native nature powers the character only of darkness — to which, also, a negative moral judgment now was added.[10]

This shift is epitomized in Babylon's creation myth. The universe grew from the serpent *Tiamat's* menstrual blood. The hero *Marduk* killed her, making Heaven and Earth from her body. Then he created men, forcing them to serve the gods. In addition to marking a new age, the story of Tiamat portrays the heroic, male ego's fear of the dark, the mysteries of nature and *human* nature, and its need to vigilantly suppress the Other. This story, recited annually for over 1,000 years, deeply influenced all subsequent Mediterranean mythologies.

The process evolved in stages, each taking hundreds of years:

1. The Great Goddess creates the world. She is *virgin:* complete and alone (only much later will *virgin* be reduced to a woman who hasn't had sex.)
2. The world is born of a goddess *fertilized by a consort,* originally her own son, who periodically dies and re-unites with her.
3. The son (embodying creation) permanently separates from the mother (now symbolizing destruction). Conquering her and fashioning the world from her dead body, he inverts the original myth. Previously, she'd sacrificed him; now he sacrifices *her,* who becomes Other, and in myths from Babylon to Ireland, a *serpent.* Marduk, Baal, Ptah, Zeus,

Apollo, Perseus, Indra, Beowulf, Saints Michael and George — even Yahweh — all defeat serpents or dragons.

4.   Finally, while the goddess *was* Heaven and Earth, a male god — *alone* — creates the world out of the waters of the abyss, or "the deep" (*Tehom* in Hebrew, related to Tiamat). *The world itself becomes Other*, and dualism is born. Spirit and nature are no longer complementary aspects of a primal unity; spirit is greater than matter (Latin: *mater*, mother). The sun dominates the moon, light the darkness, and mind the body. Light and spirit have divine sanction, while matter is *fallen*. War becomes *holy* war, and time itself (beginning around 600 B.C.E.) loses its cyclical nature, becoming a linear drive toward good's triumph over evil.

The rest is history: myth and history became intertwined. Conquerors told their history as myth, legitimizing themselves through birth from the gods. And they told myth as history: Jehovah gave mankind dominion "over every living thing..." Two great traditions, Greek and Hebrew, eventually formed Christianity. "Woman/Nature" became the model of the Other at the base of patriarchal culture; and it lies behind the racism that is so fundamental to American consciousness. It is myth because we subscribe fully without examining the contradictions described by Simone de Beauvoir:

> ...woman is at once Eve and the Virgin...an idol, a servant, the source of life, a power of darkness...artifice, gossip and falsehood...healing presence and sorceress; she is man's prey, his downfall, she is everything that he is not and that he longs for...[11]

THE GREEKS

The Greek polytheistic imagination has much to teach us. Athenian society, however, was deeply flawed. The *Pandora* myth implied that women caused all evils. Actual women couldn't vote or choose whom to marry. Rape of a married woman was considered an offense against her husband's property. There was nearly constant warfare. Later, as the color black took on negative associations, Africans became Other. And with narrowing interpretations of masculinity, homosexuals would also carry the mask.

The collective consciousness required a mythic image of the Other, and Dionysus, with his connection to the loosening properties of the grape, fulfilled this need. He became the only male divinity to be worshipped in all-women's rituals.

THE HEBREWS

Jehovah — a creator god *without parents, wife or children* — is absolutely unique in myth. His religions of the desert attempted to completely exclude the Goddess, except as temptress. Tiamat became the serpent that counseled Eve to sin, for which human females were punished with childbirth pain and submission to their husbands. Female virginity was enforced with savage violence. If the *"tokens of virginity"* were not apparent on a bride, then *"the men of her city shall stone her with stones that she die, because she hath wrought folly in Israel.* "[12]

Prophets and poets imagined their god less as a benign father and more as a jealous husband so embittered by his spouse's promiscuity that he threatens brutal vengeance: *"You sullied your beauty and spread your legs to every passerby,"* he rages... *"like the adulterous wife...I will direct bloody and impassioned fury against you.* "[13]

Their polytheistic neighbors worshipped Dionysus by various names. Indeed, the Hebrews themselves had a long tradition of collective ecstasy, which we know about only through the composers of the Old Testament. For hundreds of years, these writers grumbled that Israel was reverting to paganism. Eventually, with the triumph of monotheism and reason, they almost totally suppressed the Dionysian principle. They commanded, *"Thou shall not seethe a kid in its mother's milk.* "[14]

In Greek Orphism, however, the image of the kid in its mother's milk symbolized initiation through mystic sacrifice and infantile bliss with the mother. They inscribed in their tombs, *"From man thou hast become a god; a kid, thou hast fallen into milk.* "[15] The kid or infant become god was reunited with the Great Mother, as Dionysus had reunited with Semele. In this patriarchal world, the collective consciousness still referred to the old cycles, although *now it was the mother who had died, rather than the son.*

Neither Judaism nor Islam, in their ecstatic Hassidic and Sufi traditions, could totally suppress bodily worship. Christianity was more successful, at least until African-Americans brought Dionysian elements back into the church. But nothing in the psyche — personal or collective — is ever lost. When one culture destroys another, its values don't vanish. They fall into the collective unconscious, grow stronger and nurse their vengeance.

Gylany and Deep Masculinity

Rianne Eisler proposes a new term: *gylany,* formed from *gyne* (woman) and *andros* (man) and linked by the letter L, which recalls a word we've already encountered. *Lysis* is the root of *Lusios,* whose spell loosens boundaries between masculine and feminine. When these values are no longer banished to the cold war of polar opposites, they can interact creatively. The indigenous soul remembers its birth in gylany, and the collective unconscious periodically erupts in resurgences of gylanic values. This, however, doesn't imply a mushy mix of opposites. At the unitary level, as mystics tell us, such distinctions fade away. But we need them to live in the world.

Nor should gylanic thinking indicate an artificial construction of masculinity. Indeed, masculine archetypes seem to express themselves in hierarchies: God(s) → Sacred King → Father → Son. Such "deep masculinity" implies non-violent assertiveness, stewardship and creativity. But patriarchy, or "andocracy" (rule of men over women), literalized it into the dominator model that pervades western civilization. It creates *domination hierarchies* such as: (single, male) God → (divine-right) king → male priest → father → son → women → slaves.

In nature, however, we find *actualization hierarchies:* systems within systems arising from below toward more complex levels of function. Old Europeans imagined this one: Goddess-as-Creation ← male consort/ fertilizing principle ← Sacred king-and-queen ← community ← the individual.

Before proceeding, we must consider three more points. First is acknowledging the 7,000-year-old well of grief and rage in women. Second, masculinity does not equal patriarchy. Indeed, repressing deep masculinity actually helps to sustain this narrative. Although women's rage is older and deeper, men suffer as well under patriarchy. Third, the way out is *further in*, not for men to be more like women, but to be more authentic men by reviving initiation rites for younger men.

THE FEMININE THREAT

This book constantly poses a question: *what were they so afraid of?* Here is one answer: the universal fact of gender relations is "...not male hatred of women," writes Paglia, "but male *fear* of women."[16] Just below the heroic Greek psyche lay dread of the feminine. Most monsters were female: *Sphinx, Chimera, Python, Medusa, Gorgons, Harpies, Sirens, Charibdis, Scylla* and the *Furies*. As recently as the 1960s Greek folklore told of evil female spirits: *lamiae, gelloudes*, and child-devouring *striges*. The threatening feminine is often beautiful. *Glamour* is Scottish for a witch's power over men. The "nightmare" was originally an evil *female* spirit who afflicted sleepers. Greek men perceived images of mature female sexuality or assertiveness as threats. They imagined Athena as virginal and somewhat masculine, while Hera, who retained her femininity, was portrayed as a vindictive and persecutory bitch.

For 3,000 years male intellectuals have buttressed the lie of female inferiority because their ideas about women are based on male fantasies. Statements of rational, scientific, masculine consciousness arise from a mind that has discarded part of itself. We call this thinking Apollonic, says Hillman: "...like its name sake...it kills from a distance (its distance kills)..." Claiming objectivity, "it never merges with or 'marries' its material..." It defines our "very notion of consciousness itself."[17]

Athenian fathers, absent from the household most of the time, left boys in female-dominated environments. Their contempt for women and their brittle masculine self-confidence masked their insecurity and feelings of dependence. But playwrights terrified their audiences with powerful female characters: *Clytemnestra, Medea, Hecuba and Antigone*. By contrast, no

Shakespearean drama has a woman as its sole, main character (Cleopatra and Juliet share double billing.)

Woman, stereotyped as weak and unreasonable, is also mysterious and disturbing. The scene in *The Bacchae* when Dionysus dresses Pentheus in woman's clothes symbolizes both that threat and its transformative potential. Tragic heroines enacted the worst fears — and hidden desires — of male theatergoers. Psychologists might suggest that the fear represented the infant's terror of losing his primary love-object, his mother, or of being re-absorbed back into her. But the myths spoke of *revenge*, of the women of Lemnos, who murdered their men, or of Medea, who killed her own children just to spite her husband. This is dread of a different order. Athens stood upon a very unstable mountain of misogyny, and simple answers don't suffice.

At What Cost?

In asking what the Greeks had given up, we turn a mirror upon America. Modernity has rejected true diversity for monotheism, Dionysus for Apollo and communal values for individualism. We have long forgotten the unity of mind and body. Has there ever been a people like us who have been so uncomfortable in our bodies, who have allowed those bodies so little pleasure? Dionysus is not alone, of course, in the underworld. Aphrodite is there, too.

Freud argued that culture obtains much of its mental energy "by subtracting it from sexuality."[18] *By creating demand,* capitalism makes potential consumers feel deprived. Artificial scarcity of gratification assures surplus energy to drive the fevers of production and conquest. To generate scarcity, it attaches sexual interest to inaccessible, nonexistent, or irrelevant objects. Thus, writes Phillip Slater, "...making his most plentiful resource scarce, (man) managed...to make most of his scarce ones plentiful."[19]

Greek and Hebrew repression of the feminine set the mold for capitalism's trade-off, gratification for consumption. "The feminine," however, is a metaphor for *any* repressed mode: race; gender; class; etc. I perceive four levels of meaning. First: actual women's struggle for equality. Second, all peoples suffering the long-term consequences of colonialism and racism. Third, the so-called feminine *values* of receptivity and relatedness. Finally, the "lower" halves of *all* polarities: white/black; thinking/feeling; mind/body; life/death; spirit/soul; culture/nature; sacred/profane.

As without so as within. The mechanics of repression — and *return* of the repressed — are the same in both psyche and society. All indigenous modes that patriarchy, capitalism, consumerism and willful innocence have obscured await their opportunity. This is where Dionysus steps in. The "Loosener" invites the women to drop their veils, raise their skirts, declare their "virgin" independence and take their vengeance.

What is "revenge?" In myth, gods, especially Dionysus, commonly punish mortals who oppose or disrespect them. When Athens didn't receive his statue properly, Dionysus afflicted the men's genitals. They were cured only when they honored him by fashioning great phalluses for his worship.

Are these gods so fragile and insecure that myth justifies such immature behavior? Well, *yes,* since the Greeks created the Olympians in their own image. But if we imagine them less as impulsive, narcissistic superheroes and more as mentors in cosmic rituals of *telos*, or purpose, we ask, *"What do they want from us?"* Then, etymology helps. "Vengeance" (Latin: *vindicare*) means to claim, show authority, and curiously, to *set free*. What if we imagined vengeance as the setting-free, through symbolic death, of a soul or nation caught in the webs of illusion, distracted from its true purpose? Dionysus *demands* that we pay attention, and he determines the consequences of our refusal.

Paying Attention

How does an entire society welcome this vengeful, unpredictable god in hopes that he *won't* take vengeance? The Athenians were deeply aware of the seduction of the irrational. Every February, during the *Anthesteria*, they invoked him as purifier, rather than as destroyer. For over 1,000 years, this all-soul's festival welcomed the spirits of the dead — and Dionysus, who brought with him the new wine — for three days of drinking, processions, insults and merry-making. But it was also a period of deep solemnity, because the people knew that they couldn't go to one extreme without invoking its opposite.

Impersonated by a priest wearing a two-faced mask, Dionysus returned from Hades on a wheeled ship crowned with vine tendrils and pulled by panthers. People masked themselves as ancestral spirits who had emerged from the wine casks and were roaming the city. "Wild laughter," writes Walter Burkett, "is acted out against the backdrop of terror..."[20]

In similar Egyptian, Babylonian and Roman New Year's festivals ritual purification announced the end of one cosmic cycle and the beginning of another. Later, Christian Europe celebrated Carnival at this time, and the King and Queen still arrive on a wheeled ship. Dionysian revels are followed by the austerities of Lent, the grieving of Good Friday and Easter. Clearly, the *Anthesteria* was a model for this holiday.

Temporary inversion of the social order and breaking of taboos characterized carnival. Entire communities participated as temporary equals, with little distinction between performers and audience. In the "Feast of Fools" pent-up repression exploded in mock rituals and wild excess within churches, sometimes with clergy participating. Amid the merriment, we still observe the ancient theme of welcoming the masked spirits of the dead. Modernity, however, has reduced Carnival to the consumer spectacles of Mardi Gras, New Year's, "spring break" and the Superbowl. But the Greek town of Monoklissia still celebrates the *Gynaecocracy* ("rule of women") festival, when women and men trade roles for a day.

The Anthesteria was all this and more. The *basilinna*, wife of the religious leader, ritually copulated with Dionysus. While scholars consider this a fertility ritual that ensured good crops, she was also re-enacting the ancient *hieros gamos* marriage of goddess and consort, of the *inner* queen and king meeting in the sea — the deep Self. It recalled and evoked the unity behind all dualities. Indigenous knowledge was still alive: the proximity of decomposition and fertility, of pollution and the sacred, of death and new life.

We will never know exactly what occurred, or how people interpreted it. Who the basillina slept with, or whether they consummated literally, doesn't matter. This does: the Other symbolically invaded the royal household and claimed her. Then the Athenians donned masks, got drunk, and ignored gender-roles and rules of fidelity. Master and slave briefly exchanged roles.

Next morning, however, they symbolically fed the spirits, swept through the streets and chased them away for another year.

We have here a partial record of how an advanced urban civilization acknowledges the irrational. The rich certainly hoped these rituals would minimize the eruption of energies that could topple their palaces, that because of the attention they paid to the Lord of the Darkness there might *not* be a catastrophic return of the repressed, in the city or in their souls.

Clearly, the deep tensions in Athenian life could only be partially resolved by such festivals as the Anthesteria. Dionysus inhabited the center of this paradox, representing the return of the repressed needs of women and slaves, return of the non-rational part of the self, and return of the ancient connection to the living unity of nature.

After generations of war, however, Euripides announced with his final play that the subtle balance between citizen, psyche and city was broken. The repressed was returning as barbarians from without and demons within. Was it a pessimistic statement? As history, it certainly is; he predicted the end of Athens' Golden Age. But *The Bacchae* also imagines the transformative experiences that make young men (and perhaps young nations) grow up. In this sense, it offers a glimmer of hope for the future, but not without a considerable dose of "learning through suffering."

*Every increase in knowledge is an increase
in sorrow.*
TRADITIONAL

Every act of creation is first an act of destruction.
PABLO PICASSO

Whoever isn't busy being born is busy dying.
BOB DYLAN

He acts as if he has no relatives.
NAVAJO INSULT

---

*A man needs a little madness, or else he never
dares cut the rope and be free!*
NIKOS KAZANTZAKIS

---

*The true mission of American sports is to prepare
young men for war.*
DWIGHT EISENHOWER

---

*You teach a child to read, and he or her will be
able to pass a literacy test.*
GEORGE W. BUSH

05

INITIATION

WHAT IS A MAN? Are uninitiated men really men? The theme of initiation, and of men who don't know themselves, lies at the core of this examination of American innocence. Indigenous people believe that initiation is absolutely indispensable for the continuation of culture. From this perspective, all our major dilemmas — alienation, racism, environmental destruction and endless war — result from the breakdown of the myths that bind people together, and of the ritual initiations of youth that, for millennia, cleansed and restored society.

How does this theme emerge from our story? Pentheus epitomizes misogyny, self-control and Puritanical sublimation of *Eros* to the goals of the state. *And he is young.* Where is his father? Stories provide clues in their structure to the problems they address. Echion's absence indicates an interruption in the transmission of authentic masculine values. We never learn why Cadmus has abdicated in favor of this untested young man. Why did Euripides choose to present Pentheus as an *ephebe,* a youth just at the point of transition to adulthood?

A powerful man who remains a boy emotionally endangers the *polis.*

He lacks the wisdom that comes from having suffered into experience. Pentheus' youth symbolizes the uninitiated masculine psyche at *any* chronological age. Boy-kings, born to royalty (or chosen by Supreme Courts), cannot distinguish the greater good from the narrow interests of their social class. Such autocrats reduce the vast majority of their people to the status of Other. In extreme cases they become inflated with the archetype of the King. "L'etat, c'est Moi," said Louis XIV, "I *am* the State." Such men lack gravity; like adolescents everywhere, they live in reaction to the ground that bore them, killing the snake-dragons of the feminine, preferring force over persuasion and power over love. As Dionysus tells Pentheus, such men do not know themselves.

LITIMA, OR WHY INITIATION?

What does society need from young men, and what do they need from their elders? Indigenous cultures have always known the social consequences of what science now understands: the sudden, thirty-fold increase of testosterone in the blood of adolescent boys. Michael Meade describes this in terms of the Gisu people of Uganda:

> *Litima* is the violent emotion peculiar to the masculine...
> source of quarrels, ruthless competition, possessiveness...
> and brutality, and that is also the source of independence,
> courage...and meaningful ideals...the willful emotional force
> that fuels the process of becoming an individual...source of
> the... aggression necessary to undergo radical change. But
> Litima is ambiguous ... both the capacity to erupt in violence
> and the capacity to defend others, both the aggression that
> breaks things and the force that builds and protects.[1]

Litima poses a dilemma: how to transform those raging hormones from anti-social expression into something positive? This cannot be stated too strongly: uninitiated men cause universal suffering. Either they burn with creativity or they burn everything down. This *biological* issue transcends debates over gender socialization. Although patriarchal conditioning legitimates and perpetuates it, their *nature* drives young men to violent excess.

Rites of passage provide metaphor and symbol so that boys don't have to act their inner urges out. Even in ancient matricentric societies, this was true. *Boys must be transformed into men;* without deliberate intervention by elders, they remain boys. It is tempting to idealize indigenous culture. Thousands of independent societies were crushed under the weight of colonialism. While some were relatively non-aggressive, others did have brutal warrior traditions. However, we cannot know if they had always been aggressive and patriarchal, or whether they had undergone earlier transitions from matricentric culture. Nor can we know just how far back in the past such cultures lost their original initiation rituals and degenerated into brutal circumcision ceremonies (for girls as well as boys).

Pursuing the mystery further, we discover that although *litima* can drive everyone crazy, it is *always* connected to one's sense of purpose. Martin Prechtel, of the Guatemalan Tzutujil Mayans, writes that his people called adolescence the "holy illness." They believed that both young men and the world itself needed to be re-made regularly. The two rituals were intimately connected: "Without initiation, renewal ceases and the flower withers."[2]

"Adolescence" is related to "nourish." Something *already present* in a youth needs to be identified, cultivated and educated ("to lead out"), rather than instructed ("to pile on"). Without being seen and encouraged by one's elders, however, purpose rarely emerges in a socially positive manner. It festers and turns sour. So initiation pulls someone deeper into life than he would normally choose to go, or in Jung's words, away from "neurotic suffering" toward "authentic suffering."

Since bonding with mother is so strong in the tribal world, an abrupt break is necessary. The male psyche intuits that this shift requires a kind of death. Mayan youths traditionally got captured in whirlwinds of emotion: "...the madness of their holy pollinating illness made them run directly toward death and ruin."[3]

Psychology argues that frustration produces aggression. But *holy illness* indicates something more profound than dysfunctional families. Malidoma Somé observes: "...they say in the village that an unruly youth is asking in his own way for someone to guide him."[4] An archetypal hunger for renewal drives his self-destructive behavior. Something must die. The symbolic death of initiation, however, can substitute for actual death. Mircea Eliade writes:

> The central moment of every initiation is…the ceremony symbolizing the death of the novice and his return to the fellowship of the living. But he returns to life a new man… "death" corresponds to…the end of a mode of being… a state cannot be changed without first being annihilated.[5]

LIMINALITY

Initiatory transitions are marked by three phases. Leaving a well-defined status or identity, one enters the *separation* stage. Then he moves into the *ordeals,* the *liminal* ("threshold") state. He is "betwixt and between," timeless, ambiguous, in sacred space for as long as required. The third phase is *re-incorporation* into his community with a new identity.

Indigenous people imagine spiritual worlds existing alongside this one. Their myths represent liminality with images of death, or with bridges, crossroads and borderlands — places where one world meets another — or by dawn and dusk, when one time fades into another. To know themselves, boys must first endure liminality and suffer psychological dismemberment. If they refuse, they remain children in the eyes of the community.

First, the older men separate them from everything familiar. Since these are generally communal rituals (but boys only undergo the process when their individuality becomes apparent), they relate to no one but each other and their ritual elders. Possessing no property, they are considered impure, invisible or genderless. They are, as Mathew Arnold wrote, "…wandering between two worlds; one dead, the other powerless to be born."

The elders teach ancestral myths that relate to each initiate's life purpose. Identity shifts from vertical connections with family into horizontal bonds with clan. The objective is to awaken the elder in the youth. Outcomes, however, are not pre-determined; the ordeal of symbolic death and rebirth risks actual death or madness. Inevitably, some fall over that line.

Those who survive are welcomed back as men. This acknowledgement implies permanent change. Elders may mark the irreversible nature of the occasion by bestowing new names upon the youths. Ritual scarification, if it occurs, is intended to leave outer evidence of inner changes: affirmation of limitation, mystery, ambiguity and kinship with the Other in ever-widening spheres of meaning and participation.

Joseph Campbell universally observed exactly this same initiatory process in hero myths. Descents to the underworld expressed the awareness that something must die for something new to be born. The *Hero With a Thousand Faces* endured separation and initiation. Having accomplished his tasks, he returned with his prize of consciousness or spiritual abundance and took his place in his community. His newly attained wisdom was for *their* benefit. He became a citizen, one who gave more than he took. That symbolic journey, however, had to be protected within a strong container or crucible. If it was too weak or too hot, then it wasn't safe enough for the necessary psychological dismemberment to occur.

DISMEMBERMENT

The boundaries of identity continually shift. If they become inflexible, some god will instigate another initiation. Extreme rigidity evokes extreme responses. The destruction of old forms that changes boys into men is analogous to the shamanic experience, writes Eliade. "The profane man is being 'dissolved' and a new personality...prepared for birth." Siberian initiates are *torn apart:* "... they 'die' and...are cut up by demons... their bones are cleaned, the flesh scraped off..."[6] In modern cultures such images can appear in the visions of those who descend into madness. "If they are not supplied from without," writes Campbell, "...they will have to be announced again, through dream, from within."[7]

What is being "dis-membered"? In fact, it is phallic, heroic masculinity that breaks down so a certain psychological bisexuality may emerge. Dismemberment has one advantage, writes Nor Hall: "...we get to see all the parts."[8] The initiate re-members an interior marriage of his active and passive natures that he once had in childhood. The hero dies so an elder may be born.

In *The Bacchae's* final scenes, Cadmus addresses Pentheus as "boy" or "child" several times. *This boy is being killed symbolically* so that something else may arise. Pentheus cannot discover his mature form — "man of sorrow" — until his immature form is dead. As Yeats wrote, *"...nothing can be sole or whole that has not been rent."* The play declared to the *epheboi* in the audience that they must die as boys to become men. Perhaps Euripides was speaking to the entire male leadership; only men of sorrow, with compassion born from shared suffering, could be citizens of his Polis.

Dionysus tells Pentheus, "You do not know who you are." Pentheus interprets the statement literally and responds, "I am Pentheus, son of Echion and Agave." He knows his lineage but not his soul. Later, Dionysus ironically predicts: "You go to an extraordinary experience," and the chorus announces that Pentheus' youthful grandiosity will soon be punctured: "They humble us with death, that we remember what we are...not god, but men."

The messenger sings that the greatest prize mortals may win is humility (related to *human, humor, humble* and *humus*). The women had discovered Pentheus observing them from the top of a pine tree, far from the ground. Now his body parts lie upon the real source of power and renewal, the earth. Cadmus supervises the body's reassembly, because initiating a boy is a man's work.

Pentheus was immature, but he was still the King. Some scholars argue that myths of the killing of the king recall literal regicide. But indigenous people know that when young men don't transform into men, catastrophe results: outwardly, against the Other, or inwardly, in depression, addiction or suicide. This is the meaning of the killing of the king: when a youth is denied initiation, his *nobility* dies.

Initiation Throughout Life

Initiates periodically undergo new transformations. No single event awards permanent status. Each initiation is a temporary qualification to enter the next period of change, when something new will break open. Although the core of the Self doesn't change, initiates keep being made, unmade and remade.

This is possible, however, only if individuals are rooted in communities which in turn are held in broad, mythic containers. This allows them to enter into continually deeper transformations, to endure authentic, rather than neurotic, suffering. Mayan adolescents, writes Prechtel, realized that everyone's goal was "eventual admission into the pursuit and maintenance of the sacred."[9] Eventually, when one completes his worldly responsibilities, he enters elderhood. Then his concerns become initiation of the young and his final transition to the ancestral realm. Having faced many "small" initiatory deaths, he no longer fears the "big" death. A West African proverb says, "When death comes, let it find you alive!"

Indigenous cultures gave ritual higher priority than production. Ironically, Europeans observed such spiritual preoccupations and pronounced tribal people "lazy." How could they or we, living in our demythologized world, make sense of this comment by Somé: "In my village, people spend seventy-five percent to eighty-five percent of their time either doing ritual, or talking about ritual, or recovering from ritual."[10]

As initiation rites have disappeared, so have the clear distinctions between life's developmental stages. Consequently, adolescence in America seems to continue indefinitely. This is not to say that there are no initiations in modern life. The dizzying pace of change evokes liminality in everyone, and the psyche reacts to separation and loss as if initiations were underway. But we endure theses transitions alone and unprotected by ritual and community. From childhood trauma to divorce and war, no one puts our suffering into a larger context or welcomes us home. This drains our capacity to express our purpose, and we live lifetimes of *incomplete* initiations. Victor Turner, the anthropologist who popularized the term liminality, coined another term to describe this modern condition. The "liminoid" is the depotentiated, degraded toxic mimic of liminality; such people typically hide their own sense of unworthiness even from themselves, preferring to project upon the Other.

There are many theories of alienation, but from the indigenous perspective, it is simple: modern people simply don't know who we are. We harden around our unfinished initiations, and our wounds fester. Childhood abuse is the most extreme but also the best example: initiation at the wrong time, by the wrong people for the wrong reasons produces isolated, anxious, untrusting adults who are likely to re-enact their wounds or inflict them upon the young. Such people have not experienced enough bonding with parents and clan; they need to spend the effort to re-establish a sense of self before they can risk having it dismembered in initiation ritual. Then they can begin to look back at those events in life that had an initiatory character and determine what remains incomplete.

These are the consequences of the loss of initiation. Those who refuse to enter the cauldron force others to suffer. Youth carry the load of generations who never received (and cannot give) initiation. The *Litima* in young men must be engaged before it turns literal. Traditional people channel it into art, but modern society prefers to ignore it until self-destructive behavior demands our attention. Every army and gang is made up of youths fascinated with danger, searching for that brush with death, and for some transpersonal cause to surrender to. If society doesn't respond to this intensity, writes Somé, "…it becomes an incinerating fire directed at the entire society."[11] At each initiation something must die — an outdated self-concept — before new growth can occur; and this process involves confronting the Other within.

MALE INITIATION AND THE FEMININE

Prechtel writes, "Only an initiated man could marry a woman and not be miserable."[12] By rooting men in their essential masculinity, initiation also brought them into mature relationship with the feminine. Initiation always preceded courtship and marriage, because untransformed men were likely to abuse women. It was obvious to them that when rape is the only way to get what a man wants, as Paglia writes, "…he is confessing to a weakness… She is abused, but he is utterly tragic and pathetic."[13]

Consider circumcision: at best, modern circumcision bestows tribal membership, or identification in terms of the Other (what the Other doesn't do); at worst, it is meaningless suffering. But among the Australian Aborigines, wrote Campbell, such rites tore boys from the comforting maternal world and compensated them for loss of the mother: "…the male phallus, instead of the female breast, is made the central point… of the imagination."[14] Boys learned that they could be nurtured from male elders as well as from their mothers. Paradoxically, temporary separation from women activated their *non-violent* relational capacity and directed their *litima* toward protecting the feminine. Such men do not define their masculinity in contrast to the feminine.

Those who define themselves as *not*-women, however, must either keep separate to maintain their purity or dominate women to enforce mastery. Uninitiated men are preoccupied with literal sexuality rather than with the erotic, which they reject as effeminate. They require women to carry it all — feeling, fantasy, loving, relating, inspiration. We retain a vague memory of the secret male societies common among tribal people in all-male clubs, barbershops, poker nights and taverns. But, writes psychologist Jerome Bernstein, such events serve primarily as "places where men…hide from the Devouring Mother, rather than to gear up for a final wrenching free of her."[15] This truth underlies TV caricatures of American men, from *The Honeymooners* in the 1950s to *The Simpsons* in the 2000s.

Authentic masculinity *serves* the feminine. Holding it within, a mature man does not need to project and demonize it outwardly. Initiation encourages youths to leave the primal relationship with mother, to be held by something larger: nature. They are introduced to "the Great Mother in nature and to the Mother of Inspiration, who presides over the well of memory and art," writes Meade.[16]

"King" and "Queen" are gendered terms referring to a quality of soul — *nobility* (related to *gnosis*, to know) that is unrelated to gender. Nobility may be found in men or women, with a *tone* that is generally more or less male or female. It may be helpful to substitute "active and passive" for male and female, or even to use words like "dynamic" and "magnetic." Nobles know themselves; and no one attains nobility without enduring continual initiation. This leads to *sophia*, the wisdom that characterizes the sacred king or queen of the psyche.

WOMEN'S INITIATIONS

Young women went through initiations throughout the pre-modern world. *The Bacchae* is a male initiation story, so we will visit the topic of female initiation briefly to note some general contrasts. First, male rites were generally communal, while female initiations were not. Tribal societies celebrated individual girls as women upon first menstruation, whereas the holy madness could afflict boys at any time. The elders took on groups of boys who had shown their readiness by their *behavior,* regardless of their age.

Second, since girls generally mature through biological changes, their initiations were primarily confirmation rites; nature had already turned them into women. By contrast, a boy's *litima* didn't make him a man. He was *made into a man through the intervention of representatives of culture.* So male initiations were rituals of transformation rather than of confirmation.

Third, uninitiated women may be narcissistic or depressed, filling their meaningless lives with eating disorders, consumerism and early pregnancy. I don't minimize their plight. Unlike uninitiated males, however, they generally don't seek their souls by going to war.

I KNOW WHO I AM

Campbell taught that a living *myth refers past itself* to the ineffable, serving four distinct functions. First of all, the *mystical* function introduces the individual to that which underlies all names and forms. It awakens religious awe, humility and respect. Second, the *cosmological* function explains how the universe works. Third, the *pedagogical* function defines a moral life in terms of the particular culture.

Fourth — and most pervasive — the *social* function validates the social order and integrates individuals within the community. Originally, it oriented people to the mystery by presenting noble figures at the center of the realm or psyche who radiated the blessings that flowed through them from the other world. These figures *served* this order and showed that everyone carried such potential within. If people still revere royalty, it is from vestigial memory of what the sacred King once meant.

"It is this sociological function of myth that has taken over," wrote Campbell, "...and it is out of date."[17] Myth, however, shapes our values, organizes our experience, brings emotion to our festivals, sets the boundaries of dissent, names the children, sends them off to war and justifies their sacrifice. It is the most compelling story we tell ourselves about who we are. And frequently it is the story of who we are *not* — the Other.

We experience reality through this sociological level and regularly engage in cognitive dissonance. If facts disagree with strongly held beliefs, then *the facts* must change. "Myth," writes historian Ira Chernus, "appeals to us because it lifts us out of history."[18]

A *living* myth, however, nourishes at all levels. The greatest stories can be heard throughout life because each level of meaning provides an imaginative opening to other levels. In other words, it isn't simple political indoctrination that prevents people from questioning their national stories. There must be something else, some profound truths that compel their attention and point to the cosmic and mystical levels, to what could be trying to be born.

Perhaps we can say the same thing about knowledge. The statement "I know who I am," indicates solid roots in ethnic, class, gender and/or national identity. But it can also imply anything from memory of ancestry to a completely unexamined life. "Know thyself" can be a reminder of mortal limits, a euphemism for not questioning authority or an indicator of the massive weight of original sin and Man's irredeemably evil nature.

Too often "I know who I am" means, "I am not one of them. *Woman is Other.*" This is how patriarchy constructs masculinity. Men have often tried to create lineages entirely free of women, where only battle makes a warrior out of a boy, and his rebirth as a warrior, like his original birth, is marked by blood. After the U.S. invasion of Panama in 1989, the press hailed President Bush for succeeding in an "initiation rite" by demonstrating his "willingness to shed blood."[19]

We can also interpret "Know thyself" mystically — to *experience* the divine as Hinduism and western esotericism describe it. It could mean aligning the Jungian "ego-self axis," or "serving the right god," as poets write. It could imply removing the veil of amnesia, remembering the primordial unity that one once knew in the other world or realizing the essential non-existence of the ego. In some cultures, successful aspirants receive new or secret names to indicate their new status. Not to have completed the transition is to live in *ignominy* (literally, not to have a name), as Yeats wrote:

The ignominy of boyhood; the distress
Of boyhood turning into man;
The unfinished man and his pain
Brought face to face with his own clumsiness...

We live at the intersections of many myths. Since chronological time is irrelevant in psyche or myth, we may simultaneously identify as child in one story, as deity in another, as animal in a third. The essence of soul work is to identify these intersections, so as to come further into alignment with purpose. These are the cosmological and mystical levels. But we live, more or less unconsciously, inside the sociological and pedagogical levels — our culture's *non*-universal myths.

INITIATION IN AMERICA

A society that begins by denying the soul's longing cannot possibly satisfy it. Instead, our rites of passage socialize children into consumer lifestyles and gender roles. Boys begin to mute their emotional expression around age five, while girls do so around twelve. This, writes psychologist Carol Gilligan, is a "process of initiation...akin to trauma."[20] First through gender and later through race, American boys confront the Other. By *resisting* it, they learn the restrained self-mastery of middle class masculinity. They also learn, through dozens of subtle lessons in which they are pitted against others, that competition is America's primary value, and that consumerism is the emblem of success. Television in particular offers images and therefore expectations, with no means of fulfillment other than the consumption of commodities. Hundreds of times a day, boys are told that they don't have to die before being reborn as men — they only have to purchase a different set of products.

Our initiations are class-based. Middle-class youth experience conventional celebrations such as bar mitzvahs. Afterwards, however, few feel significantly different. These events (and most weddings) typically mark the *parents'* social status. Debutant cotillions and beauty pageants do recall female initiation, announcing that young women are available for marriage. However, these ceremonies are all rituals of *confirmation* rather than transformation.

Baptism is rooted in ancient rituals in which water represented the womb of a second birth. It evokes the third phase of initiation, re-incorporating the initiate into the community. These rituals occurred not once, but whenever a person lost touch with his/her purpose or place in the community. Modern baptism, however, offers no risk and asks little of the initiate, who — again — may not feel fundamentally different, let alone transformed.

Our ceremonies lack another critical factor. One reason for the decline of the religious vocation is the possibility of breaking one's vows and leaving the priesthood. Such *reversibility* deprives the choice of its radically transformative character. Clearly, this is also true of marriage.

Fraternity initiations can seem quite realistic. But they typically allow boys to remain boys while cementing future business and political unions. In these *ceremonies of entitlement,* their elite group identity excludes the vast majority of their own social class, let alone the rest of the *polis.*

Public education, writes Noam Chomsky, is a system of imposed ignorance in which the most highly educated people are the most highly indoctrinated. In political terms, "A good education instills in you the intuitive comprehension — it becomes unconscious and reflexive — that you just don't *think* certain things...that are threatening to power interests."[21] In psychological terms, America is still deeply influenced by its heritage of Puritanism. This has left a residue of moralistic education that teaches and schools through denial, both of the wisdom of the body as well as of the innate needs for initiation and purpose. It is more concerned with restrictions on behavior and speech than on hearing what may be emerging from a young person's soul.

Since tribal societies valued *all* their young men, their initiations were communal and usually mandatory. The dangers were real, but all were encouraged to *complete* the transition. By contrast, the primary function of our advanced degrees, professional licensing exams and corporate promotion is to choose *who* will succeed, not to ensure that all will. In business, academics and sports, definitions of success and masculinity require the *failure* of others. Thus, money and consumer goods, rather than wisdom, mark successfully socialized men.

Countless others, defined as losers, are excluded from the initiatory group. In 2004, Four million American eighteen to thirty-four-year old men were unemployed, were not in school and lacked a degree beyond high school. Some respond to the pseudo-rituals of hate groups, which accept them solely on the basis of race and offer both belonging and privilege through identification in terms of the Other.

Without authentic rituals, we make our own informal — and unconscious — ones. Many youths create personal initiations by intentionally approaching that brush with death with fast cars or extreme sports. Though these experiences can validate their sense of ability and self-worth, there is a shadow side. Surviving danger feels so good that one wants to repeat it. This happens if the danger lacks symbolic components, occurs without community ritual or has no spiritual context. The youths experience the thrill of potency *without* the satisfaction of being acknowledged and welcomed by their community. And accidents are the leading cause of death in this age group. For many men, Samuel Johnson's eighteenth century quote, "Every man thinks meanly of himself for not having been a soldier," is still applicable.

Working-class men receive their initiations in the military. Boot-camp instructors, who know ritual better than clergymen, work with three components of adolescence: *litima;* a tendency to associate in groups; and the desperate desire to fit in and serve a cause. They break down recruits symbolically by shaving their heads, replacing individual egos with membership in closed initiatory groups, and presenting obstacles that evoke the Hero's journey. Typically however, they assign those obstacles the stereotyped, racist characteristics of the Other. This literalizes what could be a symbolic defeat of one's *inner* demons. Philip Caputo describes his experience: "Soon, each platoon (was) transformed from a group of individuals to... a machine of which we were merely parts."[22]

Armies have no interest in encouraging individual purpose, despite the cloying invitation to "be all you can be." Indoctrination is a particularly cruel mimic of the real thing, writes Robert Moore, that "amplifies the striving for power and control in… an adolescent form regulated by other adolescents."[23] Fathers often make the ritual pronouncement, *"We sent a boy, and we're getting a man back,"* but this is merely initiation into the culture of death. It is a tragic irony that childhood's death is precisely what young men desire. Undeniably, combat burns away their innocence. They return wiser, but in this third phase of the hero's journey, they bring their communities no gifts. If they have sought initiation they are usually disappointed, because loss of innocence does not equal new status — and for this reason it can become addictive.

An odd paradox centers on the question of choice. Tribal people often dragged boys abruptly out of childhood and thrust them, terrified, into the ordeals with little warning and little choice to participate or not. But in class-based ceremonies of social advancement, there is *no* question of either danger *or* of transformation. In a modern, pluralistic society, millions choose to *not* make the attempt, but this very freedom reinforces the weakness of our ceremonies.

Poor youth, with little opportunity to channel their *litima* into business or often even into the military, may choose the only alternative. *Gangs* provide protection, identification of the Other (other gangs), territoriality, discipline, allegiance to leaders (adults actually lead most "youth" gangs), identification through clothing, and ritual scarification. Tattooing and body piercing are traditional attempts to leave permanent proof of an intense experience or group identification. Indeed, we cannot tease the issue of body art from that of self-mutilation. Thirty-six percent of Americans age 18 to 29 have tattoos. Nearly twenty percent of *Ivy League* students report purposely burning or cutting themselves. What seems to be pathology at one level is ritual at another.[24] Few of the youth realize that they are unconsciously recreating indigenous ritual, where the scar inflicted by the true initiators indicates that they have identified both a wound in the soul and a connection to deep purpose.

Gangs provide another factor that constellates the archetype of initiation: *irreversibility*. When youths join gangs (which may require violent acts in addition to tattoos as proof of their commitment) they sense their changed status. Extreme penalties for reversing that status ensure its permanence. And gang violence merely distorts the mainstream capitalistic value of "survival of the fittest." But with no mythology, and no true elders to guide them or place their suffering into context, they find rituals of death, not of life. For gang members and soldiers alike, a sense of betrayal and cynicism about their elders may develop. Those who survive the brush with death often become the new pseudo-elders, passing their rage onto the younger generations.

Pseudo-initiations have another factor in common: *ritual humiliation.* In such patriarchal ceremonies, the group welcomes new members with violence. Some gang initiations require all members to participate in severely beating the initiates. The military does so through verbal abuse, while fraternities utilize absurd, alcohol-soaked challenges. And, to those who could see, the 2009 Supreme Court confirmation hearings for Sonia Sotomayor involved humiliation that was no less intense for being symbolic. Paradoxically, these actions are a twisted form of love, because in these worlds love itself is twisted.

Youths may find "spirits" in the bottle. Addiction can be an unconscious search for rebirth, but it inverts the initiatory process, bringing a form of euphoric rebirth without any symbolic death. In Meade's words, such attempts become "… miscarriages of meaning… repeating the same alchemical mistake and mov(ing) toward actual death when real change was the desire… the sacrifice doesn't work."[25]

Drugs and gangs lead to another pseudo-initiation. A jail cell curiously evokes a ritual container, and many inner-city youth perceive prison as precisely the place for their rites of passage. For most, the possibility of incarceration remains a deterrent, but not, writes Luis Rodriguez, "for those who see incarceration as directly tied to their cultural identity..."[26] They become soldiers who turn their rage against their own people. Since prison rituals encourage them to identify men who look like themselves as the Other, most minority crime is directed against other minorities.

The further we investigate initiation by social class, the more important becomes an unbiased view of mandatory — *forced* — public education. Former New York State "Teacher of the Tear" John Gatto asks, "Could it be that our schools are designed to make sure that not one (child) ever really grows up?"[27] America's educational system was modeled on that of nineteenth century Prussia. Six generations of us have endured a routine designed to restrain dissent and originality and reduce everyone to a uniform, standardized level.

Gatto, quoting from early texts, distills schooling's intent into six functions:

1. *Adjusting:* establishing fixed habits of reaction to authority to preclude critical judgment.
2. *Integrating:* making people as alike as possible.
3. *Diagnosing:* determining everyone's proper social role.
4. *Differentiating:* sorting children by role and training them "only so far as their destination in the social machine permits."
5. *Selecting:* identifying the unfit at an early age.
6. Finally, the *propaedeutic* function: teaching a minority to manage the rest, who are "deliberately dumbed down and declawed..."[28]

Public schooling teaches children that they can exchange obedience for favors and advantages. It was never intended to create citizens, but servile laborers and consumers. It leaves children vulnerable to marketing, which ensures that they will grow older but never grow up. And it reverses the age-old tradition of identifying a child's unique gifts. The latest insult, standardized testing, continues to convert hope into docility and narcissism. An unexpected bi-product has been an epidemic of illiteracy. In 1909, Woodrow Wilson, then president of Princeton University, told teachers, "We want one class of persons to have a liberal education, and we want another class *...a very much larger class...* to forgo the privilege..." From precisely that point, just before World War I (when the system was installed universally), literacy declined from nearly one hundred percent to a point when, in 1973, twenty-seven percent of men were rejected from military service because of functional illiteracy. Now, claims Gatto, "forty percent of blacks and seventeen percent of whites can't read at all."[29]

Our transitions reflect our cult of individualism. Americans often feel a compulsion to *leave home* that isn't necessarily shared by youth in other cultures. Historian James Robertson writes, "The ritual American act of courage is the declaration of independence-rebellion-migration of the American adolescent."[30] Since cars symbolize independence, driver's license tests have become our primary rites of passage. But passing them doesn't indicate a shift to adulthood, because, for most Americans, it never really happens.

Male "midlife crises," however, are strikingly similar to initiation. Often beginning with job loss or divorce, men enter the separation period of regrets about the past. Then comes liminality, loosening of identity and emergence of personality aspects that were dormant during earlier, heroic years. Most pass quickly to the re-integration phase without significant change. But some are fundamentally altered and committed to continual self-examination. For them, writes Psychologist Murray Stein, liminality is a "permanent dimension...that threads through all time and occupies a space in every period of life."[31]

One of Jung's fundamental insights was that in midlife new issues emerge from the repressed unconscious. Men appropriately turn inward, emphasize the "inferior function" (usually their emotions), and ponder their mortality. But Jung and Freud treated repressed, middle-class Europeans. Midlife crisis may be a modern construct, something that people with intact initiation traditions never endured. They experienced two unequal halves of life: childhood and adulthood. "Midlife" occurred in the brief period of physical maturation, what we call adolescence. An Aboriginal elder says, "For us, adolescence lasts five days — the time of the initiation. Before initiation he is a child, after initiation, he is an adult."[32] *Modern men endure midlife crises because they don't experience initiation as teenagers.* This is why the three-phase structures of both transitions are similar. Stated differently, nature brings forth in us what pagans deliberately provoked from long experience with adolescent *litima.*

The culture of consumerism, however, invites us to remain forever young. From Peter Pan to Michael Jackson's "Neverland" Ranch, we idolize boys who won't grow up and celebrities who never age. In the 1980s, with hair-dyed Ronald Reagan as President, the nation laughed nervously to *"Darling, you look... marvelous!"* The joke was on us all. Three popular TV shows of the 1990s (*Seinfeld, Friends* and *Sex and the City*) about adults who hadn't quite escaped adolescence, played at the same time as Bill Clinton's frat-house-style sex scandal. In 2005 American women endured nine million cosmetic surgeries.[33] "Looking old," writes journalist Joan Ryan, "has become abnormal...a character defect, a sign of laziness, negligence..."[34]

Elevating this condition to high status, capitalism has inverted one of humanity's oldest relationships. Elders — who, in tribal cultures initiate the young — have no value. Rather than asking them for spiritual guidance, we imprison them in nursing homes and gated communities, because they remind us of that enemy, old age. We ask nothing of them but to be consumers.

Desperate to appear young, we ignore the massive evidence of cruelty to our *actual* children. Below our idealization of youth lies the myth of the Killing of the Children. This is one of America's greatest paradoxes, which we will closely examine in the next chapter.

A final point about American initiation: To attain serious political power, many women have been forced to reject feminine — and even human — values. Secretary of State Madeline Albright, asked on television about the deaths of a half million Iraqi children caused by American economic sanctions *prior* to the 2003 invasion, responded, "...it's worth it."[35] Condoleeza Rice pursued the same policies and worse. Such accommodation to the demands of *realpolitik* indicates that to be accepted in the world of uninitiated men, women must emphasize *their own uninitiated masculine natures,* which untransformed, will seek out and cause literal death.

ANCIENT GREEK INITIATION

By the fifth century B.C.E., initiation rites were preserved only partially in the indoctrination ceremonies of societies that were perpetually at war.

In the paranoid police state of Sparta, a minority of citizens dominated thousands of serfs. Teachers took young boys from their parents and disciplined them to be unaffected by pain or compassion. Youths constantly trained for war and didn't attain full adult status until age thirty. Around eighteen, they endured public whipping and were expected to show no signs of pain. According to reports, some actually died, but did not cry. The survivors became men capable of both self-sacrifice and extreme cruelty.

Upper-class Athenian youths ceremonially cut their long hair at puberty and spent much time at gymnastics preparing for military service. Male clans welcomed new members in rituals called *apellai,* after Apollo, who embodied the turning point in the flower of youth. The *kouros,* or the beautiful adolescent male, was the central image of Greek art. Such men knew who they were, even if identity required near-total suppression of the feminine.

Male rites followed the universal, three-part pattern. Men took the boys away, subjected them to trials and returned them in great public ceremonies. The first stage was the *pompé* (procession). The *agon* (contest or ordeal) corresponded to the liminal stage. Indeed, the main characters in drama, the *prot*agonist and the *ant*agonist, conflicted in an agon of purification. Thus Tragedy itself reflected initiation patterns. The third stage, or *komos,* (root of comedy) was the triumphal return.

Others went further, toward Dionysus or Demeter, whose Eleusinian mysteries lasted for over 1,000 years. Ultimately, these initiations prepared them for the final transition. They did not fear death, because they had already experienced another life. Plato said, "To die is to be initiated."

INITIATION IN MYTH

Greek myth is a tangled amalgam of stories. Some are extremely old and do honor the feminine. Stories justifying patriarchy replaced many others, but we can still identify the initiation theme in them. The blinding of Oedipus and Tiresias revealed deeper "in-sight." The *Odyssey* is a series of initiations in which a one-dimensional hero becomes a mature king. All descents to the underworld — endured by Dionysus, Psyche (in a Roman myth), Persephone, Odysseus, Orpheus, Theseus and Heracles — are initiations.

A man's most fundamental transition is separation from his mother. Greek myth does not deal directly with it, but the theme lies just below the surface. Consider three young heroes: Pentheus, Orestes, and Telemachus. All three were the only sons of kings, yet none knew their fathers, and each underwent a more or less successful separation from his mother.

Telemachus had not seen Odysseus since infancy. His lack of fathering was evident in his inability to confront the suitors who threatened his inheritance. Athena intervened, sending him on a dangerous night-sea journey. In Sparta, the fabled Helen and Menelaos bestowed blessings upon Telemachus during this voyage into liminality. He returned to Ithaka a man, "strong with magic," according to Homer, ready to meet Odysseus and defeat the suitors. His initiation was relatively painless, partially because his mother was willing to let him go. He died as boy without having to symbolically harm the feminine.

Orestes inherited a barbarous family curse. Apollo demanded that he murder his mother Clytemnestra, the ultimate "bad mother" who had killed his father. Orestes obeyed, but tormented by guilt and the vengeful Furies, he went insane. Much wandering, grief and purification passed before he was healed. Orestes killed his mother *complex* — that flawed inner relationship with the feminine. The murder of the bad mother was necessary before he could own his own nobility. He survived the symbolic death of his old self.

Although Pentheus is already king in *The Bacchae,* his rule is barely legitimate. Things begin to fall apart; he is begging for trouble. His initiation by Dionysus is the most extreme. Whereas Telemachus has a good mother, and Orestes kills his mother, Pentheus is killed *by* his mother.

In the most famous mother-son story of all, Oedipus *married* his mother and provided Freud's most fundamental metaphor. His tale is even more ambivalent than the others. Did he ensure his demise through his incestuous union? Or was the great error part of the initiation that moved his life into his elderhood as an honored sage?

Whereas Dionysus descended to Hades to resurrect Semele and heal their relationship, both Pentheus and Agave succumbed to the madness caused by repressing him. Too often, these *symbolic* murders become literalized. Men who can't overcome their mother complexes perpetuate patriarchy by turning their anger onto real women. They can't realize their nobility and purpose, their *souls* die and both nature and women take the blame. Because they reject the archetypal Other, Dionysus, *literal* Others suffer.

Is *The Bacchae* an Initiation Story?

Pentheus is not evil. He is, however, profoundly ignorant of his motivations. As an *ephebe* thrust into the role of king, he has yet to suffer into wisdom.

The story is either a successful or a failed initiation, depending on which version we read. The original text of *The Bacchae* that ancient librarians copied for posterity lacked a small but critical section — about fifty lines during which Agave and Cadmus reassemble Pentheus's body. Scholars have "re-membered" them from fragments and later material.[36] Some of the many translations include Agave's words:

> *Come, Father. We must restore his head*
> *to this unhappy boy. As best we can, we shall make him whole*
> *again.*

Are they making Pentheus "whole again" for burial, or has he returned from *psychological* dismemberment as a whole person? Charles Segal writes, "Pentheus does not make his way through the shadowy forest of adolescent trials... (he is) 'initiated' only to death and suffering."[37]

After the reassembly, however, the chorus sings of "...his famous *prize* of grief... fold your child in your arms, streaming with his blood!" What are these "prizes" of humility and grief? For young men, humility — reconnection with the ground of being — implies initiation, the *ground*: earth, mother in the deepest sense. For older men the experience is indeed grief. The longer the period of adolescent grandiosity, the deeper the grief when it is finally punctured. Then, writes Vachel Lindsay,

> *Men thank God for tears,*
> *Alone with the memory of their dead.*
> *Alone with lost years.*

When the Loosener destroys the walls of the heroic ego, new voices may express something other than *"I know who I am."* They may declare, *"I am not who I thought I was,"* or even *"I am you,"* a sentiment otherwise known as compassion.

DIONYSUS THE INITIATOR

A closer look at the story of how Dionysus released Hera from the golden chair reveals another initiation tale. Disgusted by her lame, ugly son, Hera had hurled Hephaestus out of Olympus. He survived and was ultimately accepted on Olympus, but he never forgot his early abuse. Hephaestus took his vengeance by tricking Hera into the infamous chair. Behind the rejection of the son is the rejection of the mother under Patriarchy. The result is a cycle of mutual ambivalence and hostility.

In Jungian terms, a man's repressed feminine "marries" his shadow complex of repressed masculinity, giving the feminine an evil tone. Projected onto actual women, this "evil" feminine justifies his unwillingness to become emotionally intimate.

But this story entertains the possibility of an integrated masculine identity. Ares could not force Hephaestus to relent, so the gods called upon Dionysus, who got him drunk. When he woke from his stupor, Hephaestus beheld Aphrodite and fell in love. They married, Hera was released and peace was restored, all because of Dionysus.

Getting Hephaestus drunk symbolizes initiation into a relaxed masculinity that has made peace with the mother complex. Dionysus is both the agent and the product of initiation, who integrates feminine soul with masculine spirit. This initiation reveals the Other as oneself; the unity of the two adds up to something greater than the sum of its parts.

Now comes the fundamental question: must America's necessary changes come through the violent initiations symbolized by Pentheus' death, or through Hephaestus' happy relaxation, the "letting go" of outmoded values? In order to answer this question, we must first immerse ourselves in the myths underlying our history.

*It is well that war is so terrible. We would grow
too fond of it.*
ROBERT E. LEE

———

I love it more than my life.
GEORGE PATTON

———

¡Que viva la muerte!
FRANCISCO FRANCO

———

*If any question why we died, tell them, because
our fathers lied.*
RUDYARD KIPLING

———

You can't stop me. I spend 30,000 men a month.
NAPOLEON

———

*I would rather have a dead son than a
disobedient one.*
MARTIN LUTHER

———

*For democracy, any man would give his only
begotten son.*
DALTON TRUMBO, *JOHNNY GOT HIS GUN*

06

THE KILLING OF THE CHILDREN

Roman generals declared that it was "a sweet and noble thing to die for your country." Why would anyone sacrifice his life for an abstract concept? What is *country* — real estate, beliefs, language? Does it include the Other?

A De-mythologized World

Joseph Campbell argued that we've lived in a "demythologized world" since Christianity began to lose potency in the twelfth century.[1] I suggest that myth has been breaking down for much longer. What remain, exposed like archeological layers, are immensely old stories: the myths of father/son and brother/brother conflict, and the literalization of initiation into the brutal socialization of children.

Myths once symbolically described *macrocosmic* dimensions of the world in terms that enabled people to situate themselves individually, or *microcosmically*. Ritual, with its *mesocosmic* function, mediated between the two. By analogy, consider the atmospheric ozone layer. It mediates between living things and necessary but harmful solar radiation, allowing an appropriate flow between the worlds.

The macrocosm is the unitary dimension of experience in which all polarities are resolved. It is both transcendent and immanent in nature. Humanity makes up the microcosm that *reflects* it. But direct, unmediated experience of the macrocosm — the rush of overwhelming archetypal energies — is too intense for humans. Recall how Semele demanded that Zeus appear in his true form. With the mesocosm (his human form) removed, she was exposed to intensity that no mortal could endure. In psychological terms, she went mad. The mystic vision opens up new worlds of perception, but only at great cost to one's ego boundaries. Or in mythic terms, the birth of Dionysus results in the collapse of the walls.

Culture used to make up the mesocosm. It wrapped individuals and societies in protective containers of myth, and its rituals produced continually creative relationships between macro- and microcosm, between this world and the other world, between personal and transpersonal and between self and Other.

The Renaissance and the Enlightenment brought new emphasis on individualism and rational science rather than revealed truth. These changes, however, accelerated the breakdown of the mythic containers that had long given humanity meaning. The mesocosm collapsed, the veils were lifted and Western man found himself alone and alienated, desperate for authoritarian leaders and the distractions of nationalist wars.

Religious revivals periodically occur, despite the inexorable trend toward a secular world. However, they are generally characterized by grim, literal interpretations of their own myths. The decline of mythic thinking produced a polarity: individualistic, secular materialism, which expresses the predatory imagination; and fundamentalism, the voice of the paranoid imagination. Sociologist Max Weber called this condition the "disenchantment of the world."

We can barely imagine the price we pay for living in a demythologized world or even conceive of times when culture and nature together held and protected our ancestors. Assuming that disconnection and constant violence are natural, we "normal neurotics" rely upon ego defenses that substitute for the old mesocosmic structures. Ernest Becker wrote that only psychological repression "...makes it possible to live decisively in an overwhelmingly miraculous and incomprehensible world..."[2]

It is also a deeply frightening world. Social institutions rarely offer meaning, except in times of great crisis. Then, with our paranoid imaginations racing out of control, we project evil upon convenient scapegoats. And we exchange liberty for security. We offer our allegiance to political leaders, upon whom we project the archetypal image of the King. The demythologized world equals an unprecedented diminishment of the creative imagination. In many places, it has replaced mythical Kings who served the entire cosmos with rulers beholden to increasingly smaller circles of "us" bounded by increasingly larger circles of "them." The logical conclusion of this process is rule by narcissists who, like Louis XIV, claim to *be* the state, or George W. Bush, who claimed to hear directly from God.

But if we slow down and allow ourselves to feel, we feel *exposed*. The sacred, with both its awesome and terrible faces, burns us like direct, cancerous solar rays. This is a *dispirited* world, since we long ago rejected the mesocosmic "spirits" who connected us to this immense and incomprehensible universe. We stand exposed to old, patriarchal conditions: raw opposition between irreconcilable polarities. Our myths no longer nourish us.

THE KILLING OF THE CHILDREN IN MYTH

We idealize the family as the ultimate "safe container." Yet we experience the breakdown of myth most directly in the crimes and betrayals that adults inflict upon children. Myth suggests that it has always been this way — or at least since the triumph of patriarchy. Greek myth is replete with stories of family violence. Although *Ouranos* (Heaven) ruled the universe, he feared a prophecy that predicted his overthrow by one of his children. So one by one, he rejected them as they were born, pushing them back into the body of his wife *Gaia* (Earth).

Gaia helped one son, *Kronos,* escape. When Ouranos came to mate with her, Kronos emerged and castrated him. The successful rebellion of Kronos and his siblings — the *Titans* — was the original return of the repressed, but it resulted in more tyranny. Kronos, now king of Heaven, also heard a prophecy that a son would overthrow him. So he *ate* his children as they were born. Kronos (Latin: Saturn) personifies Time, who devours all things.[3]

Kronos' wife Rhea bore a son in secret. Zeus grew to adulthood, freed his siblings, defeated Kronos and banished him and most of the Titans to *Tartarus,* the underworld's deepest region. Eventually Zeus heard the same prophecy. After mating with Metis (Intelligence), he consumed *her* to prevent conception of a child who might overthrow him. This resulted in Athena's birth from his forehead, implying that her wisdom had been inherited from Zeus instead of from her mother.

The Norse gods also heard a prophecy of their demise. They cast a number of suspects, including a hag known as *Hel,* into the underworld. But the gods live to this day obsessed with the fear that Hel and her siblings will return to take revenge.

Ouranos and Kronos are the original patriarchal fathers — distant sky gods — who symbolize the paranoid and predatory imaginations. The paranoid impulse arose from fear of those (significantly, one's own children) who desired to claim their inheritance. Once the Other was defined by being rejected from the clan, the predatory mind could exploit him. These stories set the stage for generational conflicts that have been literalized throughout history.

Innocent children suffer in countless legends. Tantalos killed his son Pelops and served the meat to the gods. Pelops' son Atreus had the children of his brother Thyestes killed, cooked and served to their unknowing father. Atreus's son Agamemnon sacrificed a daughter before the Trojan War. In return, his wife Clytemnestra murdered him. Their son Orestes avenged him by killing her.

Medea killed her sons just to spite their father. Procne killed her son, cooked him, and served him to her husband, who'd raped her sister. Zeus had an affair with Lamia, who bore him children. When Hera found out, she killed the children. Driven insane with grief, Lamia began devouring other children. Hera also caused Heracles to murder six of his children by mistake. The infant Oedipus was left exposed on a mountaintop because of another prophecy that a child would be the father's undoing. And on it goes…the innocent suffered for their parents' sins.

When (in the Bible) Ham accidentally discovered his father Noah naked, Noah cursed Canaan, one of Ham's *sons, and all of his descendants.*[4] Noah's other sons escaped the curse by covering their eyes to not see him naked. Assenting to Ham's curse, they gained Noah's approval. Indeed, biblical brothers often fight *each other* (Cain/Abel, Jacob/Esau, Joseph and his brothers, Amnon/Absolom) instead of their fathers. Unlike the Greeks, the Hebrew patriarchs seemed to deliberately promote sibling rivalry, knowing that if brothers were to love each other, they would unite and overthrow them.

Child sacrifice is a common Old Testament theme. Jehovah accused the Israelites: "… you slaughtered my children and presented them as offerings!"[5] Like the pagans, they "shed innocent blood, even the blood of their sons and daughters," wrote the Psalmist, "whom they sacrificed unto the altars of Canaan…"[6] When Phineas murdered a Hebrew for sleeping with a pagan woman (he murdered her as well), God was pleased: "Phineas turned my wrath away…he was zealous for my sake, so that I consumed not the children of Israel in my jealousy."[7] Lot offered Sodom his two virgin daughters to "do ye to them as is good in your eyes."[8]

Most significantly, Abraham, father of Judeo-Christian-Moslem monotheism, was willing to sacrifice Isaac to prove his loyalty to God. Bruce Chilton writes, "Different versions of Genesis 22 circulated in an immensely varied tradition called the Aqedah or "Binding" of Isaac in Rabbinic sources and — with key changes — in both Christian and Islamic texts."[9]

In many of these later versions, Isaac was indeed sacrificed, and he came to embody the only sacrifice acceptable to God. Generally, however, the patriarchs couldn't openly admit such barbaric capability, so mythmakers projected child sacrifice onto the gods (such as the terrible *Moloch*) of other people.

God confirmed the most fundamental theme of Western culture when he abandoned *his* only son. Herod, hearing of Jesus' birth, had murdered all boys of two years or less in Bethlehem.[10] Later, when Jesus asked, "Father, why have you forsaken me?" he was quoting Psalm 22. Already quite old, it

acknowledged centuries of abuse, betrayal and the profound depression —
or unquenchable desire for vengeance — they produce. Whether Hebrew
or Greek, patriarchs feared rivals among their subjects or children, pursued
the most terrible of initiations and slaughtered the innocent, while the
survivors became killers themselves.

These patriarchs display different styles of fathering and authority, but
they have two things in common. First, they are narcissists who refuse to
acknowledge the independent, subjective, personal souls of their children.
Second, by refusing to bless their children equally, to share the abundance
of life with them, they encourage sibling rivalry and establish the belief that
all good things, from food to petroleum to love itself, are scarce, and must
be earned through sacrifice.

Freud argued that civilization requires control of instinctual forces.
This generates guilt and aggressive efforts to displace and deny the power
of conscience. So the devouring of the children represents refusal to let
new generations replace older ones. Jungians suggest that the father is less
a sexual rival to his sons than an obstructive personification of the old order
necessary for the ego to emerge from the unconscious.

The stories connected with Dionysus, however, are uniquely horrifying,
because he threatens to *destroy* the ego. In many stories he *drives people
mad enough to kill their own children by mistake.* On one level they reflect
historical opposition to his cult. But what are the archetypal implications?
Why does the gentle god of ecstasy arrive with such ferocity?

King Lykourgos persecuted young Dionysus, who hid under the sea,
protected by goddesses. He re-emerged, no longer ecstatic but furious,
driving Lykourgos mad enough to kill his own son. Boutes, who chased
the maenads into the sea, went mad and drowned himself. Perseus killed
some of Dionysus' followers. The god responded by entrancing the Argive
women, who devoured their own infants.

The three daughters of Minyas scolded Dionysus' devotees. Disguised
as a maiden, he warned them of their folly, but they ignored her. So he
changed himself into a lion, then a bull and then a panther. Ivy and vines
grew over their looms. In their madness they dismembered and devoured

one of their children, then roamed the mountains until Dionysus finally changed them into birds.

When Dionysus approached Eleuther's three daughters wearing a black goatskin, they rejected him and he drove them mad. They were cured only when their town instituted the worship of Dionysus *Melanaigis* ("of the black goatskin — in league with the dead.") Similarly, King Proetus' three daughters went mad, infecting other women, and all left their families. Some ate their own children and wandered as cows in heat, fitting partners for the bull-god. It might have been different, writes Nor Hall: "Had they joined the Dionysian company willingly, they would have enacted this state of wild abandon within a protective circle."[11]

The gods victimized the House of Thebes repeatedly. Agave, Pentheus' mother, had three sisters. One was Semele, whose son Dionysus was himself torn apart by the Titans. Autonoe's son Acteaon innocently chanced upon Artemis bathing with her nymphs. The goddess turned him into a stag, which was torn apart by his own hounds. Zeus asked the third sister Ino and her husband Athamas to hide the baby Dionysus from Hera. But she discovered the ruse and struck them with madness. Athamas killed one of his sons, thinking he was a stag, and Ino threw the other into boiling water.

In these stories the children are usually boys. And, surprisingly, mothers commit much of the violence. Agave's insane slaughter of her son Pentheus connects my first two themes, the return of the repressed and initiation. The broader context is repression of the feminine, but once Dionysus arises he liberates those feminine energies, which take their vengeance *upon immature males.*

Fifteen hundred years after Euripides, we encounter the German legend of the Pied Piper of Hamelin. This odd character who was dressed in bright red and yellow cured a plague of rats. When the city fathers refused to pay him, he enchanted Hamelin's children and led them into a mountain cave — an image of the underworld. It closed upon them forever, and the fathers were left to mourn and regret their greed.

KILLING THE CHILDREN THROUGHOUT HISTORY

These stories are absolutely central to Western consciousness. They describe basic father-son relationships and indicate how long it has been since initiation rituals broke down. For at least three millennia, patriarchs have conducted *pseudo-initiations*, feeding their sons into the infinite maw of literalized violence. Indeed, it was their great genius and their primordial crime to extend child-sacrifice from the family to the state. Boys eventually were forced to *participate* in the sacrifice. No longer surrendering to symbolic death, they learned to, in a sense, overcome death by inflicting it on others.

Ultimately, sacrifice, *dying* for the cause, became as important as physical survival. Martyrdom became an ethical virtue that every believer must be prepared to emulate. "Uniquely among the religions of the world," writes Chilton, "the three that center on Abraham have made the willingness to offer the lives of children — an action they all symbolize with versions of the Aqedah — a central virtue for the faithful as a whole."[12]

When the state replaces the fathers, boys must become *patriots* (Latin: *pater*, father) to become men. Those who most excel in this madness become sociopathic killers and mentors to future generations. Such fathers feel pride, but also fear the possibility of being overthrown. Thus initiations always contain both a threat and a deal: *You will sacrifice your emotions and relational capacity, submit to our authority in all matters and become our mirror image. In exchange you may dominate your women, your children and the Earth as we abuse you.*

Yet don't we idealize our children? Parents commonly deny their own needs so that "the children" might have a better future, and government demonizes and punishes those suspected of harming them. We go to war so the children may be free, and so on. We love children because the archetypal child symbolizes rebirth, transformation and innocence. Christ said that to enter "the kingdom" one must be as innocent as those whose minds and bodies are still undivided by civilization. So the child personifies the lost unity adults long for — which adults, however, cannot recover without being psychologically "dismembered." Thus children *also* evoke the suffering to be endured on the road back to wholeness, and the grief over what we have lost. Consequently, many adults are compelled to destroy that image, to remove it from consciousness and replace it with idealization.

Why else would we emphasize family values and threats to "the children" while destroying social programs proven to keep families together, or punish children simply because their parents are poor? This can only happen in a society that is deeply ambivalent about its own children. "Some things," writes psychologist David Bakan, "are simply too terrible to think about if one believes them. Thus one does not believe them in order to make it possible to think about them."[13] Idealization is the way we keep the secret that our culture is built upon sacrifice of our actual children.

Lloyd de Mause begins his survey of the vast literature on European child-raising: "The history of childhood is a nightmare from which we have only recently begun to awake."[14] Christians long believed that children were inherently perverse: "The new-born babe is full of the stains and pollution of sin, which it inherits from our first parents through our loins."[15] They required extreme discipline and early baptism, which used to include actual exorcism of the Devil. Initiation rites became literalized in child abuse, with customs ranging from tight swaddling and steel collars to foot binding, genital circumcision and rape.

There is considerable evidence of the literal killing of both illegitimate children (at least as late as the nineteenth century) and legitimate ones, especially girls, in Europe. As a result, there was a large imbalance of males over females well into the Middle Ages. Physical and sexual abuse was so common that most children born prior to the eighteenth century were what would today be termed "battered children." However, the medical syndrome itself didn't arise among doctors until 1962, when regular use of x-rays revealed widespread multiple fractures in the limbs of small children who were too young to complain verbally.

What kind of people do these patterns produce? De Mause argues that war and genocide do "...not occur in the absence of widespread early abuse and neglect," that nations with particularly abusive and punitive childrearing practices emphasize military solutions and state violence in resolving social conflicts. Furthermore, "Children brought up with love and respect simply do not scapegoat..."[16]

"Americans," says Hillman, "love the idea of childhood no matter how brutal or vacuous their actual childhoods may have been."[17] Finally, we idealize childhood because our actual childhood did not serve its purpose, which was to provide a container of welcome into the world that would be the necessary precursor for initiation into mature adulthood. Without such preparation, we assume that alienation is the true nature of maturity. And if humans have no true animating spark, neither does the natural world. So generation after generation of young men will be motivated to *project their own need for rebirth onto the world* and set out to literally destroy it. This is how Patriarchy perpetuates itself. In each generation, millions of abused children identify with their adult oppressors and become violent perpetrators themselves. In a demythologized world, they have no choice but to act out the myths of the killing of the children on a massive scale.

THE LOVE OF WAR

War is *attractive* because it promises to resolve the tension between individual and collective. Like Dionysus, it takes us out of ourselves into something greater. But why do some attain that experience through meditation or art, and why do others achieve it through violence against the Other?

An essential, archetypal characteristic of men is that they long to serve a great, transpersonal cause. "War," writes veteran William Broyles Jr., "is an escape from the everyday into a special world where the bonds that hold us to our duties... family, community, work — disappear."[18] Combat may be the closest approximation to ritual liminality that modern men ever know. Many report that they feel more *alive* and deeply connected with others than at any other time. Indeed, war may attract us more because of our need to be closer to others than for the need to release hostility.

War has both the intensity and the justification of religion; we sum up its passions in the word "sacrifice." Men sacrifice themselves to defend the realm — or the "hood." But Broyles admits, "...from the joy of being alive in death's presence to the joy of causing death is, unfortunately, not that great a step."[19]

In some places boys are still not accepted as men until they have shed blood. At its very core, war is about initiation and the brush with death. But patriarchy inverted the sacrifice: whereas youths once encountered their own symbolic demise, initiation became literal destruction, projected upon *other* youths. However, since no authentic transformations occur, "baptisms of fire" are temporary. As with all addicts, some are drawn to re-enact the sacrifice hoping to find satisfaction. Thus many ex-soldiers, accustomed to liminality without resolution, or unable to adjust to the "profane space" of civilian life, continually re-enlist.

This is war's attraction — it allows men to enact their longing for initiation while serving a transpersonal cause. Thus, as long as we have uninitiated men we will have war. Robert Moore writes, "There is no way to understand the attractiveness of war without understanding the unconscious seduction of the archetype of initiation."[20] Rational minds recoil at the thought of war, but young men react mainly to *images*. This is why the film director Francois Truffault is reported to have said that it is impossible to make a truly anti-war movie. Even if films show war's horrors and absurdities, the images go to the oldest parts of the brain and beyond: to the drive for initiation.

And what of those who direct the carnage? War allows the old to enact the sacrifice of the children. They project their ambivalence toward their own uninitiated, "inner" children onto actual soldiers, while safely and vicariously experiencing Dionysian intensity. War is an end disguised as a means: deferred infanticide, the revenge of the old upon the young.

RITUAL WARFARE

All societies experience conflict, but those with intact ritual traditions were able to limit its expression and minimize its consequences. Certain tribes equated their enemies with the chaos to be overcome annually if the cosmos was to be sustained, and fighting ceased as soon as enemy blood was spilled. They created human versions of animal rituals to avoid seriously hurting members of their own species. In *ritual warfare*, killing was often unnecessary, even irrelevant. One of its functions was the exhilaration of competition in a relatively safe container. In small-scale tribal environments, adversaries often knew each other, hurling more eloquent insults than weapons. Deliberate steps were taken to ensure that the killing did not get too efficient. Plains Indians "counted coup" as *symbolic* victory, striking their foes with coup sticks and leaving them unharmed. Some California Indians always fit feathers to their hunting arrows for greater accuracy but *left them off* their war arrows, making it harder to shoot straight.

Another function was *expressing beauty.* New Guinean tribes postponed battles when rain threatened to ruin their elaborate feather headdresses. Until the Napoleonic Wars, warships were gilded and crammed with sculpture, and cannons were works of art as well as destruction. As late as World War I, Austrian military uniforms sported *ten shades of red.*

Dozens of societies were essentially peaceful.[21] And, while many others were known for their belligerence, there is no way to know for how long their ritual structures had broken down (as they had in Europe). Indeed, some researchers argue that it was contact with Europeans that frequently intensified war or generated war among groups who previously had lived in peace.[22]

For centuries, European warfare was governed — and limited — by elaborate rules of conduct. Ancient Greek armies camped near each other without fear of surprise attack. There were formal challenges prior to battle and truces for everyone to mourn and bury their dead. Mediaeval knights wouldn't strike unarmed opponents. Eleventh-Century Spaniards *negotiated* the dates of battles with their Moorish adversaries.

Heroic literature valued the tradition of the "worthy opponent." Two aristocrats met eye-to eye as entire armies watched. The *Iliad* includes a daylong battle between Ajax and Hector ending in a draw and a gift exchange, when Hector proclaims:

> … *afterward they'll say… "These two fought and gave no quarter in close combat, yet they parted friends."*[23]

In another scene, while the armies watch, Helen's husband Menelaos and her lover Paris engage in personal combat, intending to determine the outcome of the entire war. Memory of this ritual *com-petition* survives in sports and in movie fight scenes that end with the antagonists dusting each other off and sharing drinks. Alternatively, when a movie villain grabs a knife and escalates a fistfight into lethal combat, he is breaking the unspoken rules of ritual combat. Only then will the hero respond in kind.

De-mythologized Warfare

European *conquistadores* played by different rules than tribal people, whose ritual traditions were still alive. To the invaders, the locals were Other, to be converted or eliminated, while native warriors naively expected to engage in symbolic conflict with honorable opponents. The European mythic world, however, had already collapsed. Long before, Jehovah had specifically applauded genocide.[24] Warfare is now more literalized than ritualized. Since its purpose is absolute victory and capture of resources, any strategies, including obliterating non-combatants, are acceptable.

Now all armies regularly ignore legal conventions. In actual practice, there are few "rules of engagement," and *ninety percent of casualties are non-combatants*. What long before was initiation and strictly ritualized conflict is now the dreadful, catastrophic experience of total war. And what indigenous communities once celebrated as a creative, protective, integrated masculinity is now a brittle shell of destructive, misogynistic heroism that barely veils the grief within. It is the worst aspect of our demythologized world.

———◆———

The killing of the children is the sacred secret — sacred because no one will speak its name — underlying all of our civilized values. Indeed, all three themes that I have explored in *The Bacchae* intersect with each other. The regular sacrifice of millions of youth in war and the repression of women engender tremendous grief and rage, which modern society represses with its patriotic rituals and consumer culture. The rage of uninitiated men always threatens to emerge as the return of the repressed. If allowed full voice, such rage would tear society apart (as it almost did in the 1960s); hence the need to identify and demonize scapegoats. Periodically, and especially during times of rapid social change, our traditional Others are not sufficient to siphon off our destructive violence and keep it to a manageable level. Something else is needed. So we send the young off to war.

The first part of this inquiry ends here. Part Two moves from myth into history and invites you to consider how our collective loss of mythic thinking and repression of Dionysus are expressed in our specifically American myths. Europeans brought more than greed, dreams of freedom and missionary zeal to America. They carried an ancient load of self-loathing. They were looking for someone to bear it for them, so they could return to innocence.

PART TWO

THE MYTH OF AMERICAN INNOCENCE

INTRODUCTION

This city must learn its lesson: it lacks initiation in my mysteries.

DIONYSUS (BACCHAE, PROLOGUE)

⁓⁂⁓

THEBES AS ATHENS

A walled city can be a metaphor for a soul or for a nation. In writing about Thebes of the distant, mythic past, Euripides was implicitly comparing it to democratic Athens. This Thebes is a misogynistic, totalitarian state. But the feminine principle, held down so long, has finally exploded like the "Big Bang." Women are running wild, capable of anything. Their grief over forced marriage, prostitution, foot-binding, dieting, the veil, witch-burnings, honor killings, rape, punishment for *being* raped — echoes down through the centuries in the Bacchants' lament:

> *Dionysus, do you see how in shackles we are held unbreakably, in the bonds of oppressors?*

Ultimately Pentheus dies dressed as a maenad, the very shadow of the heroic ideal. His death exonerates the population of the city. Dionysus tells him, *"You and you alone will suffer for your city."* Cadmus, however, realizes that *"All our house the god has utterly destroyed and, with it, me."* A soul has been dismembered. And he knows that removing Pentheus without *communal* atonement merely invites his replacement by a similar figure. Denial, innocence and the need to find future scapegoats would survive unchanged.

Alternatively, Pentheus' death could signal a healing transformation. The *polis* is facing an initiation. At the end, Cadmus cries:

> *If there is still any mortal man who despises or defies the gods, let him look on this boy's death and believe in the gods.*

Euripides, however, was not calling for religious conversion. Nor was he attacking religion. He was describing the harsh force of necessity that inevitably breaks through, creating the conditions for healing. Indeed, writes Somé, the true purpose of *all* indigenous ritual (as opposed to ceremonies that merely confirm the status quo) is not the reduction of suffering but the restoration of balance.[1]

Does the ending do this? Some think not.[2] But if we accept the speculative additions to the text, Thebes does achieve wisdom when Agave re-assembles her son as a "man of sorrow." The survivors of the House of Thebes discover compassion born of shared suffering. Dionysus, however, demands even more. He exiles the royal family and all of Thebes' men. Agave, Ino and Autonoe must leave the city in expiation of their crime. What survives of Thebes is a "city of sorrow," so to speak, a city of compassion, a city that "knows who it is." It has lost its innocence.

Still, no initiation is permanent, as the audience knew. In a few generations, another mythical descendant of Cadmus — Oedipus — would rule Thebes, and a new cast of characters would repeat the cycle of innocence and experience.

ATHENS AS AMERICA

In ancient myths chaos precedes rebirth. During the *Anthesteria*, Dionysus fertilized city and psyche by mating with the queen. His disruptive, ritual madness reminded everyone to honor life's darker energies. His gift of Drama, Athens' greatest artistic achievement, expressed a commitment to freedom, to speaking truth to power. Yet Athens undermined its own ideals by denying that freedom to women, as well as to thousands of slaves.

Athens' democracy, philosophy, architecture, science and art were all constructed upon a mountain of human misery. Only fifteen percent of the actual population were male citizens. Forty percent were slaves. To Plato and Aristotle, fathers of European philosophy, slavery and subordination of women were part of the natural order. The growth of the empire led to the concentration of wealth and required constant expansion. Athens, like America, maintained liberty at home by suppressing it abroad. And perpetual warfare required the sacrifice of the children. The designers of the Parthenon inscribed a long sculptural frieze around its interior wall depicting Athens' mythical original queen willingly offering her daughter as a sacrifice to save the city from defeat. This was their creation myth, and the bloody sacrifice of their children lay at its heart.

The Peloponnesian War, begun in 431 B.C.E. and grinding on for twenty-five years, was destroying Athens' soul. Dissenters like Socrates were persecuted for heresy. Zealots burned books. In 416, Athens attacked the rebellious island of Melos, slaughtering every adult male.

The next year, swollen with grandiosity, the ruling class of Athens considered invading Sicily. Warmongers overwhelmed men of reason. Thucydides wrote, "…the few who were actually opposed to the expedition were afraid of being thought unpatriotic if they voted against it, and therefore kept quiet." A great armada set sail, only to be completely destroyed. Eleven years later, with no end to the war in sight, Euripides wrote *The Bacchae,* but Athens ignored him.

Within three generations the Greeks were too exhausted and distrustful of each other to resist Alexander's Macedonians. Democracy died, not to resurface for 2000 years. And the creative imagination almost died with it.

Now we collude with men who deny the obvious and buttress the veneer of innocence. From Aristotle to Henry Kissinger (*"We can't allow a country to go communist due to the ignorance of its own people!"*), state-sponsored intellectuals justify the empire's crimes and offer a thin sense of security in exchange for a thinner sense of freedom. Dionysus, however, invites us to awaken from the mad dream of heroism and dominance. He offers a path of awareness, grief, atonement — and joy. His last words in *The Bacchae* are:

> *If then…you had muzzled your madness, you should have an ally now in the son of Zeus.*

These words, sung in March, 405 B.C.E., predicted the next twenty-four centuries of western history.

When the American opens a…door in his psychology, there is a dangerous open gap, dropping hundreds of feet… he will then be faced with an Indian or Negro shadow.

CARL JUNG

———

As long as we are at home in the body, we are absent from the Lord.

INCREASE MATHER

———

Cut loose from the earth's soul, they insisted on purchase of its soil, and like all orphans they were insatiable. It was their destiny to chew up the world and spit out a horribleness that would destroy all primary peoples.

TONI MORRISON, *A MERCY*

———

…the world's fairest hope linked with man's foulest crime.

HERMAN MELVILLE

———

…the only good Indians are the dead Indians.

THEODORE ROOSEVELT

———

There are no kings inside the gates of Eden.

BOB DYLAN

07

RED, WHITE AND BLACK

THE ORIGINS OF AMERICAN INNOCENCE

What an ambiguous and conflicted mix of crusading moralism, anxious consumerism, cutthroat competition, aggressive practicality, racist brutality, apocalyptic fear, arrogant optimism, cheerful naiveté, willful ignorance, celebrity worship, generous goodwill and rollicking bad taste constitutes our public lives! The myth of innocence holds it all together.

In attempting to understand myth, language can fail us. We all have a deep, innate need for authentic narratives that will give us meaning and guide us in the eternal quest to know who we are and why we have been born. Lacking them, we settle for their "toxic mimics," the stories that define us in terms of who we are not and rationalize our otherwise unjustifiable actions. Each type of narrative is a form of myth.

One purpose of myth — Campbell's *sociological* function — is reconciling the gulf between ideals and realities. It temporarily resolves ambivalence, links us spontaneously to the priorities of the state and determines our reactions when someone questions our unexamined habits and beliefs.

In simple terms, this type of myth equals ideology plus narrative. *Stories* help us digest the ideology. Myths determine perception, like the lenses of a pair of glasses. They are not what we see, but what we see *with*. We can't see outside our bubble (but outsiders can see us.) We give our attention to one set of possibilities rather than another, and our intentions and dreams follow. So *myth creates fact*. Indeed, *myth trumps fact*.

We draw stories from our past and abstract them into evocative icons (Plymouth Rock, the Alamo, etc.) that contain the essential elements of our worldview. They are so obvious that they never have to be "explained." They transform history into sacred legends that describe reality to us and *pre*scribe our choices and behavior within acceptable limits. "Myth," writes Richard Slotkin, "is history successfully disguised as archetype."[1]

To understand the sociological power of myth, consider some questions. Why do millions of Americans who support unions, environmental protection, progressive taxation, women's equality and universal health care continue to vote Republican, or still believe that Saddam Hussein caused 9/11? Why, with 12,000 nuclear warheads, do we demonize nations that develop their own? Why do most of us assume — wrongly — that well-educated Americans are more anti-war than less-educated people? Why does the American flag appear in front of every public school, at every university commencement speech, at the New York Stock Exchange and at most auto dealerships, mortuaries and *churches?* Why do both civil rights activists and the Ku Klux Klan carry it? Why do we sing the national anthem before ball games?

In totalitarian societies, the dictator's version of reality must be obeyed or else. Americans, however, *believe* the myths underlying our fascination with innocence. When nearly everyone shares the common mythic language of "Americanism," vigorous argument is encouraged — but only within the limits imposed by unstated doctrinal orthodoxy. In reality, the corporate-owned media carefully frame all controversies to minimize real debate.

Yet this still doesn't get to the heart of the issue. Why did *New York Times* writers *believe* that impoverished Sandinistas threatened us? Why do federally subsidized academics *believe* their odes to free markets? If intellectuals are absolutely convinced of benign American intentions, what can we expect from the rest of us? A mythic framework holds it all together.

The myth of innocence justified the original colonization effort. Later, in changing conditions, it helped account for America's unique and rapid expansion and its worldwide economic and cultural domination. Though it must change periodically to do so, its essential elements remain. However, seeing it as *only* justifying racism and imperialism, we forget that millions of people still sacrifice everything to come here, hoping to start anew. We lose the mystical interpretation of our myth, as well as the imagination necessary to transform it.

SEARCHING FOR THE OTHER

Europe's invasion of the Americas destroyed "countless tens of millions of people," writes historian David Stannard.[2] The *conquistadors* had barely recovered from three centuries of crusades and 700 years of Muslim control in Spain. To a great extent Christianity defined itself in terms of this *external* Other who, seemingly forever, had threatened its borders. Soon after ousting them, however, Europe imploded into a century of religious warfare. Catholics and Protestants slaughtered each other with the same fury that they'd inflicted upon Muslims and Jews, Europe's *internal* Other. In the same year that Spain expelled the Jews, Columbus discovered America, bringing concepts of racial purity that had been honed in the crusades.

For generations, the Inquisition — Catholicism's ritual of purification — had produced a constant state of fear across Europe. A Protestant version took strong root in America, and it periodically re-surfaces in epidemics of scapegoating. Inquisitions are characterized by *highly imaginative cruelty perpetrated for the good of the accused.* As Blaise Pascal wrote, "Men never do evil so fully and cheerfully as when we do it out of conscience." This idea of "therapeutic coercion" can be traced back to St. Augustine, who wrote of "forcibly returning the heretics to the real banquet of the Lord." More recently, American officers in Viet Nam claimed that they had to "destroy the village in order to save it."

Linguistic research indicates that some languages have only one color distinction: black and white. In languages with a third color term, that term is invariably red. How ironic that over time, in a curious blend of history and archetype, the American soul projected itself in red, white and black images. White, of course, speaks to us of our national sense of innocence, while in our language and mythology, black and red came to represent the "Others" who threaten us from within and from without.

THE PARANOID IMAGINATION

European fear and loathing of the Other stems from an ancient, paranoid imagination. The Old Testament repeatedly celebrates genocidal yet redemptive violence: *"The righteous will be glad when they are avenged, when they bathe their feet in the blood of the wicked."*[3] Medieval art depicts the Last Judgment with detailed scenes of naked bodies subjected to (almost) inconceivable torture. The blessed, however, will *enjoy* these scenes. Saint Thomas Aquinas declared that in Heaven, *"...a perfect view is granted them of the tortures of the damned."* Eighteenth-century evangelist Jonathan Edwards agreed: *"The sight of hell-torments will exalt the happiness of the saints forever."*

The paranoid imagination combines eternal vigilance, constant anxiety, obsessive voyeurism, creative sadism, contempt for the erotic and an impenetrable wall of innocence. We can find it at least as far back as Rome, where authorities claimed that Christians: "... burn with incestuous passions...with unspeakable lust they copulate in random unions..."

This heritage was 3,000 years old when sixteenth century revolts against church corruption, but not its brutality, set the tone of life in British America (Martin Luther initiated the Reformation in 1517, six months before the Spanish first attacked Mexico). Protestantism's new way to live acceptably to God — the "calling" — was no longer through renunciation but by fulfilling worldly obligations. It gave capitalists a new freedom; they no longer felt guilty about generating wealth. Recognizing "calling" in the concept of career, we note both its similarity and its profound difference from the indigenous notion of purpose. The calling is imposed by social position, while purpose comes from within.

John Calvin took the next step by emphasizing *predestination*. The unknowable, transcendent deity had decreed long before that a tiny minority, the elect, were already saved. The vast majority would never rise above their sinful nature. One was either in a state of grace or not. "Therefore," wrote Luther, "we... deny free will altogether." America's foundation myth has enshrined these Pilgrims and Puritans as the first to settle the barren wilderness, even though other English settlers had arrived earlier. They put a fundamental — and fundamentalist — stamp on American consciousness: human nature was utterly corrupt, and the only escape was through grace.

Never *certain* of salvation, however, these people experienced constant anxiety. So they worked unceasingly, hoping that grace would show itself through the results of the work ethic. Calvinism replaced the external order of the church with a far stricter *internal* order. Never in history had so many people willingly imposed such restraints on themselves. Medieval peasants had created festivities as an escape from work, writes Barbara Ehrenreich, but "the Puritan embraced work as an escape from terror."[4] Some believed in preparing themselves for the conversion experience that might *prove* their salvation, but only after utterly debasing their sense of self-worth. They were at war with the self yet unable to escape it.

Their only respite from the weight of original sin was to project their guilt onto others. So they defined *loss of self-control* as the basis for all sins, and their answer to the perceived disorder in the world was unrelenting discipline. Once converted, they turned their critical energies (formerly directed upon themselves) into converting those who still sinned — and failing in that attempt, to eliminate them. Others believed in free will but still emphasized individual responsibility. Either way, all worked relentlessly to glorify God, *prove* one's state of grace and make a fallen world more holy.

The Catholic Church no longer controlled them, but freedom came at a price. They could relate to God directly, but he was both more abstract (no longer accessed through Catholicism's rich visual symbolism) and more remote. It turned out that the more remote their goal, the more passionately men pursued it. And the more they strove for perfection, the less they enjoyed anything.

Christianity's hatred of the body (and the rage it engendered) reached its extreme in Puritanism. Unlike Catholics, who had assurance of salvation

through works and prayer, Puritans loathed sensuality. They mistrusted
(and envied) those who didn't "crucify their lusts."[5] Their anxiety had few
outlets, except through physical work, proselytizing — and violence. Their
theology confirmed their psychology. *Revelation* was their favorite Bible
passage.

Their repressed aggression (and desire) surfaced in their confrontation
with the Other. The first Puritan migrations coincided with the height of
the witch craze that was engulfing Europe. The English were crushing
Ireland with genocidal fury and racist stereotypes that reduced the Irish to
sub-human status. They constructed their sense of innocence by projecting
their own savagery upon their victims.

In addition, these English Puritans were displaying another aspect of
the Paranoid Imagination: the fear and hatred of *images*. Under Oliver
Cromwell, they were desecrating the artwork in thousands of English
churches, continuing a tradition of iconoclasm dating back to Byzantium,
Islam and the Biblical hatred of idolatry. This tradition would resurface in
their twentieth century crusades against pornography.

Similarly, American Puritans displaced their self-hatred by persecuting
Catholics, Indians and even other Protestants. And within one generation,
they became slaveholders. White supremacy, normally considered a
characteristic of the southern opportunists, fit perfectly with the doctrine of
predestination. By 1693 (the same year as the Salem trials), Cotton Mather
was teaching blacks that they were enslaved because they were sinners. God,
not their masters, had enslaved them.

With mutual love within the community but expulsion (or worse)
for dissenters, they evolved a paranoid style that continues to re-surface
throughout American history. The Salem witch trials reveal how the
Puritans dealt with the Other within the community. Witches could be
anyone, anywhere, but were generally believed to be independent women
who consorted with the Devil or with the natives who worshipped him. In
this paranoid atmosphere some girls became "possessed" (as in *The Bacchae*)
and upset the order of careful self-control. They "named names" (as they
would in 1918, 1950 and 2001) of others — overwhelmingly women — who

had bewitched them. Public executions of these scapegoats intimidated and purified the community.

The paranoid imagination seeks itself: it constantly projects its fantasies outward onto the Other and then proceeds to demonize it. Therefore, it finds conspiracies everywhere. In 1798, ministers whipped up hysteria about a tiny Masonic group. Anticipating McCarthyism by 150 years, one minister ranted: *"I have now in my possession...*authenticated list of names." In 1835, future President John Tyler blamed abolitionism on "a reptile who had crawled from some of the sinks of Europe...to sow the seeds of discord among us."

Propriety and cleanliness were external indications of a clean soul, and bodily needs continually reminded them of their original, corrupt nature. Since they experienced constant fear — and fantasies — of pollution, they rigidly enforced moral standards, denouncing music, theater and dance and declaring capital punishment for adultery (for women). Calvinism's "most urgent task," wrote sociologist Max Weber, was "the destruction of spontaneous, impulsive enjoyment."[6]

Although both salvation and perdition fell on the individual, the entire community might suffer for one person's sins; so each person was responsible for upholding group morality. Individual sin *polluted,* with consequences for all New England. Ministers addressed condemned criminals (and indirectly everyone else) with "execution sermons:"

> You must be cut off by a violent and dreadful death. For indeed the anger of the Lord would fall upon this whole Country where your sin hath been committed, if you should be suffered to live.[7]

The Puritan was desperate to prove himself, *and* he was tightly controlled. He was obsessive-compulsive, punctual, thrifty, prudent, proper and distant. His only earthly reward was virtue, because he couldn't allow himself to enjoy his gains. He was a literalized Apollo, sending his arrows to kill from a distance, who hated his Dionysian soul. "Puritanical" prudishness set the tone for a reserved, middle-class decorum that still endures, leading to H.L. Mencken's sarcastic definition of Puritanism as "the haunting fear that someone, somewhere, may be happy."

Eventually the quest for perfection turned outward, occasionally manifesting as compassion for the poor. Far more often, however, Puritan crusades targeted those groups and individuals who were perceived as unable to control their bodily desires. Originally having emigrated for religious freedom, they enforced a brutal uniformity, even executing several Quakers.

What did Puritans repress? How do we know our contemporary Puritans? Remember Pentheus:

> ... if I climbed that towering fir...then I could see their shameless orgies better.

It is not simply desire, but *images* of desire, that they project upon the Other. We find so many examples of such bizarre and intimately detailed moralizing, that we must ask, *what were they so afraid of? Don't those images come from their own obsessed imaginations?*

This is fairly basic psychology, but my intention is not to reduce these people to a pathological dead-end. We must understand their genocidal projections on another level entirely, as a blundering and childish search for healing through re-connection to the Other. Some have called this "America's Alchemical history."[8]

In this fallen world, wealth distracted from life's only purpose — glorifying God. When, however, one felt *called* to prove one's state of salvation by acquiring wealth, such activity was acceptable, but only if one didn't enjoy it. Here is the essential Puritan contradiction: work hard, get rich, spend little. They delayed their gratification, for rest would come only in the next world. *Waste of time* was sinful. Later, Benjamin Franklin advised everyone to become what we now call workaholics: *"Be always ashamed to catch thyself idle."*

But this was a fateful step. While missionaries informed the Indians of a new god, Americans actually (and unconsciously) acknowledged an even stronger one. With our most common and most unexamined proverb, *Time is money,* Franklin declared Time — *Kronos* — as capitalism's highest value. This practical asceticism made hard labor the expression of the highest ethics, and it *drove* America toward great material accomplishment. Until the advent of mid-twentieth-century consumerism, Americans believed that they established their worth in the eyes of neighbors and God through drudgery and saving. We still ask strangers, "What do you *do?*" We have always been "what we do," as well as "not the Other," who we often perceive as doing nothing productive. But behind Franklin's proverbs ("The sleeping fox catches no poultry," etc.) lies a severe judgment: one who is doing nothing must be up to no good.

The paradox of the British conquest of North America is that Puritanical asceticism eventually produced the world's most materialistic society. The uniformity that underlies capitalist standardization of production had its foundation, wrote Weber, "in the repudiation of all idolatry of the flesh."[9] The urban northeast and to a great extent all American values came to be dominated by money, because *wealth indicated spiritual grace.* The rich, by the way, had no problem with the doctrine of predestination. By displaying their wealth, they were merely showing proof of their salvation.

These beliefs spawned radical new ideas of social obligation. "Individualism in religion," wrote historian R.H. Tawney, "led to an individualist morality."[10] As wealth became a sign of grace, poverty — for the first time — now indicated *moral* failure. Poor people were damned by nature. Furthermore, the rich were now justified in feeling only scorn for them. Since they were lazy and sinful, *or they wouldn't be poor,* to be charitable merely encouraged idleness. It was a waste. Only later was race added to the equation. Two hundred years later, Henry Ward Beecher wrote, "God has intended the great to be great and the little to be little." Ministers preached, "It is your duty to get rich," and "To sympathize with a man whom God has punished for his sins… is to do wrong." Despite many exceptions, this brutal, uniquely American contempt for poor people still justifies official neglect because it has a religious foundation. The belief has long been established in the core of the American psyche.

Britain evolved a version of capitalism without the spiritual underpinnings, because continuing persecution and civil war resulted in more emigration. Zealots continually left to maintain their purity, both diluting Europe of its Calvinists and adding to the ferment of American religiosity. Ironically, the most enthusiastic ascetics (who as Catholics might well have been monks) became the greatest moneymakers.

As generations passed and the strictly religious fervor dissipated, the competitive quest for efficiency, productivity, wealth and the self-validation they symbolized became established as our most fundamental values. This "American Dream" is so durable because, like no other myth, it promises fulfillment both in this world and the next. The obsession with self-improvement soon became the most recognizable aspect of American national character. By the 1830s the Frenchman Alexis De Toqueville wrote, "I know of no country…where the love of money has taken stronger hold on the affections of men." Another visitor, the Englishman Charles Latrobe, claimed that, "…dollar is the word most frequently in their mouths."

Capitalism's relentless logic eventually transformed this religious, if flawed, impulse into conspicuous consumption. Over three centuries, Americans gradually shifted from being producers to being consumers. They began by enshrining gain without pleasure and ended with addiction to "stuff." But underneath the surface, work still equals salvation. It has been said that Europeans work to live, while Americans live to work. Journalist Lewis Lapham, however, argues that they misunderstand us: "…material objects serve as testimonials to the desired states of immateriality — not what the money buys but what the money says about our…standing in the company of the saved."[11]

Now, zealots for wealth, we still suffer neurotic obsession and fear moral failure. America literalizes service to the *mater* into its toxic mimic, materialism. It judges a person either by how hard he works or by what he has accumulated; and it carries a hatred of the body lying just below the surface of our seemingly hedonistic lifestyles. The Puritan ethic sublimated man's Dionysian nature into a poor version of the Apollonic.

Immense contradictions lay at America's foundations. The Puritan retained his asceticism long after Europeans had dropped theirs. This "individualist" demanded conformity. He was unsure of his own salvation, yet his doctrines justified his luck. Longing for the spirit, he was aggressively pragmatic. Working unceasingly, he never enjoyed himself. Loving God, he hated his body. Hoping to convert the Indians, he massacred them. And his religious retreat became an empire.

With the second major influence on early America these contradictions grow even larger.

THE PREDATORY IMAGINATION

The children of these Northern religious extremists amassed the first great mercantile fortunes. Southerners, however, had more worldly motivations. Their first *History of Virginia* boasted, "The chief design of all parties concerned was to fetch away the Treasure from thence, aiming more at sudden gain than to form any regular colony." Aristocrats like Sir Walter Raleigh were not interested in the city on a hill but in the golden *El Dorado* that Spaniards had been chasing for decades. "In that sense," writes Michael Ventura, "America had Las Vegas a century before it had Plymouth Rock."[12] Our history has been caught between the paranoid nightmares of the Puritans and the greedy, predatory fantasies of these opportunists ever since.

Outside of Spanish and French territories and the original settlers of the colony of Maryland, large numbers of Catholics didn't arrive until the 1840s. "Americans" were essentially white, Anglo-Saxon and Protestant for two centuries.

The opportunists received vast tracts of free land and required large numbers of workers. Having first enslaved thousands of Indians, they convinced many British to emigrate, but treated these indentured servants harshly; only one in five lived to attain freedom. In addition, many free but desperately poor Scots-Irish arrived to work Virginia's plantations until about 1700, when the western migration extended the frontier across the Appalachian Mountains.

The masters needed so many workers because their crops (tobacco, rice and cotton) were highly labor-intensive. These conditions led to the enslavement of 50,000 criminals and 100,000 Irish, including perhaps 20,000 poor children. The word *kidnapping* ("kid-nabbing") entered the language. Prior to 1800, perhaps two-thirds (250,000) of white colonists came as slaves.

White survivors of this brutal system needed outlets for their rage.
But rather than revolting, they came to identify with their former masters.
Economically insecure small landholders, they learned to hold black slaves
in contempt even if few could afford to own one, and they showed little
mercy for Indians.

Whereas the northern myth involved fear of pollution by the Other,
southerners originally perceived themselves in the evolving narrative of the
lone hunter who learned from the natives and took what he wanted. Living
alone or in isolated communities, they resisted religious structures but
responded in great numbers to what historians call the "great awakenings,"
and their conversion experiences seeded the optimistic energy that
drove the westward expansion. Later, they formed the backbone of the
Revolutionary and Confederate armies. To this day, most military officers
are southerners.

So, colonial America consisted mainly of two hungry groups: grim,
puritanical northerners and southerners who suffered from generations of
poverty. Both shared a restless zeal, what psychologist Joel Kovel calls "…
that singular transformation of body into spirit and spirit into action that
is the hallmark of our civilization."[13] Both saw the land as an unparalleled
opportunity for enrichment and freedom. Both digested narratives that
substituted the symbolism of savage war against the natives for the class
struggle. And both, like none before them, were composed of *individuals*.
Geography, religion and myth were making them into solitary, isolated
figures.

A New Myth

Indigenous myths, the dreams of entire cultures, emerge from the land
itself and from the infinite depths of the past; no one "creates" them. Myths
speak of origins, of the divine figures present at the beginning, of how the
sacred breaks through into the material world. By contrast, mythic *literature*
is created by specific individuals out of oral traditions, as Homer utilized
stories that Greek bards had told for centuries.

Americans populated their political, religious and commercial
narratives with ancestry (Columbus, the Pilgrims and the Founding

Fathers), amplifying their historical experiences into literature until it assumed mythic proportions. Myth and art exerted reciprocal pressure on each other until they shaped our sense of reality. Thus, writes Slotkin, "...a national mythology may come to exercise the same unconscious appeal as the archetypal myths of which they are the variants."[14] Some use the terms "civic religion" or simply "Americanism." Myths are ambiguous, like dreams vaguely remembered. So our most common descriptive phrase (although not coined until the 1930s) is "American Dream."

Hearing these metaphors of national myth through popular culture, we gloss over our troubled history with illusory solutions. We have been telling ourselves these stories about ourselves all our lives. They glide through our dreams so smoothly that even liberals — *especially* liberals — rarely notice how deeply they hold us. Many, for example, lament America's "mistakes" in Iraq and Afghanistan, yet continue to praise our "good intentions." In speaking this way, we may easily (and this is critical) substitute Viet Nam, Nicaragua, Cuba, the Philippines, Haiti, Mexico, Chile, Iran, Guatemala, etc, for Iraq.

But myth (in Campbell's terms, the cosmological and mystical levels of myth) points beyond the social order toward essential questions of truth, justice, beauty and purpose. We study the myth of innocence to imagine ways of bringing America back into alignment with its purpose.

When Europeans "discovered" the new world, the power of myth enveloped their images of its indigenous inhabitants. Columbus initially wavered between the "noble savage" projection (innocent, generous natives) and its opposite (sub-human, untrustworthy). Quickly, the latter won out. "Indians" were shameless, naked fornicators and idolaters. Perhaps more importantly, their notions of *ownership* condemned them: in maintaining the land collectively, they were the original red communists. "They are fit to be ruled," wrote Columbus; they could be trained to be industrious slaves. When this prediction proved unrealistic, the Spaniards responded with genocide.

The new story described essentially *empty* land. However, wrote John Locke, "...land that is left wholly to nature is...waste." By the 1570s, allegorical personifications of America as a female nude appeared in European art.

"Virgin" land evokes fantasies of defloration. Raleigh was clear about that: Guiana "hath yet her maydenhead." This is deliberately constructed mythic language. The indigenous people had, of course, worked the land for centuries. And it was hardly empty. Its pre-1492 population was over 100 million. However, by 1600 epidemics had already wiped out entire native populations. The British built over fifty New England settlements on the remains of native towns.

Whites merged sexual and racial ideology to differentiate themselves from these people. Although the natives had never known prostitution or venereal disease, the process of "othering" *required* that they be perceived as unable to control themselves. Intellectuals debated whether they had souls. Some argued that they were children, to be protected and civilized, while others claimed they were "natural slaves" (Aristotle's term), set apart by God to serve those born for more lofty pursuits.

This is America's creation myth. It sings of people who came seeking freedom, charged with a holy mission to destroy evil, save souls, carve civilization out of darkness — *and get rich*. R.W.B. Lewis wrote that this story saw "... a divinely granted second chance for the human race...emancipated from history... Adam before the Fall."[15] It was a return to innocence, and the entire world was watching.

This new story recalled an older "heliotropic myth" in which history follows the sun, moving from the old empires of the east — China, India, Persia — toward dominance by western empires — Greece, Rome, Spain, Britain. Many were convinced that Christ would return in America and history would end. The millennium was at hand: "The Gospel hath crossed the western ocean."

Biblical myth justified the entire adventure. Columbus called his voyages the "enterprise of Jerusalem," and the Pilgrims saw themselves as "Israelites," leaving Egypt/England for the "New Jerusalem." Unfortunately, however, the Exodus story is intertwined with the original *invasion of Palestine*. Since God saved us, they reasoned, we have the sacred responsibility (have license) to seize (their) land. From the start, our stories of domination came packaged in the language of liberation. Everyone had a role to play: whites were the Chosen People, America was the Promised Land and Indians were the Philistines.

This dream-story was built up over three centuries of storytelling, preaching, oratory, fiction, poetry, textbooks, advertisements, films and television. *America* was neither South nor Central America, nor Mexico nor Canada. Its essence was that anything was possible. America, writes Jacob Needleman, "...was the future... not to be born anything at all" — an *idea* formed by unique philosophical ideals.[16]

In the land of opportunity, greatness was limited only by one's own desire. The Founding Fathers were steeped in the new humanistic philosophy; they contradicted their Puritan predecessors and declared the demise of original sin. Since then, Americans have maintained a superficial belief in the *tabula rasa,* the "clean slate" that we can fill with anything, that competes with our vestigial belief in predestination. Even now, TV commercials for the military encourage us to "be all you can be." The cliché is effective because it hints at purpose. Assuming unlimited opportunity, however, we believe we can be anything we *want* to be. This is a characteristically inflated and innocent American misinterpretation of the indigenous teaching that we were born to be *one* thing, and that the task of soul making is to discover it.

Cooperation between northerners and southerners birthed a paradoxical mix of extreme religious and modern Enlightenment values. Man was fallen and sinful, yet he could become whatever he wanted. Indeed, in 1776 — for the first time in history — a nation proclaimed the *pursuit of happiness* as its prime value. Soon, Toqueville observed of American preachers, "...it is often difficult to be sure when listening to them whether the main object of religion is to procure eternal felicity in the next world or prosperity in this."[17]

Eventually, religion and business merged as they did nowhere else. Without the support of a state religion or centralized Catholicism, and with Protestant churches constantly splitting in schisms, each individual preacher was forced to become an entrepreneur of souls, a salesman, in order to distinguish his church from other churches and increase its membership. Consequently, a business-growth mentality grew within American Protestantism, and its philosophy of optimistic self-improvement merged with the capitalist ideology of greed and perpetual growth. The shadow of this narcissistic, blind optimism is the wounded innocence of the missionary who simply cannot understand why the natives don't appreciate his benign efforts. To him it is obvious, as George W. Bush said in 2002: "American values are right and true for every person in every society."

Freedom became a holy term that meant all things to all people. *Liberty* (from a Roman epithet for Dionysus, *Liber)* implies release — the return of the repressed — and *liberation,* in both its Marxist and Buddhist meanings. Americans struggled for a while with the difference between *positive liberty* (the power and resources to act to fulfill one's own potential), and *negative liberty* (freedom from restraint, what one *didn't have to do).* Eventually, the two forms of liberty birthed a monster: freedom became *entitlement* to do what one wants, regardless of the needs of the community, the power to achieve it and the privilege to *take liberties* with others ("to liberate" is military slang for looting). This interpretation of the pursuit of happiness led eventually to the liberties extended to *non-human* entities, corporations.

The Enlightenment and the commercial revolution offered freedom without responsibility, but it had unexpected results, writes Historian John Hope Franklin. The passionate pursuit of liberty by some resulted in the "destruction of the rights of others to pursue the same ends…the freedom to destroy freedom."[18]

The Puritan's obsession with personal salvation met the opportunist's rejection of social class. Cheap western land served as a safety valve for the discontented, so abject poverty (among whites) was, for a while, relatively uncommon. To an extent unimaginable in Europe, Americans became landowners, and land meant freedom. Historian Richard Hofstadter points out that farming in America took on a "…commercially minded and speculative style. The farmer was constantly tempted to engross more land…hold it speculatively… to mine and deplete the soil, then to sell out and move."[19]

But when extremes of wealth and poverty did appear, the rich felt little obligation. Belief in predestination survived long after formal Puritanism declined. The myth taught that poverty was one's own fault, *not* that of the economy. The object then as now was to "get ahead," to constantly improve one's economic status relative to one's neighbors or family. Each man was free to make something of himself or to fail. Either way, he was a "self-made man," a phrase coined in 1832. By the early nineteenth century, the first "self-help" manuals appeared, often written by clergymen, extolling the Protestant virtues of hard work and perseverance necessary for success.

But if individuals were blank slates, *the nation* had a purpose unique in history: God had chosen it to spread freedom and opportunity. Eventually, America extrapolated this idea onto world affairs. The nation of individualists became an individual among nations, bringing the good news to others, generally without asking their permission. Although empires always fabricate ideologies to rationalize conquest, only Americans justify invasion, enslavement and genocide with stories of idealism, good intentions and "manifest destiny." A minister encouraged his flock: "There are 3,000 miles of wilderness behind these Indians... *We must free our land of strangers,* even if each mile is a marsh of blood." The Bush II administration eventually carried this magical notion to its extreme, but it has been the bedrock foundation of our foreign policy — or at least of our *beliefs* about it — since Day One.

The myth equated mobility with progress. History itself was heliotropic, moving constantly westward. Men easily forgot its lessons, because they continually existed in a "new" America. *America The Beautiful* (1895) sings:

> *O beautiful for Pilgrim feet*
> *Whose stern impassioned stress*
> *A thoroughfare for freedom beat*
> *Across the wilderness!*

Always moving towards something better, they looked condescendingly upon those who stayed home. For the upwardly mobile, to *be* is to be *stuck.* Tocqueville observed,

> A man builds a house in which to spend his old age, and
> he sells it before the roof is on... he soon afterwards leaves

>to carry his changeable longings elsewhere... he will travel
>fifteen hundred miles to shake off his happiness.[20]

Mobility (symbolized eventually by the automobile) expresses an enduring aspect of the myth of innocence: *starting over.* One could always pull up stakes, move on, try something new or join a different church. One needed to constantly expand and grow geographically, economically, socially and spiritually. This led to wildly divergent yet philosophically similar ideals, from infinitely expanding consumer economies to "New Age" spirituality. But always it means movement: in 2005, only six percent of the million inhabitants of Las Vegas, the ultimate place of the New Start, had been born there.

"New Start" implies a familiar archetype. Tribal initiation takes boys out of their community before returning them with their sense of purpose revitalized. It is *points in time rooted within space* (the ancestral land). America inverted this ancient relationship — a person could simply leave home to acquire a new identity. Our toxic mimic of initiation became *points in space rooted in time.* As early as 1600 America symbolized the New Start for all of Europe, humanity reborn into innocence. And this version of the myth remains nearly as strong today.

Americans characteristically emphasize individual rights over the needs of the community (although we periodically suffer the eruption of the shadow — moral crusades and inquisitions). Sociologist Robert Bellah writes, "...radical individualism is what I call the default mode of American culture. It is where we go when things are relatively stable... But (this) individualist tradition finds the very idea of the common good incomprehensible."[21]

Opportunists demonize government regulation, while Puritans emphasize individual spiritual (and financial) responsibility. Obsession with self-improvement and personal achievement keeps them both ignorant of the suffering around them. *Wealth* remains proof of grace — and poverty indicates the opposite — even if the religious terminology has fallen away.

But there is a price, because individualism, entitlement and mobility

facilitate a mask of innocence; and *innocence always evokes its opposite.*
Historian Greil Marcus writes,

> To be an American is to feel the promise as a birthright, and
> to feel alone and haunted when the promise fails. No failure
> in America, whether of love or money, is ever simple; it is
> always a kind of betrayal.[22]

Americans, like no people before them, strive for self-improvement.
But within the word "improve" lies the anxiety of those who can never *know*
if they've attained the otherworldly goal. Thus we must continually "prove"
our status in this one.

AMERICAN DUALITIES

All societies must mediate the perennial conflict between individual and
community. In America the unsteady truce between opportunistic mania
and Puritan obsessions led to a division in the national psyche (the *hero*
versus the *victim*) and a bewildering series of dualities that only temporarily
resolve this tension.

Our basic struggle over the opposing values of *freedom* and *equality,*
or individualism versus conformism, implies different views of human
nature. To Puritans, since we are all innately sinful and human nature is
immutable, society exists only to keep us under control. Descendents of the
opportunists, from robber barons to libertarians, care little for theology. To
them, less government is simply better. Giving people things they haven't
earned (unless they've inherited their wealth) creates dependency and
robs them of their freedom. Conservatives rarely acknowledge how deeply
rooted in theology such arguments are. Progressives, on the other hand,
argue that we aren't innately sinful, and that government can help people
change.

The pendulum has swung back and forth. After religious repression
relaxed, freedom "rang." Narrow interpretations of equality (excluding
blacks, Indians and women) prevailed from the Revolution through the
mid-nineteenth century. Then came the Gilded Age, unrestrained capitalism

and conspicuous consumption. In the 1930s the emphasis shifted toward equality. The decline of liberalism in the 1970s shifted the pendulum back to a superficial focus on freedom. Many still favor legislating morality — while asserting local rights over federal authority.

Wherever one of these values predominates, its shadow is nearby. Conflict emerges as tension between libertarianism and wartime conformism, or between opportunity and meritocracy — and the old-boy networks that actually ensure WASP dominance of our institutions. George W. Bush, the ultimate Yale "legacy," opposed affirmative action. Yet he never would have been admitted to Yale based on his own academic performance. Since all start on a "level playing field" with equal access to education and jobs, the myth implies, "May the best man win." The legal system is based on this notion: if (a very big if) each side retains adequate counsel, then truth and justice will naturally emerge.

Conflicts also emerge as *fairness* vs. *cheating*. Fairness implies that all who play by the rules will prosper. Cheating, however, reveals capitalism's core values and the realities of privilege. We love our fictional villains precisely because they will do anything to win. Even in losing, they briefly unveil the shadow of our heroic ideals: competition actually trumps fairness.

Why are so many outraged at drug use in sports? Our moral indignation expresses our innocent longing for ritual fields of play where the pursuit of money doesn't overcome the purity of fairness. Eldridge Cleaver, however, saw that when all secretly subscribe to the notion of "every man for himself:"

> ...the weak are seen as the natural and just prey of the strong. But since this dark principle violates our democratic ideals... we force it underground...spectator sports are geared to disguise, while affording expression to, the acting out in elaborate pageantry of the myth of the fittest in the process of surviving.[23]

More than fair, countless Western heroes offer the first blow to the villains. Since striking first would violate the rules, we must create the illusion that the Other (Indians, Mexicans, Spaniards, Germans, Japanese,

Russians, Vietnamese, Nicaraguans, Iraqis, Al Queda, Taliban, Iranians, North Koreans) has struck, or *might* strike first. Here, ideals of fairness disguise both the predatory impulse and the paranoid imagination that it manipulates.

Ours is a political myth not because it is untrue, but because its pervasiveness and its unexamined assumptions produce a consensus reality. It is a container of multiple and inconsistent meanings; its very ambiguity gives it the mythic energy that motivates us.

It allows the privileged and those who control the media to manipulate the two polar ideals. Segregation ("separate but equal") was legal for sixty years. Reactionaries invoke equality by claiming that legal equality is sufficient and calling affirmative action "reverse discrimination" and ethnic liberals "reverse racists." Some even argue that since prejudice no longer exists, minorities should require no assistance (which only encourages the sin of laziness). This false argument has potency because it contains some truth; since individuals have occasionally "pulled themselves up by their own bootstraps," then conservatives claim that *everyone* should. If they can't, says the myth, Puritan at its core, then failure is their own fault. To attack economic redistribution, however, conservatives invoke the other pole of individualism. "Freedom" becomes the right to accumulate and invest wealth without government regulation. Banking on a long tradition of anti-intellectualism, they have (since 1980) convinced millions that progressive candidates are elitist and corporate apologists are populists.

Marketing exploits both sides. Toqueville noticed tendencies toward conformity that resulted from an ideology of equality in a materialistic society. Now, we purchase millions of identical sunglasses, cigarettes, leather jackets and motorcycles because they symbolize *rebellion against conformity*. Fashion is a simultaneous declaration of freedom and membership: we present a unique self to the world while deliberately copying selected others. We "individualists" look and think, for the most part, within narrow parameters.

Military recruiters exploit romantic images of individual warriors while simultaneously emphasizing the satisfactions of forgetting oneself. They seduce young men with images of knights in heroic, *solo* combat, conquering dragons in video game conditions to entrain them in the automatic responses of the large, anonymous military *group*.

Each of the opposing values contains the seed of its shadow, especially in lifestyle choices. Moralists display stunningly imaginative voyeurism in their crusades, while sensualists reveal adolescent exhibitionism behind their rebellious gestures. Images of completely irresponsible behavior mirror unrealistic calls for abstinence.

Meanwhile, conservatives who criticize government intervention in private life demonize abortion providers, support agricultural subsidies and jail millions of non-violent pot smokers. Congressman Newt Gingrich, for example, crusaded for smaller government in the 1990s, yet quietly secured enough federal money for his home district to make it third in the nation in subsidies per capita. George W. Bush, in his second inaugural address, used "freedom," "free," and "liberty" forty-nine times — while establishing a terrorist alert list that came to include over a million Americans.

Eventually, Puritans and Opportunists merged, perceiving freedom in autonomy and material possessions rather than in social relatedness or introspection. The grand product of this mix was the American: enthusiastic, confident, practical, optimistic, classless, casual, cheerful and competitive yet helpful. But to those who endured his excesses, he was arrogant, judgmental, prejudiced, narcissistic, unreflective and contemptuous of the past. He preferred character to intellect and almost universally assumed, wrote Hofstadter, that "the two somehow stand in opposition to each other."[24] And he was *belligerent*, a childlike giant, the "Ugly American," making fine distinctions between the elect and the damned, or crushing the weak with astonishing cruelty. D.H. Lawrence called the American soul, "...hard, isolate, stoic, and a killer."

Generally, a unique if superficial balance has ruled. We love to tell ourselves that America is the land of freedom *and* equality. To Needleman, this ideal touched the hearts of people everywhere "who yearned not only for wealth...or comfort, but also for meaning and transcendence." He sees in the idea of *rights* the Jeffersonian notion that all people have the intrinsic "capacity to intuit the good..."[25]

However, we have a Bill of Rights but no Bill of Responsibilities (indeed, since government has shown that it can arbitrarily remove our rights, as it did with the Japanese-Americans during World War Two, or with the Espionage Act of 1917, which criminalized free speech, then it can be argued that all we really have are certain *privileges*). Since America, like any adolescent, emphasizes rights over responsibilities, freedom often outweighs equality. Radical thinkers, however, highlight the difference between what the nation is and its potential. The source of the paradox of freedom and equality lies in our unexamined definitions of who is and who is not a member of the *polis*. When only a small percentage of the population is admitted to that rarified atmosphere and Others are arbitrarily excluded, then both the contradiction in the rhetoric and the sense of denial and innocence are heightened. As Malcolm X said, "Sitting at the table doesn't make you a diner, unless you eat some of what's on that plate… Being born here in America doesn't make you an American."[26]

How much is our freedom worth? When dealing with *political* (as opposed to financial) freedom, we're on unsteady ground. Despite the narrative of liberty, we regularly trade freedom for a dubious sense of security. Franklin had contempt for this attitude, writing, "Those who would give up Essential Liberty to purchase a little Temporary Safety, deserve neither Liberty nor Safety."

The paranoid imagination often outranks the predatory imagination. During wartime or periods of inquisition we quickly forget the civil liberties the nation was founded upon. Terrorized by fear of the Other, we condone gross persecutions of dissenters. This is Tocqueville's tyranny of the majority. For all their emphasis on individual rights, Americans had put so much emphasis on equality rather than upon *diversity* that they became intolerant of the freedom to be different. He wrote, "I know of no country in which there is so little independence of mind and real freedom of discussion as in America."[27]

Periods of capitalist fervor have provoked responses such as the New Deal. Franklin Roosevelt reframed freedom: of speech, of religion, from want and from fear. But after FDR's death, Harry Truman replaced the last two with freedom of *enterprise*.

More fundamental to American myth than freedom or equality, *getting ahead,* or the *unrestrained quest for wealth* trumps them both. And yet, it's all relative: under Eisenhower, the rich paid extremely high income taxes. After decades of corporate welfare, both big business and big agriculture would be horrified at a *truly* free market.

The 1950s saw demands for both freedom and equality, or freedom defined as inclusion. Civil Rights activists argued that freedom is only a precondition for equality. The pendulum continues to swing. Media pundits often claim that we have it all: freedom of expression, equal pursuit of happiness and the admiration of all nations. The myth is durable, and Americans respond to myths, not facts.

Consider another duality: we could describe left-wing activism as a rational response to economic, racial or gender-based victimization. *Right-*wing extremism, however, is often a response by the relatively privileged (and *every* white male, regardless of his wealth, has privilege) to the *perception* of being victimized by women or minorities. Demonizing of scapegoats distracts millions from understanding the real sources of their troubles. This is true everywhere. But our conditions are unique, because we confuse class with race, as I will show. Similarly, American foreign policy attempts to convert legitimate anger into irrational violence. After Viet Nam, the U.S. deliberately eliminated secular activists throughout the Mid-East, thus forcing most dissent into religious extremism, which is inherently conservative and easily manipulated.

THE WILDERNESS AND THE SAVIOR

Like the Biblical story, American history moved through wilderness. The Puritans considered this a necessary stage, a test of their faith, and saw only two choices: either heroically penetrate and overcome it, or become its captive. It was the abode of savages (Latin: *silva,* forest), in "...a waste and howling wilderness where none inhabited but hellish fiends, and brutish men that devils worshipped."

By 1800 a more nuanced vision of the wilderness emerged. Nature could be a source of strength and virtue if one took a Romantic viewpoint. Emerson wrote, "...within these plantations of God, a decorum and sanctity reign."[28]

Legions of opportunists, however, were relentlessly imposing order upon the wilderness. The American soul was split; now there were two "Wests" as well, wrote Henry Nash Smith. For those who pushed beyond the frontier (and those who vicariously followed their exploits) the *agricultural* West was a tedious place. But the *Wild* West was "… an exhilarating region of adventure and comradeship in the open air. Its heroes… were…noble anarchs owing no master…"[29]

The appeal of these adventurers lay in the fact that they had embarked on the hero's journey. That they often failed mattered little because they carried the aspirations of millions. The heroes of the western expansion became the stock characters of American myth. The greatest of them, Daniel Boone, continually moved as civilization encroached, allegedly complaining, "I had not been two years at the licks before a d—d Yankee came, and settled down *within an hundred miles of me!"*

Whether Boone actually said that is irrelevant. Americans *needed* him to, because the developing myth divided the Apollonian City from the Dionysian Wilderness. The advancing line of the Frontier created a safety valve of free western land when urban conditions became unmanageable. Like the Hebrew narrative, it linked military triumph with civilization's progress and with the moral character of its heroes, who distinguished themselves by saving white women from the Indians. Biographers turned Boone into the "Achilles of the West."

Portraying history as a metaphoric, extended Indian war, their narratives insisted on the racial basis of difference. Progress could occur only by subjugating nature and exterminating the savages. Native myths had arisen from the ground out of vast antiquity. The new stories, however, were fashioned by a fledgling and characteristically American *public relations industry.* Thousands of "dime novels" depicted the west as a source of regeneration, even as actual wilderness was disappearing and transforming into a *myth* of wilderness. The cowboy (and urban detective) heroes of these novels violently resolved all challenges. This literature, writes Smith, was "an objectified mass dream." When competition among publishers arose, writers merely had to kill a few more Indians to keep readers interested, "exaggerating violence and bloodshed… to the point of…overt sadism."[30]

After Boone, "Buffalo Bill" Cody was America's greatest hero. Writers so exaggerated his deeds (while he was still alive) that one couldn't tell where the actual left off and where fiction began. Into the 1920s one publisher kept 200 titles about him in print. For years Cody took his band of cowboys and Indians on tour, further impressing the myth of the Frontier on countless Americans, including a young Joseph Campbell.

The other, less exciting West partook of the official cult of progress. Hunters blazed trails and defeated beasts and Indians, and *farmers* — the vast majority — followed, establishing new communities. A new mythic promise of America developed, expressing fecundity, growth and the happy labor of idealized, Jeffersonian farmers: the "garden of the world."

Although this story is no more accurate than that of the cowboy, it survives because it embodies fantasies of simpler, happier times and independent ownership of land. Such ownership (for whites) was possible, of course, only if the frontier continued to expand into Indian Territory. These "sturdy" family farmers, backbone of the country in war and peace, were the spirit of democracy. Neither rich nor poor, they owed no one and exploited no one. They gave to the myth of the garden another fundamental characteristic: the West (the Midwest, the *heart*land) was racially homogeneous and classless. This powerful and historically unique narrative attracted millions of immigrants in the last quarter of the nineteenth century. Americans were free *and* equal.

Another agrarian myth was the romantic and harmonious southern plantation, whose benign patriarch cared only to protect his charming heroines and happy slaves. Although the image of the garden ultimately prevailed, the romance of the South lingered for generations. After the Civil War, it was transformed into the "Lost Cause," a civic religion of white superiority that lamented the destruction of the graceful southern lifestyle by blacks and Yankee carpetbaggers. Many northerners, eager to forget Reconstruction, embraced the myth as well. The nation told itself a new story, how brothers had healed their differences and become united.

Despite the massive crime of slavery, these stories rarely acknowledged anything but purity and good within the utopian garden. Outside, however, was darkness — and dark people. The Frontier myth, or the *American*

Monomyth, was repeated endlessly: a small, harmonious, innocent community, often symbolized by a young woman, is threatened. The chosen people find themselves under *unprovoked, racial* attack. Democratic institutions are impotent against the absolute evil symbolized by the Other.

Western tales offered the original American superhero, a mysterious outsider who intervened, redeemed captives, destroyed evildoers, cleansed the wilderness and violently regenerated the community. This figure combined Jesus, willing to sacrifice himself for us, and Jehovah, furiously condemning the unrighteous. He knew the Indians better than normal white people. And, like Dionysus, he straddled the boundaries between civilization and savagery, arriving out of nowhere and disappearing when his work was finished. Eden, innocent yet powerless, had no choice but to rely on this lone hero.

In two centuries of popular literature, the enigmatic stranger, in literally thousands of incarnations, intervened at the last moment to save the day. *Redemption through violence — righteous, merciless confrontation with the Other —* became America's fundamental narrative. Invested with the power and unexamined depth of myth, the lone, uncompromisingly violent crusader inhabits the very center of the American character. All he needs to act is provocation by evil and a woman to save.

THE RED OTHER

Patriarchy's original Others were women ("not male") and nature ("not culture.") These prejudices were models for the demonizing of "primitive" people shared by all Europeans. What made America unique, however, was the combination of Puritan and opportunist philosophies. No other nation has gone to such lengths, for so long, to define itself by *excluding* so many from full membership, while simultaneously telling itself pervasive stories of freedom and opportunity.

To the settlers, the ecological and communal values of the natives were proof of their sub-human condition. Since Indians didn't utilize their resources, reasoned whites, their lands were empty, and whites should have them. Indeed, Adolph Hitler would write: "Neither Spain nor Britain should be models of German expansionism, but the Nordics of North America, who...ruthlessly pushed aside an inferior race..."[31]

The myth of the Frontier defined Indians as bloodthirsty killers who swept out of the dark forests. The relationship of white to red is so shrouded in legend that modern people cannot grasp the extent to which whites feared and utterly loathed the original "reds." Herman Melville wrote that by 1840 Indian hating had become a "metaphysic." It was a unique dimension in which religious zeal, barbaric atrocity and sacrificial ritual merged to create genocide. In 1636, while founding Harvard College, Puritans massacred and burned 500-700 Pequots:

> ...It was a fearfull sight to see them thus frying in the fryer, and the streams of blood ... horrible was the stincke and sente there of, but the victory seemed a sweete sacrifice, and they gave the prays thereof to God, who had wrought so wonderfully for them...

Hatred — and joy — of this intensity expresses a "metaphysic" that begins in abstraction and alienation from the body and drapes itself in innocence. Ritual sacrifice (fire and blood) gives its practitioners a consistent moral self-image. It enabled the My Lai massacre and dozens like it in Viet Nam. It lies behind the communal celebration of whiteness known as the lynch mob, and it enables us to casually dismiss the torture of *suspected* terrorists. But it does not completely insulate us from guilt. For that to occur, one more step is required: the erasure of memory. After the Pequot massacre, the Puritans passed a law making it a crime to utter the word *Pequot.*

The myth of innocence is so attractive because it inverts guilt. The *settlers* became the virgins — captured, tormented and raped by savages. In 1682 the first of thousands of "captivity narratives" was published. For the next half-century, *all but one of America's best-selling books* were captivity tales. These highly popular and symbolically potent stories constituted our first coherent myth-literature, and they haunted Americans for ten generations, long enough to lodge permanently in our psyche.

Innocence required that "whiteness" be clearly distinguished. So captivity narratives imagined capture by the Other as the destruction of all that was good, and rape (*pollution* by the Other's bodily fluids) as a fate worse than death. This threat enforced conformism by graphically depicting the horrors experienced by those who ventured outside the gates. Americans both feared and fantasized about "alien abductions," as their descendents would three centuries later.

The narrative of regeneration through violence was a toxic mimic of initiation that superficially resembled ancient hero myths. Both the hunter (willingly) and the captive (unwillingly) entered a primal world. By maintaining their racial/cultural integrity and defeating its denizens, they might seize its power, return to civilization and morally renew their community.

In truth, however, large numbers of captives, including over sixty percent of young women captives, preferred native life and *refused to return.* Preachers warned, "...people are ready to run wild into the woods again...to be as Heathenish as ever..." Even Franklin admitted, "No European who has tasted Savage Life can afterwards bear to live in our societies." While whites considered idleness sinful, the natives appeared happy without laboring constantly. They had few sexual taboos, relative gender equality and great affection for their children, whereas whites were known to execute children for simple transgressions. One white woman who chose life with her captors testified, "Here I have no master..."

Since native lifestyles were so appealing, it was doubly necessary to demonize them. Whites often treated ex-captives as pariahs who'd been "polluted" by intimacy with the Other. Periodicals regularly featured the theme of rape by Indian captors, despite little evidence. In fact, ubiquitous images in art of bound and near-naked virgins begging mercy from hulking red brutes revealed seductive fantasies of relations with the Other. But if Puritans were sexually restrained, European culture was not. Both rape and prostitution were common Biblical themes. *White* men had been raping, beating, mutilating and whoring their women since the Bronze Age.

The wilderness and its inhabitants inevitably reminded the Puritan of his essential oneness with his body. Therefore culture set out to destroy nature to erase the pain of remembering what it had lost.

Hundreds of (mostly fictional) captivity tales accompanied the migration west, expressing our assumptions of how civilization progresses. They served as recruiting tools for the revolutionary army. Later writers used them to re-tell stories of male incompetence as counter-narratives with female victims. Barbary pirates captured American sailors in the early 1800s, but the stories were printed as accounts of fictional *woman* captives. "The myth," writes Susan Faludi, "was now in final form…ready to be reactivated whenever a homeland threat might call for its protective services."[32]

With the basic theme firmly implanted in the American psyche, politicians easily substituted villains, manipulating fear of abduction by blacks during Reconstruction and the "white slavery" panic of 1909. In the 1970s, Patricia Hearst's kidnapping by black radicals contributed to the conservative backlash, while Richard Nixon reframed American prisoners of war as "innocent" captives. The Iran hostage crisis helped elect Ronald Reagan. Propaganda prior to the invasions of Panama and Greneda and the Gulf War utilized lurid and entirely bogus captivity stories.

The paranoid imagination continues to run wild. The 1990s saw hysteria over child abuse, predatory daycare teachers, alien abductions and satanic cults. In 1994, after a (blond) girl was actually kidnapped and murdered, California enacted the "Three Strikes" law, and thousands went to prison for life.

In 2003, Americans thrilled when Jessica Lynch was captured in Iraq and then "liberated." It hardly mattered that she was part of an invading army, nor that the Iraqis had been taking good care of her, nor that her own shadow-figure, Lyndie England, would soon become a scapegoat for the Abu Ghraib torture scenes. Indeed, the U.S. Army delayed Lynch's "rescue" until the cameramen arrived.

Hostage crises provide pretexts for intervention. In this "protection racket," writes Faludi, no wonder "fetuses in antiabortion literature are most often depicted as little girls."[33]

This potent theme remains basic to romance novels, science fiction (including *Star Wars*), superhero tales from *Superman* to *Rambo*, and, of course, westerns. The classic version is John Ford's *The Searchers* of 1956, which has been described as "the most flattered movie of all time." Jaime Weinman writes, "The very idea of a distraught relative going into an alien world to bring out of it another relative or a friend — those movies have proliferated in the last 25 years, and all of them can be traced back to *The Searchers* in one form or another."[34] But the theme itself was already 270 years old when Ford made *The Searchers*.

The City on a Hill, like the Thebes of Pentheus, was by definition utterly innocent. If it couldn't admit any imperfections, then evil was outside, and therefore Indians deserved their fate. When increasing population pushed the settlers beyond Eden's boundaries, they had *liberty* to cut the natives down like trees. By 1717, all the New England colonial governments (and by 1758 almost all northern colonies) were paying lucrative bounties for bloody Indian scalps, regardless of whether the victims were friend or foe. This led to the first use of the term "redskin." Indeed, some scholars argue that the British brought the large-scale practice of scalping to the Indians, not the reverse.[35]

There were fundamental differences between the violence perpetrated by the Spanish and the British. In the south, genocide was a by-product of enslavement and harvesting of mineral riches. The British, however, engaged in long-term development because the north lacked gold. For them, Indians were simply in the way. But their system produced the same results, and both were justified by holy texts. Rapid collapse of indigenous populations reminded whites of Biblical narratives, proving that it was all divinely ordained.

Thus it was a simple step for intellectuals to support the myth of innocence by identifying America's self-interest with God's plan. Franklin: "If it be the design of Providence to extirpate these savages…to make room for the cultivators of the earth… rum may be the appointed means." Jefferson: Whites should "pursue them to extermination." Horace Greeley: "These people must die out…vain to struggle against (God's) righteous decree." *Historian* Francis Parkman: The natives' "own ferocity and intractable indolence" caused their demise. Parkman didn't notice or care that he'd confused two opposite traits, because both aggression and laziness were sins in the eyes of the Puritan, and "othering" does not have to be logical, even for academics.

Eventually the Indian's image alternated between an ecological symbol of humanity's childhood and the cruel violator of the pastoral peace, both the victim (of the hunter) and the violator (of the captive).

America's growth required the near-total extermination of an entire civilization and a myth of innocence to cover up the guilt. Shortly after the final massacre at Wounded Knee, Theodore Roosevelt proclaimed, "… this great continent could not have been kept as a game preserve for squalid savages."

THE BLACK OTHER

Genocide created two problems: it didn't leave enough survivors to be identified as Other, and it didn't leave enough laborers. Whites required someone to act both roles. So they uprooted millions of Africans to form the foundation of the Southern economy.

In the European mind, blackness had long lacked the virtues associated with whiteness. In 1488 it was nothing unusual for Pope Innocent (!) VIII to give black slaves as presents to his cardinals. Africans first arrived in Cuba in1510, after the Spanish had decimated the aboriginal population, and in Jamestown in 1619.

But neither "blackness" nor "whiteness" firmly established themselves in the American mind until the defeat of Bacon's Rebellion of 1676, when indentured servants of both races challenged the landowners. This was a watershed moment. Historian Theodore Allen writes: "…laboring-class African-Americans and European-Americans fought side by side for the abolition of slavery…If the plan had succeeded, the history of…America might have taken a much different path."[36]

Previously, there had been little distinction between dark- and light-skinned laborers. Afterwards, Virginia codified its bondage system. In the first example of "affirmative action," it replaced the terms "Christian" or "free" with *"white,"* gave new privileges to Caucasians, removed rights from free blacks and banned interracial marriage. Other laws contributed to what Allen calls the "absolutely unique American form of male supremacism" — the right of *any* Euro-American to rape any African-American without fear of reprisal.[37]

This new allegiance to whiteness eliminated class competition and provided a sub-class of poor whites to intimidate slaves and suppress rebellion. Copied everywhere, the pattern merged with the myth of racial war: America's primary model for class distinction (and class conflict) became *relations between white planters and black slaves, rather than between rich and poor.* The new system, writes Allen, insisted on "the social distinction between the *poorest* member of the oppressor group and any member, however propertied, of the oppressed group."[38] Eventually, southern class discrimination merged with northern religious stereotyping. Since poverty equaled sinfulness (to the Puritan) and black equaled poor (to the Opportunist), then it became obvious that blackness equaled sin.

Regardless of their economic status, whites pledged allegiance to a state that was defined by the perpetual threat of the return of the repressed. The predatory imagination found the secret to perpetuating itself — as it would in the1870s, 1890s, 1930s, 1950s, 1980s and today — by manipulating the paranoid imagination.

It was exquisite timing: southerners encoded their brutal system just as northerners breathlessly read of both Salem and the first captivity narratives. *Red, White and Black were born together in the American soul.* All the darker elements of the myth of innocence were in place: race, sex, victimization, repressive religion and witch hunting. Psychologically speaking, this was America's "birth trauma" — the events that formed our essential character, our fatal flaw.

On the national level, racist fear mongering appeared at least as early as1844, when Democrats attempted to arouse laborers against abolitionists, threatening that free blacks would take their jobs. "Nativist" movements attained considerable electoral power by turning Protestant fear of the Other upon more recent Catholic immigrants.

Over three centuries after Bacon's Rebellion, scholars still wonder why a strong socialist movement never developed in America, as it did almost everywhere else. Characteristically, they rarely consider the overwhelming presence of the Other: *no other nation* combined irresistible myths of opportunity with rigid legal systems deliberately intended to divide natural allies. Whiteness implies both purity (which demands removal of *im*purities) and privilege. No matter how impoverished a white, male American feels, he hears hundreds of subtle messages every day that divide him from the impure. Without racial privilege the concept of whiteness is meaningless. Often, Americans have had nothing to call their own except white privilege, yet they cling to it and support those whose coded rhetoric promises to maintain it.

The process of exclusion and subordination required a massive lie about black inferiority that has been enshrined in our national narrative. "After all," writes activist Tim Wise, "to accept that all men and women were truly equal, while still mightily oppressing large segments of that same national population on the basis of skin color, would be to lay bare the falsity of the American creed."[39] Similarly, the French philosopher Montesquieu wrote, "It is impossible for us to suppose these creatures to be men, because, allowing them to be men, a suspicion would follow that we ourselves are not Christian."

The sheer quantities of this second American genocide stagger the imagination. We literally can't believe it — and this is a powerful marker of our innocence. *Africa lost fifty million persons.*[40] Indeed, more Africans than Europeans came to the Americas between 1500 and 1800. It is critical to understand that slavery and its effects were not secondary consequences, mere exceptions to the grand themes of liberty and democracy, writes Historian George Frederickson. They "constitute its central theme...its original sin."[41]

America in the twenty-first century simply wouldn't be America (economically, politically, psychologically or socially) without slavery and its legacy. Prior to 1860 most presidents and Supreme Court justices were Southern slaveholders. Except for precious metals, Africans produced almost all major American exports to Europe. Slave-grown cotton accounted for seventy percent of the raw material fueling Britain's industrial revolution. Slaves were America's most valuable assets after the land itself. All areas of the country, especially the northern cities, profited. But what about arguments that America grew because of the "free market?" Noam Chomsky counters them in one sentence. "Genocide and slavery: try to imagine a more severe market distortion than that."[42]

It is critical to understand that in certain fundamental respects this situation has remained essentially unchanged. Between 1900 and 1970, Southern Senators held a deadlock on Congress due to their disenfranchisement of blacks. Southern whites had nearly double the representation in Congress than they could have earned by their own population. Since then, the "solid South" has simply changed its allegiance from Democrat to Republican, with enough votes to wreck or water down any progressive legislation. In the age of Obama, race continues to be the unacknowledged subtext of our politics.

Consider the intersection of myths centering on Southern plantations: the myth of free markets; the myth of the pastoral plantation, with everyone happily playing their role, protected by benevolent masters and Protestant ministers; the myth of pure Southern Womanhood; and the complex images of the slaves themselves. Indeed, the North long held to yet another myth, that discrimination occurred only in the South. In reality, *Northern* mobs attacked abolitionists on over two hundred occasions.

Joel Kovel asserts that there are two kinds of racism. One is the obvious *dominative* racism that developed in close contact (including the privilege of rape) between master and slave. The second, *aversive* racism, arose from Puritan associations of blackness with filth. Tocquevile noticed that prejudice "appears to be stronger in the states that have abolished slavery than in those where it still exists; and nowhere is it so intolerant as in those states where servitude has never been known."[43]

Indeed, New England had about 13,000 slaves in 1750. In 1720, New York City's population of seven thousand included 1,600 blacks, most of them slaves. Not until 1664 (22 years after Massachusetts) did Maryland declare that all blacks held in the colony and all those imported in the future would serve for life, as would their offspring. And the two colonies with the strongest religious foundations — Massachusetts and Pennsylvania — were the ones that first outlawed "miscegenation."

When northern states expanded the voting franchise for whites in the 1830s, they explicitly abolished it for blacks. Andrew Jackson is the major figure in this context, the key figure of the first half of the nineteenth century. "Jacksonian Democracy" increased participation for white men, while simultaneously denying it to and then removing thousands of Indians.

With the broadening of the franchise for whites, the sense of "us" grew, but the sense of "not-us" also grew. Jackson ensured that race would trump culture as the primary determinant of citizenship.

Later, several states including Indiana and Illinois literally banned all blacks from entering. Oregon (1859), however, was the only free state *admitted to the Union with an exclusion clause in its constitution.* The ban remained in place until it was finally repealed in 1927. Well into the 1950s (as any black entertainer or athlete can attest), thousands of "sundown towns" in thirty states prevented blacks from residing overnight.

As whiteness took on increasing significance, so did the fear of "mongrelization." Below the fear, however, was *envy* and the desire to achieve authentic psychological integration. To cover up such unacceptable fantasies, whites projected their desires onto blacks. Even the great humanist Jefferson apparently felt that black men had a preference for white women over black women "as uniformly...as the preference of the Oran-utan for the black woman over those of his own species."

As the Native American population east of the Appalachian Mountains shrunk into relative insignificance, African-Americans assumed the role of the Other. What (in the white mind) were their characteristics? First, they were childish, lazy and unreliable — the shadow of the Protestant Ethic. It was necessary to *force* them to be productive.

White performers began to wear blackface in the 1840s. LeRoi Jones (Amiri Baraka) writes,

> "... the only consistent way of justifying what had been done to him — now that he had reached what can be called a post-bestial stage — was to demonstrate the ridiculousness of his inability to act as a "normal" human being."[44]

Whites *needed* to believe that blacks were slow, dumb and happy, so blacks *acted* that way. Whites created fictional characters, from Jim Crow to *Gone With the Wind's* Mammy: loveable and loyal, yet lacking any concern for intellect or freedom. Blackface minstrelsy was America's primary form of entertainment throughout the nineteenth century. Forms of it *(Amos 'n*

Andy) survived into the 1950s, tutoring millions in racist stereotyping. But it provided something else: impersonating blacks, whites could briefly inhabit their own bodies.

A second aspect contradicted the first, but no one cared. This Other was intensely sexual and aggressive. Like Dionysus, he might sneak in and corrupt the children. Class society assigns the mind to the masters and the body to the servants. In racially homogeneous societies, where leaders racially resemble followers, these images are not mutually exclusive. The poor can potentially join the elite. But in *racial* caste systems masters are physically different from servants, and the images are mutually exclusive. The mind/body division coincides with the racial gulf, and this distinction becomes sacred.

It took abstraction to new levels. Whites hated the body's needs and feared that they might be judged by how well they controlled them. Here is a clue to slavery's appeal. This terror, writes Ventura, "...was compacted into a tension that gave Western man the need to control every body he found." In slavery, "the body could be both reviled and controlled."[45]

Third, it was necessary to confine this Black Other of the South, unlike the Red Other (now primarily west of the Mississippi River), *within* the gates of Eden. Whites could savagely defend their women from him, but they couldn't exterminate or isolate him in concentration camps (otherwise known as reservations), because he was critical to economic prosperity. Slavery fit the model of an *internal* Other that had appeared earlier in the Witch craze (There was one exception. By the time of Florida's Seminole wars, black and red intermarriage had been going on for generations, and blacks joined reds as the external Other for a time).

After emancipation, racism remained the foundation of a political economy predicated upon fear, the constant threat of violence, division of the working class and further refinements of whiteness. The law long assumed that blacks were persons with *any* African ancestry. The "one-drop rule," used by no other nation, made one a black person. "Octoroons," who had *seven white great-grandparents out of eight,* were considered to be black.

Curiously, in the case of Native American admixture with whites, courts enforced the one-drop rule more selectively. The "Pocahontas exception" existed because many influential Virginia families claimed descent from Pocahontas. To avoid classifying them as non-white the Assembly declared that a person could be considered white as long as they had no more than one-sixteenth Indian blood.

After 1865, "freedom" no longer defined whiteness. So new laws prevented most blacks from acquiring western land and kept them *de facto* slaves in the south. Homesteading became a privilege of whiteness, another example of affirmative action. In the southwest, similar systems targeted Latinos. No wonder our picture of the hardy "pioneers" is lily-white.

When poor whites and blacks again threatened to unite, the Jim Crow system arose, held in place by the threat of lynching. Between 1868 and 1871, the Ku Klux Klan murdered several thousand persons. In the 1890s, when workers and farmers organized the Populist Movement, there were 200 lynchings per year. The dream of unity collapsed (as it would again in the 1970s) under the fear and the temptation to identify as *white.*

This systemic violence might have provoked more outrage but for a rationale that silenced criticism. Sexuality was a means of reasserting both white control over blacks and male domination of women, even though fewer than a quarter of lynchings resulted from allegations of sexual assault. When agriculture mechanized and the South no longer required them, many blacks left, only to be confined within northern ghettoes, where many black women could find work only as prostitutes. By 1900 the mythmakers had succeeded: most whites believed that blacks hadn't been ready for freedom because they couldn't "sacrifice their lusts."

Like ancient Athenians, Victorian Americans saw themselves as Apollonian, hardworking, rational and progressive. Meanwhile, the Other appeared in a form the Greeks would have recognized, but burdened with Christian sinfulness. There was no place for him or her within the pure American psyche, but it was necessary to keep them close. The descendents of the slaves, in both their stereotyped, earthy physicality and the implied threat of their vengeance, became America's dark incarnation of Dionysus, our collectively repressed memory and imagination. Since whites desperately needed to project him, to *see* him, they created exactly those conditions

— segregation and discrimination — that dehumanized him and fostered behavior that whites could demonize.

Violent thugs where not the only whites to perpetuate these conditions; respected intellectuals have always done their part. The "Dunning School" of racist historians dominated the writing of post-Civil War history well into the 1950s. William Dunning, founder of the American Historical Association, taught Columbia students that blacks were incapable of self-government. Yale's Ulrich Phillips defended slaveholders and claimed they did much to civilize the slaves. Henry Commager and (Harvard's) Samuel Morison's *The Growth of the American Republic,* read by generations of college freshmen, perpetuated the myth of the plantation and claimed that slaves "suffered less than any other class in the South...The majority...were apparently happy."[46] Daniel Boorstin's *The Americans: The Colonial Experience* doesn't mention slavery at all. Similarly, Arthur Schlesinger's Pulitzer Prize-winning *The Age of Jackson* never mentions the Trail of Tears.

American democracy is one of the greatest achievements in world history. Yet the unique conditions of its founding led to deeper abstraction, a widened gap between mind and body, genocide and a universal culture of fear. White Americans filled their imaginary underworld with monsters: the outer, Red Other and the inner, Black Other. In 1960, novelist James Baldwin concluded,

> We would never, never allow Negroes to starve, to grow bitter, and to die in ghettos all over the country if we were not driven by some nameless fear that has nothing to do with Negroes... most white people imagine that (what) they can salvage from the storm of life is really, in sum, their innocence.[47]

Don't you get the idea I'm one of those goddamn radicals. Don't get the idea I'm knocking the American system.

AL CAPONE

Being black has taught him how to allow white people their innocence... like taking care of babies...whom you cannot punish, because they're babies. Eventually you direct that anger at yourself — it has nowhere else to go.

HILTON ALS

I was a racketeer, a gangster for capitalism.

GENERAL SMEDLEY BUTLER

I laughed to myself... "Here we go. I'm starting a war under false pretenses."

ADMIRAL JAMES STOCKDALE, ON THE GULF OF TONKIN INCIDENT

I will never apologize for the United States of America. I don't care what the facts are.

GEORGE H.W. BUSH

08

AMERICANISM AND THE OTHER

AN EMPIRE FOR LIBERTY

Understanding the myth of innocence requires that we reassess the American Revolution and its leaders. Twelve generations of schoolchildren have learned that the colonies revolted over "unfair taxation," a phrase so basic to our vocabulary that "unfair" has long been a universal, silent qualifier of "taxation." Despite our historically *low* tax rates, Americans often feel victimized by some substitute for King George III.

Who was being taxed? Colonial aristocrats were uninterested in sharing their profits either domestically or with England. They contrived a language of liberty intended to unite enough whites to win independence without ending inequality. Indeed, they defined slavery not in terms of what they were inflicting upon blacks but as what Britain was doing to *them*. Taxation without representation *was* slavery, claimed pamphlets like *The Misery and Duty of an Enslaved People*. Jefferson spoke of extending America's boundaries in an "empire for liberty." He opposed British imperialism in the East but favored *American* imperialism in the West.

Historian Page Smith writes that the Founding Fathers intended "to inspire people everywhere to create agencies of government and forms of common social life that would offer greater dignity and hope to the exploited and suppressed."[1] However, almost half of these men, including Patrick Henry (*"Give me liberty or give me death"*), owned human beings as slaves. It was no accident that they looked to classical times for inspiration. They chose Virgil's *Novus Ordo Seclorum* ("A new age now begins.") for the motto on the Great Seal of the United States. The new American citizen resembled the Athenian of two thousand years before: a white, male property-owner, who had prospered in an economy based upon slavery.

What some called the popular will, the leadership considered the tyranny of the majority. Madison, who wrote of "protecting the minority of the opulent from the majority," and Jefferson, who preferred an elected "natural aristocracy," wrote a Constitution that *prevented* full democracy. It ensured stable class relations, kept the South within the republic, never used the word "slavery" and defined blacks as three-fifths of a Caucasian. Seven states forbade interracial marriage.

Although Toqueville described America as the most egalitarian society in history, restrictions on white male suffrage and property qualifications for office were not removed until the 1830s. Underneath the secular veneer, America retained aspects of European theocracy. Despite the constitutional separation of church and state, for fifty years many states required citizens to prove active membership in a Protestant church to hold public office. Congressmen were elected, but state legislatures — the wealthy elite — appointed senators.

Virginia's legal definition of race in 1680 was the first instance of affirmative action for whites. The second was the 1790 Naturalization Act, which allowed virtually any European immigrant to become a citizen, while denying the privilege to Asians. Over the next 120 years Congress passed many other definitions of who was "us" and who wasn't, and they served as models for the almost entirely invisible white privilege that bolstered the Reagan "revolution" many decades later. By then, structures of oppression would be so effective precisely because they seemed so natural.

An unveiled look at American history reveals an enormous catalogue of injustice. It also requires, however, that we be willing to imagine a different story. America has two histories; the first is our political and economic story. As painful as it is to contemplate, knowing the truth enables us to see how the dominant myths of innocence and good intentions were constructed to serve the privileged few.

If we persist in the "search for the Other" — Dionysus in America — we may recover a *second* history that psychologist Stephen Diggs calls "unconscious and alchemical." This story describes and predicts America's slow process of transformation and descent from the Apollonian heights of the heroic, isolated ego and the abstract, distanced killing of life. It tells of America's return to its body, to the communal experience of shared joy and suffering. America's healing will be the gift of the Other. From this perspective we can think of the Revolution and the long isolationism from Europe that followed as "a sealing of the vessel so that the alchemy of the white mind could begin."[2]

Americans have proved to be exceptional in many respects, including our naïve belief in the benign motives of our leaders and our willingness to participate in our own exploitation. This is the manufacture of consent. We live in an insidious political-cultural matrix that we cannot call tyrannical. America is not a police state; people do what is expected of them without being forced to by external authority. Unlike many people in the Third World, white Americans rarely question our dominant paradigms; indeed, we *believe* them.

WITHIN THE WALLS (1)

The Industrial Revolution in the United States required millions of new workers, yet immigration policy was highly restrictive. For over a century, the Supreme Court periodically determined who was Other. Admission to whiteness was an invitation to emerge from darkness and walk in innocence. In a thousand small but consistent ways law and custom defined white persons in terms of what they weren't. The "boundaries of whiteness," writes historian Judy Helfand, "were constructed by exclusion."[3]

The 1838 *Trail of Tears* tells us much. The Cherokees, known as the "civilized tribes," were prosperous, literate, Christian farmers who passed all the *cultural* tests of whiteness. But Andrew Jackson was determined to remove them and eventually exiled and killed thousands. Unable to dispossess Indians for not utilizing the land, he could still claim they were *biologically* inferior. Later, few white Americans saw any irony when Jackson referred to the annexation of slaveholding Texas as "expanding the area of freedom."

Images of the black person shifted after the Civil War. Previously, he was considered permanently inferior. The Fugitive Slave Act of 1850 had allowed even free Blacks in the North to be conscripted into slavery. Now, however, the emancipated black man threatened the concept of whiteness, because white had been defined as *free* for nearly 200 years. Anxiety among whites skyrocketed, and the result was large-scale terrorism throughout the South and benign neglect in the North. While the temperance movement, the daughters of the Puritans, marched against Dionysus in his liquid form, *American* Dionysus experienced unprecedented repression.

Following Reconstruction, whites everywhere colluded in the "Lost Cause" myth. Northerners forgot the ex-slaves, consigning them to the reign of terror that lasted for another century. In 1892, as the nation celebrated the 400th anniversary of the discovery of the New World, 240 blacks were lynched. By 1896 legal segregation was in place throughout the South. Thirty states enforced anti-miscegenation laws, sixteen of these laws lasting until 1967.

Meanwhile, millions of Catholic Irish had arrived. By 1860 one in seven Caucasians was foreign-born, and the struggle to define "us" accelerated. The Irish were forced to compete with free blacks for the lowest-paying urban jobs, but had some privilege based on their color. Predictably, Irish-black tensions erupted into the New York draft riots of 1863, in which hundreds perished.

As more "foreigners" arrived from Mexico, Scandinavia and southern and eastern Europe, nativistic reactionaries forced each group to temporarily carry the mantel of the Other. In the west, since Chinese, blacks and Indians weren't allowed to testify against whites, hundreds of murders went unprosecuted. Congress passed the Chinese Exclusion Act and amended it regularly until it was repealed in 1943. Filipino immigration was limited to fifty persons per year until 1965. Until 1931, "native" white women who married Chinese men *lost* their citizenship. Some argue that whites hated the Chinese because, like Jews, many Chinese stubbornly retained their cultural identity, thus insisting on their otherness. This example illuminates one of the rules of othering: only whites may determine who the Other is. Another rule: when privilege and white identity are questioned, enormous rage can erupt.

Simultaneously, white Californians were exterminating entire native communities. James Wilson writes, "More Indians probably died as a result of deliberate, cold-blooded genocide in California than anywhere else in North America."[4]

Between 1890 and 1920, the migration of eleven million rural people to the cities and the influx of *twenty* million immigrants resulted in new fears that the spiritual and physical Apollonian essence of America would be cheapened by this Dionysian element. Nativists responded by cranking up the machinery of propaganda once again. Scientists and intellectuals (including the president of Stanford) argued that moral character was inherited, that "inferior" southern and eastern Europeans polluted Anglo-Saxon racial purity. Woodrow Wilson of Princeton contrasted "the men of the sturdy stocks of the north" with "the more sordid and hopeless elements" of southern Europe, who had "neither skill nor quick intelligence."[5] As a result, twenty-seven states passed eugenics laws to sterilize "undesirables." A 1911 Carnegie Foundation "Report on the Best Practical Means for Cutting Off the Defective Germ-Plasm in the Human Population" recommended euthanasia of the mentally retarded through the use of *gas chambers*. The solution was too controversial, but in 1927 the Supreme Court, in a ruling written by Oliver Wendell Holmes, allowed coercive sterilization, ultimately of 60,000 Americans. The last of these laws were not struck down until the 1970s. Meanwhile, in *Mein Kampf*, Hitler praised American eugenic ideology, and in the 1930s, Germany copied *American* racial and sterilization laws. Years later, at the Nuremberg trials, the Nazis would quote Holmes's words in their own defense.[6]

The 1908 play *The Melting Pot* instructed recent immigrants that the route to happiness was through whiteness, individualism, "pulling oneself up by one's bootstraps" and distancing oneself from ethnicity. As they assimilated, media and politicians projected Dionysian qualities onto newer immigrants.

America's internal Other, however, remained deeply mired in institutional racism. Two years before, Roosevelt's State of the Union Message said, "The greatest existing cause of lynching is the perpetration, especially by black men, of the hideous crime of rape — the most abominable in all the category of crimes, even worse than murder." Why did his audience understand that (alleged) rape by a black man was worse than murder? Since white women were the essence of purity, rape was *pollution* by the bodily fluids of the Other; it was *penetration* through the veil of innocence.

Each immigrant group quickly vaulted past blacks and Latinos in the social hierarchy. Interracial worker solidarity was nullified by the constant threat of blacks coveting the jobs and the daughters of white workers. The pattern set in 1680 Virginia held everywhere. Wilson instituted racial job segregation at the federal level. In a society constructed on dreams of progress ("getting ahead") and nightmares of race, no one could afford to fall backwards. Recent immigrants who had been accepted as white feared contamination by non-whites. In America, "under-class" meant "underworld."

By 1920, large-scale immigration essentially ended. Eventually, many ethnic whites entered the middle class, but narratives arose in which each immigrant family had done so *alone*. "Collective struggle," says politician Tom Hayden, "is almost entirely missing from our national immigrant myth."[7]

In 1915 Wilson showed *Birth Of A Nation* in the White House, giving semi-official sanction to the movies' first mega-hit. It depicted heroic whites rescuing young women from the clutches of their drooling black abductors. Soon, the resurgent Klan unleashed a wave of hatred, attracting four million members, including 30,000 ministers. With the end of economic recession, it lost its appeal, but its descendents still divert white rage away from the system itself and toward our favorite scapegoats.

OUTSIDE THE WALLS

The Predatory Imagination constantly moved outwards. Although America long insisted on isolation from European affairs, it continued expanding to the south and west, swallowing up huge swaths of lands and peoples. Jefferson coined the phrase "American Exceptionalism" and claimed that "a different code of natural law" governing relations with other countries applied to America. The nation could do no wrong with God on its side. The promise of a new start in a new, secular world replaced Christianity in progressive minds everywhere, inspiring revolutions from Mexico to Greece.

The Founding Fathers, however, would not jeopardize their fragile coalition of Yankee industrialists and southern planters. In 1804, former Haitian slaves established the New World's second republic. The U.S. refused to recognize it, having previously authorized money to help the French recover control. *America's first foreign aid was intended to preserve slavery.*

The 1823 Monroe Doctrine announced America's intention to protect Latin America from Europe — and take over the role of overseer. In the 1840s politicians and poets alike proclaimed America's "manifest destiny," arguing that expansion was not imperialism but "enforced salvation." The Mexican War established the model: The first step was to demonize Mexicans. Then contrived border incidents provided the pretext for invasion. Once "they" had attacked "us," Americans were duty-bound to exterminate the threat and then to enlighten Mexico's backward people. Such lies were effective then, as they are now, because white Americans had already been subject to 150 years of captivity narratives regarding the external Red Other.

Throughout the first half of the century, the only brake on the drive for expansion (certainly not Indian treaties) was the question of whether territories would join the union as free or slave states.

The Civil War, writes Howard Zinn, "… was not a clash of peoples… but of elites."[8] Three factors made it so terribly destructive. War became impersonal and industrialized, with the objective of maximizing the killing. But even though technology had changed things irrevocably, tactics didn't change; old men sent young men marching in closed ranks against massed cannonry and repeating rifles. Six hundred thousand died and 500,000 were wounded, in a country of thirty million. One-fifth of the South's adult white male population perished.

The second factor was derived from the images each side projected upon the other, much of which came from the differing forms of racism they practiced. Northerners demonized the South as backwards, claimed moral superiority and rationalized their own aversive discrimination with a moralistic crusade. They did this in part by burying their own complicity in slavery and re-visioning New England in a triumphant narrative of free, white labor.[9]

Southerners could deny the sexual license with black women that they had always assumed with fantasies of preserving a "way of life." A hundred and fifty years later, we wonder why several hundred thousand dirt-poor whites who couldn't afford to own slaves defended this cause so savagely. We must conclude that they fought not to save slavery (which was against their own economic interests), but to perpetuate *white privilege*. It was all they had.

Both sides shared a third factor. Two centuries of racialized Indian conflict and the resultant literature had so justified violence in the national mind as to make the adversary, any adversary, so alien, so Other, as to be inhuman. By 1860, argues Slotkin, a new norm had been established. Americans would see all future conflicts, even against other white nations, as wars of *annihilation*.

The war pitted the urban children of the Puritans against the rural children of the Opportunists, with their original roles somewhat reversed. By 1860, religion in the north was being overshadowed by the Industrial Revolution, while fundamentalism was rising in the South as an aspect of racial domination. *Fratricide* perfectly describes the impact of the war upon the American soul, which more than that of any other nation is split against itself. The word evokes such emotion precisely because Americans still hope to heal that split in the psyche. Contemporary battle re-enactments express this longing. Because the issue of race went unresolved, however, the nation achieved only a superficial healing.

After the war, unrestrained capitalism, urbanization and the centralized, bureaucratic state overwhelmed small-town Eden. The discipline required by the factories obliterated old ideals of democracy, craftsmanship and individualism. Disillusionment, the breakdown of myth and religion and the loss of innocence created a void that was filled by *nationalism.* Western man's primary loyalty was shifting from God and his church to the nation authorized *by* God. *Every* nation, symbolized first by its royalty and later by its political leadership, became the "one nation under God."

Something else was happening. This was perhaps the first generation in history to experience major, prolonged separation between fathers and sons. For as long as anyone could remember, fathers had taught society's notions of mature masculinity in regular, physical proximity to their sons. Now, rather abruptly, thousands, and then millions of men were leaving the farms where they had been independent producers to work in factories and offices. They no longer spent most of the day in constant physical contact with their sons. Rather than growing food, they operated, repaired and served the machines that made their consumer goods. Historian Oscar Handlin writes, "The factory regime detached work from nature and from all other aspects of life."[10] The word "stress" took on its contemporary meaning of psychological overload. "Alienation" would soon become a common term, and fathers, in a few generations, would become irrelevant.[11]

Here we must take a brief detour back into mythology. The great, culture-binding myths had been slowly breaking down for centuries. The Industrial Revolution, however, greatly accelerated this trend, damaging father-son bonds in particular. In mythic terms, it brought forth the ascendancy of the god *Ouranos.*

Although both Ouranos and his son Kronos are archetypal patriarchs, utterly disconnected from the feminine, there are significant differences. Recall how Ouranos pushed his children away, down into the body of Mother Earth, Gaia. He symbolizes *distance,* from complete paternal absence to contemporary fathers who, returning from work, are physically present but emotionally unavailable. They are appendages to the family, ghostly figures existing at the edges, concerned more with the outside world. Meanwhile, mothers conduct the family's relational world, and sons lack masculine role models. Large institutions have long understood this situation, writes James Robertson, "... the armed forces and large corporations deliberately move their management employees from place to place periodically, in order to destroy the influence of those familiarities and replace them with institutional ones."[12]

As this image came to dominate fathering, its opposite was evoked as well. By eating his children, Kronos symbolizes inappropriate *proximity*. He consumes their *individuality* by demanding loyalty to monolithic standards and shaming the children for not living up to them. He may physically or sexually abuse them, or send them off to die for abstractions like patriotism. While Ouranos *neglects* the children in his pursuit of spirit(s) or success, forcing them into inappropriate identification with the mother, it is Kronos — Time — who kills them. Like his blood brother Jehovah, he demands that fathers prove their loyalty by sacrificing their sons. Time/Kronos became literalized, from measurement of natural cycles and sacred points in the calendar to the objective time of clocks and schedules.

By the second half of the nineteenth century, just as boys everywhere were experiencing the loss of meaningful fathering, the archetypal image of Kronos was fully constellated as *the national state*. Germany and Italy, for example, had only recently evolved from loose confederations of principalities into unified entities. In 1700 there had been more than 500 separate entities governing Europe; by 1900 there were about twenty-five. In countless ways, young men were encouraged to surrender their allegiance, indeed their very identity, to an abstraction, its flag symbols and its demand for sacrifice.

What had humanity lost? First, the ancient father-son connection had been severed. Second, science undermined religious faith. Third, migration and urbanization further diminished the sense of ancestry. People were separated from each other in ways no one could have predicted a few generations before. Millions of autonomous individuals, newly liberated from ties to family, religion and the land, searched for new identities.

To convince them to give it their allegiance, the national state created origin myths, heroes and elaborate rituals. It eliminated pockets of diversity, replaced regional dialects with a common language and established standardized, free, *mandatory* schooling. Schools were designed to resemble the factories and offices that most people would spend most of their lives inside. They produced citizens who, despite traditional class hatred, eventually came to feel that they shared a common past and destiny. These first generations to attend school en mass were more law-abiding and more patriotic than any that came before or since.

When old myths break down, writes Slotkin, ideology generates "a new narrative or myth...to create the basis for a new cultural consensus."[13] Many longed to submerge themselves within some larger, immortal community. They discovered that the primary function of the great nation-state was war (Prussia was spending *ninety* percent of its revenue on the military). In dying to defend it, they might participate in its immortality. Nationalism provided an alternative receptacle for the emotions they had always formerly directed toward family and church. It took on the intensity of religion, because it *replaced* religion. Indeed, the certificate which grammar school graduates received at about age thirteen replaced first communion or confirmation as a symbol of growing up.

The American South, however, retained its zealous religiosity. How did Puritanism continue to grow there long after it had been greatly transformed into the capitalist impulse in the North? As free land became scarce in the east, most immigrants (including thousands of Scots-Irish Presbyterians) headed toward southern and western frontier areas. There, they fought savage wars with the Indians long after New England's indigenous population had ceased to be a threat. In the Deep South in particular they lived side-by-side with millions of blacks and the constant fear of both race war and sexual predation. In addition, one can imagine that they felt guilt, conscious or not, for participating directly in the systematic dehumanization of the slaves. This meant that rural Southerners, far more than Northerners, were obsessed with evil in their daily lives.

The Bible occupied a prominent place on the frontier. With few educated clergy around, people were often unaware of its symbolic context. It was venerated more than it was read, and read more than it was understood. The Bible was often the *only* book in the house (this situation still prevails in many American homes). The result was a dogmatism and anti-intellectual literalism that became characteristic of this part of the country.

So, while urban Northerners transmuted their self-abnegation into the sense of deferred gratification required to amass wealth, rural Southerners built up their fear of the Other to such a fever pitch that the Devil — and their own sense of sinfulness — remained as constant presences. Belief in predestination died out, but Original Sin remained. This meant fear of judgment, repressed sexuality, longing for Apocalypse and an older sense of deferred gratification, not to wealth but to the next life. Obsession with the other world meant dismissal of this one and contempt for political participation. As a result, most fundamentalists didn't vote until the 1970s.

The nation as a whole, however, experienced migration, urbanization and alienation within its unique mythological framework, swinging wildly between extremes of individualism and conformism. Between 1867 and 1880, Horatio Alger's dime-novel melodramas affirmed the Protestant virtues of frugality, hard work and delayed gratification. His young heroes "pulled themselves up by their own bootstraps." Meanwhile, as a few white men accumulated massive fortunes, millions fell into deep poverty and threatened once again to unite with blacks. Alger's myth of *personal* success, however, counteracted populist agitation, and his name became synonymous with the economic triumph of his plucky heroes. A decade after his 1899 death, his books were still selling a million copies per year.

After the Civil War, Americans were proud of having stayed free of European political entanglements. Despite their growing domination of Latin America, they sincerely believed in non-interventionism. Yet they also assumed that America's *mission* was to save a corrupted world. It took some time, but Americans of both North and South overcame this dilemma. First, they swept the question of institutionalized racism under the table by ending Reconstruction and literally agreeing to forget about their disagreements on race. Whites everywhere could now identify with each other (rather than with their geographical regions) in their common disdain for non-whites, their common optimism and their collusion in believing that they had resolved the question of slavery. Second, turning their eyes outward, they so convinced themselves of their utter goodness that they came to believe that prying into others' affairs was a demand made upon them by Providence. Without irony, Senator Albert Beveridge declared, "God has...been preparing our English-speaking and Teutonic peoples for a thousand years ...marked us as his chosen people, henceforth to lead in the regeneration of the world."[14] The intoxication of innocent belligerence proved to be overwhelming for millions of Americans, North and South, who found new unity in their moral crusades. It was America's second birth, "one nation indivisible."

But the capitalist system could not provide stability. The financial Panic of 1873 lasted until 1877, when urban strikes broke out everywhere. The government sent troops into several cities to quell the violence, which newspapers blamed on "*Communism* — a poison introduced into our social system by European laborers."

Despite George Custer's defeat at the Little Big Horn, 1876-7 marked the point at which conflict between labor and capital replaced the Indian wars as the stage where dread of the external Other was played out. Anti-union writers adapted old frontier stereotypes — "savage," "slave" and "pauper" — to disparage workers, metaphorically substituting Indian warfare for class conflict. Another phrase, the "Red Spectre of the Commune," often appeared in newspapers. The torrent of propaganda had its effect: "worker" essentially equaled "Indian," and many came to perceive those who rejected the sacred totem of private property as race traitors. By 1886 (when there were over 1,400 strikes), the image of the external devil passed from one "red" to another, and the groundwork for future crusades was laid.

Meanwhile, the vast continent existed for anyone, living or hypothetical, to grab. That year the Supreme Court declared corporations to be "natural persons," with constitutional rights — and *no* responsibilities. Courts redefined the common good to mean the corporate use of humans and the Earth for maximum profit. In 1898 Texas ranchers bragged: "*Resolved,* that none of us know, or care to know, anything about grasses...outside of the fact that for the present there are lots of them... and we are after getting the most out of them while they last."

But one continent was insufficient. Capitalists demanded other markets and resources, as well as protection. America had experienced depressions

— "panics" — in every generation (1819, 1837, 1857 and 1873). With the loss of the wilderness and a new panic in 1893, business elites searched for means to revitalize the economy. Their solution, the "Open Door" foreign policy, demanded unlimited access to markets everywhere.

With the American wilderness under control, new versions of Manifest Destiny metaphorically described other lands as *spiritual* wilderness that needed America's benign influence. This mission (known as the white man's burden, bringing the good news, making the world safe for democracy, nation-building, etc.) has four assumptions. First: unique, divinely sanctioned *purpose*. Second: generous, idealistic intentions, never financial gain. Third, unenlightened, *oppressed people* who longed for our help. Fourth, a pretext for intervention: *unprovoked attack*.

The gunboat diplomacy of the 1890s didn't begin this pattern; it was already enshrined in American myth. Between 1798 and 1895 (the year conventional historians consider the *beginning* of American empirical designs), the U.S. had already intervened in other countries over 100 times.[15] Such policies protected business while allowing Americans to innocently believe that they benefited mankind. In 1907, however, future President Wilson admitted (or bragged): "Concessions obtained by financiers must be safeguarded... even if the sovereignty of unwilling nations be outraged... the doors of the nations which are closed must be battered down."[16]

The story remains deeply embedded in our psyches as well. When economic pressure and clandestine operations or political assassinations fail, American leaders, whether Republican or Democrat, fabricate provocations and attack. Our self-image, however, remains staunchly innocent because the myth teaches that redemption (for both ourselves and those we would save) comes not through peace but through righteous violence. "The distance between such noble principles and such self-serving aggressiveness," writes historian Walter Nugent, " is the measure of hypocrisy."[17]

But Americans, though naïve, are no more inherently violent than other peoples. To give one example of both our ignorance as well as our innate ethics, a 1989 college survey revealed that over fifty percent believed that the Communist Manifesto phrase "from each according to his ability, to each according to his need," formed part of the U. S. Constitution.

The *state* must regularly administer massive dosages of indoctrination to reanimate our sense of innocence. Propaganda merges with belief; every student learns that America never starts wars but always aids those in need. The mythic appeal is so fundamental that occasional disclosures of the truth do little to alter popular consciousness. Still, the narrative of innocence requires regular ceremonial maintenance.

Americanism (there is no equivalent term in other countries, no "Brittanism" or "Chinaism") requires many ceremonies, holidays and regular invocations of god in order to make war sacred. Long before George H.W. Bush, Theodore Roosevelt called for a "new world order" and stirred supporters with songs like "We stand at Armageddon and we battle for the Lord."

Our civil religion is composed of basic, non-sectarian convictions: divine guidance, reward of virtue, absolute goodness of the nation, survival of the fittest, success at all costs and moral condemnation of failure. Its ritual calendar includes Thanksgiving, Memorial Day, Independence Day and Veteran's Day. Our sacred shrine is Arlington National Cemetery. Public education, writes Bellah, "serves as a particularly important context for the cultic celebration of the civic rituals."[18]

A fundamental aspect of America's civil religion is our unique cult of the flag. Curiously, we display it in our churches as well as in many places of business, as if to reinforce the notion that in America there is little difference between them. We worship it by pledging allegiance, and occasionally by kneeling and kissing it. And we are horrified at the thought of its desecration, because, write Carolyn Marvin and David Ingle, it is "the ritual instrument of group cohesion…the god of nationalism."[19] Such rituals nearly equate God with America, writes Bellah. Often "…the most jingoistic identity of nation and church has come not from our political leaders but from the churches themselves."[20]

Eventually, popular culture replaced most of our sacred national ceremonies. Now, films, TV and video games deliver the myths of innocence, competition and violent redemption, and the Super Bowl is more significant than a Presidential inauguration.

The civic religion is summed up in two words: "American Dream."

The phrase appears in over 700 book titles, yet historian Jim Cullen writes that most take its definition for granted. Perhaps the consensus is that "...anything is possible if you want it badly enough."[21] *You can have it all, in this life and the next.* This mix of Puritan spirituality and Opportunist materialism is an ambiguous source of power. America as opportunity and potential remains an idea more than a place, available to everyone, yet compromised by nightmares of failure, of *falling behind.*

A unique logic connects Exodus to Promised Land, and to empire. *God chose* America's destiny. Similarly, anyone can choose to participate in Americanism by rejecting ethnicity and accumulating our cultural symbols of success. Conversely, those who reject private property are considered "un-American." Therefore, since God wants everyone to have those opportunities (both spiritual and material), he calls us to *bring* them to the underprivileged and, like the Puritan missionaries to Hawaii, to "do well by doing good."

This religious nationalism has as its model the *Book of Revelation,* where furious battle drives history toward redemption (or in secular terms, the happy ending). Missionaries easily raise money for proselytizing abroad, since their requests, by definition, assert their and our superiority. Such assumptions, however, invariably poison relations between them and their objects. In the 1830s missionaries failed to convert many people in China. One described the Chinese as "the most craven... and selfish as heathenism can make men, *so we must be backed by force if we wish them to listen to reason.* " It was the old choice of conversion or death.

Twisting the idea of natural selection into "Social Darwinism," intellectuals claimed that America's wealth *proved* its virtue. Exploitation and elimination of the weak were natural processes and competition produced the survival of the fittest. The next step was to infer that only the affluent were *worthy* of survival. They were, of course, merely restating the Calvinist view of poverty as a condition of the spirit. Life was a harsh, unsatisfying prelude to the afterlife, redeemable only through discipline. Deeply religious people passionately argued that the suffering of the poor was *good* because it provoked remorse and repentance, and that political movements to relieve their condition were unnatural. Secular apologists, meanwhile, simply substituted "nature" for "God."

Social Darwinism justified colonialism. Competition for survival had produced a new human type, the Anglo-Saxon, with the moral sense to accept the White Man's burden. Such men were uniquely qualified to help civilize those who couldn't improve themselves without the prolonged tutelage of enlightened colonial rule.

Despite such generosity, however, class warfare remained a threat. Americanism became a safety valve against an explosive return of the repressed. Zealots flocked to the Spanish-American War to make men free, and quick victory proved America's pure motives. But in its aftermath, Americans slaughtered *several hundred thousand* Filipinos, a larger percentage of the population, and with far less sophisticated weaponry, than they would later kill in Viet Nam.

Ouranos and *Kronos* ruled the unconscious of modern man. Now everyone was judged by how useful they were under capitalism. In 1900 George Simmel wrote that existence in the urban factories had diminished human passions in favor of a reserved, cynical attitude. This had created a compensatory craving for excitement and sensation, which for some was partially satisfied by the emerging consumer culture. But others needed something even more extreme, *more Dionysian,* to make them feel alive.

This damage to the soul occurred along with the most rapid technological changes in history. One Frenchman fated to die in the first weeks of the Great War said that the world had changed more since he had been in school than it had since the Romans. In the thirty years between 1884 and 1914, humanity encountered mass electrification, automobiles, radio, movies, airplanes, submarines, elevators, refrigeration, radioactivity, feminism, Darwin, Marx (who wrote, "All that is solid melts into air"), Picasso and Freud. It is particularly ironic that just as modern people were learning of the unconscious, they were forced to act out the old myths of the sacrifice of the children. The pace of technological change simply exceeded humanity's capacity to understand it, and the pressure upon the soul of the world exploded into *World War.*

The international socialist movement had been exerting considerable pressure for worker solidarity. But very quickly, nationalist propaganda in each European nation created artificially shared interest between rich and poor by channeling class rage into war fever, or hatred of the Other.

Most Americans, however, remained uninterested and refused to get involved. Ever since, schoolchildren have been taught that our country entered World War One to save democracy. In fact, the war was a conflict among colonial powers for domination of the Third World. By 1917 it was going badly for Britain, which had taken out huge loans from American bankers, who soon convinced Wilson to intervene. To overcome the reluctance of the population, he responded with a massive propaganda campaign that demonized Germans, played upon images of heroism and honor and criminalized most forms of dissent.

Afterwards, however, the year 1919 saw 3,600 strikes in America involving over four million workers (as well as twenty-six major race riots). When bombs exploded outside the residences of lawmakers in several cities, the *New York Times* quickly announced that "Bolsheviks" were responsible. The Red Scare, America's first anti-communist hysteria, enabled the government, in the infamous Palmer Raids, to deport 4,000 radicals. Over 10,000 were arrested and many were tortured. By then, the U.S. indirectly controlled the finances of much of Latin America. This is not left-wing propaganda. Former Defense Secretary Robert MacNamara admitted (in a declassified document) that the "role of the military in Latin American societies is to overthrow civilian governments..."[22]

This is a significant event in American history, marking the latest in a series of points (recall Andrew Jackson's expansion of voting rights with his simultaneous Trail of Tears) when the inclusion of one Other was marked by the exclusion of a second. In 1920, decades of heroic protest culminated with women achieving the right to vote. Meanwhile, however, the Klan grew to include 4–5 million men, and Congress severely limited further immigration. But class anger persisted. Capitalism desperately needed a diversion, a new external Other, and it found one with the birth of the Soviet Union.

The *Times* blared, "Bolshevik assault on civilization... Menace to world by Reds... Reds seek war with America."[23] The U.S. and twelve other nations attacked Russia in an unsuccessful attempt to prevent consolidation of communist rule. Afterwards, compliant intellectuals inverted history; historian John Gaddis terms this invasion a "defensive" action. The U.S.S.R would exist in a permanent state of mistrust regarding America's "good intentions." And, like an abused child, it would grow up to become a perpetrator.

With this new, external, *red* Other, America found a bottomless well of paranoia to exploit. The Dionysian menace, once again seeping through the gates of the Apollonian city, was now an *international conspiracy* to deprive Americans of their property, freedom and dreams. Wherever workers organized for their rights, the media and churches framed their actions as Soviet-inspired hooliganism. Attorney General Palmer described radicals as "moral rats," whose "sly and crafty eyes" revealed "cruelty, insanity and crime." They had "sloping brows and misshapen features."[24] To Wilson, they were "apostle(s) of Lenin...of the night, of chaos, of disorder." J. Edgar Hoover collected several hundred thousand names, while ignoring murders of leftists. The Red Scare ended quickly, having served its purpose: white America, where blacks were still being lynched, had repulsed the red hordes and was free.

But Satan himself was still out there, just beyond the gates. By now, one could well ask, could "America" exist without its Others? Massive, continuous, *daily* anti-communist propaganda pictured an immense evil that was not motivated by normal morality but dedicated to enslaving the world. "This is how it looks to the simple folk of America," writes Historian William Blum, "...the sophisticated, when probed slightly beneath the surface of their academic language, see it exactly the same way."[25]

In the 1930s, *Life Magazine* published articles such as "The Trojan Horse Policy of Communism in America" and "If the Communists Seized America." Hollywood helped demonize communists with *Ninotchka, Comrade X* and *Red Salute;* this continued into the cold war *(The Iron Curtain, The Red Menace)* and beyond *(Invasion, U.S.A.).* The only break was from 1942-1945, when the U.S. and the U.S.S.R. were hesitant partners against Germany. Then, Hollywood dutifully produced pro-Russian movies: *Mission to Moscow* and *Song of Russia.*

American nightmares persisted in their common fantasy of this red, external Other for seven decades. In the 1980s, when Ronald Reagan denounced Nicaraguans as Soviet proxies, he never mentioned that America had been invading Nicaragua (six times) since long before there *was* a Soviet Union.

WITHIN THE WALLS (2)

The economy eventually absorbed most immigrants, and for many of them America really was the land of opportunity. Meanwhile, a huge *internal* migration occurred when southern agriculture mechanized in the 1940s. Many blacks left, hoping to improve their lives. This migration had its own mythic quality. After the generations of sorrow, high-paying northern jobs beckoned to them like the Promised Land, though many undoubtedly hated to leave their age-old connection the soil.

However, for minorities America never really recovered from the Depression. Even permanent military mobilization couldn't employ everyone. Growing industries required relatively high levels of education, and trade unions remained racially segregated. These internal immigrants, writes Chomsky, were "herded into concentration camps, which we…call 'cities.'"[26]

Race continued to be the subtext of national politics and the economy. As the Founders had done in 1776, Franklin Roosevelt unified northern liberals and southern conservatives. But, like them, he had to maintain silence on race, fearing that the coalition would disintegrate. Southern politicians, who had defeated over two hundred anti-lynching bills, supported Social Security only if it *excluded* agricultural laborers and domestic servants. This compromise, the fourth instance of affirmative action for whites, deliberately kept most blacks outside of the welfare state. And even black industrial workers discovered that Social Security itself was unfair, because it used monies they contributed to pay benefits disproportionately to affluent whites, who lived longer than most blacks.

After fourteen generations of slavery and another five of apartheid, Blacks (and Latinos) arrived in the cities to encounter *de facto* discrimination.

The familiar cycle of segregation, unemployment, bad schools, alcoholism, police violence and hopelessness developed in scores of ghettoes.

The G.I. Bill financed ninety percent of the 13 million houses constructed in the 1950s. However, Southern senators made sure that ninety-eight percent went to whites. Of 350,000 federally subsidized homes built in Northern California between 1946 and 1960, fewer than 100 went to blacks, as did *none* of the 82,000 homes built in archetypal Levittown, New York.[27] People of color remained locked in the inner cities, their dwellings and businesses often torn down to make room for the interstates that would shuttle whites to the suburbs where only they could live. This fifth degree of affirmative action for whites had long-term impact. Due to home equity inflation and resulting family inheritance, as well as the exclusion from Social Security and unequal access to capital, an average black family still has *one eleventh* of the wealth of a white family, even when they make the same income.

The northward migration of blacks created a counter-migration. Retreating to the suburbs, whites imagined the internal Other as a denizen of the dark, unclean city (in mythic terms, the prison where Pentheus cast Dionysus.) They lived entire lives within cocoons of unexamined privilege, never encountering an African- or Mexican-American except as a servant. This isolation perpetuated racist beliefs and kept white cultural norms invisible. In 1963, two out of three whites innocently told pollsters that blacks were treated equally, and *ninety percent* said black children had equal educational opportunity.

Puritanism's bedrock assumption remained as powerful as ever: poverty and the dysfunctional behavior it engendered was the *individual's* fault, not that of the system. The myth of innocence reached its most solid manifestation. America had saved the world from Fascism; but to minorities, it was still a plantation.

AMERICA AFTER WORLD WAR TWO

This is the mystery of *xenos* as both stranger and guest. The repressed or marginalized parts of our souls and our culture desire more than anything to be welcomed home. And like Pentheus, those of us within the pale also long unconsciously for that moment, because we all want completion. However, like posters on a wall illuminated by a moving spotlight, our picture of the Other can shift quickly. None of its images alone can carry its fullness. So, healing is possible only with the acknowledgement of all of those images which we envy, fear or desire so much that we feel like owning — or destroying — them. We achieve wholeness by meeting, acknowledging and suffering together. This is the gift the Other offers.

Roosevelt said, "...the only thing we have to fear is fear itself." But in 1938, when CBS Radio broadcast *The War of the Worlds,* millions panicked, believing that Martians had attacked the Earth. In truth, world war was approaching. Once again the government required a new Other to overcome an entrenched sense of isolationism. And this required manipulating the old myths of Indian attack upon innocent Eden.

America fought a *race* war in the Pacific. Mendacious posters of ape-like "Japs" raping white women helped mobilize bellicosity and led to a savagery by U.S. soldiers against the Japanese that they rarely exhibited against the Germans. This behavior resulted from official policy. Years later, Robert MacNamara who had assisted General Curtis LeMay's bombing of Tokyo (which killed 100,000 civilians), admitted, "He, and I'd say I, were behaving as war criminals."[28]

From the Japanese-American perspective, however, the war was bounded by two enormous lies. One was that America was betrayed by a surprise attack on Pearl Harbor (which resulted in them, *not* German-Americans, being imprisoned in internment camps).[29] The second was the atomic attacks that ended the war. Years later, Dwight Eisenhower admitted, "...the Japanese were ready to surrender and it wasn't necessary to hit them with that awful thing."[30]

Ultimately, Japanese-Americans were too few to carry the role of internal Other for long. Blacks, who were far more numerous, widespread and impoverished, remained the ideal scapegoat, and many race riots broke out during the war.

For once, America actually confronted genuine evil, but victory also buttressed the myths of innocence and the chosen people. And the shadow of America's crusade (Prescott Bush's financing of Hitler and FDR's refusal to bomb Auschwitz) was edited from the popular record.[31] Elites, however, knew that the real roadblock to economic domination was Russia, and that Stalin would be most valuable as the post-war face of the Other. Many scholars now argue that the atomic attacks were meant primarily to threaten the Soviets, that Hiroshima was the opening salvo of the Cold War.

America, essentially undamaged by the war, was now the world's strongest nation. However, the fact remains that only military spending ended the depression. As in the 1890s, many argued that further economic expansion (investing surplus capital in foreign markets) would prevent unrest. This would require force and, for the first time, *a permanent* war economy.

Domestic spending increased, but millions, still remembering the Depression, favored moderation and thrift. So businesses learned to play "mood music," subtly giving customers permission to have guiltless fun. By 1990, Americans would be exposed to 3,000 daily advertisements. The onslaught of images eventually reversed the logic of Puritanism. Previously, excess consumption had been sinful, but advertising made people envious of others. Now, *not* owning the best possessions ("keeping up with the Jones's") meant that one wasn't part of the elect. Eventually, when *not* consuming became the emotional equivalent of sin, Americans would suffer new forms of anxiety. For a while, however, it seemed that a consumer paradise had arrived.

Government aid boosted ten million (white) families out of poverty with welfare, the minimum wage, Social Security, Medicare, the G.I. Bill and subsidized education, business loans and home mortgages. For the first time, a society claimed to offer everyone comfort and security.

However, forty million were still mired in extreme poverty. Prior to this time, few poor people had seen how others lived. Now, in displaying the consumer culture, television was implying that everyone but *you* was prospering. Despite the optimism, an immense rage was growing among people of color, but also among working-class whites, who would eventually come to perceive themselves as *victims* of those same people of color.

America had amassed great moral credit for having saved Europe. Soon, however, the U.S. was covertly undermining democracy in France,

Italy, Greece, Indochina, Africa and Latin America. Determined to split the European labor movement, it allowed organized crime to reconstitute the heroin trade. This fact establishes early complicity in drug smuggling that would eventually support counter-revolution in Latin America, Southeast Asia, and Afghanistan, all places where the U.S. military would follow. Nevertheless, America's myth of opportunity beckoned to millions.

THE COLD WAR AND THE EXTERNAL OTHER

The range of acceptable discourse in our corporate media still frames the Cold War in terms of America's heroic containment of "Soviet expansionism." Government documents, however, acknowledged that the primary threat was *Europe's* "...refusal to subordinate their economies to...the West."[32]

Let's take another detour through myth: the birth of the national security state coincided precisely with the peak popularity of western movies. Westerns had been central to the movies from the beginning. In 1910, more than twenty percent were westerns, and the trend continued. In 1959, westerns comprised one quarter of all prime-time network hours. Eleven of the top twenty-five shows were westerns.

The genre attracted audiences worldwide, but also evoked ambivalence. People throughout the Third World understood perfectly well that *they* were the Indians. Many connected American affluence to the theft of their resources by post-colonial oligarchs. While they lived in darkness, Americans enjoyed the brilliant light of their all-electric kitchens.

It is certainly true that the Soviets dominated Eastern Europe. However, we simply don't know to what degree their policies expressed the excesses of totalitarianism, or to what degree they were a paranoid reaction to two generations of German — and American — aggression. What we do know is that in May 1945, Brittan once again prepared plans for invading the U.S.S.R., "to impose upon Russia the will of the United States and the British Empire."[33]

"The purpose of propaganda," writes psychologist Sam Keen, "is to paralyze thought, to prevent discrimination, and to condition individuals to act as a mass."[34] It is critical to understand how quickly our institutions (government, media, universities and churches) converted post-war optimism into *hysteria,* since this was neither the first nor the last time this happened. In demonizing communists, they utilized the mythic narratives that fifteen generations of Americans had already consumed.

Mere months after Hiroshima, *Life* depicted rockets raining down from the east, predicting millions of dead. Advisors told President Truman in 1947 that in order to win approval for his foreign policy he would have to "scare hell out of the country." His Attorney General warned: *"They are everywhere* — in factories, offices — and each carries with him the germs of death for society." In 1950, Hoover declared that "Communists are today at work *within the very gates of America. "*

Propaganda films (known as "newsreels") portrayed Russia threatening Europe with its tentacles, or as a grapevine (the perfect image of Dionysus) spreading over the map. Week after week, they depicted a state of crisis, and with no opposition, reality was what appeared onscreen. Politicians brayed, "Like apples in a barrel infected by one rotten one, the corruption of Greece would *infect* Iran..." and, "...this red tide... like some vile creeping thing...spreading its web westward..."[35]

Americanism now had a "higher power" (the state), dogma (anticommunism), zealots (the F.B.I.), modes of excommunication (the Hollywood blacklist) and clergy. Billy Graham declared that communism was "a religion inspired...by the Devil himself." *Religion:* what other word can describe the all-encompassing force that anticommunism injected into American life, how the fear, *as well as the sense of identity,* spread?

In this sense, 1950s Americanism can be called a negative ideology, of mere opposition to or fear of another way of thinking. Or we could call it a religion of denial, because it allowed nuclear bellicosity, neo-colonialism and *de facto* segregation to coincide with the ideals of freedom and opportunity. Millions resolved this dilemma by accepting the unrelenting propaganda; to be American *was* to be anticommunist. "If Americans could only band together against the common red foe," writes Kovel, "they would know who they were."[36]

Terror of the external Other was also bound up with an internal issue, gender anxiety, as it is now. The press attacked feminists as neurotic, sexually frigid and communist. In 1948 the *Kinsey Report* revealed a huge gap between public morality and private behavior. Suddenly, deviants were everywhere inside the gates. Crusaders accused Truman's administration of protecting a communist "homosexual underground." Hoover asked, "How Safe Is Your Daughter?" In 1952, Eisenhower barred gays from federal jobs. Businesses and local governments forced workers to swear to their "moral purity."

Contagion and *pollution* are scientific terms, yet in our context, they have mythic potency. A half-century before the "Neo-Cons," reactionaries were willing to say absolutely anything to amplify fear. From this point on, we can follow the predatory imagination to its logical extreme — *doing* whatever is necessary. But the myth of Good Intentions is so pervasive that generations would pass before liberals, innocent believers in "fair play," would begin to acknowledge that conservatives had never played by the rules.

The major media casually dismiss "conspiracy theories." Indeed, the phrase itself clearly demarcates the range of acceptable discourse; it is a verbal symbol of the walls of the *polis*. But any objective person must at least acknowledge the sheer numbers of questionable events: multiple political assassinations; Operations Paper Clip and Northwoods; mind control experiments; the CIA's two-decade-long MK Ultra program; several mysterious plane crashes of political candidates and whistleblowers; Watergate; the "October Surprise" of 1980; the Iran-Contra scandal; CIA involvement in drug smuggling; the 9/11 attacks; and the theft of the 2000 and 2004 presidential elections; not to mention several undeclared wars.[37]

These events fit a tradition extending backwards, past Pearl Harbor, the Palmer raids, the sinkings of the *Lusitania* and the *Maine,* the Mexican War and the Witch craze. The 1950s, however, saw a quantum leap in terror. America was producing leaders who would drastically heighten both the predatory and the paranoid imaginations.

It was the time of HUAC, McCarthyism and bomb shelters. Children crawled under desks as practice for protection from atomic blasts, while the U.S. Air Force decimated Korea. The FBI intimidated unions, school boards and universities, where 600 instructors were fired. Some 2,700 federal workers lost jobs, and 12,000 resigned. As in Salem, one could save oneself by naming names. The hysteria was a sobering reminder of how thin a veil our modern temperament is, how mythic furies still drive our imagination.

What makes this period so maddening, and so similar to our present time, is that millions managed to deny the hysteria by immersing themselves in consumer delights, vacuous sitcoms or paranoid narratives *(Foreign Intrigue, I Spy, Passport to Danger, I Led Three Lives, The Day North America Is Attacked* and *Nightmare In Red).* Subtler film allegories *(Invaders from Mars, The Manchurian Candidate and Invasion of the Body Snatchers)* expressed the fear — or fantasy — of pollution. The 1953 version of *The War of the Worlds* ends by warning: *"Keep watching the Sky. Stay vigilant against another attack."* 1958's *The Blob* featured a shapeless, *red* jelly that, like Dionysus, seeped effortlessly through all man-made boundaries. People reported alien abductions. Later, Hollywood mythologized the C.I.A. James Bond, with his "license to kill," reincarnated the Redemption Hero, exempt from all laws.

The doctrine of "Mutually Assured Destruction" (MAD) implied that neither side could instigate nuclear strikes without being destroyed itself. The Cold War, however, rarely involved direct confrontation. Instead, as Chomsky has argued, a tacit compact developed that allowed a sharing of world management. The Soviets dominated their satellites in Eastern Europe, while the U.S. was free to overthrow Third World democracies. From this perspective, consider this 1960 statement by General Thomas Power, commander of the Strategic Air Command: "At the end of the war, if there are two Americans and one Russian left alive, we win." Was it the joke of a psychopath or cynical hyperbole deliberately intended to maximize anxiety? Or would only the former do the latter?

Before the hysteria dissipated, complete trust in anyone was impossible because "they" could be anyone or anywhere. In its fear, the public supported undemocratic security measures that the government (as it would in 2001) claimed were necessary to protect democracy. In 1954, seventy-eight percent agreed that it was a good idea to report any neighbors they suspected of being Communists. Indeed, for a decade the red supplanted the black as both inner and outer Other. Later, however — much later — George

Kennan, the architect of "containment," admitted, "...there was not the slightest danger of a Soviet military attack."[38]

By 1960, however, millions were fed up with both the tension and the conformism. John F. Kennedy's "New Frontier" (characteristically mythic terminology) challenged Americans to defeat injustice everywhere. Unlike the benign but boring Eisenhower, this confidant aristocrat could hold the projection of nobility. Tapping into a massive longing for meaning, he briefly reframed "opportunity" from consuming to service.

"Camelot" is our modern tragic narrative. Many baby-boomers date their disillusionment from this point. Sociologist Linda Brigance writes that without their heroic king, Americans began to feel a "...paradoxical combination of romantic yearning and fatalistic inevitability... (that) set the stage for the political cynicism and civic disengagement that characterized post-assassination America."[39]

Our innocence, however, runs deeper; it is profoundly critical to the myth of innocence that a so-called *troubled individual* supposedly killed Kennedy. If Lee Harvey Oswald didn't act alone, if in fact a wide-ranging military-industrial conspiracy was responsible, then America is not exceptional, no different, no freer, no better than any other nation.

Lyndon Johnson exploited dread of the Other from *both* the right and the left. During the 1964 election, he portrayed himself as a pacifist alternative to the warmonger Barry Goldwater. Immediately *after* the election, however, he invoked the "domino theory." If America didn't fight in Asia, Communists would again be at our doors. Chomsky, however, argues that America *invaded* Viet Nam, to prevent it "...from becoming a successful model of economic and social development..."[40] Johnson required elaborate lies to justify intervention. Once again, and certainly not for the last time, politicians argued that scheming outsiders had assaulted innocent Americans.

The essential tragedy of 1964 parallels the events of 1920 and the 1830s. Just as the power elite was inviting the internal, black Other into the *Polis* with the War on Poverty, they were destroying the possibility of national healing by pursuing a new external, *yellow* Other in Viet Nam. Johnson signed the Civil Rights Act in July. In August, his military contrived the Gulf of Tonkin incident that gave him an excuse to invade.

In Viet Nam, America enacted its "red, white and black" narrative, with white generals sending black and brown soldiers into what everyone called "Indian country." At least three million Asians died, the vast majority being civilians. The U.S. dropped seven million tons of bombs. Significantly, most were dropped from 30,000 feet, so pilots never heard the explosions or saw the results. They took Apollonic killing at a distance to its extreme: bombing peasants "back to the Stone Age." New phrases included "defoliation," "anti-personnel bombs" and "free-fire zones."

On the ground, however, obsession with the *body count*, rather than control of territory, became an end in itself. General Westmoreland set the tone when he smugly dismissed civilian casualties: "It does deprive the enemy of the population, doesn't it?" With this kind of permission coming from the top, massacres became commonplace, as they had been in Korea and would continue to be, wherever the U.S. would oppose dark-skinned people. Phillip Slater argues, "This transfer of killing from a means to an end in itself constitutes a practical definition of genocide." He asks, "Do Americans hate life? Has there ever been a people who have destroyed so many living things?"[41]

The anti-communist crusades would continue until the Soviet Union collapsed in 1989. Here is a partial list of the human consequences:

Spain:	1,000,000
Greece:	150,000
Korea:	3,000,000
Indochina:	3,000,000
Indonesia:	1,000,000
East Timor:	300,000
Mozambique/Angola:	2,000,000
Guatemala:	200,000
El Salvador:	75,000
Nicaragua:	70,000
Chile:	30,000

Argentina: 30,000
Colombia: 500,000
Afghanistan: 1,000,000

CIVIL RIGHTS AND THE INTERNAL OTHER

Around 1955, the servants asked to share the table with the masters. The Civil Rights movement insisted that America confront its Otherness, that it acknowledge that its historical narrative bore virtually no resemblance to reality. We notice several things in films of the demonstrations, especially of Selma, Alabama in 1965. First, the religious fervor, but also the dignity of the African-Americans. Second, northern whites accompanying them. Third, when the camera pans back, we comprehend the broader context: hundreds of local whites, absolutely consumed with hatred. We see burning crosses, police dogs, fire hoses, leather-clad thugs and housewives in high heels taunting the marchers with astonishing profanity.

What we *don't* see is three centuries of fear in which poor whites and blacks were forced to become adversaries. We don't see the Puritan heritage that turned whites against their own bodies. We don't see the heart-numbing alienation that required an entire race of scapegoats.

The demonstrators are sitting quietly, singing or marching in silence. They have deliberately intended to provoke a sense of shame, both across the nation and among the local whites. So why is there such *rage* on the white faces? Since the blacks aren't "shuffling and jiving" or lowering their heads, but *looking the whites directly in the eyes,* the whites are facing a profound dilemma. They can't project self-contempt for their own sexuality, their bodily connection to the old pagan gods, to *Dionysus,* onto the blacks. They must contemplate people *more self-controlled than themselves,* Others who refuse to be Other.

The whites were not intending to merely disrupt the marches; they were inciting blacks into *retaliating.* They were hoping to make blacks re-inhabit the psychic space of the Other, so that *they, the whites,* could be free of the oppressive weight of awareness, to remove it from their own shoulders and replace it where it belonged. But how could they do that when blacks were soon chanting, *Black is beautiful?* If the Other was everything that the citizen of the *polis* wasn't, and the Other was self-controlled — *or beautiful* — what did that make the white citizen?

The Civil Rights miracle is not in the relatively trivial legal victories but in the fact that African-Americans could remain so hopeful amid such hatred. Eventually, they asked why America appeared to admire non-violence only in black people. The movement died when they could no longer restrain their anger. So much had been promised. Even poor families now had TV and could view the good life (in 1957 households with TV sets surpassed those receiving daily newspapers), yet so little was delivered. Johnson's War on Poverty failed because his war on the Vietnamese was bankrupting the nation. Historian Milton Viorst writes, "…rising expectations prevalent in the mid-1960s had transformed everyday discontent into an angry rejection of the status quo."[42]

In the long and sordid history of large-scale racial violence in America, the Watts riot of 1965 was the first to be an essentially black-on-white event. Afterwards, a new phrase articulated the return of the repressed: *Black Power!* In 1967, twenty-three cities rioted. Once Blacks refused to submit, two things resulted. First, many others — students, women, Native Americans, Latinos, prisoners, disabled people, environmentalists and gays — also rose up. The year 1968 exploded in televised war carnage, anti-draft demonstrations, assassinations, riots and mayhem in Chicago.

Secondly, public opinion, which had favored racial progress, began to change. Television displayed not only the rage but also ecstatic images of blacks looting only blocks from the White House. Violence was familiar, but this was new: the internal Other was refusing to be the *victim* of American violence. By 1970, the white middle class was exhausted, disenchanted and vulnerable to backlash. Hollywood responded with vigilante movies starring Charles Bronson and Clint Eastwood in which lone redeemer-heroes cleaned up the urban chaos.

Working-class whites had struggled so hard to achieve their Dream, only to hear radicals condemning their patriotism and materialistic lifestyles. They retreated into willful ignorance and innocence. Forty-nine percent of the public simply refused to believe that the shameful massacre at My Lai (not to mention dozens of other such events) had occurred. If American boys actually acted in this manner, then once again America was no different from any other nation.

Conservatives were quick to manipulate this fatal flaw of class difference. When the National Guard exploded at Kent State in 1970, writes Viorst, many local people were outraged at the *students,* not the killers, and rejoiced that, "...the act had been done at last... the students deserved what they got."[43]

"The act" was mythic, ritual sacrifice of the children. So many youth had rejected American values so completely that they had seemingly *become* Other. Although America had been slaughtering children in Viet Nam and in the ghettoes for years, the message was unmistakable: *You will be like the fathers or die.* Shortly after Kent State, as students struck on 450 campuses, thugs attacked demonstrators and police watched approvingly. Years later, after exonerating the students, Kent State commissioned a monument. However, it rejected sculptor George Segal's model of Abraham poised with a knife over Isaac. It would not accept the mythic implications of the murders.

The myth of innocence had weathered many shocks, but its stereotype of the internal Other had survived. By 1970, African-Americans were no longer seen as discreet, non-violent saints in the white imagination. They were now *dashiki*-wearing, "afro"-haired, foul-mouthed terrorists who ruled the city at night. They were "Black Panthers." Curiously, in Greek iconography, the panther was one of Dionysus' animals. The projection of American Dionysus was nearly back where whites needed it, but not quite. In the next ten years, the F.B.I. made sure that most black, red and brown activists were discredited, imprisoned or (in two dozen cases) dead. Black rage turned inward again, in drug addiction, gangs and internalized violence. In 1981, Hollywood gave cultural approval by releasing *Fort Apache the Bronx.* The film's title acknowledged a hideous mix of mythic and racial stereotypes. A beleaguered police station stood as a small outpost of civilized values within a wilderness of black and brown savagery, which itself was surrounded by affluent white suburbs. In the South Bronx, the inner Outer was the outer Other.

Except for a few highly publicized, isolated extremists, student protest diminished once the war ended. Even though relations with Russia and

China improved, communists remained the external Other. The myth of innocence had been shaken but restored. The old story was the new story: blacks were back in their place; and the tragedy in Viet Nam (fast forward to Iraq and Afghanistan) had resulted from *good intentions* gone wrong. Since then, writes Chomsky, intellectuals have emphasized negative aspects of the Sixties: "... naturally it has a very bad name — because they *hated* it."[44]

America After Viet Nam

Popular culture conveys American myth to the world with narratives of its divinely inspired mission. We saved the world from fascist tyranny (even though the U.S. sustained only two percent of Allied deaths in World War Two, compared to Russia's *sixty-five* percent). We represent opportunity and freedom. We tolerate alternative lifestyles. We welcome many refugees, who send money home to support their kin. We *are* the good life.

With the arrival of television and eventually computers in even remote villages, the infectious rhythm of the American Dream has become a world dream. In the late 1990s a *billion* people were watching *Baywatch*. Materialism is a much stronger spell than the deteriorating oral traditions of tribal cultures. "The modern American empire," writes Mark Hertsgaard, "colonizes minds, not territory."[45] The media's speed and frivolity charms everyone, conveying American values primarily through two film and TV styles. In one, action films, the violent redemption hero rules. The other is the ubiquitous Disney-style cartoon, in which, writes Todd Gitlin, characters incarnate "...an innocence that can never be dispelled."[46]

Much of the world however, is well aware of America's support of oppression. *U.S. soldiers are stationed in 135 countries,* and our military expenditures surpass those of the rest of the world combined.[47] Peasants recognize "U.S.A." labels on armaments shipments. They hear English spoken in their mine offices, logging companies, *maquiladores* and torture chambers. They see the consumer culture packaged in New York and Los Angeles replacing their indigenous ways. Outside the walled compounds, their children starve while listening to the rock music that emanates from inside. They envy us and they hate us, because, as former Attorney General Ramsey Clark admits, "U.S. trade policies are driven by the exploitation of poor people the world over."[48] Sound bites fool only those who are committed to innocence. Few Third World laborers or "urban" Americans recognize any distinction between neo-liberals and neo-conservatives. They've seen it all before.

The end of the Viet Nam war marked a unique moment. This first failure of an "Indian war" coincided almost exactly with the collapse of our privileged expectations of perpetual affluence and growth. It was a disruption in the story we tell ourselves about ourselves. For the first time since the Depression, cracks appeared in the façade of the myth of innocence.

No one can predict the consequences when mythic narratives break down. Punctured innocence releases enormous energy that can either remake one's world or spiral downward toward cynicism and backlash. Many felt inspired to imagine the dawn of a new age. But political assassinations, urban violence and Watergate produced disillusionment. Fantasies of an American utopia froze into (at best) emphasis on personal, spiritual quests and (at worst) narcissistic disengagement, turning the 1970s into the "Me Decade." Quickly, voter turnout approached the lowest in the world. Let us put this last statement in context: in 2008, if Americans had turned out in the same proportion as they had in 1960, there would have been about *24 million more (primarily working-class) voters.*[49]

By 1975, trust in all major institutions slipped to dreadfully low numbers that would continue declining until 9/11/2001. Permanent war, corporate welfare and voter apathy joined race as the unacknowledged subtexts of public life. In the 1980s, it was commonly noted that voters had turned rightward. But TV pundits (whose primary functions are to resurrect the myth of innocence and perpetuate the demonization of the Other) never acknowledged that large majorities supported welfare, environmental protection, defense cuts, national health insurance and abortion rights. When citizens perceive little difference between candidates, however, they are likely to stop voting.

Several factors led to this situation, including the media's exclusion of divergent views, the distractions of single-issue politics and the perception that the Democrats have abandoned traditional liberalism. Decline in participation, of course, is welcome news to the rich. It also means, however, that fewer people reflexively accept the assumptions of Americanism; hence the periodic need for government, schools, media and church to re-invigorate the myth of innocence.

SHOCK AND AWE: RE-INVIGORATING THE MYTH

This has occurred, since long before 9/11, in three major ways. On the positive side, pundits present a unified front of denial. *"Doom-and-gloomers" overrate problems; global warming is a fiction; racism is history; Iraqis welcome us,* etc. Television idealizes the nuclear family and small-town values in cloying commercials that convey a ubiquitous, Disney-style innocence. Sitcom protagonists are young, attractive, middle-class whites whose problems (caused individually, not by the system) consistently resolve themselves. Reality shows are Social Darwinist fables in which the ablest triumph, but everyone gets a hug. Reassuringly calm, unemotional, authoritative newscasters place even bad news in the wider context of progress. It's all good. Michael Ventura, however, measures how deeply "...people know that 'it' is *not* all right...by how much money they are willing to pay to be ceaselessly told it is."[50]

The negative side involves both sanitized violence and a constant, low-level atmosphere of electronically-induced dread: stories of illegal immigrants, teen pregnancy, drugs, urban violence, satanic cults and child molesters; "security" rituals at airports (do we laugh or cry when we give up our water bottles?); and TV news, where "if it bleeds it leads." Fifty-five percent of local newscast coverage of children concerns violence. As a result, three out of four parents worry that strangers will kidnap their children. Between 1990 and 1998, as murder rates declined dramatically, murder stories on *network* newscasts increased by 600 percent (*not* counting O.J. Simpson stories).

Ignoring global warming, poverty, race and the political-economic sources of terrorism, we fret about issues that TV *chooses* for us. Everyone can avoid discussing gun control when newspapers editorialize, "It's Not Guns, It's Killer Kids."[51] We dread the disturbed *individual,* the bad seed, the Viet Nam veteran, rather than systemic inequities or corporate corruption.

Thus, our emphasis on individualism links happy denial to this constant, low-level background of fear. Periodically, when actual — or *contrived* — episodes of terror evoke the old frontier paranoia, Americans jettison their moral concerns like recycled computers.

Most of this bizarre mix of denial and fear mongering settles upon the black, internal Other. A great deal of the fear, of course, has had a black face for so long that urban, African-American men commonly observe how whites (especially women) cross the street instead of bypassing them. On the other hand, countless TV shows and films offer a vision of racial sameness by portraying blacks and whites as "buddies," many of whom are policemen who team up to restore order in the *polis*. The (mixed) message is: *It's really dangerous out there, but together we've solved the racial issue and banished hatred.* As a result of all these feel-good images, writes Benjamin DeMott, "The nearer at hand the perfect place and good life can be made to seem, the more needless politics becomes."[52]

A third factor that contributes to the re-vitalization of the myth of innocence is the mania produced by our technologically enhanced environment. In most public spaces (stores, shopping malls and sports arenas) we endure unrelenting onslaughts of loud music, blinking lights and high-definition visual images. Restaurants are designed with floors and walls that reflect sound and force patrons to shout just to be heard (thereby increasing the noise). In many places, especially those catering to adolescents, the atmosphere approaches that of gambling casinos, which are deliberately designed to create "altered states" of consciousness. The object is to heighten anxiety and encourage consumerism. However, the anxiety never fully dissipates, and we continually acclimate to greater levels of it.

This awkward combination of fear, denial and stimulation has ruled our consciousness during the sixty years of television, which was born amid both the new consumerism and McCarthyism. Lucille Ball diverted us while Richard Nixon admitted, "People react to fear, not love." As we have seen, however, the roots of this madness go back to the original confrontation of Puritans and Indians. Ever since, we have held the contradictory notions of chosen people and eternal vigilance. If we *are* attacked, the release of disillusioned energy drives us to violent extremes. Our lost innocence — *we have done so much good* — justifies our Biblical fury. Bad dreams constantly interrupt our 400-year sleep of denial, and we awake exhausted.

For thirty years we have flocked by the millions to disaster films. This genre works both sides of the fear/denial dichotomy by heightening fear of apocalyptic retribution and then cleanly resolving the threat to Eden through the intercession of selfless heroes.

To combine all these factors, the pathology of this condition is that it subjects us to overwhelmingly persistent messages that completely discount our emotional, intuitive and moral intelligence. It is exactly the same wounding that children receive if adults tell them that they (the children) don't really feel something; and this happens all day long, every day of our lives. We all learn this: *My ways of evaluating reality are failures.* And, since failure in America is always *moral* failure, *I am also a failure.* The result is epidemics of depression and desperate attempts to self-medicate through substance abuse (legal or otherwise), consumerism and vicarious violence.

After 9/11, the mad fusion of fear and denial reached cliché proportions. Throughout the Bush II years, the government manipulated anxiety with its color-coded terrorist alerts. Americans awakened daily to a degree of apprehension that shifted according to suspicious and unconfirmable "findings."[53] However, most (employed) people had the existential experience of nothing being particularly wrong in their personal lives. By 2006, seventy-nine percent expected another terrorist attack soon, but only twenty percent were *personally* concerned. In psychology experiments, such "intermittent reinforcement" drives lab animals mad. And it drives humans to release the tension by sacrificing a scapegoat.

Except for brief periods of wartime cohesion, these conditions also drive us toward further disengagement. Bellah documents declining membership in service clubs and unions. The alternative, talk radio, merely "mobilizes private opinion, not public opinion, and trades on anxiety, anger and distrust, all of which are deadly to civic culture." Almost the only groups that have grown are *support* groups, which are "oriented primarily to the needs of the individual."[54]

Isolated individuals, we seek safety within our cars. In 2008, more commuters than ever before, over a hundred million, were driving to work solo. As other aspects of the myth weaken, mobility retains its value; we can still broadcast our status by getting away. For many, driving an attractive car may be the last way to engage the *polis* at all, once we emerge from behind the walls of our gated communities. A century after the last Indian fight, whites are circling the wagons again. Ten to twenty million Americans live behind walls. *Madness at the gates:* as we retreat into homogeneous, suburban ghettoes, we simultaneously warehouse millions of elders and imprison more people than any other nation.

At the center of the madness, mass media offers distractions, ignores or mocks authentic alternatives and reduces debate to sound bites and infotainment. The Watergate scandal revealed Nixon's criminal pettiness. The media, however, never related it to deeper crimes (COINTELPRO assassinations, secret bombings in Southeast Asia, prolonging of the war and overthrowing of Chilean democracy). The *values* and many of the individuals that produced Watergate remained, while America celebrated a peaceful transition. Despite the occasional bad seed, the system, we were told, still worked.

BACKLASH

The increasing pace of change provoked the paranoid imagination once again. In 1970, the publication of Hal Lindsey's *The Late Great Planet Earth* roused previously apolitical fundamentalists. It was the decade's best-selling non-fiction book, selling 35 million copies and spawning over 60 million copies of "Left Behind" fiction as well as several movies. It addressed a huge population that became Ronald Reagan's core constituency. These people felt deeply impacted by modernism and the excesses of the sixties. And, like all Puritans, they were obsessed with sin.

The demythologized world has two primary expressions: consumerism and its mirror opposite, biblical literalism, which leads millions to anticipate the end of history. Its primary image is *the Beast,* an "ancient serpent" rising "out of the sea."[55] The Beast, however, was that same *feminine* presence the ancients knew as Tiamat, later as all those female dragons, and eventually as the giant shark in 1975's *Jaws*. Emerging from the collective unconscious, the Beast is all that patriarchy has repressed. It was no coincidence that both the religious reactionaries and the disaster films emerged shortly after the arrival of feminism.

This was also the period in which spiritual cults appeared and revealed the shadow of American individualism — the willingness to give up one's autonomy to a king/savior figure. The most extreme, paranoid examples, such as the People's Temple, recalled the old western image of the community under attack. They were more American than they knew.

It must be acknowledged that fundamentalists were persuasive. Many of them genuinely hoped to counter the madness of consumerism by re-emphasizing communal spirituality. But they missed two essential points: their religion reflected outdated, literalized myths; and their "family values" were bound up with racism, misogyny and innocence, all factors that those with less spiritual motives could manipulate. In the short run, however, they could displace their anger upon the Other.

Openly religious and rural-based, Jimmy Carter appeared to challenge entrenched Washington interests. Since then, most major presidential candidates have been self-described Jacksonian "outsiders," despite their Ivy League backgrounds and Wall Street connections. And each has trumpeted his religiosity.

After Nixon's pardon, investigations of the C.I.A. withheld reports of the overthrow of governments, involvement in drugs, and complicity in the Kennedy and King assassinations. The media also failed to report the Trilateral Commission's proposal of "limits to the extension of political democracy" in America.

Carter attempted to reverse declining faith in America's intentions by emphasizing human rights. However, he covertly supported the world's worst human rights *offenders* (Nicaragua, El Salvador, Guatemala, Chile, Argentina, Iran, the Philippines, Indonesia, Cambodia, etc.) When moderate domestic policies failed, he turned to the traditional solution and re-kindled the Cold War. He set another precedent by attempting to "out-Republican" the Republicans, and still another during the Iran hostage crisis: a foreign dilemma of questionable origin suddenly made an unpopular president (temporarily) popular.

The defeat in Viet Nam occurred during the first decade in 150 years (including the Depression) in which real earnings had not grown. Working people had always enjoyed rising standards of living and had come to define success as something within reach. They had internalized the assumption that one's children would do better than oneself.

Real raises stopped in the 1970s and have never resumed since. The economy was shifting from manufacturing to service work, and Baby Boomers, realizing that they were doomed to make less than their parents, were susceptible to the temptation of backlash. Now, observing George Wallace's popularity, conservatives began to masquerade as *rebels against the establishment.* They subsidized scholarly presses and academic endowments, and trained hundreds of "populist" shock-jocks to manipulate the backlash. All they needed was a figurehead "communicator."

Their new narrative took full advantage of the fact that American myth offers only one alternative to the hero, and that is the victim. It emphasized "values" over "interests," redefining class war, again, in racial and cultural rather than economic terms (precisely 100 years earlier, the media had substituted "red communist" for "red Indian" as the external Other). Seventy-five percent of TV stories on welfare featured blacks, even though forty percent of the poor were white. Extremists bombed birth-control clinics and murdered doctors. School boards fought desegregation, tax revolts spread to forty states and support for capital punishment increased.

White males, oblivious to their privilege, identified as *victims* — not of the rich, but of the minorities who were competing with them, the women claiming equality with them, the gays who publicly questioned the value of their masculinity and the intellectuals who appeared to be telling them how to live. The conservative media barrage took advantage of the old tradition of anti-intellectualism. "Elite" now meant stuffy, superior, arrogant liberals who ignored or trivialized the concerns of ordinary people. The investment paid off; by 2000, only a fifth of Americans would describe themselves as liberal.

Sure of their base constituencies, Republicans disguised policies that concentrated power with mythic language that emphasized "wedge" issues: abortion, pornography, crime, immigration and (later) gay marriage. Since

Democrats, caught between their working-class roots and their corporate masters, could not articulate a consistent vision, more voters gave up each year, at least until 2008.

Half of Americans didn't vote in the 1980 election (in fact, Reagan entered office with the support of only twenty-seven percent of the actual electorate). Those who did vote understood that "getting government off your backs" meant "no tax money for black welfare cheats." Their fear of the Other and their longing for a return to innocence prevented them from seeing that his policies would wreck *both* their affluence and the stability of their families. They could not foresee that he would preside over a massive shift of wealth, turning the world's most affluent nation into its greatest debtor.

He announced his candidacy in Philadelphia, Mississippi, where racists had murdered civil rights workers in 1963. This was a highly contrived yet easily understood statement of his intention to reverse racial progress. Well aware that captivity narratives were at the core of American myth, he celebrated the return of the Iranian hostages as his first Presidential gesture. His political genius was to articulate hate within a mythic language of inclusiveness. He rhapsodized, "This land was placed here by...divine plan...to be found by a special kind of people, a new breed of humans...to begin the world over again." But his supporters understood his consistently encoded messages. Garry Wills writes:

> ...no one has undergone a more thorough initiation into
> every aspect of the American legend than Reagan has, and no
> one has found so many conduits...for bringing that legend
> to us in the freshest way. He is the perfect carrier: the ancient
> messages travel through him without friction.[56]

Evoking both ends of the mythic spectrum, he told Americans they could have it both ways. They could get rich *and* have their traditional values, while paying no price. They could be *both* Puritans and Opportunists. Reagan resolved white men of all responsibility when he called unemployment insurance "vacation for freeloaders" and claimed that people were homeless "by choice." A spokeswoman conflated New Age philosophy with Social Darwinism: "...a person's external circumstances do fit his level of inner spiritual development."[57] And the media, writes Zinn, never asked, "why babies...should be penalized — to the point of death — for growing up in a poor family."[58]

Reagan deregulated the fairness doctrine, which had mandated balanced opinion in the media. This freed the shock jocks to attack minorities without fear of retaliation and to motivate people to vote their fears rather than their hopes.

Then, just as government was withdrawing its commitment to reducing poverty, America experienced the crack cocaine epidemic. This resulted in thousands of deaths, *hundreds* of thousands of new prison inmates and new levels of anti-minority scapegoating. A large majority of blacks remain convinced that Reagan deliberately allowed this tragedy in order to reverse the inclusion of minorities into the American mainstream. And, sick of the compliant Democrats, many stopped voting.

In times of stress the soul is revealed — in our case, a *Puritan* soul. Recall how Calvin had given sixteenth century merchants theological justification for their greed. Whether the message comes in the form of old-right attacks on big government, new-right sermons or New Age clichés, it is remarkably consistent. Lewis Lapham distills it: free money makes rich people strong and wise, while it *corrupts* poor people, making them stupid and weak.[59]

Still, there were cracks in the myth. Most of the public regarded the Viet Nam War as fundamentally wrong, not a mere mistake. Massive crowds protested the nuclear buildup and intervention in Central America. The U.S. could no longer attack anyone it wanted to.

So it attacked *covertly*, utilizing mercenary states like Israel and South Africa. "Other countries hire terrorists;" says Chomsky, "we hire terrorist states."[60] Quick victories in Grenada and Panama offset more expensive interventions elsewhere. Investigations of "Contragate" merely removed — temporarily — a few players. No significant critique of secrecy in government resulted. The U.S. cast a solitary "no" vote at the United Nations on 150 occasions between 1984 and 1987.

However, since Viet Nam remained a blemish on the skin of American myth, Hollywood was given the task of re-writing the war. Revenge fantasies starring lone, persecuted heroes such as Sylvester Stallone and Chuck Morris made men feel better about themselves and about war. These films deliberately inverted reality: now the *Vietnamese* (in over a dozen films) were the torturers, although *Russians* commonly directed them. "Myth," writes James Gibson, "readily substitutes one enemy for another...If Russian white men really controlled and directed the yellow Vietnamese, then the U.S. defeat becomes more understandable and belief in white supremacy is confirmed."[61]

Reagan mastered the intermittent reinforcement of denial and fear, reassuring whites that Eden was secure, and terrifying them with prospects of immanent nuclear war. He described the external, Communist Other with demonizing rhetoric: *evil empire, shadowy, fanatics, satanic* and *profane.* The corporate media complied. *Time, Newsweek,* and *U.S. News & World Report* commonly described Russians as *savages, dupes, adventurers, despots* and *barbarians.* Their methods were *brutal, treacherous, conniving, unmanly, aggressive and animalistic.*[62] "Unmanly" yet "aggressive" — only the Prince of Darkness himself (or Dionysus) could hold such contradictory projections.

Despite their 12,000 nuclear warheads, Americans were told that they needed the "Star Wars" missile defense. The greatest power in history couldn't protect itself from the barbarians outside without appealing to the high-tech gods. Nor could it solve the internal threat without building more prisons and establishing SWAT teams in every city.

With both Washington and Hollywood depicting the cities as crime-ridden, the suburban exodus drastically increased. Nearly one-sixth of the land developed in the nation's entire history occurred during the 1980s and 1990s.[63] This massive demographic shift resulted in sprawl, the defining characteristic of the new American landscape. Millions expected to fulfill their dreams in the suburbs; instead, they found long commutes, uniformity and isolation.

Reagan's damage to the economy and the environment can be repaired. His assault on American values, however, will take longer to heal. In a thousand subtle ways, he announced that the 300-year-old balance between freedom and equality was broken. The theme of his revolution was traditional values, but its subtext proclaimed racism, narcissism and the predatory imagination. Financier Ivan Boesky summed it all up: "You can be greedy and still feel good about yourself."

The long, painful inclusion of the Other had brought blacks, browns, reds, yellows, women, gays and the disabled within the gates of the City. Reagan reversed everything, circled the wagons, retreated within the pale (pale skin) and reduced the *polis,* once again, to a minority. The ancient Athenians called those who ignored the general welfare *idiots.* Reagan gave Americans permission to be idiots.

THE HUMAN FACE OF EVIL

After seventy years and *trillions* wasted, the U.S.S.R. collapsed. The result was worldwide euphoria.[64] Sixty percent of Americans favored huge cuts in defense and a "peace dividend" that would eliminate poverty. But visions of infinite wealth drove the opportunists, who demanded further deregulation and *increased* military spending. Other visions drove the Puritans. Psychologist Lionel Corbett suggests that such people cannot tolerate peace, because happiness produces guilt and the desire to be punished, especially if we feel too greedy.[65] But neither greed nor guilt could generate support for new aggressive policies. *Fear* could do that, and this required a new external Other.

Over the years, the image of the external Other had shifted from the Indians, resting briefly on Mexicans, Spanish, Germans and Japanese before finding its home among the Communists. However, there was always a problem with othering the grey-suited and anonymous Russians: despite their slightly exotic, Slavic features, they were *white.*

Around 1985, the Other became more personal when television identified many charismatic Third World villains. After the first generation (Ho Chi Minh and Fidel Castro) came Moammar Khadaffy, Idi Amin, Yasser Arafat, Ayatollah Khomeini, Manuel Noriega, Kim Il Sung, Slobodan Milosevic, Hugo Chavez, Saddam Hussein, Osama Bin Laden and the greatest of all, Mahmoud Ahmadinejad, who was too good to be true: a Holocaust denier who sought to possess nuclear weapons.

Note three themes here. First, U.S. propaganda attacks were often timed to impact (or obscure) *domestic* issues. Second, only Milosevic was white (but Slavic). Third, several of these men had previously worked for the U.S. Back in 1932, Roosevelt had said of Nicaragua's Anastacio Somoza, "He's an S.O.B., but he's *our* S.O.B.!" It is as if the U.S. keeps them on ice, allowing them to quietly do their work until it needs to reveal them as the Devil's latest incarnation. Then they become expendable, or, as with Bin Laden, even *more* valuable as fugitives, hiding in caves and bazaars, plotting more evil.

When Communists became our friends, it was a dizzying experience for older Americans, who grew up fearing Russians, then Germans and Japanese, then Russians again, along with Chinese, Koreans, Vietnamese, Nicaraguans, Iranians and Arabs, while Germans and Japanese became allies. Still, Hollywood took years to portray Russians (in 2001's *Enemy at the Gates*) or Vietnamese (in 2002's *We Were Soldiers*) as moral agents. By then, the image of the Other had shifted.

Renewing the myth requires something more than small-time dictators. As Communism disappeared, conservatives found the answer. *Terrorists* hated freedom and meant to destroy our way of life. Wily, shifty, turbaned, bearded, *they almost invariably had dark skin.* And they were already among us; once again, no one could be trusted.

An American general had lamented, "The drug war is the only war we've got."[66] The Gulf War, however, made violence acceptable again, and pacifist euphoria dissipated. George Bush boasted, "Viet Nam has been buried forever in the desert sands." Saddam, more valuable to the myth as the face of evil than as ex-dictator, remained in power for another twelve years. One official candidly admitted, "Saddam...*saved us from the peace dividend.*"[67] Sensing the opportunity, Hollywood contributed *Rules of Engagement, Iron Eagle, True Lies, The Siege, Delta Force, Harem, Executive Decision*, etc.

Awash in a sea of yellow ribbons, Americans barely noticed the massive economic shift. In 1985, one percent owned a third of the nation's wealth. By 1995, they owned forty percent, while eighty percent of the people received no increase in income.

Bill Clinton appeared to represent a generation that rejected Cold

War values. But after winning election only because of a schism among conservatives (Independent Ross Perot won nineteen percent), he quickly chose to "out-Republican" the Republicans. Clinton expanded the military, maintained the murderous embargoes of Iraq and Cuba, supported the usual dictators and sold more arms (by 1997) than the rest of the world combined.

Militant Islam was growing for three reasons. First, the U.S. had eliminated almost all *secular* forms of resistance to Western domination, while staunchly supporting Israel. Second, it spent billions supporting fundamentalists in Afghanistan and Saudi Arabia. Third, it needed an Other.

Clinton offered "globalization." But in the inner cities, those *outside* the bubble of innocence knew that such policies, whether instigated by Republicans or Democrats, had the same goals: lowering labor costs by shifting production abroad. The NAFTA trade agreement would eventually eliminate 900,000 American jobs. Nearly half of those it created paid minimum wage.

The media proclaimed unprecedented prosperity as Clinton reduced both taxes and services in a country that was already at the bottom among industrialized nations in social spending. Then, despite bloated military budgets and increased corporate welfare, he proclaimed the end of the "era of big government." His "welfare reform" declared war on the internal Other. In 1995, he identified *teenage pregnancy* (not racism or poverty) as America's "most serious social problem." Meanwhile, politicians warned of incorrigible (black) "superpredators," while southern states reintroduced the rural chain gang.

Ongoing demonizing of the inner cities combined with lost manufacturing jobs to swell new internal migrations. Between 1990 and 1995, New York City and Los Angeles each lost a million residents to the Sun Belt, to be replaced by immigrants. Cities became darker and poorer, while the suburbs became whiter and poorer.

The "economic miracle of the 1990s" was a lie: two million discouraged workers dropped out of the workforce; one in four children lived in poverty; forty (now fifty) million lacked health insurance; and two million were prisoners. Since the mid-1970s, profits had risen, but not wages. To compensate, Americans worked more and retired later, their spouses went to work, and they used up savings. Then they started borrowing. By 2008 (prior to the financial crisis), the average family would be paying fourteen percent of annual income in interest, and thirty percent of working families would be living in poverty.

In the year 2000, the U.S. had *over a thousand* military bases in other countries.[68] Pundits bragged, "Others welcome our power." Exactly the same pompous yet mythically effective rhetoric had rallied the innocents in 1900 as Americans massacred Filipinos, in 1800 as they subsidized repression in Haiti, and in 1700 as they slaughtered Indians and took over their lands.

Half of Americans no longer participated in the *polis.* "Limits to the extension of political democracy" arrived *before* the 2000 election. Having abandoned liberalism, Democrats were nearly indistinguishable from Republicans on most issues other than abortion. But the Republicans owned the "values" voters. Nebraska's McPherson County (the poorest in the nation) voted for Bush II by eighty percent.[69] Still, it took massive fraud and the Supreme Court's bizarre mendacity to finalize the results. With the media carefully framing the limits of discussion, public protest was mild and brief.

Bush's tax cuts exacerbated income disparities and provoked another economic downturn. Quickly, his popularity dropped to record lows. Cracks in the myth appeared again; the nation had to be shocked back into compliance. The new oligarchs had recently suggested that "a new Pearl Harbor" might be necessary.[70] That something was 9/11.

"DADDY, WHY DO THEY HATE US SO?"

On the morning of September 11, TV commentators repeatedly assured viewers that Bush was "in touch" with vice-president Cheney; an elder was guiding the young, illegitimate leader. Things were *under control,* despite the carnage on the screen. Spokesmen unanimously declared America's goodness and the sure, quick retribution it would exact. Several politicians repeated, "Make no mistake about it."

The next day, a second wave of commentators offered more nuanced interpretations. Rabbi Marc Gelman, asked if America would be changed by this event, responded, "Yes, we have lost our innocence. We now know there is radical evil in the world." It was *out there,* and Americans, mysteriously, had never heard about it. Psychologist Robert Butterworth's son had asked him, "Daddy, why do they hate us so?" Staring mutely and miserably at the camera, he really didn't know. His non-response assumed that viewers didn't either. Such laments could have followed the Oklahoma City bombing, 1993's WTC bombing, the TWA airliner bombing, the bombings of the destroyer Cole and Lebanon barracks, or any of the recent college or high school shootings. America, we were told, had lost her innocence.

On September thirteenth, Clear Channel, owner of 1,200 radio stations, banned the airplay of 150 popular songs, including *Peace Train* and *Imagine.* On the fourteenth, Bush promised to "...rid the world of evil." Later, he verbalized the consensus of innocence betrayed: "... (although) in some Islamic countries there is vitriolic hatred...like most Americans...I know how good we are."

Bush's popularity speedily soared to over ninety percent. The prince was no longer illegitimate. *Time* dubbed him our "Lone Ranger" and proclaimed, "America Unites," with "new faith in our oldest values." Although the hyper-inflated, phallic towers had collapsed, America stood erect behind Bush, who had symbolically absorbed the strike without flinching. He exhorted Americans to show the world that they too were unfazed. *Americans were to continue consuming* — while the poor, who had grown to thirty-three million, were *being* consumed. A million black children were living in "extreme poverty."

By October, Bush was arguably the most popular person in the world, and Bin Laden (who repeatedly claimed that he'd had nothing to do with the WTC attacks) was probably second. The "terrorist mastermind," ruler of the evil hordes, was already a stock character in American myth; the role had been rehearsed in countless movies. The two fundamentalists stood like the cousins Dionysus and Pentheus, mirror images of each other.

While eighty-nine percent of Americans supported the invasion of Afghanistan, the government enforced drastic reductions in personal freedoms, incarcerating hundreds of citizens and legal aliens. New phrases entered the language: Homeland Security; weapons of mass destruction; regime change; axis of evil; preventive war; and the Patriot Act. Meanwhile, Attorney General Ashcroft spent $8,000 to veil a nude statue of *Justice.*

Americans, terrified by the Anthrax scare, barely noticed that Congress passed the entire Republican agenda.[71] Confidence in the president and the military climbed to their highest levels since Watergate. Everywhere, cars displayed American flags. As sales of SUVs passed sales of regular cars, people commonly spoke of how life had changed forever. Others, resisting the war fever, spoke of a magnificent opportunity. America, said Cornel West, could know how other nations, women and blacks have suffered; America had been "niggerized."[72] But the moment passed.

The year 2002 was a blur of layoffs, corporate scandals, color-coded predictions of immanent danger, "nation-building" in Afghanistan, "duct tape security" and consistent, public lies about Iraq.[73] Forty-eight percent of Americans agreed that America has special protection from God. But just beneath the confidence was a tooth-grinding fear of the future. The cadaverous face of evil was waiting, just beyond, or possibly already within the walls. This was a new experience, claimed the pundits.

Or was it? Hadn't Americans feared Indian attacks for three centuries? Hadn't they been terrorized for seventy years by red hordes from the east? Hadn't every President since Truman managed a war economy that perpetuated itself on fear of the Other? Hadn't politicians played the "race card" for two centuries? Hadn't gun sales continued to rise even as crime rates had plummeted? Weren't Americans already armed to the teeth?

Had they forgotten the missile gap, the domino theory, the window of vulnerability and the Evil Empire? Hadn't AIDS ended the sexual revolution? Hadn't they been stuffing themselves with anti-depressants, hormone replacements and potency drugs? Hadn't *fear of losing* property, status, security, virility, youth, freedom — and innocence — always been at the core of the American experience? Hadn't we bounced between denial and terror for our entire history?

On 9/11/ 2002, newspapers gushed: "The President... the Statue of Liberty behind him... praised the unsinkable character of America...That character shone all day." Toby Keith's song, *"Courtesy of the Red, White and Blue,"* was number one:

> *You'll be sorry that you messed with the U.S. of A.*
> *'Cuz we'll put a boot in your ass — It's the American way.*

The Other had a new face; forty percent of Americans were now convinced that Saddam Hussein had caused 9/11. In February 2003, Colin Powell forced the U.N. to veil its copy of Picasso's *Guernica* before threatening to attack Iraq. Then came embedded reporters, video game war graphics and yellow ribbons. Bush revealed that God had instructed him to invade Iraq. In May, he crowed, "Mission Accomplished!"

"BRING IT ON!"

After opposing and delaying a commission to investigate the WTC attacks, the administration finally relented. Half a million viewers complained about the exposure of a breast during the 2004 Super Bowl. Two weeks later, the U.S. overthrew Haiti's government again, after having failed to do so in Venezuela. In March, atmospheric carbon dioxide reached record levels, and the U.S. became a net importer of food. In May, pictures of torture at Abu Ghraib circulated. The gap between America's rich and poor was the widest since 1929. Single mothers headed twenty-six percent of families. The black male unemployment rate in New York City was fifty percent. Several "immanent" terrorist attacks never happened. Reagan's death provoked a frenzy of hagiography. Ten percent of American workers labored in fast-food outlets. The word "McJob" entered the *Merriam-Webster Dictionary*.

The *9/11 Report* blamed everyone and punished no one. A poll revealed: "Half of New Yorkers Believe US Leaders Had Foreknowledge of Impending 9/11 Attacks and 'Consciously Failed' To Act." No major media reported the results for almost a year.[74] The Education Department admitted having destroyed 300,000 copies of *Helping Your Child Learn History*. Republicans warned that John Kerry would ban the Bible. Fear of terrorist attacks was strongest in small towns far from the big cities. After the election, the media ignored the differentials between exit polls and vote totals, while lamenting voter fraud in the Ukraine.[75] The war's purpose was now to spread democracy.

Infant mortality rose for the first time in forty-four years. Three million manufacturing jobs had been lost, and 3.5 million people had exhausted their unemployment benefits, but corporate profits were the highest in seventy-five years. America was emitting more greenhouse gases than ever before. There was a record of 772,000 marijuana arrests. Alberto Gonzales, architect of the legalization of torture, announced his highest priority as Attorney General: *obscenity*.

In 2005, the national debt increased by $2 billion/day. Congress prevented doctors from pulling the plug from brain-dead Terry Schiavo. Bush, who had overseen 152 executions as Governor of Texas, lectured, "We should always err on the side of life."

The Pentagon couldn't account for a *trillion* dollars.[76] A million Americans had HIV, nearly half of them blacks. The Arctic ice cap was the smallest in a century. Thirty-eight million were living in poverty, seven million more than in 1999. Lobbyists in Washington had doubled since 2000 to nearly 35,000. Five hundred people died trying to enter America illegally. Pat Robertson, America's best-known theologian, publicly suggested assassinating Hugo Chavez.

Then Katrina hit New Orleans. The media acknowledged government incompetence, but the dominant images were of black "looters." Barbara Bush announced that the victims "...were underprivileged anyway, so this is working very well for them." Sixty percent of blacks said that race and class were factors in the government's slow response; nine in ten whites disagreed.

The next week, Congress removed food stamps from 300,000 people. All three major TV networks introduced series about alien invasions. The year 2005 was the hottest year on record, until 2007. There was a record trade deficit for the fourth consecutive year. Hate groups increased from 600 in 2000 to 800 in 2005. More phrases entered the vocabulary: extraordinary rendition; outsourcing of torture; warrantless wiretapping; data mining; evildoers; Islamo-fascism; and signing statements.

In 2006, conservatives revived the old scapegoat, immigration. Congress passed the sixth tax cut in six years and its seventh raise, but refused to increase the minimum wage. One percent of households owned fifty-three percent of all stock. Thirty-nine percent agreed that Muslim-Americans should carry special identification.

The national database of critical terrorist targets grew to 300,000 localities, and *Indiana* had more than California and New York combined. Fox TV's *"24"* featured an American hero reluctantly yet expertly torturing terrorist suspects. Bush bragged that he had ignored the law on hundreds of occasions. The IRS cut in half the number of lawyers auditing the super-rich. Half of all taxpayer audits were on people earning $25,000 or less. The EPA was forced to close most of its research libraries. Congress raised the national debt limit for the fourth time in six years. Bush distilled the American mystery into, "Today we are safer, but we are not yet safe." Then he abolished *habeas corpus*. Pundits calmly discussed nuking Iran, while ignoring reports that 600,000 Iraqis were dead.

Republican fear-mongering couldn't prevent the loss of Congress in the 2006 election. Six in ten people expected a terrorist attack in 2007, while twenty-five percent anticipated the second coming of Christ. Ignoring the winner of its own reader's poll (Hugo Chavez) *Time* declared "You" to be "Person of the Year."

In 2007, Paul Bremer admitted to Congress that he couldn't account for $12 billion in cash he had distributed to Iraqi politicians. America had 371 billionaires, while sixteen million were severely poor. Over 750,000 were homeless. One in four Americans were making under $9.00/hour. The nation was spending more than a billion dollars/year incarcerating its citizens for pot possession. Exxon-Mobil reported another record profit. The media crucified a black athlete for torturing dogs, while Texas executed its 400th prisoner. The Supreme Court struck down *voluntary* desegregation. After the shootings at Virginia Tech, pundits announced the end of innocence.

In 2008, the housing market collapsed, followed by the financial system. The government bailout paid billions to those responsible. Two-thirds of corporations had paid no income tax for several years. A record thirty million people received food stamps. A million Americans were on the Terrorist Watch List. The wars were costing $12 billion/month. Military spending exceeded $1 trillion, pushing the federal debt past $9 trillion. Forty-five hundred U.S. soldiers were dead, 150,000 recent veterans were already receiving disability benefits, and the backlog at the V.A. was over a million. The U.S. had attacked, directly or indirectly, *forty-three countries* since the end of World War Two. Barack Obama was the new president. Yet after years of headlines, over fifty percent of the public was not opposed to torturing suspected terrorists. There was madness at the gates, but on which side?

MADNESS AT THE GATES

We could debate whether the administration had prior knowledge of 9/11 or whether it merely took advantage of it. Or we could psychoanalyze George Bush and his cronies. But I want to identify the deeper mythic implications.

From a Third World perspective, he was just one more leader whose genocidal actions belied his inspirational rhetoric, whose policies were entirely consistent with those of his predecessors and with historic American attitudes toward the Other. Focusing on Bush's crimes, however, may only cloud the picture. It is more useful to consider that the most dysfunctional among us (like Pentheus) enact our national myths most clearly. In this sense, Bush and the entire political class do us a favor: they invite us to step out of our innocence.

Since the fathers of 1914 sacrificed millions of their sons to the new gods of the age, much has shifted. Four generations later, the rate of change, the literalization of war, the madness of consumerism, the demythologizing of the world and the depths of our alienation have only increased. In Morris Berman's words, "We have inherited a civilization in which the things that really matter in human life exist at the margin of our culture."[77]

Bush represents the logical extreme of uninitiated rulers that has manifested progressively for centuries. "We may now be the possessors of the world's flimsiest identity structure," writes Paul Shepard, "...where history, masquerading as myth, authorizes men...to alter the world to match their regressive moods of omnipotence and insecurity."[78] We are talking about psychopaths, men who speak with reassuringly sincere voices yet are completely amoral.[79]

Perhaps we can understand deeply religious men who sponsor torturers and drug smugglers only by comparing them to the original *conquistadores*. Such men, writes James Wilson, lived "an apparently insoluble compound" of greed, cruelty, deceit, opportunism — *and* an absolutely literal, legalistic, church-sanctioned piety that assured them of their own salvation.[80] This is the bizarre logic of the modern Calvinists. Since they are already saved, then they are infinitely entitled, and evil deeds are irrelevant to their salvation. The "chosen" are above morality. What are we to make of a Supreme Court Justice — Antonin Scalia — who has publicly stated that there is nothing unconstitutional about executing innocent people? "The normal rules don't apply," brags Doug Coe, spiritual mentor to several conservative, Christian Congressmen.[81] *Their "morality" demands contempt for ethics.*

Is history cyclic? Perhaps the Paranoid and Predatory imaginations have merged once again, as they did during the crusades and the early colonial period. Or perhaps, like antibiotic-resistant bacteria, a new strain of reactionary has evolved: true believers, whose ends justify any means; grandiose boy-men who murder not *despite* their faith but *because* of it. They see no ethical dilemma in corruption and violence because their twisted mix of smug righteousness and social Darwinism assures them that their victims deserve their fate. Anyone who isn't a hero is a victim, and all but the inner circle are now Other. And these men, beginning with Ronald Reagan, have taught us well; it was no coincidence that the hugely popular "reality shows," many of which regularly featured extended, ritual abuse of the losers, as well as the "torture-porn" program *24*, appeared in the same years that news commentators and politicians calmly debated the torture of suspected terrorists.

Again, I suggest: only a mythic perspective can make any sense of this. America's rulers are not ignorant; they are fully aware of our human and environmental tragedies. The fathers no longer send only the young to be sacrificed; now they offer everything to the sky-gods. Whether or not we take their religious rhetoric literally, they are deliberately (if unconsciously) provoking both personal and global apocalypse. They are like children driving a truck with a cargo of high explosives, with the rest of us in the back.

Recall Pentheus, emerging from his collapsed palace, even more determined to confront (or to merge with) Dionysus. Thebes/America is a city of uninitiated men, fanatically devoted to the systematic destruction of their own children. A boy-king, who secretly longed for the symbolic death that might effect his transition to manhood, was leading this city. The entire world could almost feel it as a desperate, visceral *prayer* when, in June 2003, Bush, the self-appointed embodiment of American heroism, challenged the Iraqi resistance to "bring it on!"

OBAMA

In 1972, Chinese Premier Chou En-Lai, questioned by Richard Nixon about the impact of the French Revolution, responded, "Too early to tell." We can't say yet if Barack Obama's all-too conventional cabinet appointments and the vast sums he raised from Wall Street will prevent him from producing concrete change, let alone a significant shift at the mythic level.

After one year in office, Obama had expanded the Afghanistan war into Pakistan, causing hundreds of civilian and scores of American deaths. He had increased the defense budget, pushed to renew the Patriot Act, doubled arms sales abroad and subtly condoned both the Israeli invasion of Gaza and the military coup in Honduras. He was continuing Bush's secrecy policies, the outsourcing of torture, "signing statements," the embargo of Cuba and the demonization of Iran and North Korea. He would not re-institute the Fairness Doctrine or endorse the ban on land mines. He refused to prosecute either torturers or Wall Street financial swindlers. He reconfirmed "No Child Left Behind" and backtracked on countless civil-liberties issues. His climate bill offered record subsidies to Big Coal, while his health bill promised vast profits to Big Insurance. His response to the economic crisis socialized the risk, privatized the gains and rewarded the same bankers who had caused it. Hurricane Katrina relief? Louisiana's 2nd Congressional District was dead last in the nation in stimulus funds.

He is, argues Chris Hedges, merely a new "brand," designed to pacify the public with convincing fantasies while business continues as usual. "Brand Obama does not threaten the core of the corporate state any more than did Brand George W. Bush."[82] In the eternal gentleman's dispute within the ruling class, Wall Street's man defeated John McCain, the candidate of Big Oil. Obama is merely the newest, more palatable face of empire, with the clear assignment to re-invigorate the myth of innocence.

His role, writes Greg Palast, is to "...soothe America's conscience with the happy fairy tale that his election marked the end of racism in the USA."[83] If the more blatant forms of traditional bigotry have receded somewhat, a newer, more insidious version may have appeared. Tim Wise writes that "Racism 2.0" allows whites to celebrate the achievements of certain acceptable, non-threatening individuals such as Obama who have "transcended their blackness," while continuing to fear and discriminate against the great majority of blacks, reds and browns. This suggests the "fluid and shape-shifting nature of racism."[84] Obama himself has fed the post-racial narrative by lecturing black audiences with condescending talk of personal responsibility.

Perhaps the most generous assessment of Obama is that he and his party have been "spineless" in confronting the right-wing media backlash. From the start, by negotiating from the middle rather than from a position of strength, he has allowed the Republicans to set the terms of debate. In this view, he is the latest example of liberal innocence, the would-be savior who is truly ignorant of political reality. By trying to remain above the fray and not using his office to stand for anything substantial, he has allowed himself to become — in the eyes of whites — the Other, the President as Other, in a nation still obsessed with race.

In his defense, we must note that seven former godfathers of a fifty billion dollar crime syndicate known for assassinating public figures — the CIA — very publicly warned him not to probe too deeply into allegations of prisoner abuse by that same gang. It was, perhaps, a declaration of just who is really in charge to a man who receives over thirty death threats per day.

Ultimately, however, the symbolism of a black man in the slave-built White House may be far more significant in terms of the long-term effort to welcome the Other into the *polis,* which the politics of the last thirty years have reversed. This is despite the paradoxical truth that as of this same election, forty-three states had restricted marriage to two persons of the opposite sex. Just as in 1680, 1838, 1920 and 1964, it seems that mild progress in the inclusion of one Other requires the exclusion or further demonization of another Other.

Perhaps his election does represent a change in consciousness. Millions of whites rejected the negative politics and were finally willing to "vote their pocketbooks" instead of voting their fears. Suddenly, if grudgingly, the media have acknowledged the possibility of all kinds of radical rethinking, from green energy and appropriate transportation to the banking system, gay marriage and legal marijuana. Obama himself has stated that change must come from below, that he can't act without popular pressure.

Once again, cracks are showing in the walls of the myth of innocence. "It's not that Obama is the change;" writes Michael Ventura, "it's that his election is an expression of decades of painful, difficult, incremental changes." Furthermore,

> It was Obama's genius to know that the hardened crust of
> American habit and prejudice could be broken…that for
> many Americans, (it)… was only a crust, and, if that crust
> could be broken, what lay beneath was essentially good and
> invaluable. But… it would take oodles and oodles of money
> to break through that hardened crust…A paradox consists
> of at least two aspects that are opposite yet equally true…It is
> equally true that Obama inspired his way into the Oval Office
> and that he bought it. Obama won by the power of a paradox,
> and his administration, for good and for ill, will be a paradox
> of power.[85]

Perhaps only the language of paradox will work to facilitate the breakdown of a crust so hardened as American myth. In the short run, that myth has actually been strengthened by the philosophy of "Yes we can." Only in America (we are told) could such a mixed-race person rise so high from such humble beginnings. The story is so familiar: an exceptionally extraordinary man — the Hero — comes out of nowhere and takes power in a dangerous time.

Millions of new, young, black and brown voters are thrilled to feel included in the polis for the first time. But hope taken to the extreme can make people inappropriately dependent on specific individuals, rather than on their own capabilities. The risk of pursuing a philosophy of inclusion in a madhouse is that it may easily evoke its shadow of disillusionment, deflation and further disengagement when things go wrong. For now, we need to look much deeper into our own belief systems and be willing to confront the demons within those walls.

If we have to use force, it is because we are America! We are the indispensable nation. We stand tall, and we see further into the future.
MADELEINE ALBRIGHT

———

This cowboy doesn't have to be courageous. All he needs is to be alone... he rides into the town and does everything by himself.
HENRY KISSINGER

———

Show me a hero and I will write you a tragedy.
F. SCOTT FITZGERALD

———

Progress is our most important product.
RONALD REAGAN FOR GENERAL ELECTRIC

———

When the President does it, that means it is not illegal.
RICHARD NIXON

———

I believe in God and I believe in free markets.
KEN LAY

———

Never give a sword to a man who can't dance.
CONFUCIUS

09

THE HERO

An Intersection of Myths

The indigenous soul remembers being held by myth and ritual, being embedded in a web of cyclic time, being connected to worlds of spirit, ancestry and purpose. It remembers incomprehensibly vast prehistory. It knows that things *have* been this bad before, that cultures have unraveled, that there have been times when, as Yeats wrote, "…the center cannot hold." And the indigenous soul possesses the code for regeneration.

We live at the intersections of many different myths, or with myths layered on top of each other. Our "bone-memory" is covered over by many veils of relatively newer mythologies, each deeply influencing our beliefs and behavior, all the more so because we don't realize how firmly they hold us. If we lift those veils and examine the stories we tell ourselves about ourselves, we'll see that some fit consistent patterns, while others conflict with each other, thus requiring still *other* stories to resolve the contradictions.

THE MYTH OF PATRIARCHY

Our world has been conditioned by 5,000 years of patriarchy (or *andocracy*, the rule of men); in other words, all of recorded history. Its stories are of domination, hierarchy ("rule by the high priest"), conquest, jealousy and violent betrayal of fathers and sons. These stories sing of heroes who create the world by killing mother-serpents and set the mold for masculine identity almost everywhere. And they remain so influential because older stories of deep, initiated masculinity — identity *not* in terms of the Other — have nearly disappeared.

As far as fathers and *daughters* are concerned, of course, the cruel heritage remains very much alive in the lands running from West Africa to India and beyond. Foot-binding, arranged marriages, veiled faces, genital mutilation and "honor killings" indicate this story's enduring strength. And fundamentalist backlash shows how tentative our own feminist progress is.

THE MYTH OF TIME

The winners produce myths that become accepted as history. Through all our stories strides the colossus of *Kronos* — Father Time — with his irresistible pressure to perform, compete, accomplish, build, destroy and rebuild before he eats his children; he can never rest or be satisfied. Nearby stand his brothers, Yahweh and Allah, each regularly *testing the faith* of his followers. Time, we are told, is linear; it began at a single point.

Then we are offered a paradox. On the one hand, earlier ages of Man are said to have been nobler than ours. We can never approach the standards of the fathers; our choices are limited to fruitless rebellion or to conformity that passes the accumulated rage of the generations onto our children. On the other hand, we will find a happy ending in heaven at the end of time.

Perhaps the essence of civilization is the deferral of pleasure and desire; the more satisfaction is moved out of reach, the more time becomes palpable. Mathematically divisible, linear time led to the factory system of production. The twentieth century's precise standardization of *world* time, writes John Zerzan, was a "victory for the efficient/machine society, a universalism that undoes particularity..."[1]

In Jonathan Swift's *Gulliver's Travels* (1726), The hero told his captors that his watch pointed out the time for every action of his life. They concluded that the watch was his god. Who is *our* greatest diety? Jesus, whom we visit once a week for a few hours, or Kronos, whom we equate with money, whose temple we carry on our wrists? In a demythologized culture, clocks are constant reminders of time running down and out, toward death. Death, who carries the scythe that Kronos himself used to castrate his father, leers at us from the future, hinting that only grandiose, heroic deeds can slow him down.

For indigenous people, however, both time and death are parts of the natural cycle. Death is not the opposite of life but the opposite of *birth*. The Dagara language has no word for time. Somé writes, "The absence of 'time' generates a mode of life whose focus is on the state of one's spirit," rather than on production.[2] The Dagara had no word for art either, because like the Balinese, they did art (as ritual) constantly. Older Greek tradition tells us that time is defeated not by heroism but by memory and its creations. Kronos's sister *Mnemosyne* (Memory) birthed the nine Muses. Only in the ritual imagination, where "time stands still," can we truly "kill time."

Modern people, however, stand exposed to and often identify with the god who eats his children. Kronos presides over an ironic mythic space that emphasizes youthfulness in all things, while offering no future to the young. Today's elders — who benefited from the G.I. Bill, *history's most generous welfare program* — have overwhelmingly supported policies that deny similar benefits to their own grandchildren. Desperate to beat Time by *looking* young, Americans apparently despise those who actually are.

THE JUDEO-CHRISTIAN MYTHS
We are told that linear time will end with the final accounting. Overlaying older patriarchal myths is the 3,000-year-old Judeo-Christian tradition. One version awaits the coming of the messiah, while another claims that he came once and was sacrificed by his father. Both stories predict a spectacular conclusion. Millions feel assured that they (and not others) will be saved, and millions of others worry that they won't make the cut.

Whereas indigenous traditions often have multiple origin myths, monotheism has only one, which is interwoven with woman's guilt. Man falls from innocence into original sin. Since the time of Saint Augustine, the normal act of birth has been considered to be an instrument of God's eternal punishment to women.

Scholars may debate the allegorical nature of Genesis, but monotheism has inexorably ground down the indigenous human capacity to *think* metaphorically. Millions of fundamentalists interpret these stories (or their Koranic alternatives) quite literally. Even secular thinkers rarely identify the Puritanical biases within our collective unconscious. Augustine also wrote, "Filled with fear myself, I fill *you* with fear."

Monotheism breaks up the primordial union of opposites into the duality of spirit over matter. It follows that the spiritual world is *more real* than the physical world. The Earth, writes Riane Eisler, becomes a "testing ground where human beings...are trained and disciplined for their ultimate destination."[3] This radical separation becomes a crucial feature of both the Christian myth and the Western psyche. The transcendental deity communicates only through revelation, which calcifies into dogma. New revelations lead to new beliefs and black-or-white schisms. In the Old Testament, the elect *destroy* vast numbers of the Other; in the New Testament, they *convert* equally vast numbers. Both texts are obsessed with temptation. Anticipating an actual Israeli wall by three millennia, Ezra (9:11-12) speaks of erecting a virtual wall of purity around the Holy Land.

Men dominate women and whites subjugate blacks. Any images, like Dionysus, that dissolve these artificial dualities are relegated to the darkness. The only way out of this condition is renunciation. Women must reject the feminine, Africans must deny their tribal heritage and all must condemn the body. Whether that repudiation occurs through asceticism, capitalist sublimation or alcohol — *spirits* — hardly matters. All long to escape matter, *mater*, the mother. The founder of the influential Catholic group Opus Dei, wrote, "If you know that your body is your enemy and the enemy of God's glory, why do you treat it so gently?"[4] But repression of one's nature always constellates its shadow of libertinism. And the repressed always returns.

We move from revealed dogma to theological exclusivity to demonizing difference. Outside the pale, the Other questions our fragile self-definition by his or her mere existence. So the final, logical step is *jihad* or crusade. The Israelites, then the Christian Church, then the Puritans, and finally America itself are on missions from God.

The Pagan Greeks, no strangers to conflict, had more nuanced views. The gods and goddesses *take sides* in the *Iliad*. Heaven itself is conflicted; there is dignity and truth on both sides. Moreover, the poem ends with a funeral, not a victory. But, writes Joseph Campbell, the Old Testament God is "a single-minded single deity, with his sympathies forever on one side," who repeatedly commands his people to destroy every living being in the cities they capture.[5] Again, we can interpret such passages metaphorically, *but metaphorical thinking requires the ability to imagine the subjectivity of the Other,* a skill that monotheism deliberately and specifically destroys.

Thus, once the religious mesocosm began collapsing, secular movements (nationalism, fascism and communism) motivated millions to similar extremes of sacrifice. Although religious symbols have largely lost their power, the heritage of "chosen people" and "holy war" persists in the modern psyche, which still equates the salvation of one people with the destruction of another. One only needs to consider the 3,000-year-old conflict between Hebrews and Palestinians to see this dynamic in action.

Monotheism attacks the imagination like a virus. When Christ says, *"Everyone that looketh on a woman to lust after her hath committed adultery with her already in his heart"* (Mathew 5:28), he diminishes our capacity to discriminate, to tell fantasy from action. Once the Puritan *thinks* about pleasure, he has already sinned.

Some can understand metaphors and tolerate ambiguity. To do this, however, is to *resist* a profoundly durable inheritance, and we easily slip into the default mode of literalism. Hillman writes, "...we are each... like it or not, children of the Biblical God. It is a fact, the essential American fact."[6] Our monotheistic heritage determines our thinking about identity, race, gender, body, war, time, sin, self and other. Regina Schwartz concludes, "... if we do not think about the Bible, it will think (for) us."[7]

THE MYTH OF INDIVIDUALISM
In an odd reversal of initiation motifs, the American heroic son is supposed

to "kill" his father symbolically — if he has one — by individuating, moving away and repudiating everything the father stands for. In truth, we perceive family as at best a necessary evil, something to be escaped, so that one may get on with the pursuit of happiness. Progress (see below) happens through separation.

Americans generally consider the infant to be so fused with its mother that we make every effort to develop its ability to stand on its own as early as possible. It is held and carried less than in most societies. Very early, we admonish it to be a "big boy" or "big girl." The Japanese, by contrast, have a different myth of the child. They consider the infant to be utterly alien, from some strange, other world. Like many traditional people, they make every effort to enfold it within community as early as possible Neither view of the child is right or wrong, says Hillman; both are myths, because they are "lived unconsciously, collectively as truths, performed unwaveringly as rituals."[8]

One story we tell ourselves about ourselves is that purpose can be divorced from community. The desire to be seen as special contributes to the quest for expensive symbols — a quest that is ultimately futile, says Slater, "...since it is individualism itself that produces uniformity."[9] Paradoxically, our American obsession with individualism produces persons who "cannot recognize the nature of their distress." This results in a desire to relinquish responsibility for control and decision-making to the *images* provided by the media. Here lies a great paradox of American life: our emphasis on the needs of the individual has contributed toward cultural and political conformism.

But conformism and rebellious individualism are not our only choices. For tribal people, true community exists in order to identify and nurture the *individuality* of every one of its members, who are, in turn, necessary for the community to thrive and reproduce its values. Malidoma Somé writes that in West Africa, "Individuality is synonymous with uniqueness. This means that a person and his or her unique gifts are irreplaceable... A healthy community not only supports diversity, it requires diversity."[10]

SCIENCE AND THE MYTH OF A DEAD WORLD

Monotheistic thinking initiated the process that culminated in the disenchantment of the world. It had once been a world in which humans weren't the only beings with consciousness, in which animals, trees and stones were the abodes of ancestral spirits. It had been a world in which the material and the spiritual were in close contact, with neither subordinate to the other; it had been a living, *animated* world. Christianity declared such thinking heretical. Soul or consciousness resided only in the body, indeed only in the head. Most philosophical thinking for two thousand years has perceived life only in the biological. Everything else was dead. Spirit (if it existed) was invisible and inaccessible.

Scientific rationality, the new, infallible arbiter of objective truth, inherited and amplified this dead world. Tribal thinking, however, sees more similarities than differences between science and religion. Both science and religion assume a de-animated world. Both implicitly devalue nature. When the two came into direct competition in the sixteenth century, mankind fell upon the natural world as colonizer, as organizer of her "resources," as rapist. When men agreed that the world was dead, *the world itself* became Other.

THE MYTH OF PROGRESS

The Greeks envisioned a gradual and cumulative advancement of material knowledge, embodied in the arts and sciences. They expected that primitive, mythical thinking would evolve toward reason. Ultimately, they discounted their own myths as expressions of a childish past. The Hebrews, who believed in *spiritual* improvement, literalized their myths: God guided history. For them, life began in lost innocence and progressed toward the perfection of human nature.

When these traditions merged in early Christianity, progress became inseparable from linear time. Things progressed from ignorance to knowledge, from the local to the universal, from the particular to the abstract, from fall to redemption. Consequently, for a hundred generations, people deferred earthly gratification for fulfillment in a heavenly paradise.

The eighteenth century Enlightenment began to replace religion with faith in a *secular* idea of progress. Right reasoning and increasing knowledge would result in increased freedom. America's founders expected to free mankind from obsolete ideas through "self-improvement," actively participating in progress by bettering one's material condition as well as one's spirit. The sum total of each individual's improvement would equal the improvement of the community. Within a few generations, assumptions of progress, democracy and a classless society contributed to a characteristically American mood of optimism and cheerfulness.

The more openly religious have seen America as the millennial nation, the place where history will end with Christ's return. Historian Robert Nisbet writes that by 1850 the concept of progress as the means for personal freedom had become sacred, "grass-roots evangelism in America from one coast to the other."[11]

But millennialism gets tangled up with innocence. Imperialists whipped up support for their wars with the florid language of progress and America's responsibility to civilize primitive people, and they still do today. Once it became clear that Iraq had no weapons of mass destruction, Bush administration propaganda shifted to the old crusade to bring democracy to the ignorant. Because of our faith in progress and our own good intentions, we remain susceptible to rhetoric that justifies impulses that are polar opposites of each other: generosity and greed, freedom and conquest.

After Darwin, progress got confused with evolution. Fervent capitalists substituted "destiny" and the "natural law of growth" for "providence" as the determinant of history. This faith in progress promoted the status quo because it implied that in order to progress, one must simply do more of the same, and that the poor should ignore social injustice as long as the economic pie continued getting bigger. Millennialism served up in scientific terms allowed racists to define non-whites as less developed in evolution, unable to progress without the benevolent intervention of Euro-Americans. Indeed, without the notion of progress there would be no "primitive" people. Labeling poor nations as "developing" allowed rich nations to deny the obvious social stratification, as well as the fact that development made poor nations even poorer.

Socialists also believed in progress. Freedom, writes Nesbit, became inseparable from "membership in some collective or community...and from the creation...of *a new type of human being.* "[12] The religious expectation that had driven men for centuries shifted to socialism's secular dream without losing intensity. Marx put the golden age at the end of history rather than at the beginning. Communism would be "the solution of the riddle of history." Its universally compelling appeal had overtones of the Book of Revelation. People everywhere sang the words of *The Internationale:* "Tis the final conflict."

Eventually the word "progressive" came to describe activists for justice and equality, those who opposed "reactionaries." People assume faith in progress and worship of the new everywhere in modern culture: progressive education, art, music, jazz, poetry, literature and architecture.

Progress, however, has other implications. It typically runs from simple, dark, slow, primitive and natural to complex, light, speedy, rational and enlightened; in other words, *from feminine to masculine.* It sees women, like tribal people, embedded in the relational world of nature, representing tradition and the unconscious. Thus our notions of masculinity itself are tied up with the myth of progress and the imperative to transcend nature.

Furthermore, in linear time the shadow of progress is regression. If progress halts, we fall backwards. At any time the *Loosener* may penetrate the walls of the disciplined, masculine self, release all its repressed energies and destroy everything we've worked for. Hence the need for eternal vigilance. Nineteenth century missionaries believed that they risked corruption by the natives they were saving. As one asked, "Can a man touch pitch and not be himself defiled?"[13]

Of course, twentieth century literature is full of doubt and disillusionment. Since Viet Nam we have seen declines in both optimism and interest in past glories that support faith in future ones. As we question old assumptions of history, religion, race and gender, little is left to bind Americans together except for the myths of innocence and progress — and for consumerism.

Advertising addresses people steeped for centuries in ideas of self-improvement and sustains deep faith in technology. Ninety percent of us still believe that "Science and technology are making our lives healthier, easier and more comfortable." Whatever is newest and most complicated is most desirable. But since few can understand how their electronics work they cannot participate *directly* in the myth of progress. Advertising offers a solution: by owning gizmos we identify with those geniuses who, like Jehovah, made such wonders. Instead of making things we buy them, and consuming technology substitutes for real creativity. So the myth of progress meets the Puritan drive to prove salvation through material striving. "Work your way into the highest happiness bracket," preaches a bus advertisement.

Some contend that Americans are genetically self-selected toward our mania for self-improvement. Those who strive, risk and compete, who chafe most under restrictions, have always made up a disproportionate number of immigrants. Arriving here, they continually reinforce the myth of progress.

Americans naturally assume that our values are the most advanced of all societies. Our faith in progress justifies the status quo and marginalizes alternative voices, dismissing them as "going backwards," which in this story is an unforgivable sin. Without *justice,* however, progress for a few means ruin for most. Automation typically increases both productivity and unemployment. After 9/11 Bush urged Americans to go shopping and focus on a brilliant future of air-conditioned SUVs. But as fuel becomes expensive and jobs scarce, the notions of progress and grandiosity revert to their shadow, depression, in both its economic and psychological meanings.

The Myth of Growth

The goal of *Survivor,* television's most influential recent series, is to manipulate and scheme against other participants until only one winner is left. This perfectly exemplifies the American dogma of *unlimited economic growth,* which teaches that all must be free to achieve their potential through independent, meritorious (and if not meritorious, then creatively dishonest) action. Its relentless logic, however, turns nature into a resource and humans into individual rather than social animals. All motivation becomes self-interest, and no winners exist without losers.

Simplistic faith in "the market" mirrors fundamentalist faith in scriptural authority. In this story, the greatest sins are not violence but personal laziness (the crime of the Puritan) and social intrusion (the nightmare of the Opportunist.) Government, by taxing successful individuals to sustain the needy, calls this faith into question: if everyone, even the poor, is entitled to basic human rights, then no one is automatically among the elect. In reality, of course, the corporate world is terrified of truly unrestricted ("cutthroat") competition.

But we are talking about a *belief* system. The individual should be free to build, buy or waste whatever he wants. Then, the "rising boat" of generalized wealth may lift the less deserving along with it. Capitalism, argued J.M. Keynes, is the extraordinary belief that the nastiest of men, for the nastiest of reasons, will somehow work for everyone's benefit. When the freedom to grow trumps responsibility to the *polis,* however, "productivity" becomes a euphemism for "increased unemployment."

The myth of growth has enshrined the idea that abstract concepts devoted solely to accumulating capital — corporations — have all the rights of persons, plus limited liability and the freedom to externalize costs. Who are the gods of this theology? Corporations can live forever; they are immortal. They can reside in many places simultaneously, transform themselves at will and do virtually whatever they choose, but they can't be imprisoned. And they know more about us than we do. Corporate headquarters, like medieval religious shrines, are housed in America's tallest buildings. Americans express our aspiration to greatness through the metaphors of size, speed, height, expansion, acceleration and constant action. Both territorial expansion and cultural influence have been our manifest destinies. We outrun the competition and climb out of ignorance, up the rungs of the ladder of evolution. Great music "uplifts" us. The Greater grows by "rising" out of the lesser. Consider some books on American history: *The Rise of American Civilization, The Rise of the Common Man* and *The Rise of the City.* Both intoxication and euphoria are "highs." Depressive individuals are "down" and bad news is a "downer."

Counter-arguments produce anxiety, because we perceive them as attacks upon the faith itself. If one grows from wet/dark/feminine to dry/light/masculine, then appeals to sustainability become entwined with threats to masculinity. Male identity converges with the imperative to grow;

everything is bound up in "potential" and "potency." *Bigger* is not simply better, but the only alternative to "smaller," as "hero" is to "loser." Jimmy Carter suggested mild limits to growth and was destroyed politically for the attempt. Having studied his fate, Reagan, Clinton and the Bushes praised limits to *government*.

The belief that the imperative of growth trumps life itself underlies all corporate and most government policies. Conservatives attack big government, but praise its responsibility to support the private sector through subsidies, infrastructure and military intervention — all forms of externalizing costs.[14] The result is an economy, writes Hillman, that is "... the God we nourish with actual human blood."[15]

The holy text of this myth, the *Gross Domestic Product*, symbolizes the pathology of growth in four ways. First, it counts *all* economic activity as valuable, such as the $20 billion we annually spend on divorce lawyers, and never distinguishes between textbooks and porn magazines. It includes every aspect of a death from lung cancer — medical, hospital, pharmaceutical, legal and funereal, as well as growing, transporting, packaging, marketing and disposal of tobacco products. Increased gas expenditures add to the GDP without a corresponding *subtraction* for the toll fossil fuels take on the thermostatic and buffering functions of the atmosphere. Luxury buying by the rich covers up a lack of necessary buying by the poor. So the GDP actually disguises suffering. The ultimate absurd example is *war:* exceptionally costly, energy-intensive, requiring lengthy cleanup. By adding to the GDP, however, it builds an artificial sense of economic health.

Second, judging profitability on quarterly stock reports leads to maximizing short-term strategies (such as investing in the SUV rather than in energy-efficient cars) at the cost of long-term losses. Third, even if it were of any real value, the GDP is wildly inaccurate because it ignores the massive *underground* economy of drugs and gambling.

Fourth, it *doesn't* count the real, natural economy. Robert F. Kennedy said it "measures everything...except for that which makes life worthwhile." Most crucial life-supporting functions take place not through the market, but through social processes and voluntary activities (the help and care of families and churches) or through completely natural processes (the cooling and cleansing functions of trees, etc). None register in the GDP until something destroys them and people have to *buy* substitutes in the market. In this mad calculus, fuel conservation, stable marriages and children who exercise and eat healthy foods are *threats* to the economy.

Many "progressives" are also unaware of the pervasiveness of this story. Clearly, recession hurts the poor most. But we reveal ignorance of our myths when we demand larger shares of an ever-expanding economic pie, or lament "underdevelopment" in other nations. Growth, whether inequitable or sustainable, leads inevitably to the terrifying vision of seven billion people each driving their own SUV.

Eastern wisdom teaches that we can never satisfy the soul's hunger with material food alone. Yet self-improvement and growth are such bedrock American values that, by the 1970s, they were, once again, models for the *spiritual* life. To Hillman, the first assumption of the "therapeutic culture" is that emotional maturity entails a progressive *differentiation of self from others,* especially family. American psychology mirrors its economics: the heroic, isolated ego in a hostile world.

For a significant segment of the population, "inner growth" replaced the old ideal of the democratic citizen. Well-meaning people, more American than they knew, spoke of what they could get *from* life, rather than, to paraphrase John Kennedy, what they could give to it. Spiritual growth became another version of the pursuit of happiness, now defined by *"heightened* awareness" and *"peak"* experiences. "Feeling good," wrote psychologist Lesley Hazleton, became "no longer simply a right, but a social and personal duty."[16] And the economy provided the material symbols that gave evidence — *proof,* in Puritan terms — of spiritual "growth."

This idea takes its energy from two older ones: life-long initiation, and biological maturation. But it has split off from the natural and indigenous worlds in its unexamined assumptions. All living things die and return to Earth, but a "growing" person, by definition, cannot. Initiation requires the *death* of something that has grown past its prime. And worse, since the myth of growth (material or spiritual) is essentially a personal story, it narcissistically assumes the unlimited objectification and exploitation of others for the ultimate aggrandizement of the Self.

We find unlimited growth in neither nature nor culture, but only in the *cancer cell,* which multiplies until it destroys its host. The miracle of reproduction serves death instead of life. Growth inevitably evokes its opposite. The body produces *anti-*bodies, which destroy the twin-towered invaders of autonomy and grandiosity. There is no more basic ecological rule. Natural growth only occurs within a broader cycle that also includes decay.

But when growth, potency, happiness, pressure to be in a good mood, to "have a nice day," to be "high" are hopelessly intertwined with consumer goodies, *not* having them means a drop into powerlessness, shame and depression. In the real world of limited resources, growth is a Ponzi scheme in which our great-grandchildren subsidize our innocent and narcissistic fantasies.

THE MYTH OF SCARCITY

A South African Bushman asks, *"Why should we plant, when there are so many mongomongo nuts in the world?"*[17]

The myth of growth leads to another curious paradox. As infants assume unlimited nourishment, Americans assumed their country was so vast that its resources, and later those of the entire planet, appeared infinite. Four hundred years later, despite countless examples of the negative consequences of our way of life, we remain firmly *entitled.* As bumper stickers ask about Iraq, "How did our oil get under their sand?" Americans still take an essentially infantile view that assumes infinite resources for our comfort and delight.

We consume in order to attempt to satisfy the longing in our souls, which really *is* infinite. Pursuing happiness through material wealth is like trying to fill a sieve. We are like the "hungry ghosts" of Buddhism, constantly hungry yet unable to fit food through their pinhole mouths; or like Tantalos, whom the Greek gods condemned to the underworld, where he must lie below a tree bearing delicious fruit. When he reaches up, the branches also rise, then fall back almost within reach, "tantalizing" him forever. These myths are metaphors for life in a demythologized world, where just below our assumptions of unlimited resources lies an even more fundamental belief — scarcity.

In truth, modernity assumes *scarce* resources — fuel, food, education, power, freedom, knowledge and especially love. These assumptions begin in our monolithic creation myth, the expulsion from Eden, and lie, along with the compensating belief in progress, at the core of all western thought. The Old Testament provides occasional visions of plenitude (manna from Heaven); but these are followed by laws and restrictions, which, when disobeyed, result in expulsion. It is, writes Schwartz, a world "where lying, cheating, stealing, adultery and killing are such tempting responses to scarcity that they must be legislated against."[18]

Biblical stories of fathers and sons are utterly rooted in scarcity assumptions. Isaac cannot bless both of his sons; apparently there isn't enough to go around. Forced to compete for the blessing, they establish a pattern in which the father rejects the loser. Earlier, Jehovah preferred Abel's offering to Cain's. *Even God* doesn't have enough blessing to satisfy everyone. Jealousy, rivalry and murder all follow. This core text of monotheism defines identity as something that is won through competition, at someone else's expense.

Scarcity either imposes sibling rivalry or forces sons to conspire against fathers. It leads to monotheism, hierarchy (God must maintain his uniqueness against other gods) and transcendence, making God inaccessible. With room for only one at the top, sons cannot become their fathers and man cannot become God; an infinite longing is created. Time becomes linear and "progress" achieves mythic value when humanity learns that it can only recover its original abundance in a distant future.

The Protestant Ethic of unending labor grew strongest in Northern Europe and America where men were most at war with the flesh. Why do we work so long and hard, competing rather than cooperating? Clearly, most addictions and neuroses stem from a perceived lack of something that is desperately needed but unavailable, or available at too high a cost. Without scarcity assumptions there would be no generational conflicts, no masters or slaves and no need to invent an "Other."

Scarcity opens a theological quagmire. If there is never enough and *my* prayers are answered, will someone else be deprived? How, *and why* does one prove one's worth? How many children must be sacrificed to a jealous Yahweh? If he is omnipotent, why is he so jealous? Why is Kronos afraid of his children? Why is there never enough time?

Because scarcity is one of modernity's most pervasive and unexamined assumptions, it has the potency of myth. Many indigenous cultures, however, assumed that *abundance* flowed from the other world. Indeed, the reciprocal relations between spirit and matter meant that problems in each world were healed by adjustments in the other. For all of life's tragedies, people were held from birth to death in a web of spirits and ancestors. In this way, the Dagara people still spend most of their time preparing for, doing and recovering from ritual.

The Bushmen still do much "visiting, entertaining, and especially dancing," writes Anthropologist Marshall Sahlins. He argues that as culture evolves, the amount of work per capita increases, while leisure decreases: "The world's most primitive people have few possessions, but they are not poor…Poverty is a social status. As such it is the invention of civilization."[19] Western travelers still report that even amid extreme material poverty, many Third World people are actually *happy*, a word that stems from the same root as "happen."

This notion of abundance is communicated in countless stories. When mythic heroes attained their quests in the other world, they unlocked the secrets of life, which flowed into this world. Places where this breakthrough occurred became sacred, wrote Campbell: "Someone at this point discovered eternity."[20]

Civilization, however, invented *artificial* scarcity by restricting the availability of something that theoretically isn't scarce — sexual gratification. Although most societies do this to some extent, capitalism takes it further. Advertising attaches sexual interest to inaccessible, nonexistent or irrelevant objects and motivates people to work endlessly for rewards that may never come.

Similarly, romantic love is a scarcity mechanism based often on the intensification of the parent-child relationship. It occurs less frequently in tribal societies where the community raises all children, where bonds between child and parents are more casual. Oedipal conflicts may be the primary source of the scarcity dynamics in modern relationships. However, Freud's subjects were middle-class Victorians who lived in nuclear families. By contrast, Sobonfu Somé (another African teacher) writes, "I was almost six years old before I understood that I came out of one particular person's womb, and not *all* of the women in the village who had helped to care for me."[21] She did not assume scarcity.

If assumptions of *emotional* scarcity are based on the nearly exclusive mother/child relationships in modern families, then these dynamics exist in the extreme in America. After World War Two, when young couples left the inner cities for the suburbs, they also left their networks of extended families. With husbands away at the office, isolated suburban mothers had only their children to share their emotional lives. Baby Boomers matured in possibly the most extreme Oedipal conditions in history, expecting all emotional needs to be met from the scarce resources of one person. Such unrealistic demands led to massive disillusionment, and soon the Boomers experienced the highest divorce rates in history.

The more one's erotic energy is bound up in longing for an idealized parental fantasy image, the less he will seek pleasure in those emotional and erotic forms that are actually available. He develops an infinite longing for material goods, food or drugs (literalized Dionysus). All these objectives merely symbolize what he really wants. Others crave power. However, writes Phillip Slater,

> A man hooked on fame or power will never stop striving because there is no way to gratify a desire with a symbol… an emotional long shot that will never pay off. They will work their lives away to achieve a love that is unattainable.[22]

*A man hooked on fame or power will never stop striving…*We are back to the mythic roots of our crisis. Who rises to the top in societies dominated by competition, individualism and artificial scarcity? To pose the question in these terms is to answer it. America, like no nation in history, is led by uninitiated men. These leaders are still boys emotionally (one can see it in their faces) who have been mentored for generations by similar people, like inbred royal families. They subordinate beauty, justice and truth, even sex, to the all-consuming will to power. Like Thebes empty of women, they are disconnected from Woman, *except as they have literalized her into their addictions.* This is why they hate feminine values and fear the threat represented by repressed people. Talk of reconciliation or emotional connection simply confronts them with the proximity of the idealized mother, the great she-dragon, whom they have never served or honored in themselves.

In a world of scarcity, *men rise to power by exploiting the fear of never having enough.* But such men, like Pentheus, are utter slaves of this story, and would rather die, taking everyone with them, than examine the gaping wounds in their own souls. Ultimately, our obsession with materialism indicates a profound *lack* of connection to materiality: the body, and the body of the Earth, the *mater.*

THE MYTH OF MYTHLESSNESS

After centuries of declining faith and increasing rationalism, myth has come to mean mere superstition, or "other people's religions." But even this thinking has mythic characteristics: unconsciously held, universally *unexamined* premises. Robert Jewett and John Lawrence call this the "myth of mythlessness," the belief that modern culture has "transcended mythical forms of thought..."[23]

Our national myth rarely opens paths to the mysteries of the soul. But this is not the same as having no myths at all. Popular entertainment, advertising, education and politics are filled with mythic themes that continually reinforce our beliefs about ourselves, all the more powerfully because we are generally unconscious of them. So, on a more superficial layer — above the older stories of patriarchy, monotheism, progress, growth and scarcity, as well as the archetypal themes that make up the universal, "hard-wired" nature of all humanity — we find *the story that says that we have no stories.* All of these myths provide the general background to the American story.

AMERICAN MYTHS

Almost every modern person has internalized this five thousand-year-old heritage. In addition, white Americans incorporate the myth of innocence. For all their inadequacies, our institutions still teach that individualism, consumerism, mobility and competition, and underneath, the deeper legacy of Puritanism, define us as Americans. Above all, the media have replaced the ancient priests and storytellers who told us who we are. They regularly instruct us that we are a nation with no shadow, existing, like Christ, to enlighten and redeem the world.

Our essence, we are told, is free enterprise. Entering the world as blank slates, we make our own destiny on our own merits. We assume that everyone should, and does, have equal access to the resources needed to become anything they want to be. We believe that the gods (or forefathers) have left us the means, the sacred free market, to succeed. As a result, we believe that we live in an affluent society, the best in the world, that has resolved old problems, and that we are *meant* to do this. Curiously, this collectivity of free and purposeless libertarians thinks of itself as a nation that exists for the *purpose* of spreading those freedoms everywhere.

However, even temporary detachment from the myth quickly reveals that those rights and freedoms have rarely been available to most of us, that they were achieved only after decades of sacrifice, and that we have recently lost many of them. But the myth of innocence remains so pervasive that even in those rare moments when the nation confronts bare reality, we quickly re-veil our eyes. Recall the backlash refrain of the 1960s: *My country, right or wrong!* Americans have developed a unique and massive cognitive dissonance; if facts contradict the story, then it is *the facts* that change. Our priesthood of intellectuals continually frame information to keep it consistent with the story. The "liberal establishment" has an essentially religious function, like the Inquisition: preventing, or at least marginalizing, heresy.

THE CULT OF THE CHILD

Emerson wrote that nineteenth-century America was a country of young men. A young country symbolized new beginnings. Twentieth-century

America emphasized *looking* young, even as parents sacrificed everything to improve their children's lives and panicked over accusations of child abuse. Eventually, as popular culture promoted youthfulness as the highest standard for behavior and appearance, the differences between adults and children began to disappear. The media celebrated adults, including politicians, who refused to grow up.

Yet earlier, Benjamin Franklin had announced the ascendancy of the child-eater Kronos ("Time is money"). In America capitalism and violence ground down the lives of millions of *actual* children. By the twenty-first century, children joined minorities (and especially the children *of* minorities) as scapegoats for a mad society.

The *image* of the child represents Lost Paradise. What we say and believe about children and how we "sacrifice" for them says more about ourselves than about them. When the facts (how we actually treat them) so sharply contradict the narrative, we must conclude that America's cult of the child is not really about actual children, but about idealized images that help to cover up the disgraceful reality.

EXCEPTIONALISM (1)

Americans are unique in many ways. We are a nation of *firsts:* the first modern democracy, the first with individual freedoms and the first nation of immigrants. Other nations' identities come from common ancestry; one cannot become un-English or un-Japanese. Because of its diversity, "American" is more an ideological commitment than a matter of birth. To be considered un-American, one must reject American *values,* and few of us do. Despite occasional disillusionment, we are convinced that ours is the best system, that it is exportable to the rest of the world and that all peoples may someday arise out of darkness and ignorance to be like us.

It is an eternal mystery, however, that the world's most materialistic society, where "lifestyles" were invented, where the predatory imagination reached its apogee, also claims to be the most religious country in Christendom. Americans exhibit high acceptance of literal belief and church attendance. Ninety-four percent express faith in God, compared to seventy percent of the British. Only two percent are atheists, compared to nineteen percent in France. Over fifty percent claim that God is the guiding force of American democracy. Forty percent say that reading the Bible is very important to them, and seventy-five percent believe that it says, "God helps those who help themselves" (it doesn't).

Shared belief in personal responsibility, independent initiative, equality of opportunity and positive thinking equals optimism. As recently as 1996, seventy-five percent of us expected to improve our standard of living, when only forty percent of Europeans did. We believe that our system offers the best opportunity to fulfill our dreams. While people in other countries may be *nationalists*, we are *patriots*.

EXCEPTIONALISM (2)

But aren't those dreams equal part nightmare? Sociologist Seymour Lipset, a good liberal, reveals a stunning naiveté: "America has been a universalistic culture, slavery and the black situation apart."[24] Indeed. Howard Zinn responds, "There is not a country in world history in which racism has been more important, for so long."[25] In reality, slavery, genocide and "free" land created the economic foundations for the optimism and idealism that distinguish America from other countries. Without these protracted, unresolved (and unmourned) crimes there would be no affluence, no optimism and no innocence in America. And no white privilege.

Anyone using statistics to argue about America is lost in a dream. Since most polls question only "likely voters" on landline phones, they ignore poor people, minorities and young people and are invariably skewed toward the rosier and more conventional picture favored by older, white Americans. But this confusion provides us with a metaphor for one aspect of exceptionalism: "white thinking." *Privilege* is utterly invisible to most whites and perfectly, constantly, daily, painfully obvious to almost all minorities. An inconsequential example makes my point: we speak of "African-Americans," but never of "Euro-Americans." Language, more than law, reveals who is part of the *polis* and who isn't.

Privilege is the advantage of having views that define the norm for others. It allows one to view oneself as an *individual*, to not think of himself as any color at all. Tim Wise writes, "To even say that our group status is irrelevant…is to suggest that one has enjoyed the privilege of experiencing the world that way…"[26] It allows half of all whites to believe that blacks enjoy economic parity with them, sixty-one percent to say the average black has equal *or better* access to health care than the average white, and eighty-five percent to say that blacks have just as good a chance to get any housing they can afford, *despite the contrary views* held by the great majority of black people.[27] This means that whites are privileged to say to blacks, in effect, "I know your reality better than you do."

Privilege allows "underprivileged" whites to favor cultural advantages over economic interests, to identify as white rather than as poor. Since it offers them membership in the *polis* (even if they can't afford to live there), it creates a vicious cycle that confuses responsibility with guilt. Arguing, "My ancestors didn't own slaves," whites can believe, "I'm not guilty, so I don't have to do anything about the situation." Rejecting guilt, they also reject the responsibility to understand how slavery's legacy offers them privilege. Keeping them from *thinking about privilege,* it is the very essence of American innocence.

It allows one to *not* have to think about race every day, *not* be perceived as hyper-sexual, *not* be racially profiled, *not* assume when driving through certain areas that one will be pulled over by an officer inquiring as to one's intent, *not* be viewed with suspicion when shopping, *not* be unfairly treated when buying a home, *not* have to work twice as hard to prove oneself, or *not* be denied job interviews. It is the freedom to avoid being stigmatized by the actions of others with the same skin color. It allows white politicians and white-collar professionals to *not* have to transcend racial stereotypes.

Privilege provides a place in the social hierarchy and a belief in upward mobility for whites, who can know who they are because, as un-hyphenated Americans, they are *not* Other. But to define ourselves this way, we must periodically cleanse the *polis* by isolating or rejecting the impure. Without our paranoid imagination, we wouldn't tolerate periodic inquisitions running from Salem, the Red Scare of 1919 and McCarthyism to our post-9/11 terror anxieties and demonizing of immigrants.

I offer the following statistics and comparisons not out of gratuitous America-bashing, but to put the yawning gap between myth and reality into some perspective. Note two things: first, as I mentioned above, the conservative bias of most polls, and second, that these numbers are from around 2007, *prior* to the current depression.

We have over two million prisoners, more than in any other country except China (which has four times our population), and the criminal justice system supervises over *seven* million. With five percent of the world's population, we have twenty-two percent of its prisoners. One hundred and forty thousand Americans are serving life sentences. Of these, 7,000 were juveniles at the time of the crime. Texas alone has executed over 400 prisoners since capital punishment was reinstated.

Consequently, we also have over a million lawyers, the highest in the world in both number and per capita. More lawyers leads to the world's highest divorce rates. Americans who are very religious divorce less than the rest of us, but even they divorce more than Europeans. An American child is more likely to see his married parents break up than is a child of *unmarried* parents in Sweden. American individualism leads to early sexual intercourse compared to Europe. But greater religiosity and restricted access to sex education undermine the use of birth control. The result: a quarter of teenage girls in the U.S. have sexually transmitted diseases, and our teen pregnancy rate is twice that of Europe. Indeed, states whose residents have more conservative religious beliefs tend to have higher teenage birthrates. This in turn leads to the world's highest rate of single parent families.

This religiosity counters our official dogma of separation of church and state. Almost half of voters (including a third of college graduates) believe in the literal creation story. Twenty-five percent want it required teaching in schools. One in four Texas public school *biology* teachers believe that humans and dinosaurs lived on Earth at the same time. Forty percent of Americans believe the world will end with the battle of Armageddon. Sixty-eight percent *(including fifty-five percent of those who hold post-graduate degrees)* believe in the Devil. Sixty-two percent won't vote for an atheist for president.

While abortion and gay rights are non-issues in most parts of Europe, Puritanism still has an iron grip upon American attitudes toward pleasure. Although we engage in more premarital sex, we are far more likely to condemn it. One in four American men judges it as "always wrong," more than three times the rate of the British.

Despite such emotionally laden issues, both civic awareness and participation continue to decline. We vote in lower percentages than in any other democracy. *Eighty million eligible voters (equal to the population of Germany) stayed home in November 2008.* Of those ineligible to vote, five million have been disenfranchised over felony convictions.

America is seventeenth in the world in high school graduation rates and 49th in literacy. Over forty million adults are illiterate and another 50 million read at fourth or fifth grade level. One of four teenagers drops out of high school, and of those who graduate, one of four has the equivalent or less of an eighth grade education. Seventy percent need remedial courses upon entering community college. Forty-two percent of college graduates never read a book after they finish school.

How "dumbed-down" are we? Over half of us believe the Constitution establishes a Christian nation. One third think the press has too much freedom, and would deny freedom of worship to any group that the majority considers "extreme." Half of us fail basic civics tests, and *elected officials* score even worse. Seventy percent of us cannot name our senators or congressman. Seventy-five percent of Oklahoma high school students cannot name our first president. In 2009, twenty-one percent of New Jersey *voters* either thought that Barack Obama is the Anti-Christ or were not sure. Twenty percent believe the sun revolves around the earth. Forty percent, including most Republicans, don't believe in Evolution. Only forty percent can name more than four of the Ten Commandments. During the health care debates of 2009, thirty-nine percent wanted the government to "stay out of Medicare," and fifteen percent were not sure. *Twelve percent of American adults believe Joan of Arc was Noah's wife.*

Ignorance is a major component of innocence, and television (a third of which is advertising) functions to keep it that way. American children view 20,000 commercials a year. The generations raised on TV have been the first to be less well informed than their elders. A study of the Gulf War found that the more TV Americans watched, the less they knew. But conventional education is no answer: the more educated we are, the more likely we are to support America's wars. Millions completely misunderstand common political labels. Nineteen percent think that conservatives oppose cutting taxes. *In 2005, twelve million adults considered George Bush a liberal.* In 2009, fifty-seven percent thought the world was getting warmer, down from seventy-seven percent in 2006.

Our ignorance is both cause and result of our unique political system. The Senate reflects nineteenth century demographics that vastly under-represent the interests of minorities, liberals and cities. Since only forty-one "no" votes kill a bill with a filibuster, the eleven percent of Americans living in the least populated states have enough power to do that, even if eighty-nine percent favor the bill. This is no mistake. Fearing "mob rule," the Founders deliberately designed the voting system, with its the two-tiered legislature and "winner take all" Electoral College, to limit participation. Because of it, presidential candidates have twice won 500,000 more votes than their opponents but lost elections.

A third of American adults are not registered to vote because ours is a "self-initiated" registration system that puts the burden exclusively on the voter. In contrast, most democracies have "state-initiated" voter registration systems. And because of our federal system, even when Congress passes laws to make registration easier, individual states often refuse to comply. Most Americans still vote on a Tuesday (often in cold weather), rather than on both days of a weekend, as they do in Europe. The requirement to spend many hours in line away from work is essentially a poll tax that effectively prevents many from voting. As a result, *138 countries have higher voting rates.* This creates a vicious cycle: low turnout by working people results in two major political parties that are *each* more conservative than the population.

We twist in the storm of Americanism's contradictory values: competitive individualism and paranoid conformism; ideals of equality with subtexts of exclusion; and official church-state separation with the legislation of morality. These features come together in a truly exceptional cult of the flag. We have Flag Day, flag etiquette and a uniquely violent national anthem dedicated to the flag that we sing, curiously, at sporting events. Officially, states the U.S. Code, "The flag... is considered a living thing."[28] Twenty-seven states require school children to salute it daily. All fifty state legislatures have urged Congress to pass a constitutional amendment criminalizing defacing of it. Indeed, we consider insults to the flag as rejection of our entitlement to innocence, the ultimate "un-American" gesture.

And the ultimate American statement was made by Ben Franklin, not Jesus: "God helps those who help themselves." The myth of the opportunist meets Puritanism to form another exceptional belief. Worldly success is evidence of our elect status, and the poor have no one to blame but themselves. Prior to the economic meltdown of 2008, four million children were suffering merely because they were living with unemployed parents. Yet *six out of seven of us believe that people fail because of their own shortcomings*, not because of social conditions.[29]

We are the *only* industrialized country without a national health care system and the only one that doesn't guarantee paid maternity leave. America is not among the sixty-five countries that offer paid paternity leave, the 145 countries that mandate paid sick leave, the 134 countries that limit the length of the workweek, or the 137 countries that have paid vacation laws. Half of working Americans receive less than a week of paid vacation, a quarter have *no* paid vacation or holidays, and nearly half of all private sector workers have no paid sick days. We are 22nd in child poverty, 42nd in life expectancy, first in depression and second to the worst in the newborn death rate.

Nevertheless, due to our irrational fears of "socialized medicine," we have the world's costliest healthcare, equal to fifteen percent of our GDP, which is twice that of Britain. Forty-five thousand Americans die every year due to lack of health insurance. Medical error (200,000 deaths per year) ranks as the country's eighth leading cause of death, more deadly than breast cancer or highway accidents. We account for fifty percent of the world's prescription (legal) drug budget. Despite our strict (illegal) drug laws, we lead the world in marijuana and cocaine use. One in five of our four-year-olds is obese. We are 39th in the world in environmental performance.

America is also 67th in percentage of women in government, and one of only a handful of democratic nations that deny equal rights to women.

We are particularly ignorant on this issue. In 2001 *ninety-six percent* of U.S. adults believed that male and female citizens should have equal rights. However, seventy-two percent mistakenly assumed that the Constitution already includes such a guarantee.

The average American believes that foreign aid makes up twenty-four per cent of the federal budget. It actually consumes about one per cent, and we are 22nd in proportion of GDP devoted to it. Indeed, over half goes to a few client states in the Mid-East. While nearly seventy percent of Europeans want their governments to give more aid to poor nations, nearly half of Americans claim that rich nations are already giving too much.

Whether by choice or by necessity, we labor unceasingly. On average, Americans work *nine weeks* longer per year than Europeans. Our vacations average two weeks, compared to five to six weeks in Europe. Forty-three percent of us did not take a single week off in 2007, and only fourteen percent will take a vacation of two weeks or more this year. We spend forty percent less time with our children than we did in 1965. The American Dream emphasizes independence; yet only one working American in thirteen is self-employed, compared to one in eight in Western Europe. We relax only when we have acquired the symbols of redemption. Even then, we keep working.

One reason we work so hard is to afford our cars, which we have far more of in both total and per capita than other countries. Indeed, the average household has more cars than drivers. America is responsible for nearly half of the greenhouse gases emitted by automobiles globally, even though our vehicles make up just thirty percent of cars in use. We drive ten hours per week, parking those cars next to houses that average more than twice the size of European homes.

Americans are taxed at far lower rates than other developed nations. Consequently, we receive fewer social services, and economic inequality is the highest of all democracies. One cause of this situation is the tax code, which taxes ordinary income at up to thirty-five percent. The very rich, however, who receive most of their money from capital gains and stock gains ("unearned income"), pay only fifteen percent.

Average income (and employment) figures are meaningless: one percent of Americans own forty percent of the wealth and earn a fifth of the income, while the bottom fifty percent earn thirteen percent. Over twenty-five million households have no bank accounts. Most elders are well off, but twelve percent (again, the industrialized world's highest percentage) remain impoverished, even after Social Security.

Youths, however, are our poorest age group, because *America spends fewer public resources on children than any industrialized nation.* Where it does spend money on children is in the prisons: the U.S. is one of only two countries that refuses to sign the U.N. Convention on the Rights of the Child, because that document bans sentencing children to life imprisonment. Over two thousand American children are serving such a sentence. America, virtually alone in the world, executes non-adults. And despite the huge incarceration rate, we don't protect our young. Nearly half the children in the country were assaulted at least once in the past year; nearly one-quarter were victimized by robbery, vandalism or theft; and one in sixteen were sexually assaulted.

Inequitable taxation, perpetual war and Puritan condemnation of poverty leave little for the poor. Here we return to mythic issues: America *needs* the poor. A population of Others is absolutely crucial to perpetuating the myth of innocence. As long as *they* threaten *my* job, and as long as I desire the symbols that substitute for a genuine erotic life, I will work unceasingly.

Our compliant workforce and lack of progressive political parties is another facet of American exceptionalism. While other peoples perceived worker agitation as straightforward response to inequity, only Americans saw communists as so absolutely evil, such pollution of our innocence, that we created a Committee on *Un-American Activities.* Only Americans have preferred to be "better dead than red."

Systematic manufacture of consent based on terror of the Other is the ultimate meaning of American exceptionalism. The U.S. is the only nation that convinces victims of its own excesses (economically struggling white people) that they share in its bounty and over-taxes them to pay its imperial expenses. "How skillful," writes Zinn, "to tax the middle class to pay for the relief of the poor, building resentment on top of humiliation!"[30] An efficient system of control, a brainwashing under freedom, has flourished like nowhere else. It combines relatively free speech and press with patriotic indoctrination and marginalization of alternative voices, leaving the impression that society is really open. The system distributes just enough wealth to limit dissent, while it heightens anxiety, isolates people and turns them toward symbols that create loyalty.

The media, writes Chomsky, functions "to keep people from understanding the world."[31] By limiting debate to those who never challenge the assumptions of innocence and benevolence, it maintains the illusion that we all share a common interest. When the *boundaries* of acceptable thought are clear, debate can be permitted. But in this context, the "loyal opposition" legitimizes these unspoken limits by their very presence. *The system exists precisely because of our traditional freedom of expression.*

A 1920s public relations manual (titled *Propaganda*) acknowledges, "… manipulation of the organized habits and opinions of the masses is a central feature of a democratic system."[32] Former army officer Stan Goff writes that this "perception management" functions primarily to destroy our natural empathy for others, and our reluctance to stomach extreme violence.[33]

The media also continually reinforce a subtle characteristic of American innocent liberalism. This is the assumption that getting rid of the worst *individual* perpetrators (from Oswald to Nixon to Bush), rather than changing individual consciousness and public institutions, solves our problems. And it keeps us from seeing patterns that are obvious to others.

One of those patterns is championing human rights and presenting America as an ideal for other nations to emulate while persistently *exempting* ourselves from the most basic, common standards of decency. Abu Ghraib and Guantanamo are merely the latest examples. Perhaps only we Americans can regularly hear of atrocities, torture and bombing of civilians done in our name and yet remain convinced of our innocence and non-complicity. Such "constantly renewed ethical virginity," writes Ella Shohat, thrives "only in the magic kingdom of amnesia."[34]

Such criticism actually reflects a tribal perspective. Mass society as we know it is barely three centuries old. For most of history, humanity lived in small communities in which individuals knew everyone else and experienced their relationships within a mythic and ritual framework. In a sense, human nature has not had time to adjust to the strife and alienation of modernity. It is precisely this disconnect that advertising and nationalist propaganda manipulate. Indigenous people, by contrast, have no myths of innocence. Elites may *coerce* their consent, but they cannot manufacture it.

What is exceptional is this combination of subtle repression of dissent and willful ignorance. We *want* to believe our stories. Only in America do these gaps exist between national mythology and domination, between greed of the elite and naiveté of the people, between fathers who eat their children and youth who freely offer themselves up. Cornel West writes, "No other democratic nation revels so blatantly in such self-deceptive innocence, such self-paralyzing reluctance to confront the night-side of its own history."[35]

We are similarly ignorant about one of our most fundamental values: social mobility, or the opportunity to get ahead. The likelihood of advancing in social class has decreased significantly since the 1980s. But fifty-six percent of those *blue-collar men who correctly perceived Bush's 2003 tax cuts as favoring the rich* still supported them.[36] The myth of the self-made man is as deeply engrained as our wild, naïve optimism; in 2000, nineteen percent believed they would "soon" be in the top one percent income bracket, and *another* nineteen percent thought they *already were*. Two-thirds expect to have to pay the estate tax one day (only two percent will).

But when our assumptions of social mobility are revealed as fiction, the hero encounters his opposite — *the victim* — within himself, and we become what we really are (except for Nazi Germany), the most violent people in history. American crime is a natural by-product of our values, an alternative means of social mobility in a society where "anything goes" in the pursuit of success. "America," says mythologist Glen Slater, "has little imagination for loss and failure. It only knows how to move forward." We go ballistic when we can only imagine moving forward and that movement is blocked. Then guns become the purest expression of controlling one's fate. As such, they are "the dark epitome of the self-made way of life."[37] We as a people may well dream bigger dreams than other peoples. With great possibilities, however, come great risks. Gaps between aspiration and reality — the *lost* dream — are also far higher here than anywhere else. When we don't meet our expectations of success, when that gap gets too wide, violence often becomes the only option, the expression of a fantasy of ultimate individualism and control. In this sense, the Mafia is more American then Sicilian, and the lone, mass killer (almost all of whom have been white, middle class men with no criminal background) is an expression of social mobility gone bad.

Our frontier myths and terror of the Other prevent the gun-control legislation common in most countries. Forty percent of American adults own 260 million legal and 25 million illegal firearms. Twenty-four percent of us believe that "it is acceptable to use violence to get what we want."[38] We suffer 15,000 gun murders, 18,000 gun suicides and 1,500 "accidental" gun deaths per year. America's adult murder rate is seven times higher and its teen murder rate *twelve* times higher than in Britain, France, Italy, Australia, Canada and Germany. These nations together have 20 million teenagers; in 1990 a total of 300 were murdered. That same year, of America's 17 million teens, 3,000 were murdered, while thirty of Japan's ten million teens were murdered, a rate *one-fiftieth* of ours.[39] Slater concludes that gun violence "keeps the national psyche in a holding pattern, preventing it from a more conscious encounter with more soul-wrenching issues."

In response to such violence, America kills criminals to show that killing is wrong. However, the impulse to scapegoat the Other clashes with the temptation to deny our darkness. Executions, though common, are *private* affairs; the state no longer displays the grizzly results publicly (as commonly happened up to the nineteenth century). The result is that capital punishment has no deterrent effect.

Meanwhile, constant, massive, *fictional* death in film and TV reduces the emotional impact of actual death. By age eighteen, an American will have seen 18,000 virtual murders. "Harmless violence where no one gets hurt," writes Hillman, "breeds innocence...the innocent American is the violent American."[40]

History, too, has conspired. No one alive can recall the Civil War, and there are no film records of its carnage. There had been no warfare on American continental soil for well over a century until the recent terrorist acts. The U.S. has never suffered the full consequences of defeat. It lost comparatively few soldiers and fewer than 2,000 civilian war deaths during the twentieth century. Except for the World War II generation, we have little memory of loss comparable to other countries. Consequently, America is one of the few nations in which public figures glorify the military.

Given our beliefs about using force, it follows that we rarely object to externalizing our violence. *The U.S. spends more money on arms than the rest of the world combined.* Calculated accurately, annual military expenditures typically exceed $1.2 trillion, over half of the federal budget.[41] What are these beliefs? Forty-two percent of us (compared to eleven percent of Europeans) strongly agree that, "under some conditions, war is necessary to obtain justice." Only forty-six percent of us believe that bombing and other attacks intentionally aimed at civilians are never justified. Bullets and bombs: we are talking about Apollonian (and therefore often emotionless) violence at a distance, where we remain insulated from the human consequences. Already, forty years ago, Philip Slater identified the pattern: "America has developed more elaborate, complex, and grotesque techniques for exterminating people at a distance than any nation in the history of the world...perhaps the distance itself carries special meaning."[42]

What is extraordinary about us, writes Richard Hofstadter, is "our ability to believe that we are a peace-loving and law-abiding people."[43] The myth of innocence allows us to perpetrate mass destruction while simultaneously denying death's reality.

THE DENIAL OF DEATH
Ernest Becker asked,

> What are we to make of a creation in which the routine
> activity is for organisms to be tearing others apart... pushing
> the pulp greedily down the gullet with delight, incorporating
> its essence...and then excreting with foul stench and gasses
> the residue. Everyone reaching out to incorporate others who
> are edible to him.[44]

He argued that we construct all our myths and religions from the need to deny this fundamental anxiety. Humans must "shrink from being fully alive," because confronting the truth of mortality results in madness.[45]

This is the background to another essential American myth. Despite its religiosity and its violence, or perhaps *because* of this weird juxtaposition, America denies death more than any other society. Arnold Toynbee joked that death was "un-American," an infringement on the right to *pursue* happiness. Americans *do* things; we are masters of our fates who expect perpetual progress. To us, death represents failure.

We commonly exclude children from discussion of such a morbid subject. Hoping to repress the anxieties that arise around the terminally ill, relatives maintain the fiction of probable recovery as long as possible. Then they rush the patient to the hospital, frequently against his or her will. Doctors, rather than ministers, preside over the deathbed. They typically sedate the patient, depriving both children and the patient from consciously confronting death. Ironically, the final experience of the American "self-made man" is often complete passivity. And he usually dies alone.

Then the powerful funeral industry takes over. Many hospitals release corpses *only* to licensed funeral directors, who usually embalm the corpse. Neither law nor religion nor sanitation requires this, and *nowhere but in North America is it widely done.* Embalming insulates mourners from the process of decomposition but also minimizes cathartic expressions of grief.

The funeral director, wrote Jessica Mitford, orchestrates "a well-oiled performance in which the concept of *death* has played no part…"[46] Euphemisms abound: "the deceased" sleeps peacefully; he has "passed on" or "gone to Jesus." Mourners commonly receive only three days off before being required to return to work. The mysterious, initiatory space closes abruptly and too soon for authentic resolution. A veil that had been lifted drops.

Native Americans, with their integrated communal life, didn't have to protect and preserve an artificial sense of personal identity. Vine Deloria argued that they generally produced people unafraid of death.[47] By denying death, however, Americans also ensure that they will carry great loads of unexpressed grief. Somé observes:

> A non-Westerner arriving in this country for the first time is struck by how… (Americans) pride themselves for not showing how they feel about anything… People who do not know how to weep together are people who cannot laugh together.[48]

This succinct, tribal definition of alienation brings us back to the loss of the Dionysian experience. If we can neither grieve nor tolerate the vision of the dark goddess and her bloody, dismembered son, then we cannot experience ecstasy either. We tolerate pale substitutes: romance novels, horror movies (with characters who *refuse to die*), the spectacles of popular music and sports, Sunday church and happy endings. We learn early to emphasize the light ("lite") and exclude the dark.

It follows that we are fascinated with violence. Death's repressed energy re-emerges in *images*. As suppression of sex creates pornography, American attitudes toward death result in what some have called "necrography:" highly sensationalistic, electronic mayhem. This substitute gratification allows us to meet death and remain unharmed; thrill and pseudo-terror replace grief.

Elizabeth Kubler-Ross, however, wrote that our denial of death "has only increased our anxiety and contributed to our… aggressiveness — to kill in order to avoid…facing of our own death."[49] How does this happen? Subject to vast, impersonal, forces impacting us from remote, Apollonic distances (government, corporations, media, advertising, noise, junk phone calls), we may refrain from exploding in *personal* violence. By tolerating long-distance violence against the Third World, however, we displace our rage upon the Other in the same way we've received it, and we retain our sense of innocence.

This is nothing new. America was characterized from the start by extreme violence. It was present in the "idea" of America: not the abstract ideals of the founding fathers, but the projection of darkness onto the Other in the demythologized world of the seventeenth century. By the Industrial

Revolution, Americans had been slaughtering Indians and enslaving Africans for two centuries. Technology certainly amplified alienation. But as a seed of depression and long-distance violence, it fell on fertile soil that had been well prepared.

The final factor is TV, where news has become almost indistinguishable from entertainment. On one hand, it abets our longing to remain sheltered from the world and our impact upon it. "We are so desperate for this," writes Ventura, that we are willing to accept ignorance as a substitute for innocence."[50] On the other hand, even as programming perpetuates fear of crime and terrorism, it desensitizes us to the *actual* effects of violence. We innocently observe and quickly forget. But the body remembers.

Never having confronted either our complicity or our own suffering, we *must find a way to see them.* We are so abstracted from experience that we don't care whether death occurs on a seven-inch game-boy or on a Palestinian street. The only nation to use atomic weapons also invented napalm, cluster bombs and "anti-personnel" mines (and refuses to ban them). The nation that exports much of its electronic mayhem (American movies account for eighty percent of global box office revenue) and has more handguns than citizens is shocked — *shocked!* — each time a teenager massacres his schoolmates.

To paraphrase Mexican poet Octavio Paz: a culture that begins by denying death will end by denying life. It desperately needs someone to save it, to distract it from the black hole of death, and to vanquish, rather than to understand, the darkness. Such a nation needs heroes.

A Gallery of Heroes

Heroes are ideal figures or role models: the rugged, capitalist individualist; the lone gunfighter; the plucky "Horatio Alger" lad; the soldier or firefighter who dies protecting his buddies; the detective; the communist-hunting "G-man;" the athlete; the comic book superhero; and the rock star. He is such a fundamental actor in our mythology, yet who can actually define him? He completes the puzzle of American exceptionalism. Without understanding him, we can't fully grasp our stubborn resistance to change.

THE MYTHIC HERO AND THE TRAGIC HERO

Like the sun, the hero descends into the underworld and rises victorious. The key ideas of solar mythology are transcendence, freedom, growth, going beyond the known. This mythology focuses on the individual who differentiates himself from the collective. From Marduk and Apollo to Saint George, Beowulf and the hero of *Jaws,* he vanquishes the dragon or serpent that represents chaos, ignorance, the unconscious and the feminine. Light (as awareness) triumphs over darkness. The theme is so universal that archetypal expectations often color our memory of actual history. European legends that developed generations after the deaths of many historical figures have assigned them miraculous births, journeys to the underworld and the conquest of dragons. Forgetting their actual biographies, we replace them with mythic events, because *we need to see* these archetypal themes projected out into story.

Hero worship is connected to the ancient Greek reverence for the dead. Heroes were exceptionally powerful, semi-divine men of past ages who performed famous acts of valor that began or perpetuated noble families, established cities or furthered cultural progress. Their graves were sacred because their relics could heal, and they were more accessible than the distant and uncaring gods. Later, this function was taken over by the Christian saints.

Heroes lived by codes that ignored conventional morality. They took what they wanted, and poets praised them for their boldness, regardless of the consequences. Their greatest desire was to defeat death, not through spiritual enlightenment, but by achieving *kleos* (fame) or *timé* (honor). An heroic death and the singing of one's tales by future bards were preferable to a life lived without honor. Both Hector and Achilles died young, confidant that they had achieved victory over death. Three thousand years later, we still read of them; they live continually in our *imagination.*

The greatest heroes, such as Achilles, had some divine blood. Needleman writes that this "juxtaposition of the eternal and the finite" gives their tales a "… poignancy and mystery. And…their haunting sense of reality."[51] Most died tragically. Yet their lives hint at initiatory ritual. Psychologically, the hero represents the extroverted, outward arc of life's first half: productivity, growth, achievement, ego. This psychic figure must die, however, to begin the *inward* arc of the second half of life. In stories he is willing to die for fame. In doing so, he regenerates his community and releases the vital energies that feed the universe. But, like Odysseus, he becomes a hero in this sense only by having transformed himself and *returning.*

Tragic drama used the old legends of familiar mythic heroes as the stock themes upon which contemporary issues were played out. The tragic hero, or *prot-agonist,* contended with his *ant-agonist* in the *agon,* or ritual contest of the great principles and paradoxes of civic life. Classicists speak of the fatal flaw *(hamartia)* that brings the tragic hero down. But this is not a moral quality. The hero, wrote classicist Moses Haddas, "has pushed back the horizons of what is possible..." He is no saint; indeed, he is deeply flawed, and "... his flaws are inherent in and inseparable from the virtues which enable him to become a hero."[52] One discovered his purpose by confronting his wounds. The tragic hero often died happily in pursuing that purpose.

When (in most cases) a man, especially a *great* man of extreme character, is defeated by powers he can't control or understand, then we have tragedy. Pentheus is such an extreme individual. His unreasonable passion leads to his dying from boy into "man of suffering." When the hero dies, something else — the wisdom of experience — may be born. He fails grandly, by the degree to which his nature leads him to confront life's possibilities. In rare cases, such as in the *Oresteia,* the hero lived and prospered because he had suffered into a greater awareness. Because he could change, the world itself could change.

Audiences understood that such personal, even narcissistic suffering was ultimately for something greater. The hero appeared at those moments of crisis in a culture when the energy flow between macrocosm and microcosm had ceased. Striving and dying into something greater, he was a model for the human potential. The audience also understood that Dionysus stood outside this tradition, subverting everything that Pentheus represented. Still, the heroes suffered for us, the community, and Nietzsche paradoxically saw the suffering god as the model for all tragic heroes. He suggested that they were all "masks of Dionysus."[53]

THE MONOMYTHIC HERO AND THE FEMININE

A hero ventures forth from his familiar world to answer a call. He encounters a liminal, magical world of great challenges. He returns transfigured, dead to his old self and able to bestow boons and blessings upon his community. He teaches the lesson of renewal through suffering. The pattern of *separation-initiation-return* exactly replicates the three stages of initiation. To Joseph Campbell, it was so fundamental to all mythologies that he described it as the *monomyth,* the archetypal narrative structure that arose from the soul everywhere. The hero's quest was a metaphor for both the *inner* journey as well as the universe's grand macrocosmic cycles, both of which required some sort of periodic death. The greatest of these heroes, the "world redeemers," returned knowing that "I and the father are one."[54]

The prize he wins is often a woman, who symbolizes a previously unknown part of his own nature, " the image of his destiny."[55] Often, however, his adversary is a witch or goddess. We can interpret such stories as patriarchy's conquest of matriarchal culture. This is dualistic and unavoidably gendered language. Heroes, however, embody the archetypal masculine in *everyone.* Victory over the serpent also signifies individual consciousness gaining mastery over collective and unconscious patterns of behavior. The conflict is not between good and evil, but between ignorance and awareness.

Recall that "evil" is a poor translation of the Aramaic "unripe." The hero doesn't overcome evil, not even an evil part of himself, but his own "unripeness." This is the meaning of the trials Hera sets for Heracles: he must suffer to inhabit the meaning of his name, "Glory of Hera." Persecuting him, she is really challenging him to rise to his potential. Indeed, many heroes (such as Odysseus and Theseus) can't negotiate the terrifying descent into the unconscious without *aid* from the feminine. Woman may be temptress, combatant, or devouring mother, but she is always a necessary part of the story. Every hero must come to terms with the deeper regions of his soul and the soul of the world, both of which culture imagines as feminine.

When, however, men began to imagine the feminine as *evil,* they broke the ancient cycle, and found themselves in a desiccated, desacralized world. "When the gods have fled," says Hillman, "the Hero serves only the Ego."[56] In the solar mythology of uninitiated men he stands over and against nature, conquering and controlling it, burning it down. Solar mythology ultimately justifies male supremacy.

Instead of returning to share his boon, blessed by his contact with the Great Mother, the hero is now separate from the world, entering it only to save it or to justify himself to his remote father. This is critical; the archetypal hero emerges out of community and returns to it, bringing it a greater imagination of itself. If he has no community, the fount of material, relational embededness, then he is no hero in this sense. He becomes the toxic mimic of the hero, a cult figure of celebrity. We live vicariously through such figures. Yet, since they perpetually disappoint us, our admiration is matched only by our elation when they fall from grace.

Modernity minimizes the initiatory elements and maximizes the literal violence. Its one-dimensional heroes require demonized opposition and personifications of evil.

THE AMERICAN HERO

Consider John Wayne in five of his best-known films: *Sands of Iwo Jima, Red River, The Searchers, She Wore A Yellow Ribbon,* and *The Horse Soldiers.* His characters and literally dozens of other film, TV and comic book heroes are widowed, unrequited in love, divorced or loners who reject any erotic relationships. Such characters symbolize the man who has failed or never even attempted the initiatory confrontation with the feminine depths of his soul. He carries a sense of danger that is undeniably attractive. Through him, we live out our own longing for that initiatory death, which he approaches literally. Like the terrorist/martyr, writes Robin Morgan, "... he seeks (or risks) exalted annihilation...threatens (or promises) the same... magnetizes us as an avatar of power."[57]

This type of hero embodies the myth of violent redemption. Watching him, we are being mythically instructed, because he appeals to the unconscious mind. *Mythic* violence can evoke symbolic death and renewal. But stories in a demythologized world convey only the sociological level of the hero myth. This brings us back to innocence. This hero *never* initiates the mayhem (although once aroused, he reluctantly gives it back many-fold). He does not strike first because, above all, he embodies the Puritan quality of self-control, which proves his superior character. And since his adversaries *lack* self-control, they embody the Dionysian Other. Then, whether he is an imperfect, wounded parody, a complicated anti-hero or even a hyper-sexy female heroine, he remains innocent. Because he has little awareness of his own darkness, he cannot symbolize genuine renewal.

The cult of celebrity has further cheapened the hero archetype. For at least four generations, we have associated fictional characters (effortlessly achieving the impossible) with the actors who *portray* them. Now, few of us can distinguish between genuine heroes and fictional ones. We perceive little difference between Sylvester Stallone and Rambo, or between Arnold Schwartzenegger and the vigilantes he portrayed. We love them for being who they are, not for what they have done. In Daniel Boorstin's phrase, a celebrity is *"a person who is known for his well-knownness."*[58] The Hero was distinguished by what he had achieved; he had created himself. Celebrities are known for their personalities and distinguished by their images, which are created by the media. Ronald Reagan in particular was an expert at portraying derived values rather than anything heroic that he himself had achieved. He was so persuasive precisely because he could barely distinguish his life from his role. As President, writes Joel Kovel, he "played Ronald Reagan."[59]

Wayne, however, remains our greatest example of the confusion between actor and mythic image. Where did his stereotyped roles end and his public persona as right-wing spokesman begin? Those images were overwhelmingly present in the psyches of three generations of American men. Even now his films are required viewing for recruits at military academies, where his name is so common as to be a verb. Robert Bly jokes that the only images of masculinity available to young men in the 1960s were Wayne and his reverse-image, the "wimpy" Woody Allen.

This heroic image is now not merely American. Since the 1990s, soldiers in Chechnya, Serbia, Liberia and other places have affected Rambo-style headbands and sleeveless muscle-shirts. Barbara Ehrenreich observes that the old warrior ideal has become a commodity in global consumer culture: "With Rambo... Hollywood offers up a denationalized, generic warrior-hero, a man of few words and limited loyalties, suitable for universal emulation."[60]

Politicians commonly dilute the image further by ascribing it to persons who have done nothing courageous but have been arbitrarily victimized. When we do hear of individuals, such as the firefighters of 9/11, who actually sacrifice themselves to save others, we are left with only this depotentiated, over-used cliché to describe them. Or, acknowledging its weakness, we call them "real" heroes (as presidential candidate John McCain described himself).

Contemporary expressions of heroism tend to fall into the patriarchal trap, the erasure of feminine values. Even among progressive activists, Morgan cites examples of how women initiate political movements, only to be pushed aside once men become involved. Then, "A fatal shift in tone occurs — a slide from…spiritual integrity (now regarded as sentimental, idealistic, *womanly*) into self-righteousness."[61] The men become obsessed with a higher abstract good and shift from "living for a cause" to "dying for a cause." They reduce something that was conceived in images of integration into a duality: *with us or against us.* We find the same issue in the fields of surgery and emergency medicine. When doctors focus exclusively on prolonging life they enact two myths, the denial of death and the hero. The doctor transforms the meaning of the event from patient-centered to one that centers on *him,* as the individual savior. It becomes less about the patient's crisis and more about the doctor's heroic quest. By contrast, palliative care, with its goal of alleviating pain and facilitating a good death, expresses another mythic image: Hermes, guide between the worlds.

Heroic men disdain the feminine because they have never fully separated from the mother's orbit. Unlike Heracles who *served* the mother, modern heroes react against their fear of (or longing for) maternal engulfment by constructing a thin veneer of machismo. But its shadow is the needy, vulnerable child. *Every hero has a child in the background.* Then the cult of celebrity meets a cult of victimization: perpetually wounded "adult children" who gravitate toward saviors, simple solutions and literal thinking. The child in the psyche doesn't want mystery; all it wants is a return to innocence.

In an individualistic and competitive culture, *winners* are our highest mythic personifications. Altruism and compassion, however, merely indicate weakness, and no one wins unless someone else loses. We patronize children with clichés: "trying" makes them winners. Some adults who do not succeed in sports or business go on to compete in other arenas and find satisfaction, but these victories are not initiations. Men motivated by the myth of heroic achievement require constant challenges, because competition (the toxic mimic of the quest for knowledge) is addictive. Consider the sad spectacle of the newly retired sports star or CEO, moping around the house, until his wife pushes him out to the golf course. With both the feminine and the child existing in the shadows, heroes (and their admirers) live with *the constant fear of losing*.

Our Puritan heritage teaches unsuccessful people that failure is their own fault. So, in a meritorious society, many learn that they don't merit approval. They internalize shame, which builds until it demands release. In the mythology of innocence, the only way out of victimization is the revenge that turns the victim into a perpetrator, a fantasy that converts the paranoid imagination into the predatory imagination.

THE REDEMPTION HERO

Is America exceptional? All societies evolved versions of the monomyth — *except America*. Europeans, long alienated from their own indigenous myths, brought with them only their stories of Puritanism, materialism, progress, chosen people and othering. Conditions were ripe for the creation of something new. And that is exactly what happened.

Four centuries of unique historic circumstances, idealistic storytelling and deliberate propaganda have created an *American* monomyth, with its own American hero: individualistic, lonely, extraordinarily powerful, selfless *and sexless*. Though he first appears as the frontiersman and matures into the cowboy, he reincarnates as the detective or the superhero. Jewett and Lawrence describe him:

Whereas the classic hero is born in community, hears a call, ventures forth on his journey and returns sadder but wiser, the American hero comes from *elsewhere*, entering the community only to defend it from malevolent attacks. Its leaders, who are weak, incompetent or corrupt, often betray him. Though he cares about them, *he is not one of them*. Often his identity is a secret; he may wear a mask or bizarre costume. He is without flaw but also without depth. He is *not* re-integrated into society, and in recent versions, the community itself is not fully re-integrated. The Other — Terror — is now a permanent threat. "If the function of the enemy is to represent uncontrollable human desire," writes James Gibson, "then he must constantly be reincarnated in some form or other."[62]

Classic heroes often wed beautiful maidens, enact the *hieros gamos* and produce many children. But the American hero (with few exceptions such as James Bond and comic antiheroes) doesn't get *or even want* the girl. Even Bond remains a bachelor. Often the hero must choose between an attractive sexual partner and duty to his mission. Some (Batman, the Lone Ranger, etc.) renounce marriage altogether, preferring a male "sidekick." Wayne (in almost all of his roles), Hawkeye, the Virginian, Superman, Green Lantern, Spiderman, Rambo, Sam Spade, Indiana Jones, Robert Langdon, John Shaft, Captains Kirk, America and Marvel: all are *single*. Their sexual purity ensures moral infallibility, but it also denies both complexity and the possibility of healing.

Indeed, sexual *im*purity corrupts Eden. The hero often enacts his savior role in disaster films *(Earthquake, Towering Inferno, Tidal Wave, Jaws)*. In these films, the sexual license of certain (usually female) characters seems to trigger the destruction, and they die first. Nature responds with a moral cleansing. The pattern was set in the Old Testament: only the pure and faithful escape. The first victim in *Jaws* (one of cable TV's most popular re-runs) is a sexually provocative woman. The final scene, in which the hero (who has refused to make love to his wife) destroys the giant shark, perfectly recreates Marduk's killing of Tiamat. Once again, the hero vanquishes the serpent.

In redemption mythology, women are *excuses* for the hero's quest. Recall that captivity narratives begin with abduction and end with heroic deliverance. The capture of a pure white woman sanctifies as Christian a project that is inherently violent and un-Christian. "Without the violence done to her," writes Slotkin, " there is no motive or justification for the hero to vindicate his manhood by attacking and destroying the Indians."[63]

The classic hero endures the initiatory torments in order to suffer into knowledge and renew the world. In this pagan and tragic vision, something always dies for new life to grow. But the American hero cares only to *redeem* ("buy back") others. Born in monotheism, he saves Eden by combining elements of the sacrificial Christ who dies *for* the world and his zealous, omnipotent father. *The community begins and ends in innocence.*

The collapse of religion didn't eliminate the Puritan's longing; it merely displaced it. The hero's superhuman abilities reflect a hope for divine redemption that science has never eradicated. Only in our salvation-obsessed culture and the places our movies go does he appear. Then, he changes the lives of others *without* transforming them.

I can't emphasize this insight too strongly. The redemption hero, whom Americans admire above all others, has inherited an immensely long process of abstraction, alienation and splitting of the western psyche. He gives us the model, writes Hillman, "for that peculiar process upon which our civilization rests: dissociation."[64] He is utterly disconnected from relationship with the Other, whom he has demonized into his mirror opposite, the *irredeemably* evil. Since he never laments the violence employed in destroying such an evil presence, he reinforces our own denial of death. His appeal lies deep below rational thinking. This hero requires no nurturance, doesn't grow in wisdom, creates nothing, and teaches only violent resolution of disputes. His renunciation justifies his furious vengeance upon those who cannot control their appetites for power or sex, and this clearly has a modeling effect on millions of adolescent males. Defending democracy through fascist means, he also renounces citizenship. He offers, write Jewett and Lawrence, "vigilantism without lawlessness, sexual repression without resultant perversion, and moral infallibility without... intellect."[65]

In a parallel tradition, heroines generally perform their redemptive roles non-violently (exceptions such as Wonder Woman and Xena are mere copies of male heroes, despite their fabulous bodies). In stories ranging from *Heidi* and *Pollyanna* to *The Wizard of Oz, The Sound of Music, Little House On The Prairie* and the Nancy Drew mysteries, they are the secular replacements for a culture that has lost faith in the Virgin Mary and her angels. Untainted by sex, they transform villains with cheerful love, always producing happy endings. They restore the moral order and avert the threat of random, Dionysian chaos.

What academics call "secular displacement of religion," pagans call the "toxic mimic." Mythology creates history. Constant repetition of these images in infinite variations socializes children, some of whom will grow up to perpetuate the myths. Another generation internalizes the assumptions of innocence, because instead of *losing* his innocence, the one-dimensional hero only wants to *restore* it. Such heroes are compelled to repeat their unconscious search for the Other, whom they find in every slum breeding more terrorists. Inverting the classical hero, they are anonymous, pathological killers in search of an *enemy* with a thousand faces.

Enter George W. Bush: for eight years, we saw him *staged,* always with a crowd of supporters or soldiers standing behind him. A huge flag or patriotic motto above them completed a scene carefully composed for television. It evoked a Protestant church with chorus, the Fascist strongman, the "war president" or a TV game show host softening up the crowd with one-liners.

He enacted the myth of the lone savior, called forth by the unprovoked attack of pure evil. This ground had been well prepared. The dozens of action/disaster films of the 1990s had culminated in two films (*Independence Day* of 1996 and 1997's *Air Force One*) in which American presidents *personally* pilot jets and save the entire world. Perhaps these films were so popular because our actual President Clinton was caught up in a sex scandal; he actually *liked* women.

Bush, however, came from the countryside to battle the liberal establishment. He was both an outsider and a man of the people, playing both the savior of the innocent and an innocent one himself. Like Reagan, he cavorted at his ranch doing physical work, or staged his "mission accomplished" aircraft carrier landing. Even his (contrived?) malapropisms worked in his favor: he seemed inarticulate, *just like the rest of us,* unlike patricians like Al Gore and John Kerry. When reporters occasionally pointed out his contradictions, like Reagan he simply ignored them, as if sharing the joke with his fraternity friends. This comfort in the world of pure fiction made his lies, like those of Reagan's, seem all the more convincing.

So Bush combined the image of the lone savior with another one: the unsophisticated country boy tweaking the noses of the effete, city intellectuals. His famous smirk was the passive-aggressive gesture that adolescents make while enduring lectures on propriety. Ultimately, he was persuasive because, like Reagan, he played *himself*, a grandiose, inflated, uninitiated male, alternating between hero and clown. That so many were moved for so long by such patent insincerity speaks to the depths of our longing, the enduring strength of our myths and our unwillingness to examine our innocence.

THE PARADOX OF THE OUTSIDER

The redemption hero, like Christ, leaves once his work is done. He *must* leave; he came from somewhere else, and he must return. However, as I have suggested, innocent Eden is defined by the existence of the Other — the external Other of terrorism, and internal Other of race. The Other *is* the outsider. Or: *evil comes from outside, but so does redemption.*

Riding off into the sunset, writes James Robertson, "...the cowboy hero never integrated himself with his society."[66] But he has quite a bit in common with his villainous adversary. Each rejects conventional authority, each despises democracy and, although they serve opposing ends (like Ethan Edwards and Scar in *The Searchers*), their methods are similar. The hero often *becomes* an outlaw (think Rambo) to defeat evil, because legitimate, democratic means are ineffective. Slotkin writes that by the 1820s, the standard frontier hero rescued captives by fighting the Indian "in his own manner, becoming in the process a reflection or a double of his dark opponent."[67] Eventually, the dual relationship in the mirror shatters and the villain must die, (frequently in a *duel*). The one who can control himself defeats the one who cannot.

Yet because he takes whatever he wants, has no responsibilities and transgresses all moral codes, the villain is exciting and frankly attractive. Americans *admire* outlaws. Newspapers described an 1872 hold-up as "so diabolically daring and so utterly in contempt of fear that we are bound to admire it and *revere its perpetrators.* "[68] Fifty years later, when Al Capone and his henchmen took their seats at ballparks, people applauded. *The Godfather* as both book and movie series is a regular candidate for the Great American Novel. In the era of capitalism's greatest profits, millions identified with the families depicted in *The Sopranos* and *Growing Up Gotti.* The policeman and the criminal express contradictory impulses within American character. Puritan zeal for order clashes with its equal, the frenzied quest for wealth. Robert Warshow writes that the gangster is "what we want to be and what we are afraid we may become."[69] Both share still another characteristic: the villain's rage is a natural component of his pleasure in violating all boundaries, while the hero is also full of rage. Only by killing the villain, writes Gibson, can he "release the rage accumulated from a life of emotional self-denial."[70]

Though the hero rejects society's rules, he is hardly alone; the desperado and the hedge fund CEO, whom we can't resist admiring, join him, along with all the Others who have been pushed beyond the walls or down into the underworld (a term which was first used to describe organized crime in the 1920s).

America's post-Biblical redemption story approximates but stops short of *The Bacchae's* primary insight: *the "evil other" and the "good other" are one and the same, stranger and guest: xenos.* We seek the Other to know ourselves. Polytheism could hold the paradox of Dionysus. Monotheism, however, cannot.

BOY PSYCHOLOGY

Because boyhood generally takes place in a maternal realm, society must transform the nurturing yet constricting mother-son bond. So, the theme of heroes defeating dragons symbolizes the universal struggle to attain individuality. The dragon can symbolize the smothering mother, and the hero's aggressive stance is entirely appropriate to the first half of life.

But America provides neither a mythic framework that places heroism in the context of descent, nor authentic rituals to enact that descent. And our spiritualized heroes rarely succumb to the sticky temptations of relationship. The community is passive, weak and feminine. And the hero who on one level gallantly saves it is, on another level, trying to defeat the mother-dragon. *But he cannot kill her because he is saving her, so he does the next best thing; he leaves.* To stay — in relationship — would be to admit defeat. Boys learn this quite early. By adolescence, most are desperate to leave home, to depart literally when they cannot do so symbolically. Later, many are equally desperate to escape commitment to a woman.

Redemption mythology presents men with a simplistic duality when they experience conflict. One choice is that of Kronos, to quickly raise the ante to literal violence. The second, like Ouranos, is to leave, either out of fear of violence, or out of refusal to engage on the feminine ground of relationship. Indeed, the fear of relationship is so strong that it often makes violence seem more preferable.

These are two extreme responses; men typically combine both styles. The most common is *to remain physically while leaving emotionally*. He presents a mixed message; he is there (on her ground of relationship), but he is not. Her demands for emotional commitment exacerbate his fears of the engulfing feminine. He reacts by taking his heroic quest to work, or simply disappearing behind the newspaper, and leaving the children with her. She ends up trying to initiate them on her own while shaming him as emotionally irrelevant.

The American hero is the toxic mimic of another, more mature archetypal figure. Jungians Robert Moore and Douglas Gillette envision a four-part masculine soul divided into the *King* (image of order, blessing and fertility), *Lover* (relatedness and deep passion for life), *Magician* (awareness and insight), and *Warrior* (focused aggression and devotion to a cause). Each of these archetypes is divided into an immature, "boy psychology" image and a mature, initiated "man psychology." They lament "…that most men are fixated at an immature level of development."[71] The immature form of the warrior is what we know as the hero. This macho man overcompensates for his insecurities, either bragging of his potency or smoldering in silence. He is brittle and easily provoked.

The warrior's courage and discipline, by contrast, are intended for *service*. He hones himself into "an efficient spiritual machine… to bear the unbearable," serving a transpersonal goal.[72] The King (himself in relation, and this is critical, to a divine queen) personifies the cause or community.

The road to knowing one's masculine purpose often runs through the territory of the hero/warrior. But America provides few non-violent options beyond fireman, athlete or doctor. This vacuum offers a dangerous temptation; to serve the modern king as a warrior is *to go to war,* often in one's own neighborhood. Then we enact another myth, the killing of the children.

The indigenous soul perceives danger as opportunity. In Chinese, the word "crisis" is composed of two characters. One represents danger, the other opportunity. At the core, the adolescent hero longs to die to his old self, to be admitted into the hut of the elders. In some African tribes, adolescents were expected to demonstrate their sincerity by dancing at great length before that hut, pleading for initiation. They knew the consequences of not being admitted: remaining boys in the eyes of the community.

Greek myth acknowledged the damage that uninitiated men could do and told cautionary tales of golden youths inflated with *hybris.* Icharus flew too close to the sun and perished. Phaethon, child of the sun, borrowed his father's fiery chariot. Unable to control it, he set the world on fire and died. Grandiose King Erysichthon cut down a sacred oak. Demeter cursed him with insatiable hunger, throwing him into a frenzy of consumption. He ate everything and everyone in his kingdom, ultimately consuming himself. The king who couldn't bless ended up destroying the realm.

These are images of boy psychology. The hero may vanquish the beast. But if he doesn't enact the third part of initiation, returning with a boon for his community, or if that community is limited to a small minority of rich people, then his heroism becomes pathological. Either he turns his violence against others, especially the women and gays who remind him of his own vulnerability, or he condones such violence by others, or he turns it upon himself in depression or suicide. *He must serve a transpersonal cause, or his own image, like that of Narcissus, will become that cause.* His great towers will become targets, unconsciously provoking the Stranger who will puncture his grandiosity.

DEATH OF THE HERO

> *"All of us carry, in a hidden recess of our heart, a deadly wish*
> *towards the hero."* — *Carl Jung*

Achilles, greatest of heroes, had two choices: he could leave Troy, go home, marry and live a long and boring life; or he could die an early but honorable death and have his deeds sung forever. True to his nature, he kept fighting. But Achilles didn't complete the Hero's Journey; he never returned to bless his community. Only when he descended to Hades, where heroism is meaningless, did he realize, *"Better... to break sod as a farm hand for some poor country man... than lord it over all the exhausted dead."*[73] He tells this to Odysseus, still very much a hero himself, implying that Odysseus still has the opportunity to "die" symbolically *while still alive,* and be transformed into something greater.

Homer provides a model for this process at the end of the *Iliad* (if we see the various masculine figures as parts of a single psyche). Hector, too, chose heroic death. But Hermes guided his father Priam to the Trojan camp, where he secured permission from Achilles to bring home and mourn the corpse. Hector's burial represents *dis-identifying* from the immature pattern of the hero and indicates the soul's capability to mature.

In Campbell's terms, the Hero returns to the community and weds the inner maiden of his soul. Knowing her in himself, he is no longer threatened by feminine dragons. He is in *relationship* to the community of other archetypes, having filled the void left by the loss of his old identity. Or, like Dionysus, Osiris and the other god/consorts of the Great Goddess, he dies repeatedly only to return with the blessing of renewal in springtime.

But the *savior* hero dies only once, sacrificing himself *for* the world. Under patriarchy, the world's redemption requires no death into greater life, but the death of god's child, the sacrifice of a child for the benefit of the father. His death equals the redemption of the father's world. The empty tomb implies that Christ has returned to the ultimate abstraction, pure spirit. He refuses to remain on or even *in* the earth.

After restoring innocence to Eden, either the American hero rides away or he dies, which is also to leave and return to spirit, the realm of the distant fathers. Either way, he chooses union with the father over the tedium (or anxiety) of life among the women and children. Or, chasing after "spirits," he becomes an alcoholic. He may leave by choice (the sunset in Native American lore indicates the land of the dead), or by his father's decision ("fate"). Either way, he goes to a "better place." Unlike the universal hero who lifts the veil between the worlds to bring awareness of eternal values, the redemption hero pulls the veil back down, confirms our innocence, and puts everyone back to sleep.

Redemption mythology gets one thing right: the hero must die. But he must die symbolically, not literally. And without the return to community, initiation is incomplete and heroism becomes addictive. Because such heroes long to die into something greater, they are repeatedly compelled to challenge the Other to give them that opportunity, as Bush did on the aircraft carrier. Taunting the Iraqi resistance to "bring it on," he knew full well that actual young men would attempt to live out his hero myth and die trying. American culture is bound up in a mythic knot of heroism, individualism and adolescent innocence, stuck half way through a story.

AMERICAN SHADOW MYTHS

The myth of innocence inevitably constellated its shadow. Indians, slaves and "minorities" all resisted. Their stories are found in the margins, just as today similar stories arise from marginalized, inner-city youth.

Mexican-Americans warn that naughty children might be abducted by *La Llorona,* the weeping ghost of an Indian woman searching for her own dead children. She killed them out of grief from having been rejected by their rich, white father, or out of spite, or to keep him from taking them away from her. In a modern version, they died in a river that his factories had polluted. The common theme is that innocents die under patriarchal capitalism. This death may be literal, or it may be the death of a woman's creativity. The same theme occurs in the African-American context. Tony Morrison's *Beloved* retells the actual 1856 story of an escaped slave who murdered her children to prevent their recapture.

Hawaiians tell of *Pele,* Goddess of the volcano. Stories of her murderous eruptions often involve the deaths of grandiose, heroic men. She represents the violent return of the repressed feminine. Psychologist Rita Knipe writes, "Sooner or later, Pele will erupt and overwhelm a man's entire personality."[74]

I return briefly to this theme to restate it in its specifically American context. "The feminine" refers to *any* repressed or marginalized energy that demands recognition. "Woman" is one of the basic images of the repressed. (Dionysus, the androgynous male, is another.) Recall those vindictive women, Clytemnestra and Medea, who represent two options available to the repressed when it arises. Clytemnestra takes vengeance but suffers the consequences of her acts in further patriarchal reprisal. Medea, like *La Llarona*, takes the more common option. She turns her resentment inward, in low self-esteem, eating disorders or self-mutilation, or sacrifices her children to spite her oppressor husband, the "hero" Jason. It is her only way to exert control. Her story is repeated in millions of homes. America, again, is exceptional: it has the highest rate in the world of parents who kill their own young children.

Our modern shadow myths express our ambivalence over the mixed blessings of progress. The theme of great towers of the corrupt city inviting natural disaster dates back to *The Last Days of Pompeii, Intolerance, Noah's Ark, Deluge, S.O.S. Tidal Wave* and *When Worlds Collide*. Especially since 1950, wrote Susan Sontag, we have lived under the dual threat of "two equally fearful, but seemingly opposed, destinies," unremitting banality and the nuclear terror.[75] Both anxiety over our own personal mortality and legitimate fears of complete extinction drive us to consume these narratives.

Disaster films give expression to these fears (and the desire for new beginnings), and they also provide resolution by the redemption hero. Both *Armageddon* (second highest-grossing film of 1998, with its images of collapsing Twin Towers) and *The Day After Tomorrow* (sixth highest-grossing film of 2004) end with happy reunions of the main (white) characters. "After 9/11," writes critic Asad Heider, "it is necessary for all American disaster films to end with success...to push suffering out of the imagination."[76]

THE TWIN TOWERS

These myths of Other, growth, progress, exceptionalism, heroism and privilege were alive on 9/11. Then we lost our innocence — or did we? When society is constructed upon such myths, every assault on our assumptions seems like the first time, because the veil of innocence drops automatically after each awakening. Ignorant of history, we are always, by definition, unprepared. *The unprovoked assault against Eden is always the first assault.*

Christine Downing suggests that public trauma reawakens individual traumas of birth and childhood, long-repressed feelings of "how precarious and illusory our everyday sense of order and stability is." We are pulled back into old fears of annihilation, "and our even more repressed *longing* for death, peace, resolution and completion."[77]

A certain sense of innocence is indispensable for anyone to live productively. We need to forget the reality of death long enough to go on. Few of us, however, get the opportunity to experience a ritual container within which we might confront the great backlog of grief we carry. So by keeping us from constantly re-experiencing loss and victimization, *personal* innocence also blocks the road to healing.

National innocence, however, insulates us from our history as *perpetrators*. Europeans had been victimized, in a sense, merely by having been born into a world whose myths were no longer viable. World conquest allowed them to inflict their sense of victimhood directly upon native people, and to experience the relief of a myth of innocence. What were the padres thinking as they whipped native slaves for minor infractions? *It is for their own good!*

National innocence implies exceptionalism, uniqueness and profound ignorance. Mark Slouka taught a university seminar on early Christianity. A young woman admitted without any irony, "...*I always thought Jesus was an American.*" To Slouka, she was speaking, "as succinctly as I have ever heard it articulated ...with almost poetic compaction...the core myth of America."[78] Only such naiveté could mirror the hubris of the two thousand-foot-high towers.

The repressed longing that Downing speaks of is not yearning for actual death, but for Pentheus' *symbolic* death. Innocence always evokes betrayal.

From the point of view of humanity's two billion malnourished persons, from the perspective of Dionysus, the twin towers were a grandiose statement in steel and concrete of America's innocence and unconscious desire to be awakened. They were a dance before the elders' hut, an invitation to "bring it on," to kill the boy-hero society so that a mature society might arise.

Most Americans experienced a few weeks of shared compassion and introspection. The veils rose and the national illusion was briefly undone. Great things were possible; Americans, like Athenians in the Theater-temple of Dionysus, suffered together for perhaps the first time (the only other modern image we have of such shared suffering is John F. Kennedy's funeral). But, quickly, Bush encouraged everyone to go shopping, to move on and to re-invigorate the myth of innocence *by converting grief into the thirst for vengeance.* He was successful: as late as 2006, eighty-five percent of U.S. soldiers in Iraq believed that their mission was mainly to retaliate for Saddam's role in the 9/11 attacks.

Vengeance establishes a sense of identity and continuity, allowing us to feel powerful rather than victimized. Dissolving our sense of conscience, we perceive our violence as self-defense. Psychologist Lionel Corbett suggests that *"rage can also cover up feelings of guilt that we secretly approved of the attacks."*[79] If our longing for initiation has no other outlet than images of literal destruction, then we will feel guilty when those images become reality, and we will need to deny that guilt.

MYTHIC IMAGES OF THE TWIN TOWERS

Many mythologies share the theme of cataclysm ("wash down") or catastrophe ("turn down") and tell of disasters such as earthquakes, floods and eruptions. The Judeo-Christian tradition perceives such events as divine punishment resulting from sexual transgressions and reversions to Paganism. The Greeks saw these events as retribution *(nemesis)* for excessive arrogance and pride *(hubris),* which is symbolized as *towers* that reach toward heaven in Egyptian, Mexican, Assamese, Burmese and Native American myths.

The Tower card appears in the European Tarot Deck as a medieval castle, a Babylonian ziggurat, a skyscraper, a prison or the White House. It collapses in flames from an earthquake or lightning bolt. Sometimes human bodies fall from it, or pieces of it strike the king. Psychologically, it represents the ego defenses that hide our incomplete selves. The Tower, writes Shanti Fader, is a place of "fear and jealous, possessive pride, designed to keep out love..."[80] Recall Pentheus bellowing, *"I shall order every gate in every tower to be bolted tight."*

It also represents knowledge swollen out of control, like the Tower of Babel. Yahweh's response to it was to punish its builders by "confounding their language that they may not understand one another's speech." He "scattered them abroad upon the face of all the earth" (Genesis 11: 8-9). Hillman suggests that this isn't a bad thing: it prevents mankind from speaking with the single voice of monotheistic literalism. Unity (contrasted with *com*-munity) leads to inflation and arrogance; the correction to "vertical ascensionism" is diversity. When humans scatter horizontally across the earth they learn to speak in many languages.[81]

But the terrorists attacked the Towers for their political as well as their psychological significance. A network reporter admitted that the WTC was the "symbol of American power, democracy and world trade."[82] The terrorists would have added, "and empire." Temples in patriarchal societies are built as tall as possible, at the highest elevations. This recalls Icharus' heroic attempt to escape the ground of The Mother and the natural world, a return to the abode of the sky gods.

Polytheistic cultures acknowledge aspects of the divine that aren't conventionally positive. Some have suggested that the attacks were "a wake-up call from the Dark Feminine" (*Kali* in India, *Baba Yaga* in Russia and *Coatlique* in Mexico), the one to whom all beings return, who destroys in order to create. The Dark Mother, however, had already been calling on September *tenth*, when 35,000 children died of malnutrition, as they do every day. With all due respect to the victims of the attack, it is characteristic American narcissism to imply that 9/11 had more personal meaning than the carnage going on in any of the forty-odd wars being waged across the globe.

Euripides presents a *relationship* between the Great Mother and her children. In *The Bacchae* the palace collapses precisely at the play's halfway point. Rather than killing Pentheus, Dionysus warns, *"Friend you can still save the situation!"* Pentheus can still "re-pent" and change his fate or turn it toward destiny before his older female relatives kill and dismember him. From this perspective, 9/11 is indeed a wake-up call, rather than the simplistic "moral cleansing" of the disaster movies.

The Great Mother acts with broader strokes. If *she* reaches the point of no return, then the entire ecosystem will be dismembered. She will paint her picture with global warming, pandemics, nuclear holocaust or the collapse of agriculture, as Demeter did when Hades abducted her daughter Persephone. But she is patient. Feder sees the Tarot's destruction of the Tower as "clearing away...outmoded ideas and patterns...which may well have served a purpose at one time.[83] The Tower is like the Hero, who produces and achieves in the first half of life, but must die into something greater in the second half. Dionysus concludes *The Bacchae* implying that if uninitiated boy-kings awaken, they might "have an ally...in the son of Zeus."

THE WOMAN BEHIND THE BURKHA

One dominant image of the new millennium is the flaming collapse of the twin towers. Here is another one: the Muslim woman wearing the burkha, covered so completely that we can barely see her. Hardly able to see where she is going, she is trapped physically, economically and emotionally. The Greek term for a woman's veil, *krêdemnon,* also signifies the battlements that crown the city and the lid or stopper of a bottle. To veil a woman is to keep the lid on, ensuring purity and legitimate heirs for the husband.

Yet isn't it the privileged white male, 10,000 miles away, observing her on TV or in *National Geographic,* who can't see clearly? Does he realize that his dispassionate attention requires that she carry his unacknowledged feminine half? "Woman," writes John Jervis, embodies a powerful secret for him: She "both *is* mystery, and yet is also the *key* to mystery."[84]

Possessing the secret to life, she must also know death's mysteries. Since he doesn't know what she is thinking (he never asks), he is mystified. If he gazed long enough, what else might he feel? Pity, sympathy, terror? What does she carry under her robe? A gun, a bomb, a *vagina dentata* (the ancient image of the terrifying feminine)? If he revealed himself as Pentheus and she were Agave, would she recognize him, or would she tear him apart?

Perhaps she conceals something he *needs,* a map of his emotions, a bare breast, shoulders to hold him while he cries? A divine child? The path *home?* Below his heroic stance he is unsure of his purpose or status. Paglia observes, "The agon of male identity springs from men's humiliating sense of dependence upon women. It is women who control the emotional and sexual realms, and men know it."[85]

Does he tolerate her condition out of resentment? Does he sense some vague connection to his fears (or hopes) of impending apocalypse (again: to *lift the veil)?* Does he fear the end of time because that might mark the beginning of, or return to *her* time? Will she take vengeance or bless him and set him free? Is this why Ashcroft and Powell went to such lengths to veil the *Spirit of Justice* and *Guernica* in 2003?

In fashion-obsessed America, the equivalent of the burkha is "size six." Looking carefully at fashion models, we are as likely to see disdain, even hatred, in their eyes as we are to see charm. Ultimately, the burkha symbolizes the *persona* behind which everyone hides.

All peoples, races and modes of being that have been veiled by our patriarchal, religious and consumerist myths await their revenge. This includes the eruption of rage in the Muslim world. However, Western culture represents both a reminder of the colonial brutality their ancestors endured as well as a threat to their own fundamentalist domination of women. Thus, modernity is also a constant temptation of the Loosener himself, who invites women to drop their veils, raise their skirts, declare their "virgin" independence and take vengeance.

Psychologically, the urge for vengeance is a form of inflation; mythologically, it is identification with the gods, who punish those mortals who oppose them or do not perform appropriate sacrifices. As mentioned previously, Dionysus sent an affliction upon the genitals of the Athenian men and cured it only when they duly honored him by fashioning great phalluses for his worship. But identifying with a god is not the same as welcoming an archetypal energy.

Who are these gods who take vengeance? Are they so fragile and insecure that myth allows them such behavior? Well, *yes*, since we created them in our own image. But if we think of them less as unconcerned, or as impulsive, narcissistic superheroes with thunderbolts, and more as participants in a cosmic ritual of purpose, we reframe the question: *"What do they want from us?"* Vengeance stems from the Latin *vindicare* (to claim, to show authority and curiously, to *set free.*) What if we were to think of the vengeance of Dionysus as the setting-free, the releasing, through symbolic death, of a soul (or a nation) caught in the webs of illusion, innocence or inattention? Dionysus *demands* that we pay attention, and he alone determines the consequences of our refusal.

There is another picture that may become the dominant image of the century: the hooded man standing on a bucket in Abu Ghraib Prison, electrodes attached to his outstretched arms. It evokes both the crucified Christ and the Ku Klux Klan. But there is another meaning. The man is *veiled,* like the woman in the burkha. He is silenced and *feminized,* as Dionysus feminized Pentheus. The image reinforces to the entire Muslim world our refusal to *see* them, except as the Other. Is it any wonder that Iraqi resistance (including the videotaped executions that screamed, *Look at Us! We are the same as you!*) rose dramatically after the photos were published?

NATURE BATS LAST

This perfectly American, baseball metaphor sums up our innate, moral intelligence. *It isn't right* when someone's behavior harms the natural order. It violates *Themis* (Justice). We know that this order runs far deeper than politics or theology. But it turns into its toxic mimic, hubris, when humans heroically usurp divine will, identifying themselves with the archetype of the King, and selectively interpreting that will. Hubris inevitably evokes nemesis.

The Hero must die for America to undergo its initiation. Nature is not yet poised to tear us apart. We can still sacrifice our heroic *attitudes* without experiencing massive destruction. There are ritual acts that we can still perform to welcome back the Stranger. In Chapter Ten, I will consider how we honor Dionysus unconsciously in contemporary life. Let two poets have the last words for now:

Through the midnight streets of Babylon
between the steel towers of their arsenals,
between the torture castles with no windows,
we race by barefoot, holding tight
our candles, trying to shield
the shivering flames, crying, "Sleepers awake!"
— *Denise Levertov*

When school or mosque, tower or minaret gets torn down — then
Dervishes can begin their community. Not until faithfulness turns
into betrayal and betrayal into trust can any human being become
part of the truth.
— *Rumi*

What is madness but nobility of soul at odds
with circumstance?
THEODORE ROETHKE

———

This is America. If you're not a winner it's your
own fault.
JERRY FALWELL

———

…divide us those in darkness from the ones who
walk in light…
KURT WEILL

———

Then our possessions will turn to beasts and
devour us whole.
ZUNI PROPHESY

———

We are still as much possessed by autonomous
psychic contents as if they were Olympians.
Today they are called phobias, obsessions, and…
neurotic symptoms. The gods have become disease.
CARL JUNG

———

For where there is dance, there also is the Devil.
ST. JOHN CHRYSOSTOM

10

FIVE STYLES OF "POOR QUALITY DIONYSUS"

HERE IS OUR basic dilemma. As Jung wrote, the gods never died; they went underground and resurfaced as illness in the body, in the body politic and in the soul of the world.

The stories we tell ourselves about ourselves maximize individualism, conflict and competition while minimizing aesthetic, sensual and ecological interrelationships. Twenty centuries of literal thinking have left us without the mythic and ritual tools to comprehend the tragedy, mystery and ambiguity of existence. And the unprecedented rate of technological change has put such pressure on the collective consciousness that millions have gravitated toward the simplistic answers of consumerism, militarism or addiction, hoping to prolong our flirtation with innocence.

Our task is to facilitate the process of awakening from this fantasy, but this requires that we fully comprehend *and grieve* the diminishment of our imagination. We have settled for the minimum, the toxic mimic of the real thing, allowing Dionysus and the other divinities into American life in ways that keep us barely alive yet hungry for real nutrition. Like Tantalos in Hades, we are *tantalized,* dimly perceiving the soul's food almost within reach, but our eating muscles have atrophied. Consider this observation by Robert Johnson:

> … we hear a screech of brakes and a crash… Cold chills go up and down our spine; we say "How awful!" — and run outside to see the accident. This is poor-quality Dionysus… what happens to a basic human drive that has not been lived out for nearly four thousand years.[1]

This chapter identifies five styles of "poor-quality Dionysus," or ways in which we unconsciously honor the god: inflation; scapegoating; pornography and drugs; religion; and mental illness. They are expressions of our diminished imagination. From *his* point of view, however, they show us how he squeezes through the walls and slowly widens the fissures, leading toward either healing or collapse.

Our universal longing for ecstasy traditionally appeared as the god of wine. The route to Dionysus through alcohol is obvious; we needn't spend much time there, nor on the easing of the restrictions on sexuality of the last two generations. From the pagan perspective, acceptance of both gay people and the value of pleasure for its own sake are long overdue. What is more interesting is the continuing *resistance* to this relaxation.

It is crucial to understand the other subtle ways in which Dionysus appears. They are difficult to perceive because of their sheer commonality. As with myth itself or white privilege, when we are immersed in something, we rarely notice its power over us. These categories are not absolutely distinct from each other. I offer them as imaginative tools to help comprehend what we have lost and *how we unconsciously attempt to recover it.* But this is how he works. As Raphael Lopez-Pedraza writes, "Dionysus *always* appears in a distorted form… it is part of his nature."[2]

ONE: INFLATION, INTENSITY AND *COMMUNITAS*
When Dionysus's mother Semele endured Zeus's visitation she experienced *enthusiasm* ("filled with God"). She had demanded to see her lover in his

divine form, but instead of being a channel for the archetype, she became *inflated* with it and perished. Our urgent need to break out of the solitary and depressed self, to get *en-thused,* can become a desire to equal Dionysus, writes Ginette Paris. But instead of finding his intensity, some find only its opposite, emptiness; they are burned up like Semele. "Inflation through an archetype makes us lose the very quality with which we identify too exclusively."[3]

American teenagers are exposed to over three thousand advertisements daily, and ten million by the age of eighteen. High-volume, rapid-speech commercials whip up anxiety and offer only the temporary resolution of shopping. Satisfaction quickly diminishes and we search for new material. Consequently, inflation, which we mistake for enthusiasm, has become the cultural norm. After fifty years of television, anything must be outsized to grab our attention.

This longing for intensity drives gambling fever, which is also an alternative expression of the drive to achieve salvation by attaining wealth. The Opportunist's greed has trumped the Puritan virtues of thrift, hard work and deferred gratification; now many believe success should come quickly and effortlessly. The anxiety associated with the risk yields to the greater American fantasy of winning. Consumer culture has responded by providing an entire city way out in the desert where "anything goes," and people can briefly drop their corporate or small-town lifestyles to safely enact the shadow of Puritanism. So, a vacation in Las Vegas, America's fastest growing city, takes on the characteristics of a pilgrimage. A protected environment — a sacred space — to engage in activity that approximates the conditions of liminality, where "what happens in Vegas stays in Vegas," the entire city is a shrine to the goddess of luck *(Fortuna)* and the god of intensity.

Seventy percent of Americans engage in legal gambling, not counting the stock market. Fifty-seven percent buy lottery tickets, thirty percent visit casinos, twenty-three million play poker online, and thirteen million play fantasy football. The gambling industry had $90 billion in legal revenue in 2006, much more than music, books and movies combined. Fifteen million Americans display signs of gambling addiction.

This attraction to intensity drives our fascination with celebrity scandals, most of which tend to involve sex or money. Someone wants *more* of something than his puritan heritage entitles him to; like the Other in most of his incarnations, he cannot control his desires. The public, however (in countless "news" stories), "reacted with jaw-dropping disbelief."[4] Each new scandal elicits astonishment, which is in fact the reaction of those who have innocently suppressed their own desires to do precisely what the celebrity has been accused of.

The addiction to intensity expresses our archetypal longings for initiation and for ecstasy. Desensitized, bored or depressed, many hope that dangerous and extreme experiences such as riding motorcycles, bungie-jumping and roller coasters will sharpen their senses and shock them back into life. They achieve temporary, if ultimately unfulfilling, entrance into the world of liminality. But with few exceptions, young men have always endured initiation rituals *communally.* Such African-based religions as Voudoun and Santeria (as well as their modern expression in rock concerts) express this drive for communal ecstasy.

Fundamentalism offers this experience, but negates it with pressure toward moral conformism; and romance often seems so fleeting. What remains, for many, is the military and its substitutes. Individual violence results from frustration and the need for self-protection. But the willingness to go to war has more to do with self-*transcendence,* the need to be closer to others, than it does for the need to express hostility. Although recruitment commercials emphasize individual heroic challenges, all veterans know that what keeps men sane in combat (and makes some of them addicted to it) is shared, initiatory suffering and affection for their *comrades* (from the Spanish for "bedmate"). Hillman quotes various writers: "...the edge of the bearable... maximum of intensity and maximum of impossibility at the same time...communal ecstasy."[5]

This is *communitas,* the group experience of liminal space, where social boundaries relax and people sense that "everyone's in this together." It may occur spontaneously in situations such as shared grief, religious pilgrimage, rock concerts, sports, horror movies and political spectacles. It lies behind the vision of the Marxist classless society and other utopias in which men drop their perpetual competition for status. But we cannot institutionalize authentic *communitas;* we can only discover it, briefly enter it and lose it, because it is a gift of Dionysus. Modern attempts to create it don't result in significant initiatory change. So we endlessly repeat our attempts to achieve ecstasy, turning them into addictions.

Innocence beckons to us through the literalized Dionysus in the bottle. Why do so many get not festive and convivial, but nastily, aggressively drunk? Some may do so to verbalize what custom normally prevents us from expressing. Alcohol lowers inhibitions; afterwards we apologize, explaining "The liquor made me do it" (similarly, Homeric heroes said, "Some god made me do it"). Since the loosening of restraints allows us to evade responsibility for our actions, we return to innocence, if only temporarily. But whether we find *communitas* in the brief coming together of a community or forget ourselves in a bar fight, the haunting sense of loneliness returns.

Increasingly, we have only second-hand experience of *communitas.* "To go from a job you don't like," writes Ventura, "to watching a screen on which others live more intensely than you… is American life…"[6] Electronic media have become our immediate environment — not the land, not people, but *images* of the land and people. Millions spend their evenings alone or with their spouses watching television, or in taverns dominated by the ubiquitous TV.

Who can comprehend what a century of movies and a half-century of television have done to the soul? In the first five years of his role in *Marcus Welby MD,* the actor Robert Young received more than 250,000 letters from viewers, mostly asking for medical advice. These people were engaging in the one-sided relationships with celebrities or fictional characters that psychologists call "parasocial."

Consider that for thousands of years *everyone, everywhere* listened to storytellers at night. Sounds went directly into the ear and became pictures *in the imagination.* Eventually, when people enacted their myths, grieving and laughing together, they created Drama, which later devolved into conventional theatre, with professional actors entertaining passive spectators. For four centuries, people *read* those tales, privately. Then, they heard literalized versions of the myths on the radio, or consumed pre-formed images of beauty, courage and evil projected onto movie screens. In turn, millions returned the projection (their own inner gods and demons) onto celebrities. TV and computers increased our passivity and further diluted our imaginative capacity. Such images enter the brain directly, without even the mediation of a projector and screen.

Today's media, writes sociologist Christina Kotchemidova, foster an experience of emotion that is controlled, predictable, and undemanding without impinging on our rational lifestyles. Thus, "We can engage in mass-mediated emotions to the full while retaining control over our emotion experience and avoiding the risks of personal communication."[7] This situation is further exaggerated by texting and internet sites that make "friending" easier and less risky than actually interacting with anyone.

The public relations industry presents a literalized hero's journey. Gossip shows and Sunday supplements constantly describe celebrities who fall out of favor through scandals and divorce. They drop into the "liminal space" of anonymity, only to return with new shows, but essentially unchanged. They bring their trophies, Academy Awards and platinum albums with them, but nothing else.

Or consider the politicians upon whom we project royalty and perfection (mythologically speaking, kings *are* perfect). In America, *sexual transgression* marks imperfection (while displacing awareness of real corruption). When TV discovers their flaws and disillusionment sets in, we despise them absolutely, because if they are not perfect, then — in a Puritan society — they must be evil.

This is *vicarious intensity,* the excitement we feel when *someone else* (usually the *image* of someone else) confronts the edge of danger. Other examples include the funerals of major celebrities and the thrills we experience hearing about natural disasters or watching women go into labor, etc. Murder mysteries and crime shows are particularly appealing, writes critic Michael Wilmington, because they offer a comforting sense of "moral order restored after a holiday in chaos."[8] While the tribal mind understands that the chaos of liminal space is the necessary, fecund ground for new growth, the demythologized mind sees random screen violence as a vicarious and brief vacation, with the full, innocent expectation of a quick return to normality. We like to visit Dionysus, but we don't want to live with him.

If we were honest, we'd admit to a sense of relief and even festivity when disaster hits, because it often brings a refreshing sense of potency, community and purpose. Both the problem and the response become clear. We skip work and speak intimately with neighbors we normally ignore. Something important has grabbed our attention: the opportunity to relax our painfully rigid social boundaries.

Mythologically, Dionysus *Lusios,* the Loosener, has arrived in his non-alcoholic form, getting us drunk with excitement and temporarily unifying us. "I" become *we.* Something overrules my conditioning against any cooperation that doesn't serve my personal interests; I'm *glad,* in more ways than one, to help. Ancient Greeks experienced this "holiday in chaos" during the *Anthesteria,* and medieval people did so during Carnival. Rebecca Solnit suggests, however, that our "lack of real carnival…may be why its contents surge forth in unexpected places."[9]

At our best, we open hearts, stores, homes and wallets to each other. At our worst, however, we bar the doors and reach for the guns. Or we dissolve another boundary, between religion and nationalism. Submerged in a great cause, we anticipate holy vengeance and hope that a sacred King will allay our anxieties and bring us all together. Our most well known religious figures can be counted upon to sacralize the war, while presidential approval ratings soar. And, as the young and poor experience the actual danger, we — especially our intellectuals — enjoy the spectacle from a safe distance. After the 9/11 attacks, Christopher Hitchens, utterly insensitive to his own privileged safety, articulated the thrill experienced by the "Neocons" and others:

> …another sensation was contending for mastery…to my own surprise and pleasure, it turned out to be exhilaration. Here was the most frightful enemy…if the battle went on until the last day of my life, I would never get bored in prosecuting it to the utmost.[10]

The hope of experiencing some form of *communitas* explains why we prefer to watch major sports events among friends. "Fans" (Latin: *fanaticus,* mad, divinely inspired, *originally pertaining to a temple*) make up an emotionally engaged community holding the container for rituals of "competition" (petitioning the gods together). Shared interest and experience forge our identity. We take this same longing for communal ecstasy into rock concerts and dance clubs. Often, sexually ambiguous (long-haired but clean-shaven) young men enact the ritual on stage and provide our "minimum requirement" of Dionysus.

Watching sports, however, we're never really satisfied. We demand more vicarious intensity. Often, only the expectation of violence can penetrate our emotional armoring; then we *pay attention.* Hence the increased popularity of football, hockey, pro wrestling and auto racing, where helmeted Christs suffer for us all. Even watching alone at home, we know that we are part of a *virtual* community of fans. We belong.

But we move easily from cheering our team and wearing its logo, to taunting opponents and brawling with their fans; from "Kill the umpire!" to "Kill the Jews!" Vicarious intensity feeds upon literal violence that was once expressed symbolically under ritual conditions. In America, however, war and sports, especially football, are so closely linked that they share many of the same metaphors. Team spirit has archetypal roots, of course: we all share a deep and ancient longing to submerge our identity into clan or tribe. But when we have not been initiated into a fundamentally spiritual identity, team spirit becomes war fever. Jung wrote that people become "sick of that banal life…they want sensation…when there is a war: they say, 'Thank heaven, now something is going to happen — something bigger than ourselves!'"[11]

Authoritarian governments present *spectacles* for audiences to passively consume, instead of the organic, ecstatic festivals that once took people out of themselves and truly connected them to each other. Spectacles are scripted in every detail. They connect people not to each other but to the state.

The fourth century theologian Tertullian promised that in Heaven, Christians would have the *pleasure* of witnessing the eternal suffering of sinful pagans. American Protestantism inherited this tradition of moralized suffering and bloody redemption. Enjoying the punishment of the wicked is a fundamental aspect of our myth of innocence, especially in our ecstatic responses to crime and disaster films.

I have speculated that the archetypal meaning of vengeance is to set free and release something. We long to drop the oppressive weight of rage and alienation. "In fantasy," wrote Freud, man enjoys "...freedom from the grip of the external world, one which he has long relinquished in reality."[12] Paradoxically, we muffle the dark knowledge of mortality by viewing images of people killing each other. Clint Eastwood admitted that his early fans came to see *vengeance:* "They go to work every day for some guy who's rude and they...have to take it. Then they go see me on the screen and I...kick the shit out of him."[13]

Vicarious, voyeuristic intensity meets electronic spectacle in our recent wars. We see without being seen, writes Marita Sturken: "This tension of immediacy, sadism, and a slight tinge of complicity was thus integral to the pleasures of spectatorship. We saw, we were 'there,' yet the technology kept us...at a safe distance."[14]

Our primary leisure activity is entertainment, *being* passively entertained. Certainly we deserve relaxation and restoration. But why does it seem so unrewarding; and despite this, why do we constantly repeat the experience, as if something might change and our longing be fulfilled?

Entertain means "to hold together." But what does "together" refer to, subject or object? Two or more subjects can hold something in common. Or, one subject could hold two or more objects. Finally, a community, several subjects, could hold mutually exclusive concepts — the tension of the opposites — in a ritual container such as tragic drama, and *suffer together.* I suggest that the original meaning of entertainment was *ritual renewal of the community though shared suffering.* Athenian audiences did exactly that; viewing the clash of unbearable contradictions, they held that tension and wept together. They emerged spent but renewed, purged of their anxieties for a while.

This is why the satisfaction of entertainment is so fleeting. Certainly we hold something (hero-worship or villain-hatred) together. But since we (in our darkened rooms) rarely encounter authentic paradox or nuance, we miss the shared grief and joy that can actually unite people. Instead of embracing the mysterious and tragic coexistence of opposites, we release the tension by watching it being resolved, either violently or comically.

We identify with either redemption heroes who restore Eden, or with an endless procession of cute, ironic, self-deprecating, sharp-witted, deathless, *fun* characters who are as innocent as we'd like to be. Media entertainment satisfies nothing but our longing for innocence. Inflation and intense experiences give us so little nutrition for the soul, so little *communitas*, that sooner or later we succumb to the need for a scapegoat.

Two: Scapegoating American Dionysus

The ancient Hebrews had an atonement rite involving two goats. They killed *and burnt* the first one. Its blood placated Jehovah and purified the people, who confessed their sins and symbolically loaded them onto the second goat (Leviticus 17:22, *"And the goat shall bear upon him all their iniquities unto a land not inhabited"*). They dedicated this goat to *Azazel*, a Semitic goat-god who embodied primal creativity and sexual potency. Then they sent it away into the wilderness. Along with it they sent its unruly, Dionysian energies back to their origin in the unconscious.

By contrast, certain pagan rituals involved killing a kid, cutting it into pieces and stewing it in its mother's milk. They were symbolically and consciously returning their own Dionysian energies to the underworld. Then they ate it as a kind of communion, safely re-incorporating it. The Hebrews forbade this custom, repressing Azazel/Dionysus in favor of their god Jehovah. Whereas early paganism renewed itself through periodic festivals of ecstatic license and sacred marriage, the Hebrews did so through expelling negative elements.

The Greeks used both methods. Athens annually expelled two men to purify the city of moral pollution. *Pharmakon* (root of "pharmacy") meant both poison and its antidote, just as Dionysus both caused and cured madness. By scapegoating the *pharmakoi,* the community briefly banished its own destructive impulses. Some claim that *katharsis,* the emotional release experienced by dramatic audiences, corresponded to an earlier release that the entire community experienced in mystery plays celebrating the death and resurrection of Dionysus.

Many peoples practiced similar customs: some loaded animals with their sins or unacceptable desires and sent them away; others symbolically loaded their sins onto boats and released them into the ocean. There are countless examples of human scapegoating, in which communities chose certain men to act the part of death, evil, sickness or Dionysus himself. Symbolically or literally, the people killed or exiled these men, who took the pollution with them. Often this happened during New Year's rituals, which purified the land for the following year and hastened the end of winter. In the Roman *Saturnalia,* a mock king briefly ruled over everyone before being killed. Later, the Christian mass reenacted the sacrificial murder of Jesus to exemplify its central theme of redemption.

Medieval Carnival crowned a "King of Fools" to reign over the festivities, at the end of which he stood accused of everyone's sins and was symbolically killed. In some areas, the people hunted and symbolically killed the Dionysian "wild man of the woods" to call forth the end of winter. After these holidays in chaos, the authorities restored the regular moral order and everyone reverted to their social roles.

These are all examples from times when vestiges of the indigenous, creative imagination survived. But the mythic mesocosm had nearly completely broken down by the Renaissance. With scientific advances and the Protestant rebellion questioning the authority of the church, darker forms of scapegoating evolved. The Inquisition's *auto-de-fe,* or "test of faith," was an elaborate, communal ritual of murder, purification and warning to those who might exceed the bounds of acceptable thought. Both Catholics and Protestants brought this tradition to the New World.

Such ceremonies of human sacrifice were essentially equivalent to those practiced in Africa, Mexico and Oceania. Common components included consecrated places, fire (symbolizing the deity to be propitiated) and a tree where the deed was performed. "The victim," writes sociologist Orlando Patterson, "mediated between the sacred and the profane."[15] His sacrifice created a compact between the people and their deity, expiating their sins and reinforcing their values.

Often, when the community needed to resolve some fundamental social transition, human sacrifice became its method. American Southern whites faced precisely such a period of acute liminal transition in the decades after the Civil War, and they performed regular rituals of human sacrifice well into the 1930s.

René Girard writes that every society develops rituals to protect its members from their own potential violence, periodically identifying a victim whose violent death will cure the community. He is truly a "healing drug" because once the community has identified *him* as the source of the trouble, then they can violently rid themselves of the pollution. This action reconstitutes "…a true community, united in its hatred for one alone of its number… any community that has fallen prey to violence or has been stricken by some overwhelming catastrophe hurls itself blindly into the search for a scapegoat."[16]

The community achieves temporary unity and restored innocence by focusing its shadow upon the Other (usually identified as having the Dionysian qualities of sexuality or irrational violence) and projecting it outwards where all can safely view it. However, the need to be cleansed of the unacceptable feelings always builds up again.

Scapegoating typically involves accusations of intra-family — mythic — crimes such as incest and especially, *the killing of the children*. Romans accused early Christians of eating children. Once in power, Christians used the same ploy to justify persecutions of pagans, and later of Jews. In sixteenth-century France, as many women were executed for alleged infanticide as for witchcraft. In the twentieth century, both Jews and Germans were called baby killers. As recently as the Gulf War of 1991, pre-war U.S. propaganda claimed that Iraqis had killed Kuwaiti babies.

Consider again our fundamental Western images of fathering. Ouranos abandons his children, while Kronos *consumes* his. Abraham would sacrifice Isaac to prove himself before Yahweh, who sacrifices his own son Jesus. These figures serve as models for centuries of uninitiated men, who narcissistically manipulate their children/soldiers/supporters, etc, to curry favor with their gods. In the toxic mimic of initiation, those who forget the necessity of *symbolically* killing the child inevitably find more *literal* ways to do so.

Our demythologized culture socializes children by destroying their experience of primordial unity and instilling the basic polarities (black/white, male/female, good/evil, etc) upon which it is built. But this process, begun in original sin, leaves tremendous reservoirs of guilt in the western mind. In response, the collective unconscious dreamed up mythic images of the killing of the children and projected them onto a long series of scapegoats who, in their righteous suffering, might cleanse us of our sins.

The killing of the children, one of patriarchy's fundamental statements, is the universal substrate for scapegoating in America. No longer allowed to engage in literal child-sacrifice, we do so through abuse, battery, negligence, rape and institutionalized hopelessness. Girls eleven years old or younger make up thirty percent of rape victims, and juvenile sexual assault victims know their perpetrators ninety-three percent of the time. A quarter of American children live in poverty; over a million of them are homeless.

But aren't adolescents troublemakers? When polled, adults estimate that juveniles are responsible for forty-three percent of violent crime. Sociologist Mike Males, however, reports that teenagers commit only thirteen percent of these crimes. Yet nearly half the states prosecute children as young as *ten* as if they were adults, and over fifty percent of adults favor executing teenage killers.

In fact, argues Males, "aging baby boomers" are responsible for most drug addiction and crime, and most of them are white. Adults deny the extent and causes of our social problems by falling back upon the mythically-charged war against the children, easily substituting the code word "teenage" for "black" or "Latino."[17] Thus, the domestic war on minority children yields some stunning numbers. *American youths consistently receive prison sentences sixty percent longer than adults for the same crimes.* When adults are the victims of sex crimes, sentences are tougher than when the victims are children; and parents who abuse their children receive shorter sentences than strangers who do so.

New ways continually emerge for the sins of the fathers to fall upon the young. "Zero tolerance" policies allow school administrators no leeway for interpretation. A valedictorian is charged with a felony and banned from her graduation for mistakenly leaving a kitchen knife in her car. A thirteen-year-old who brings a model rocket to show in class is suspended. An eleven-year-old is jailed for bringing a plastic knife in her lunch box. A ten-year-old is suspended for sexual harassment for asking a boy if he liked her. Mall police turn away *girl scouts* for being "similarly dressed." A third of the students of a Chicago high school are expelled because of zero tolerance. It began not through political correctness, but because governments that cannot enact real gun control for *adults* divert the spotlight onto children. And youths convicted of *any* drug offense permanently lose federal financial aid (over 130,000 so far).

We further scapegoat children with standardized testing and the cruel euphemism of "No Child Left Behind," which relies on threats and punishment, imposes narrow agendas and simplistic tests, overrules local control, punishes entire schools for the failures of the few, and completely ignores the impact of poverty.

Where does the anger go in a culture that eats its children? We identify persons whose mere existence questions our identity, especially our notions of gender, and label them as child-molesters. If *they* are guilty, then *we* remain innocent. This relieves us of the "terror of history," says historian Teofilo Ruiz: "... at the very root of our making into civilized people lies always the fact of child sacrifice."[18]

In raising individualism to mythic status we stigmatize individuals as well as groups. It is far easier to identify priests, gays or single men as child molesters than to address unemployment, overcrowded schools, family disintegration or institutionalized violence. It is now virtually impossible for men to work in early education; they comprise only one of *eleven* elementary teachers.

Increasing visibility of gays on TV has encouraged many LGBT adolescents to publicly identify themselves. The pressure of high school and peer-group conformism, however, has resulted in much painful scapegoating. One in seven teenagers attempts suicide, but gay youth try at two to three times that rate, and comprise thirty percent of *completed* youth suicides.

Young women serve as scapegoats when other targets are unavailable. It is likely in vast areas of the country for a girl who has been raped and impregnated by a relative to have no access to abortion (family rape is the source of forty percent of teen pregnancies). She might run away with her child to escape the ongoing abuse, go on welfare (until the funds run out and the state takes the child) and become a homeless prostitute. She would be a sacrificial victim, no different in any respect from similar girls in the Middle East.

We scapegoat minorities, gays, women and youth. Three of these streams of vitriol converge on black, teenage girls (all four if they are gay). The "welfare queen" still bears the burden of an old tradition in which the legal system equated lack of chastity with lack of veracity. Courts often refused to trust the testimony of women who were considered to be promiscuous, or who "provoked" men by the way they dressed.

Economic decline leads to new forms of intolerance. Immigration and gay marriage are the current "values" issues, which follow prior panics over demonic abuse, alien abduction and poison in Halloween candy.

Long before our concern over child molesters, however, a uniquely American pattern of scapegoating existed. The grizzly murder of thousands of black men — based upon accusations of *sexual relations with white women* — remains our richest, if saddest, example of poor-quality Dionysus. Sociologist Calvin Hernton wrote in 1966 that the image of the black sexual beast was so extreme in the mind of the racist that he had to eradicate it, yet so powerful that he worshipped it:

> In taking the Black man's genitals, the hooded men in white are amputating that portion of themselves which they secretly consider vile, filthy, and most of all, inadequate...(they) hope to acquire the grotesque powers they have assigned to the Negro phallus, which they symbolically extol by the act of destroying it.[19]

The threat of lynching kept both black men and white women in their places in the rigid southern hierarchies of race and gender. Elites knew that racial violence kept poor blacks and whites from uniting politically. Patterson, however, asks that we look more deeply into the *sacrificial* nature of lynching. Of five thousand cases reported between 1880 and 1930, at least forty percent appear to be actual human sacrifices, communal rituals that identified certain individuals as the source of the community's problems and eliminated them.

Lynchings were very often *not* spontaneous mob-violence, nor were they quick and clean; they were carefully orchestrated events. All social classes participated, *clergymen* usually presided, and Sunday was the favorite day. The site, chosen in advance and advertised in newspapers, often even before the victim was apprehended, was usually a tree in the center of the community. Trees had been sacred to both pagans and Christians. Both Adam's fall and Christ's death were associated with tree-symbols. Christianity itself had been founded upon a human sacrifice.

Since white supremacy was a *religion,* wrote theologian James Sellers, all threats to it took on mythic importance. "Segregation is a system of belief that would protect its devotees from…'the powers of death and destruction'… It therefore becomes a holy path, complete with commandments, priests, theologians…"[20] The question of actual guilt was often quite irrelevant. If the mob couldn't apprehend the accused man, they'd randomly select one of his kinsmen for the sacrifice. Often, they ritually tortured him for hours before burning him at the stake. Then they distributed his remains like religious relics, for his death *and dismemberment* (think Pentheus) had cleansed and unified them.

The myth of the Old South, writes Patterson, stated that the presence of the Other, not a slavery-based economy, had caused its shameful defeat. The ex-slave symbolized both violence and sin to an obsessed society. He was "obviously" enslaved to the flesh, and his skin invited a fusion of racial and religious symbolism. His "black" malignancy was to the body politic what Satan was to the soul. "The central ritual of this version of the Southern civil religion…was the human sacrifice of the lynch mob."[21]

Reading of such astonishing brutality, we recall the crazed Agave and her sisters dismembering Pentheus:

> *...shrieking in triumph. One tore off an arm, another a foot still*
> *warm in its shoe. His ribs were clawed clean of flesh and every*
> *hand was smeared with blood...*

And we recall the delight in *detailed imagery* taken by Puritan chroniclers:

> ...to see them thus frying in the fryer, and the streams of
> blood quenching the same, and horrible was the stincke and
> sente there of, but the victory seemed a sweete sacrifice...

Approaching Dionysus forces us to encounter the potentials for horror as well as ecstasy that lie within us. We must first know who we have been and still are before we can imagine what we might someday be; the ghosts of the past require this. In 1899, before torturing him, ten thousand Texans paraded their black victim on a carnival float, like the King of Fools, like Dionysus in the *Anthesteria*, or like Christ at Calvary. Patterson writes, "... the burning cross distilled it all: sacrificed Negro joined by the torch with sacrificed Christ, burnt together and discarded..."[22]

Ninety years later, Senator Orrin Hatch explains, apparently without irony, how we perpetuate our sense of innocence: *"Capital punishment is our society's recognition of the sanctity of human life. "*[23] America executes people (eighty percent of them poor minorities) to dramatize our disapproval of violence, even though over 130 Death Row inmates have been exonerated since 1972. Race, especially if the accused is black and the victim is white, remains the primary factor in death penalty decisions.

Such attitudes survive because black men represent the violence that whites can't admit is a core part of the American soul. For over seventy years, lynching was the perfect symbolic tool to expiate it. "Today," writes Patterson, " we no longer lynch in public rituals supervised by local clergymen. Instead, the state hires the hangman to do it."[24]

Since literal sacrifice became socially unacceptable, we have found subtler means to quarantine our cultural shadow, imprisoning more of our citizens than any other country. America today has five times as many prisoners as it did in 1980, when the backlash began in earnest. Over half of them are men of color, whom we continue to police, profile and punish in hugely disproportionate numbers.[25]

The myth of innocence identifies young black men as inherently and irredeemably violent. When they show they can rise above the conditions imposed upon them, the state intervenes to prove its accusations. Los Angeles police have repeatedly, deliberately sabotaged the truces carefully crafted by youth gangs.[26]

Racism and sexism intersect in scapegoating. Throughout the 1990s, many black celebrities (Mike Tyson, Clarence Thomas, Michael Jackson, O.J. Simpson, Kobe Bryant, etc.) were accused of sexual improprieties. Although the nation needed to discuss the issue openly, the media's focus on these men confirmed racial stereotypes and allowed whites to absorb the truth of rape and harassment by displacing responsibility for it on to blacks. Again, innocence prevailed.

Scapegoating of blacks has always proceeded in long-term cycles of collusion between the federal government, the media, local elites, police, schools and trade unions. But in 2005, the cycle was condensed into a single week in New Orleans. Stage One, universal neglect of the poor, appeared in Louisiana's overt, institutional racism. Specific federal policies and intentional lack of preparedness intensified the conditions for catastrophe. When it occurred, *the Bush administration knew that the levees had been breached but refused to notify local authorities.*[27]

Stage Two: After the storm, FEMA's incompetence (including preventing the Red Cross from entering the city) resulted in massive suffering and false but well-publicized scenes of black violence and degradation. The media emphasized anarchy and crime over cooperation. TV showed blacks "looting," while whites were "finding food." Barbara Bush and televangelists offered gratuitous, racist commentary.

These media images quickly reinforced racist stereotypes, and Stage Three evolved. In the old fear of madness at the gates, white suburbanites refused entry to the "refugees." Vigilantes murdered at least eleven black men, and none of the crimes were investigated.[28] Local police ignored rescue duty to protect private property. With 200,000 blacks suddenly rendered homeless (and ineligible to vote), the conditions were set for a return of the cycle to Stage One, further neglect at the federal level. Three months later, only twenty percent of whites agreed that the federal government's failure to respond had anything to do with race (ninety percent of blacks did).

America has found countless scapegoats, but why are we periodically compelled to *lynch* only one of them? In truth, popular thinking remains polarized along racial lines: civilized vs. primitive, abstinence vs. promiscuity and sobriety vs. intoxication, all forming the opposition between *composure and impulsivity* (mythologically, Apollo and Dionysus). The worst of all sins to the Puritan is lack of self-control. Even while similar percentages of whites and blacks engage in sex, drugs and violence, whites believe stereotypes of blacks as more susceptible to such "vices." This allows whites, wrote Ralph Ellison, "...to be at home in the vast unknown world of America."[29]

Othering is not logical. As with archetypes, when one pole of a stereotype is active, so is its opposite. Even as they perceive blacks as unable to control their desires, *large majorities* of whites accuse blacks of the Puritan's second worst sin, laziness. Two thirds say that the problems suffered by blacks are due to their preference for welfare over work. This is an odd claim, writes Wise, "...seeing as how five out of six blacks don't receive any."[30]

The next step in scapegoating is manipulating the fear that those who can't control their desires will tempt us to follow them, that *we* might not be able to resist temptation. The black man is America's modern Dionysus. Like the enigmatic outsider of *The Bacchae,* he comes from beyond the gates to liberate the women, to lead them to the mountains to dance among themselves, free of patriarchal control.

The projection of American Dionysus combines scapegoating with envy of those who appear to be comfortable in their bodies and unrestrained in their desires. In a culture that elevates the dry, masculine, Apollonian virtues of *spirit* over the wet, feminine and Dionysian, blacks proudly use the word *soul* to define their music and culture in contrast to the dominant national values. White youth understand the term instinctively. Patterson observes that in only a few generations America's internal Other has expanded to include aspects of which white America is now admittedly, nervously envious. This ultimate Dionysian symbol crosses boundaries and dissolves them. "The Afro-American male body — as superathlete, as irresistible entertainer...as sexual outlaw, as gangster."[31]

Black athletes and entertainers attract a mainstream culture that is over-balanced toward Apollonian demands. In this context, African-American images have become a "Dionysian counterweight" unstably balanced with the discipline required of those who must tolerate the conditions of the modern workplace. Dionysus has free reign in the inner cities, where he remains safely contained, "...until the instinctual need for release from the Apollonian pressures...calls for its tethered, darkened presence."[32]

Blacks provide much of the cultural container that allows white youth (who purchase seventy percent of hip-hop music) to act out some mild rebellion between their suburban school years and the corporate life they must eventually submit to. This is no initiation, merely a controlled transition into consumer lifestyles. All learn to suppress their innate grandiosity of soul and project it onto celebrities. Instead of living creative lives as involved citizens, we consume the cultural products, including Dionysus, that the media feeds to us. Generally, however, we *watch* the Dionysian experience, like Pentheus in his tree spying on the maenads.

Instead of carrying Dionysus, we carry "stuff." *Brands* engage us very early. The average 10-year-old has memorized 400 brands, and the average kindergartner can identify 300 logos.[33] Rather than selling specific products, advertising is more concerned with establishing consumer allegiance to a brand, with building, writes Todd Gitlin, "...a ladder in the imagination from attention to belief..."[34] As with all symbols, logos point toward the real thing, which is our human need to proclaim a genealogy and a connection to community. That community was once with living persons, spirits, ancestors and animals. But when the snake clan disappears from memory, we turn to Nike "swatches," Michael Jordan basketball shoes, allegiance to a warlord or any symbol of shared devotion that proclaims: "Here we are! Ignore us at your peril!"

Assuming that blacks have a certain license to behave in ways the culture as a whole chooses to repress, whites project both fear and envy. Some blacks play along for profit. Others, writes historian Gerald Early, resent "the entrapment of sensuality we are forced to wear as a mask for the white imagination."[35] Meanwhile, Hip-Hop subculture reflects the killing of the children back toward the wider culture. It displays anger and self-confidence in the lyrics, but (as Michael Meade has noted) *grief* and *depression* in the clothing: baggy pants, drooping below the waste; everything pulled down; collapsed. Adolescents, especially minorities, are well aware of being forced to carry the weight of the world that their parents cannot.

From the perspective of those who bear the projection of American Dionysus, the subtext of most of our pressing domestic issues is race.

THE STREETS: WELFARE, IMMIGRATION, CRIME, HOMELESSNESS

Is Welfare a "black" problem? A million black children live in "extreme poverty" (defined as disposable annual income of less than $7,000 for a family of three). But the typical welfare recipients are a thirty-year-old woman and her two children, forced there by divorce and abandoned by their unemployed father. Realistic estimates of poverty in America prior to the current economic collapse ranged from forty to eighty million people, most of them *white*.

The narrative veils the issues of corporate welfare, financial corruption and deindustrialization and the fact that most white males vote Republican, partially because they fear affirmative action. Few admit the racial dimensions of the issue and the degree to which even poor whites have privilege. Actually, the generosity of state welfare reform varies according to demography: those with overwhelmingly white populations have stronger safety nets and impose softer sanctions.

Reagan inspired his followers with tales of black welfare mothers riding about in Cadillacs. Don't these pictures evoke Dionysus, with his frenzied women and satyrs, parading through town, spreading their "values" like Mardi Gras beads? Aren't they the essence of the sinful, fallen life to the Puritanical mind, and aren't they tantalizing? What if all that self-control didn't guarantee redemption? What if "they" really are not just happier but *better?*

Illegal immigration is a classic image of madness at the gates. In the familiar mythic pattern, conservatives project essentially the same qualities onto Latinos as they do onto blacks. Significant immigration from *northern*

Europe ended by 1900. Since then, most newcomers have arrived from countries that don't sanctify Protestant traditions of self-denial. Some haven't grasped the sacred notion of delayed gratification. Many of them *dance.*

The anxiety, as always, stems primarily from the Puritan fear of pollution by those values and physical characteristics that evoke our Dionysian shadow. A second source of the anxiety is the assumption of scarcity; in a zero-sum world, one group's (blacks) gain is another group's (whites) loss. It surfaces in the common perception that illegal immigrants are criminals and are costly burdens upon taxpaying citizens. Corporate managers, however, know very well how immigrants stabilize the economy.

Recently, the right wing has successfully conflated the issues of immigration and terrorism, especially in pork-barrel Homeland Security expenditures. As I have suggested, the Paranoid Imagination does not discriminate between inner and outer. Whenever we evoke one pole of the archetype of the Other (formerly communism, now terrorism), *the other pole (race) automatically constellates.* Immigration, not a major issue until well after 9/11, combines both. In 2007, a Republican activist said, "Some of these people may be coming in here to get jobs washing dishes, but some of them are coming in here to hijack airplanes...I can't tell Jose Cuervo from Al Queda..."[36] He was framing the issue to stress not criminality but otherness. That same year, state legislatures introduced over 1,400 immigration measures, a number that exceeded the total of the previous ten years.

Curiously, we project onto blacks and browns exactly what the heritage of discrimination ensures that they *don't* have: power and influence. Lurid headlines in the early 1990s warned of amoral "superpredators" who'd kill for basketball shoes. In fact, blacks commit only a quarter of all violent crimes, and whites are far more likely to be assaulted by other whites than by blacks. But race-based fear trumps common sense, and politicians continue to profit by promising, like Pentheus, to seize the Other and lock him up. The frenzy of prison construction and execution of minorities continues even as national crime rates drop. Over 2,000 prisoners are serving life sentences for crimes committed when they were seventeen or younger.

Black youths are serving life without parole at a rate of about 10 times that of white youths.

Black men, simply by being visible, contribute to our unique ebb-and-flow of fear and denial. Whites begin to remove their children from local schools and move out when neighborhoods become as little as eight percent black. Although the streets are safer than a generation ago, many whites concede urban space to the Other, preferring to watch easy solutions in urban crime dramas, or to bypass poor neighborhoods entirely en route to suburban malls and sports arenas.

For a generation, the exhausted and terrified white middle class has engaged in a new activity, "cocooning" (renting DVDs, surfing the net and shopping online). Ten million work at home and eight to sixteen million live in gated communities. But fear only leads to further alienation. Astonishing to Europeans and tribal people alike, households listed as "people living alone" comprise the largest category in America. The number of people who have *no one* with whom to discuss important matters has more than doubled in two decades.[37]

A major reason for urban unease is the homeless. Disheveled and sweaty, they could be infected with God knows what. Contrasting with our buzz-cut hairstyles, they are often the only people in the crowd with long hair and beards. Many (at least 250,000) remind us of America's last tragic crusade in Viet Nam. They harass us by begging or raving. They are everywhere. Three and a half million Americans, *two-fifths of them children,* are homeless at some point in a given year. They make us *feel* disgust, pity, anxiety and guilt.

And so many are black men. Hurrying to produce or consume, we find a certain comfort in their bizarre and unembarrassed behavior. Innocence beckons; we distance ourselves from the uncomfortable feelings by retreating into judgment and conclude that their misery is their own fault, proof again of *our* state of grace. We suppress the knowledge that we are all, like motherless children, far from home.

Much of the millions that cities spend on homelessness is wasted, because they are powerless to impact its systemic causes. Serving business's demands to clean up downtown, police roust the homeless and push them across arbitrary political boundaries into other cities, or in New York, into underground subway tubes, where some 5,000 people allegedly live. Like Zeus and Odin, we tolerate the Other down there, in the underworld, repressed into the unconscious. The myths, however, speak of the price those gods pay in constant vigilance because those below, like horror movie villains who refuse to die, perpetually threaten to re-emerge.

THE BODY: GAY MARRIAGE, TEEN PREGNANCY, ABORTION, CHILD ABUSE

The arguments against same-sex marriage come down to its assumed threat against marriage itself, as if rights granted to the Other would come at one's own expense, as if the institution of marriage were not already collapsing. Below that concern lie questions about one's own choices, and the Puritan hatred and envy of those who can't control themselves. And those assumptions veil the more fundamental fear of *contagion,* that mere proximity to the Other destroys one's carefully constructed boundaries, that one, or one's children, might *become* the Other. Their response to the entire sexual revolution is framed in Puritanical terms; AIDS is clearly divine judgment for the unforgivable sin of allowing one's impulses free reign, and a clear warning to those (including themselves) who might contemplate such behavior.

Shock-jocks condemn the spectacle of second-generation welfare mothers. But even though states with the lowest welfare rates have the *highest* teen pregnancy rates, the charge that public assistance promotes single motherhood has mythic power. As with homophobia, the attack on promiscuity derives its energy from Puritan rage at the notion of *pleasure without consequences.* Like maenads, these women seem to follow their god at government expense.

Framing the issue in this manner allows us to evade the question of why so many of these girls don't use contraception. The pagan explanation is that they are searching for initiation by creating new life. While boys push one edge, extending themselves outwards toward unknown challenges, girls generally push the other edge, taking that risky energy inward. Sex education doesn't impact the causes of the longing to be seen as women once they bear children. In traditional cultures, older women have always welcomed girls into the adult ranks at first menstruation, but such customs are non-existent in America. So girls often turn to older but equally uninitiated *men*, especially those who enact the role of American Dionysus, to conduct their rites of passage. As a result, two-thirds of babies born to teenage girls are fathered by *adult* men.

Liberating women from their constricted circumstances, Dionysus is an image (as much as a male figure can be) of *female* independence. As such, he becomes the archetypal object of the murderous rage the radical right directs at abortion providers, who are in essence Dionysian figures. With their images of aborted fetuses, these extremists actually project their hatred of their own inner children, as well as one of the culture's primary myths — the killing of the children — onto these convenient scapegoats.

Some argue that men whose sense of control is the most tenuous are the worst misogynists. Many anti-abortion activists are Baby Boomer males who earn less than their fathers had. They resent women's professional progress as well as their sexual freedom. Susan Faludi writes, "Sexual independence, not murder (of the unborn), may have been the feminists' greater crime."[38]

They point us toward the deeper issue, in which, once again, we invert reality to maintain our innocence. Obsession with the unborn masks the facts that we are often dealing with "the Idea of the Child" rather than *actual* children, whom America has abandoned and left to die in massive numbers. In 2008, prior to the economic meltdown, at least twenty percent of American children were living in poverty (*forty* percent in New York City), and thirty million Americans, most of them children, were hungry. These statistics resulted not from mistakes but from deliberate policy. In the 1980s, hunger declined everywhere, with two exceptions: sub-Saharan Africa and the U.S., where it increased by fifty percent, primarily due to the attack on welfare. Six hundred thousand American children are physically abused and 300,000 are sexually abused yearly. *Family members* kill two-thirds of children who are murdered.

We insulate our fantasy of national innocence by forcing both suffering and responsibility upon the *truly* innocent. The logic of Puritanism condemns millions of children because of the alleged laziness of their parents. "We" can be innocent and deserving only if we compel "them" (children, minorities and, especially the children *of* minorities, those whom American Dionysus has fathered) to bear this burden. And the logic goes a step further: *American children are taught in countless subtle ways that they are the source of their own suffering.* Such children become adults who yearn to pass on their rage to new scapegoats.

THE UNDERWORLD: PRISONS AND ASYLUMS

While thousands literally dwell underground, forced institutionalization is our symbolic underworld and the prime repository for our scapegoats. With five percent of the world's population, we have a quarter of its prisoners. Over 500,000 work in corrections, tending to a prison population that has risen by six hundred percent since 1970. Now, one in every thirty adults is in the corrections system. Over 25,000 are in solitary confinement, one third of whom, because of this treatment, will become psychotic.[39]

The U.S. is the only democracy that disenfranchises felons, over five million people, two million of whom are black. This simple fact has utterly determined the course of recent history. The more African-Americans a state contains, the more likely it is to ban felons. The average state disenfranchises 2.4 percent of its voting-age population but 8.4 percent of blacks. In fourteen states, the share of blacks stripped of the vote exceeds ten percent, and in five states it exceeds twenty percent. While seventy-five percent of whites register, only sixty percent of blacks can. Seven Republican senators owe their election to these laws. Had felons been allowed to vote in 2000, Al Gore's popular vote margin would have doubled to a million. If Florida had allowed just *ex*-felons to vote, he would have carried the state by 30,000 votes and with it the presidency.[40]

Of the mentally disturbed, sixty thousand are in asylums, 280,000 are incarcerated and 550,000 are on probation. Without funding health services, Reagan-era deinstitutionalization merely dumped them on the streets. They comprise fifteen percent of Los Angeles County Jail's 21,000 inmates (some 3,200 people on a given day), making it America's largest mental institution.

We have defined these "Others" as dangerous, beyond redemption or simply too uncomfortable to behold. Most had long been invisible to middle-class society, but the social revolutions of the 1960s forced the nation to see them. The vision was so disturbing that, beginning with Reagan, we have gone to great lengths to push them back into the underworld. There, they serve to justify the prison-industrial complex *and* the nursing-home industrial complex, and they provide cheap labor for the industries that function inside those walls. Now, Pentheus has Dionysus well secured within the towers, and Dionysus more than pays his own way.

THE OUTSIDE AGITATOR

Dionysus has a counterpart, however, outside the walls. The Other as drug dealer tempts the children, but the terrorist Other wants to destroy the palace itself. The truth is that *right-wingers* have perpetrated the vast majority of terrorist incidents in America in the past sixty years: the Kennedy and King assassinations; the Oklahoma City bombing; dozens of racially motivated church-burnings (civil rights activists called Birmingham, Alabama, "Bombingham"); and countless bombings and shootings by right-wing Cuban-Americans and anti-abortion fanatics.

But fear of the outsider is stronger than ever, and that fear was nurtured through the deliberate creation of an image. For four decades J. Edgar Hoover described those who threatened the status quo as "outside agitators," regardless of their nationality. This almost poetic image of the Dionysian menace implies three assumptions about the *polis*. The first is innocence: evil comes from abroad. It implies that communist ideas couldn't possibly originate *here*. Terrorism, quips Chomsky, is "what others do to us."[41]

A second assumption is *weakness*. Just as youths seemingly cannot resist drugs or sex, the *polis* can entertain only the mildest diversity of opinion. If allowed access to the children, communists would prevent discrimination of right from wrong and infect the national immune system with their "agit-prop."

A third assumption about us is *fairness*. Pentheus, who would attack directly, throws fastballs, while Dionysus throws curves. The terrorist could be a friend or co-worker. He is urban, possibly Jewish. He infects us through trickery rather than through direct, "manly" confrontation. And since he refuses to play by our rules, we are justified in our righteous and overpowering vengeance.

Both terrorists and black men provoke the curiosity of the innocent, white citizen because they are close, much closer than the rest of us, to death. In the psyche, death evokes initiation. Perhaps the deniers of death, writes Zoja, envy the initiate, "he or she who has contact with another dimension... someone to whom a truth has been revealed."[42] This insight leads us back to the Greek meaning of scapegoat, the *pharmakos*, who was both the poison and its antidote. Anthropologists agree that sacrifice (literally, "to make sacred") is a religious act, in which the victim is raised to the status of the deity so as to briefly bridge (Latin, *pons*, root of *pontiff*) the gap between the worlds, unite the community and wash away sin.

THREE: "GETTING OFF," THE SEARCH FOR ECSTASY IN PORNOGRAPHY AND DRUGS

Opinions about pornography do not break down into conventional right-left polarities. Both religious conservatives as well as many feminists who are concerned about the objectification of women hate it. Andrea Dworkin helped frame laws in the 1980s defining porn as "a form of discrimination... sexually explicit subordination of women."[43] To Susan Griffin, porn is "...a sadistic act" which humiliates all women.[44]

Others, however, argue that censorship always limits liberation struggles and that anti-pornography activism preserves the virgin/whore dichotomy that denies women access to erotic pleasure. The gay and feminist porn industries counter the argument that porn by definition subordinates women. Wendy McElroy suggests a "value-neutral" definition: "explicit artistic depiction of men and/or women as sexual beings."[45] Janice Radway insists on women's right to their own fantasies. In romantic novels: "... if he is 'mad with desire,' rape reflects *her* power over *him*. "[46]

But we can all agree that porn is big business. Annual U.S. profits are $6-10 billion; worldwide revenues are $100 billion. There are 15,000-20,000 adult bookstores in the U.S. The industry employs 100,000 people and produces 13,000 movies/year. Seventy percent of young men visit porn web sites monthly. Some argue that porn is the economic engine that actually drives the Internet; in 2005 there were over 6,000 sites devoted solely to child porn. So we need to ask, *Why is porn so appealing?*

James Hillman suggests that porn is the return of the repressed. Denied access to our cultural consciousness, the goddess Aphrodite has cast a spell over Western culture, reappearing in images of the female body.[47] But the only way she can reach us is through *fantasy.* He suggests replacing dictionary definitions which link "pornographic" with "obscene" with this one: "lustful images, or imaginal lust" that appear in the fantasies of those who lack Aphrodite in their *actual* lives.

Myth tells us that Aphrodite had a son with Dionysus: *Priapus,* the grotesque, hard-core character with the enormous erection. For some reason, Hera cursed the pregnant Aphrodite, and the misshapen child resulted, along with our condemnation of porn.

Hillman sees repression of Aphrodite everywhere, not simply as the lack of sexual pleasure, but also as the loss of the "sensate quality of the world" — *beauty* — from ugly buildings and tasteless tomatoes to talk radio and the soul-less language of psychotherapy. Consumerism, for all its marketing of sex and free choice, actually limits our modes of encountering the world to the economic and the therapeutic. It has banished the aesthetic; we live "an-aesthetized" lives.

This brings us back to definitions. From the start, Puritanism attempted to regulate one's *internal fantasies.* As late as 1936, the U.S. government defined smut so broadly that the circulation of birth control information through the mail remained a federal offense. But the market for sexual imagery persisted. The Hollywood production code, adopted in the early 1930s, measured a film's moral standing by its portrayal of crime and violence, but its chief criterion for a negative rating was sexual content. Images of men taking life were not obscene, while images of women giving birth were.

Cold Warriors claimed that porn would weaken America's moral fiber. In 1995, Texas still banned *heterosexual* sodomy. Just before the invasion of Iraq, North Dakota's state Senate explicitly voted not to repeal its anti-cohabitation law. The federal government has spent over $1.5 billion on abstinence-only education, despite its own studies that show that such programs have no effect on sexual behavior among youth. Why? The obsession with denial and innocence makes the obscene wholly sexualized. Dislocated from its actual daily occasions (toxic dumps, rape, clear-cut forests, TV tortures, homelessness, mangled Iraqi children, etc.), obscenity is displaced onto the body, the source of all those desires, the thing that must, above all, be controlled.

The release of tension through masturbation, presumably the goal of pornography, has been condemned by religions, philosophers (Kant, Voltaire and Rousseau) and, until recently, by scientists. Doctors have used both female genital circumcision and castration to cure or prevent "diseases" such as lesbianism that were allegedly caused by masturbation. A 1959 urology textbook advised mechanical restraints to prevent masturbation.

But the clues to the real issues are in the Puritan's own fantasies. In 1889, one firebrand ranted against babysitters who allegedly allowed children to masturbate: "...the crime could hardly have been worse had the nurse...*cut the throats* of those innocent children..."[48] Recall Ashcroft and Powell, veiling the nude statue of Justice and Picasso's *Guernica*. Why are we so obsessed not simply with defining smut, but with *describing* it?

Puritans, says the old joke, have the nagging suspicion that someone, somewhere, may be enjoying himself. What are they so afraid of? Hillman answers: "The free-flow of fantasy images. We don't know where the fantasy might go."[49] "After all," writes Jervis, "sex represents the *opposite* of mastery of the body: an irrational subordination *to* the body..."[50]

Tribal societies rarely punish masturbation. They set limits on social behavior, but through their rich, polytheistic mythologies, they encourage the development of the inner world, or the imaginative capacity. By contrast, patriarchs from the Catholic Church to the Soviet state restrict all imagination, with the exception of the *paranoid* imagination.

But the more images are controlled, the more we are obsessed with them and the more they demand recognition ("to think about again"). In 1991 the Supreme Court agreed that Indiana could close a private club that advertised nude dancing. Antonin Scalia wrote the majority opinion: "The purpose of Indiana's nudity law would be violated...if sixty thousand fully consenting adults crowded into the Hoosier Dome to display their genitals to one another, even if there were not an offended innocent in the crowd."[51]

Would Puritans be so disturbed by naked dancing if the act didn't already exist in their imagination? Nobody prodded Scalia to visualize that image. *His imagination produced it.* Similarly, Texas senator John Cornyn argues, "It does not affect your daily life...if your neighbor marries a box turtle. But that does not mean it is right..."[52] Cornyn's *imagination* conjured pictures of inter-species marriage. Pat Robertson wonders if a man who "likes to have sex with ducks" should be protected by hate crime legislation. Former Pennsylvania senator Rick Santorum muses:

> "If the Supreme Court says that you have a right to consensual sex within your home, then you have the right to bigamy...
> to polygamy... to incest...to adultery. You have the right to anything!.. That's not to pick on homosexuality. It's not, you know, man on child, man on dog..."[53]

Indeed. They care so deeply about these images because they can't stop thinking about them. But they can't allow them into awareness with a clean conscience unless they have demonized them and displaced them onto someone else. Then they feel entitled to invent images like "sixty thousand fully consenting adults" and invite the Grand Inquisitor back.

Women are justifiably concerned about objectification and desensitization. But Psychologist Michael Bader argues that countries with more porn and Internet usage than ours have much lower rates of sexual violence. His male patients feel lonely and powerless but can differentiate between fantasy and reality. They view porn because it provides imaginary scenarios that safely gratify their wishes.[54] Researchers have never correlated consumption of porn with violence. Indeed, evidence suggests that its cathartic effects reduce the likelihood of acting out. Perhaps rape results from a *deprivation* of images. While Griffin argues that porn exists to suppress real Eros, to Hillman it exists precisely *because* of that suppression, especially among conservatives. One study found that states that consume the most online porn tend to be more conservative and religious than states with lower levels of consumption. A church survey claims, "50% of all Christian men and 20% of all Christian women are addicted to pornography."[55]

Our real concern, however, is with the overwhelming presence of *soft*-core porn. Denied meaningful access to Aphrodite, we turn to her toxic mimic. She returns in the appeal of consumerism, in material goods, although she is ultimately unattainable through them. But the appeal is so strong, and our longing so infinite that we become life-long addicts who could consume the earth chasing her.

All literalists of both the right (Christian or Muslim) or left (feminist or communist) assume no difference between fantasy and action and believe that having "lust in one's heart," as Jimmy Carter confessed, is the same as enacting it. But the more we recognize the reality of the psyche, the less need we have for acting out; and the less need we have to project Aphrodite or Dionysus onto others. Hillman concludes that our fundamental liberty should be the right to fantasize (ideally, through producing one's own images, but if not, by viewing those produced by others). And that right can potentially ignite an insurrection of the imagination "...for fomenting curiosity to pry into what is concealed."[56] That curiosity could in time disentangle our obscene violence from bodily images, because *violence* is the enemy, not sexuality.

Read the myth: *Psyche* marries *Eros*. He is Aphrodite's favorite son, the beautiful, winged youth. The story tells us that the soul, Psyche, cannot mature without union with the erotic imagination, and their daughter, the product of their union, is *Voluptos* (voluptuousness). Here is Paganism's alternative to Puritanism: *The end-result of soul-making is not asceticism but voluptuousness!*

What are they so afraid of? Our cultural obsessions are always connected. The paranoid imagination has linked drugs to the Other ever since Chinese immigration stirred up hysteria about opium. The early 1900s saw headlines of black drug fiends with superhuman strength. Westerners panicked in the 1930s over Mexicans getting children hooked on marijuana. Indeed, Nixon's War on Drugs was the rare crusade that targeted mainly white users. But he was more successful when he lumped youthful rebellion and black militancy with ghetto heroin addiction and the rising crime of the 1970s. After 9/11, TV ads implied that pot smokers indirectly support terrorists.

For at least the last forty years, "...when asked to envision a drug user," writes Wise, "upwards of 95% of whites say they picture a black person."[57] The image of the drug dealer veils Dionysus himself, appearing mysteriously, tempting the youth, taking advantage of their vulnerability. In 2002, Congress considered a bill to suppress the all-night dance parties, or raves, in which MDMA ("ecstasy") is consumed. It was called the RAVE bill — *"Reducing America's Vulnerability to Ecstasy."* This is a long way from tribal cultures that consider ecstasy both a fundamental right as well as insurance against violence, or from the rites of Dionysus, in which, writes Christine Downing, "Ritually sanctioned 'raving' protected against true insanity."[58]

The government places pot, the "gateway" to hard drugs, in the same risk category as heroin. However, eighty percent of adults claim that drug abuse has never caused problems in their family. Drug-related murders did skyrocket during the "crack" epidemic of the mid-1980s, but this occurred precisely at the same time as the well-documented involvement of the CIA with Latin American cocaine smuggling.

"Gateway" is a powerful image. Under other circumstances, "gateway" means the threshold of liminality. Somé says that his people call gays and bisexuals "gateway people," because they are ideal mediators of the boundaries between the worlds. Similarly, Many Native American languages have words for gays (who often become shamans) that mean, "one who changes."

But by gateway, the drug crusaders mean an opening that invites contamination by the Other, the *black* Other. Anti-drug hysteria in America is, quite simply, inseparable from racial prejudice. Blacks, thirteen percent of the population, make up the same percent of drug users and only sixteen percent of dealers, even though they comprise thirty-five percent of arrests and *seventy-five* percent of those imprisoned for drugs. White high school students are *seven times more likely than blacks* to have used cocaine or heroin and are far more likely to sell drugs. Indeed, whites are twice as likely to bring weapons to school as are blacks.

Eighty percent of crack cocaine defendants are black, despite the fact that over two-thirds of crack users are white or Latino. In the 1990s, the average time served by blacks for drug offenses increased by seventy-seven percent, compared to twenty-eight percent for whites, while the U.S. Attorney's office in Southern California went more than five years without prosecuting a white person for crack. In overwhelmingly white Minnesota, ninety percent of the people convicted for crack were black. Blacks are twice as likely as whites to have their cars searched, even though police are twice as likely to find evidence of illegal activity in cars driven by whites. Whites over age thirty make up thirty-six percent of California's population but comprise *sixty* percent of its heavy drug users. Between 1997 and 2006, 360,000 people were jailed for marijuana offenses in New York City, ten times more than had been arrested in the decade previous. While more whites used pot, *eight times as many blacks* were arrested.[59]

Americans, five percent of the world's population, consume two-thirds of all illegal drugs. Despite the penalties, 112 million *admit* to having used them. One in ten of us admit to using psychedelics. Three-quarters used only pot (while fewer than two percent went through the "gateway" to heroin). This is no subculture of deviants; it is certainly well over half the adult population. Despite the propaganda, seventy-two percent would decriminalize pot, while fifty-three percent favor outright legalization.[60] Twenty-five million Americans will smoke pot this year.

These numbers don't include those who use legal anti-depressants, nor those who abuse alcohol, nor the six million who use prescription drugs non-medically. One in ten teenagers, or 2.3 million young people, have tried prescription stimulants without a doctor's order. Fifteen thousand doctors sell prescriptions to addicts, yet less than one percent of the War on Drugs addresses abuse of legal drugs. These numbers point to one reason for the scapegoating. American culture is indeed exceptional in the degree to which it *encourages* the consumption of legal stimulants and psychotropic drugs by its children. Due to the pharmaceutical industry's marketing strategies, drug use has become an accepted part of childhood. Two generations have been brought up to believe that most psychological problems have a pharmacological solution. Once again, maintaining the myth of innocence in a Puritan culture requires that we demonize our ambivalence about self-medication and project it onto those we define as incapable of self-control.

The Old Right, with its fear of state intervention in private life, is unconcerned with the Religious Right's war on the imagination. However, the two Rights do make a wrong when they resolve their differences by attacking scapegoats. While only one-fifth of pot smokers regret having smoked, seventy-four percent (including *ninety-four percent of parents*) would disapprove if their own children experimented — as they had and still do — with drugs.

The federal government spends about $20 billion per year on the War On Drugs, and state governments spend an *additional* $20 billion. Marijuana-related arrests more than doubled from 1990 to 2002. In 2006 there were 830,000 (740,000 merely for possession), and 2007 set a new record of 872,000. The number far exceeds the number of arrests for all violent crimes combined. We spend $7.6 billion per year on marijuana enforcement, about $10,000 per arrest. Over twenty years, there have been 13 million arrests, but pot use hasn't declined, and nearly 8,000 people try drugs for the first time every day. Marijuana is America's fourth most lucrative crop and the top cash crop in twelve states. And all this occurs while *arrests for cocaine and heroin* have sharply declined and tobacco kills a thousand Americans per day.[61]

With so many happily turning on, why do we tolerate this costly and lethal crusade? Any objective economist would acknowledge that the drug trade is so lucrative precisely because the products are illegal and, hence, relatively scarce. Legalization would end prison over-crowding, undercut the profit motive of smugglers, create vast sources of tax revenue and produce a *decrease* in the amounts of drugs actually entering the country.

In the early 1980s, pot was not seen as threatening. Even Jimmy Carter proposed that it be decriminalized, and most prisoners were in jail for serious, violent offences. Then came the end of the Cold War, the need to revive the myth of innocence and the search for new scapegoats. Marijuana (like black men) was suddenly endowed with extraordinary new powers. Soon, growing pot in fifteen states could result in life sentences. Supreme Court cases dealing specifically with marijuana led to huge increases in government power long before the Patriot Act. But almost all drug-related criminal activity occurs because the drugs are illegal, not as a result of their effects.

Although the Loosener in his other major forms runs free, protected by powerful alcohol and tobacco lobbies, the federal government still persecutes providers of marijuana to AIDS and cancer patients. Astonishingly, the rationale for refusing pot even to the terminally ill is the danger of addiction. Males, however, argues that the crusaders fight medical marijuana so fanatically because "...it changes the image of who smokes pot from rebellious teens to respectable, suffering old folks," thus weakening the effect of the scapegoating campaign.[62]

Our attitudes toward drugs mirror the basic cultural split between the Paranoid war on the imagination and the Opportunist's dream of a consumer paradise. Many prescription drugs have effects similar to those of illegal drugs. But law and custom view some users as patients and others (those who consume for pleasure) as criminals. Official culture (Pentheus and his thugs) ignores the reality of demand and concentrates on preventing supply. Meanwhile, *popular* culture (MTV, etc.) regularly celebrates our own *Bacchants* as they cavort on spring break.

All Puritan and militaristic cultures attempt to prevent the Dionysian spirit from slipping through the gates, or to *make it serve the state* when it does. Warlords know they must either suppress the erotic and ecstatic impulses, or corrupt and reduce them to mass spectacle. The Communist ideal subsumed the personal into the communal; any interest in love and pleasure, not to mention ecstasy, betrayed a criminal narcissism.

But America's most effective form of social control is maintaining the fear that wild Dionysian energies might leak in from the outside, or burst out from the inside, symbolized by the ghetto or the prison. It is as if our value system were shaped like a great donut, with both the outer spaces and the hole in the middle infected with the Other. The gated residents of Eden hold fast to their fears and their punitive philosophies, wait for a lone savior to ride into town and restore order and allow no one inside but the pizza delivery boy.

But, if after thirty years and nearly *a trillion dollars* wasted, drugs remain cheaper and more popular than ever, we must question whether the combination of availability and increasingly severe penalties serves a purpose for the corporate elite. We can look to late sixth-century BCE Greece for a parallel. The tyrant Pesistratus, in the first instance of "bread and circuses," instituted Dionysian festivals as part of the official state religion. He captured the Loosener and toned him down, securing the support of the working classes and channeling their rebellion away from politics. Dionysus, who had long been considered an outlaw by the high priests, became the "opiate of the people," as Marx would describe all religion 2,400 years later.

Similarly, by allowing massive importation of drugs and severely (but selectively) punishing their possession, elites reap many benefits. Drug use channels legitimate political anger into passivity or local violence. Felony drug convictions disenfranchise millions. The drug war supports most of the $9 billion prison economy. Business utilizes prisoners as cheap labor. And the threat of the Other emerging from the ghetto, to rob so as to maintain his habit, adds to white fear, the security industry, the lure of gated communities and toleration of restrictions on personal liberties. A right-wing fantasy: a combination of passivity, scapegoating, disenfranchisement and a police state, all *prior* to 9/11.

But economics takes us only so far. Why are the Puritans so obsessed with marijuana, while millions drink themselves to death? Why do they so stridently insist on abstinence among youth while tolerating epidemic abuse among adults?

Dionysus tells us that both drugs and alcohol are the toxic mimics of things more "spirit"-ual — the archetypes of ecstasy and initiation. The desire to alter consciousness is universal; every society has accessed the gifts of psychoactive plants. But Americans are uniquely willing to tolerate the massive costs of "reducing vulnerability to ecstasy."

In the 1960s, psychedelics opened up a mythological consciousness completely unknown to the World War II generation. Their children took to the drugs, and quite a few never stopped. They learned that "entheogens" (theologian Huston Smith's term) facilitate a heightened imagination of the soul's infinite desire for nonmaterial experience.

Ironically, the media acknowledge this infinite longing, or a literalized version of it. Advertising implies that we can never get enough money, status symbols or security. Or drugs. Users behave much like good Americans, filling spiritual needs with material products. Addicts participate in a form of consumerism, increasing dosage and frequency, wanting more and more of something. It is accurate but useless to explain that something as simple escapism. "A binge," writes Marion Woodman, "is driven both by a desire to feel all-powerful, and by a desire to surrender to something bigger than oneself...to connect with the numinous in a way that will instigate a new beginning."[63] The addict may be enacting a universal myth, searching for the lost paradise of innocent childhood. But because he lives in a literalist culture, his archetypal desire for rebirth devolves into its toxic mimic, the longing for something that will briefly restore that lost paradise. While "shopaholics" accumulate because they symbolically associate consumer goods with erotic satisfaction, he consumes his drugs because of his longing for the reverse birth into innocence, behind which lies the natural desire for initiation and spiritual ecstasy.

Dionysus, curiously, says something similar. He *always* tells us, "It's never enough." But again, to the Puritan, the ultimate sin is *lack of self-control*. Since he offers the archetypal image of uninhibited joy to a workaholic culture, much of white America perceives his surrogates (perceived as blacks and gays) as unable to control their appetites.

If we relaxed our inhibitions, would we all ease our frantic participation in the wheel of production and consumption, which we so poetically term the *rat race*? Would we work only enough to ensure our survival and spend the rest of the day sharing stories, doing art, dancing and making love? This is precisely what the *conquistadors* accused indigenous people of doing, why they envied and destroyed them, and why conservatives are revolted at memories of the sixties, which are evoked more than anything by marijuana.

The androgynous character of the counter-culture (long haired men and loosened gender distinctions) horrified both Puritans and adherents of imperial machismo, who shouted, *"You look like a girl!"* By responding, *"Make love, not war!"* hippies artfully inverted the redemption hero who rejects his emotional and erotic capacity in favor of violent retribution. "Free love" called into question the most fundamental premises of both Puritanism and capitalism. If sex (or community, or meaning, or love, or the kingdom of heaven) were readily available, would we work so hard? Wasn't this evocation of *actual* innocence and (once birth control had become available) a guilt-free erotic existence the real threat?

The promise of love unmediated by the symbols of consumerism was both the lure and the threat of the counterculture. Ehrenreich argues that drugs, by dissolving boundaries between self and object, could render the mere possession of things redundant. They were "the ultimate commodity and the negation of all other commodities."[64] Both of our faiths, Christianity and capitalism, reject momentary sensual pleasures in expectation of some future fulfillment. But pot, which immerses us in the *present,* writes Michael Pollan, "...short-circuits the metaphysics of desire on which both... depend."[65]

Other images disturbed our false innocence. By calling themselves "flower children," hippies evoked the archetypal image of the child, even as the war (by consuming Asian babies and American teenagers) revealed America's fundamental ambivalence about its own and others' children. Startled by the idea that pleasure could be an end in itself, many asked, *"What is it for?"* What was the *purpose* of beauty? And why wear Native American clothing? Why evoke things that are better left unspoken?

What is the fear really about? Perhaps what we discover in the return of the repressed is our own emotions. As devotees of Carnival know, the problem with accessing joy is that the emotional body doesn't discriminate; when the "gateway" opens, anything that has been buried may rush through. In decreasing inhibitions, pot aids in recalling deep memory. *Grief* lies just below the surface, always looking for an opportunity to erupt. The oppressive national sense of guilt — for slavery, for Wounded Knee, for Viet Nam, for the wasted centuries of hatred of our own bodies — may force itself into awareness. Just below consciousness, we are aware that we stand on stolen, shaky ground. Like the innocent Persephone, we pluck flowers while the Lord of Death awaits us.

Grief rises from within, while infection comes from without. If we relax our vigilance, the drugs, or the sexual images, will contaminate the children. What is this obsession? The answer lies again in Puritan psychology. "Contamination" implies the *irresistible* power of evil, a deep and pessimistic sense of human weakness, an inability to identify right from wrong without severe restraints, and dreadful fear of permanent pollution by the sinful. If the Loosener opened the gates, "all hell would break loose;" everything that the soul and the culture have stuffed into the underworld would arise and overwhelm the guardians of propriety.

Ultimately, we must conclude that our core values are simply too fragile, inauthentic and *unnatural* to withstand even casual contact with any alternatives. We have finally arrived at the core of the patriarch's blustering machismo and unending *Thou shalt not's*. We don't trust children to decide for themselves, because we *know* how they would react. We know how *we* would react if we loosened the armor, listened to the drums and let the body speak. The children, even the lovers of learning, *especially* the lovers of learning, would dash screaming from the schools that deaden their imaginations. They would touch each other and begin to remember. And, instead of scapegoating the powerless, they would rage at *us* for not initiating them. Ultimately, we all know that we weren't born to work, accumulate, exploit and destroy, but to serve, play, create and love. This is what American Dionysus and tribal cultures remind us of. This is why (despite our superficial idealizations) we *hate* them — and our own children — with such ferocity.

Intuitively, the addict, the gambler, the sex addict, the shopper and the sports fanatic all sense what is missing. The alcoholic especially knows what will satisfy his sickness, but he fails to see that the literalized cure may kill him. *American culture provides only artificial forms of access to the "loosened" state, and simultaneously shames those who crave it.* Whether the drugs are legal or not, we know there are few ritual containers for their enlightened use. Consequently, we have very little control over *what* gets loosened, and all of our outmoded, violent mythologies are let out "through the broken dike" (in poet William Stafford's words) of normal awareness. When we invoke Dionysus literally rather than ritually, he may show his dark side or his light side, but the choice is up to him, not us.

What of conventional alternatives? "Just say no!" means only more repression. "Getting high on life" (or Jesus) offers only surrender of individuality. "Getting high" on *anything* implies escape into the celestial, the spiritual, and a devaluing of what is "grounded" — the Earth, the body, the feminine; it is another form of low-quality Dionysus.

Ultimately, all our conventional ecstasies — inflation, communal madness, pornography, drugs and scapegoating — are unsatisfying. Each experience only temporarily quiets the longing in the depths, and for that reason each is addictive.

And who would knowingly pursue that longing in a society that provides no ritual containers? Gordon Wasson, who first conceived of hallucinogenic plants as factors at the beginnings of religion, wrote, "...ecstasy is not fun... After all, who would choose to feel undiluted awe?"[66] Dionysus has another face, which shows itself when we pursue the ecstasy too far. Or it may show itself when we don't pursue it far enough. In a demythologized world, either license or repression may break us. And if the culture can no longer tell us what is obscene, or what is sacred, can it tell us what is evil?

FOUR: CHRIST AND THE DEVIL

Western man divided the primal unity of the indigenous soul into irreconcilable opposites: mind/body; male/female; white/black; culture/nature; and ultimately, Christ and the Devil. Gone was the memory that in the great cycle of existence darkness or chaos is the necessary pre-condition for rebirth. Two interdependent aspects of a polarity, symbolized by Dionysus and Apollo, became *opposites* that excluded each other. Eventually, both Dionysus and his mother were banished. First came the split of female goddesses and the male godhead, then the split of the male sun god Apollo from his dark half-brother. Finally, writes Arthur Evans, "Christians took the last version of Dionysus as it was developed by paganism and split it in two."[67] They assigned the "good" traits (as well as much of Apollo's characteristics) to Christ and the "bad" traits to the Devil.

Images of a god-man had long flourished in Old Europe and the Middle East. For over a thousand years, the birth of a divine child associated with Dionysus was one of the central moments celebrated annually at the

Eleusinian Mysteries. He was known in Babylon as *Tammuz,* in Egypt as *Osiris* and *Serapis,* in Asia Minor as *Attis,* in Persia as *Mythra,* in Italy as *Bacchus,* in Syria as *Adonis* and as *Fufluns* among the Etruscans.

This god-man (like many of the Greek deities) had an intimate association with trees. Adonis was born from a tree, Tammuz lived in one, Osiris was reborn from one, and Dionysus had his sacred pine tree. Later, Christian artists portrayed Jesus upon a tree-symbol, and sometimes they envisioned the cross as a living tree. Both Saints Peter and Paul refer to Jesus not as crucified but as "hung on a tree" (Acts 5:30, Galatians 3:13). Sometimes the tree had grapes hanging from it.

He was God's Son, but he had to suffer dismemberment before being reborn as a divinity. His mother was mortal and a virgin. Dionysus was born of *Semele,* Attis' mother was the virgin *Cybele,* and the virgin *Myrrh* birthed Adonis. Many heroes were also born of a virgin (who had been impregnated by a god) around the winter solstice. December 25th was Mithras' birthday. Other significant events occurred at the Vernal Equinox. Jesus' death and resurrection were originally March 23rd and 25th, dates that coincided exactly with Attis' death and resurrection. Priests of the Attis cult complained that the Christians were imitating their vernal celebration.

In his various incarnations, he was a savior, an ecstatic liberator and a Prince of Peace. He sometimes had the horns of a bull or goat. He descended to the underworld and returned as ruler over death, and he turned water into wine, such as at Dionysus's wedding to Ariadne. Much later, Jesus would proclaim, *"I am the true vine"* and turn water into wine (John 15:1, 2:1-11).

Dionysus was neither the first image of this archetype, nor the last. By Jesus's time, *The Bacchae* had been known throughout the Greek world for four centuries. Elements of the New Testament's confrontation scenes between Jesus and Pontius Pilate seem to be lifted straight out of Euripedes:

> *Dionysus: You do not know what you do.*
>
> *Jesus: They know not what they are doing. (Luke 23:34)*

This isn't to imply plagiarism, only that *the scene itself is archetypal,* something played out in every human heart.

Christian mythmakers combined elements of the pagan tradition with other factors. One was the Jewish concept of salvation through the coming of the Messiah. Gradually, cyclical time had faded into chronological time, and the spell of the sensuous world that had long enfolded tribal people was replaced by a new spell of literacy. For the first time, humanity lived in *history*, a sequence of unique and unrepeatable events, rolling onward toward its end.

Since the sixth century B.C.E., the prophets had written of a single godhead: "For I am God, and there is no other" (Isaiah 45:22). His representatives would be given over "all peoples, nations... an everlasting dominion" (Daniel 12:2). During the Babylonian exile, Judaism was influenced by Persian dualism, which posited a cosmic conflict between absolute good and evil, ending with a great conflagration and the coming of the savior. The dead would be resurrected (Isaiah 26:19, 65:17). Early Christians, inheriting a pattern that would be repeated a thousand and two thousand years later, expected the immanent end of time and history.

Yet already the idea that humans are alienated from God (who regrets having created them) was firmly in place (Genesis 6: 5-6). And so was the idea that the children of light must forever war against the children of darkness. God hid from human perception and forbade men to create "graven images." This was the birth of monotheism's assault upon the imagination; repeatedly, Old Testament prophets condemn Israel for regressing into paganism.

A second system utilized by the Christian mythmakers was the Greek Orphic tradition, which had long emphasized Dionysus's return from the dead. Their myth of his rebirth out of the ashes of the Titans led ironically to the literal doctrine of original sin. In this story, humans retained a divine spark from Dionysus as well as the malevolent potential of the Titans, whom Zeus had condemned to the underworld. Men needed discipline and moral purification to control their darker side and emphasize their higher nature. Aristotle had used the word *hamartia* ("error" or "missing the mark," a term from archery) to describe the tragic hero's fatal flaw, the wound that connected him to his potential. It was, paradoxically, the very thing that made him unique. In both the Greek and the Celtic worlds, if sin had any meaning at all, it meant "failure," and potentially every failure could be reversed. But Christians were the first to interpret *hamartia* as inherent and inescapable sinfulness, mankind's literal inheritance from Adam's original mythic transgression.

The change in the meaning of hamartia is an historical marker. The Christian usage drags us into a fearsome new world in which everyone is tainted from birth with the mark of evil. By this logic, children are already corrupt and require strict discipline to keep them from polluting others. This belief led to baptizing infants soon after birth to exorcise demons. It was yet another toxic mimic of initiation. And the concept made *literal* child murder a bit more acceptable.

A third factor in the solidification of Christian dogma was the rational and ascetic Greek philosophical tradition. The Church turned Plato's notion of a realm of pure ideas into the afterlife, which was a *higher, better* place than the sensual world. Another old word took on new meaning. Plato wrote that before birth each soul receives a unique soul-companion or *daimon* that selects a pattern for it to live on earth. Hillman writes, "The daimon remembers what is in your image and belongs to your pattern, and... is the carrier of your destiny."[68]

Like hamartia, *daimon* (known as *genius* by the Romans and *jinn* or *genie* by the Arabs) was connected to purpose. But Greek dualistic thinking eventually divided good from evil. In the second century B.C.E., the men who translated the Hebrew Bible into a Greek book (the *Septuagint*) chose *daimonion* to denote "evil spirits." Thus, with two linguistic shifts, western man gradually both lost his guiding spirits and his sense of how his wounds reveal his blessings. Eventually, one's intuition, if it disputed church dogma, would express only the voice of the *demonic*, and the pagan gods, archetypal images of human and cosmic potential, became demons.

Changes in language signaled changes in cult practice. The breakdown of ritual eventually led to a condition in which human urges that were once hallowed to the gods became *evil*. The church repressed them into the personal and collective unconscious — the underworld — and eventually projected them onto the Other. The Puritanical impulse blamed all suffering upon human sinfulness. Orphism had taught that the soul (derived from

Dionysus) was potentially good; but the body (from the ashes of the Titans) was its prison, where it remained until all guilt had been expiated. This led, writes E. R. Dodds, to "a horror of the body and a revulsion against the life of the senses." The Orphics had written: *"Pleasure is in all circumstances bad; for we came here to be punished."*[69]

As the age of mythological thinking neared its end, it became more difficult to think in terms of the symbolic processes of initiation and rebirth. The holy text that emerged out of this period omitted the few metaphors of the sacred Earth that had been allowed into Hebrew scripture. As a result, writes Paul Shepard, the New Testament is "one of the world's most antiorganic and antisensuous masterpieces of abstract ideology..."[70]

All these factors were rolled into the messianic tradition. Pagan myths such as the *Odyssey* had expressed a longing for the return of the king or the divine child who was reborn in the hearts of the initiates. But as mythological thinking declined, the Jews longed for a literal messiah (*Christos* in Greek). They witnessed the quick passing of many such figures, including the historic Jesus. After his death, however, zealots turned him into "The Christ." It was a concept, writes Evans, that was molded by traditions that had "...nothing to do with his life, applied by people who never knew him, recorded in a language he never used."[71]

At first, the Roman world welcomed the new god. Their cosmos was still marked by *epiphany*, the continual manifestation of spirit in the world. Paganism never needed to create structures of belief. Toleration, indeed celebration, of multiple divine images was its most essential characteristic.

But it was precisely this animating connection between world and individual (the mesocosm of myth) that Christianity sought to destroy and replace. Its transcendent god could only enter the world through revelation, which led to dogma and reduced a world of possibilities to one of dreadful certainties. This god was kept alive through belief, not through sacrifices. Saint John of Patmos interpreted his apocalyptic dream vision not as an internal initiation experience, a lifting of the veils, but as universal destruction. His *Book of Revelation* is ecstatic poetry. Interpreted literally, however, it is the very definition of — and a prescription for — madness.

To Puritans obsessed with judgment and evil it became the Bible's most important section.

Early Christians including the Gnostics eliminated class and gender bias and shared many ecstatic practices with the pagan mystery cults. But the zealots who wrested control of the church believed that Christ had literally returned from the dead, and that metaphoric interpretation of his life was unacceptable. Theirs was a religion, write Timothy Freke and Peter Gandy, of "...outer mysteries without the inner mysteries..."[72] By the late second century, they prohibited women from participating in worship. Soon, schisms developed, and rival sects attacked each other in furious jihads.

Roman polytheism was degenerating into mere ideological justification for empire. Mobs of bored and uninitiated men craved the distraction of the "bread and circuses" held in the Coliseum. Historian Rodney Stark writes, "...watching people torn and devoured by beasts or killed in armed combat was the ultimate spectator sport..."[73] It was perhaps the first instance of state-sponsored "vicarious intensity." Suffering martyrdom in this context, Christianity grew up in an atmosphere of violence. Like other traumatized children, it became a perpetrator of abuse.

With Paganism in decline, the empire needed a mass ideology to replace it, something that would link the individual to the state. Christianity filled the vacuum, re-writing history to de-emphasize its esoteric origins and violently purging the Gnostics. In the fourth century, it became the official religion of the Empire, the Catholic (universal) faith. The notion of One True God found its political equivalent in the totalitarian Roman state. After the Council of Nicaea (325), the Church, now essentially a branch of government, taught that the Emperor expressed God's will in governing the world (and for the next thousand years, popes and kings would conflict over who had ultimate power). In 346, Pagan observance was made a capital offence.

The popes expelled the old gods, destroyed the sacred groves and either demolished their temples or rededicated them to Jesus. Their repression was far more brutal than the one early Christians had suffered. Here is Tertullian again, describing the final judgment: *"How shall I admire,*

*how laugh, how rejoice, how exult when I behold so many proud monarchs...
liquefying in fiercer fires than they ever kindled against the Christians. "*

By the end of the fourth century, Christian Zealots had free license
to burn the remaining Pagan temples and slaughter those who resisted. A
generation later, the Visigoths sacked Rome and the Dark Ages began. This
was a decisive event, writes historian Steven Karcher: "The shadow that fell
on the Gods, the flesh, and the cosmos fell on all races and cultures..."[74]

The disenchantment of the world was underway. The repression of
the spirits of the Earth led centuries later to a situation in which, as Jung
said, the Gods could only reach humans through their psychological and
physical afflictions. Missionaries spoke of "taking prisoner every thought
for Christ." In 785, the Emperor Charlemagne instituted the death penalty
for refusing baptism. The God of love presided over centuries of genocide
done in his name. Eventually this heritage would lead to an America of
innocent violence and violent innocence.

For generations, the new faith, primarily urban, maintained a suspicious
attitude toward rural people. They were the last to be converted, since they
lived closer to the natural and still magical world that had been served
by the older cults. Christians called them "country dwellers" *(paganus)*.
Eventually the term "Pagan" became so thoroughly defamed that the English
language can barely describe it in value-neutral terms. Common dictionary
definitions include "an irreligious or hedonistic person." For millennia they
had gratefully accepted the mysterious bounty of the earth in the form of
Dionysus' wine and Demeter's bread. The Eucharist eventually expressed
this same mystery, while removing both Dionysus and Demeter.

Also at the end of the fourth century, the Church set the Christian
canon, excluding much literature that had formerly been considered to be
divinely inspired. It declared that Jesus was born on December twenty-fifth.
Now, his birth coincided with the rebirth of the sun, and the symbolism
of his light conquering darkness matched a common theme in ancient
hero myths. Other old beliefs, such as reincarnation, died slowly. Early
theologians had embraced it, but eventually the church opposed it because
it promoted the idea that men could find the truth for themselves, without

intercession by religion. It wasn't until 543, however, that they declared it *anathema* ("devoted to evil").

Still, southern Greece remained substantially pagan until the ninth century. To facilitate the transition, the church introduced saints with characteristics that corresponded with many of the old gods and heroes and transferred reverence for them and their relics to the saints. Artemis became Saint Artemidos, Hermes became the Archangel Michael, Hephaestus became Saint George and Demeter became the *male* Saint Demetrius. Apollo, associated with Helios, the sun god, became the Prophet Elias. (A similar sequence took place in northern Europe; Freya became Maria, Thor became Saint Olaf, etc.) The pagan temple became the Christian basilica. The deity, no longer represented as an ideal of human beauty, moved from the center of the temple to Heaven. The eye was drawn to the altar and then *upward,* away from the Earth. And Dionysus became Saint Dionysios, who still retains his patronage of wine.

Dionysus, however, remained popular. Christ took on some of his characteristics, but the fathers deemed others inappropriate. His worship in Athens had involved deliberate inversion of the social order, including cross-dressing, and such practices persisted for centuries. As late as 691, the Council of Constantinople condemned

> …dances and initiation rites of the "gods," as they are falsely called … no man shall put on a woman's dress…nor shall any disguise themselves with comic, satyr, or tragic masks, nor call out the name of disgusting Dionysus while pressing grapes in the press or pouring wine.

Jesus had preached a radical gospel of love and non-violence. Absolutely nothing attributed to him in the Gospels suggested anything about his death as a sacrifice. Saint Paul, however, changed Christianity's central image from the birth of the Divine Child to his *death;* in his vision the *Aqedah* of Isaac was completed only with Jesus' sacrifice and resurrection. An invitation to immanence became an excuse for transcendence. A religion of love became an obsession with suffering. It taught that Christ's sacrifice had occurred *once,* not as part of an unending cycle. Emphasis on this single event and the progression from creation to salvation solidified our concept of linear time and led to the invention of clocks, which eventually contributed to the regulation of social behavior for the purpose of production (the word "calendar" came from the Latin *calends,* the first day of the month, when business accounts had to be settled). The western world understood myth literally, as actual history. Europeans came to believe that Jesus, unlike Dionysus, had died not to symbolize the cycle of creation but as a sacrifice *for* humanity's bad behavior. This subtle yet significant difference shifted the emphasis from the tragedy of the human condition to the sinfulness of human nature.

The idea of one unrepeatable sacrifice excluded any metaphorical or psychological interpretation of Christ's death as sacrifice of the *ego* and resulted in the suppression of initiation rites. But if salvation was open to everyone who chose to submit to the new belief system, then it was, in a sense, open to no one. Because it entailed little risk, it had little value. With baptism, one was no longer welcomed into the community as an adult with a unique purpose, but merely as a *believer,* as "not one of *them.* "

Having died for the sins of the world, Christ became the ultimate, if willing, scapegoat. Men left society (and women) to defeat their own sinfulness. To this day, the monks of Mount Athos in Greece still refuse to allow the presence of female *animals* onto their sacred grounds.

Many looked forward to imitating Christ's sacrifice. Ignatius longed to suffer, "but I do not know whether I am worthy." Cyprian imagined the "...flowing blood which quenches the flames and the fires of hell by its glorious gore." Christianity became the first religion to make martyrdom a demand of faith. Leonard Shlain puts this process into historical context:

> Until the Christian martyrs, there does not occur anywhere in
> the recorded history of Mesopotamia, Egypt, Persia, Greece,
> India or China a single instance in which a substantial
> segment of the population accepted torture and death rather
> than forswear their belief in an ethereal concept.[75]

The meaning of the word "martyr" gradually changed. Abraham's knife became a soldier's sword in Christian iconography. Dying *as* Christ (around 100AD) became dying *for* Christ (500), which became *killing* for Christ (1000).

Such motivation is utterly foreign to the indigenous mind. It is, however, the logical outcome of the disappearance of mythic consciousness and initiation ritual. For thousands of years, men had symbolically killed the child-nature in their boys to invite their full participation in the adult world. But with the crushing of paganism, a literalized myth (the sacrifice of a child for the glory of his *father*) came to predominate. It was a very old myth, but now Europe was about to feast on the bodies of its young.

By the early Middle Ages, both dualistic thinking and misogyny had long been absolutely basic to European thought. Men identified with mind and spirit and associated women with nature and the body. We can follow the linguistic shift. The Hebrew word *ruah* (spirit/breath) is feminine. Translated to Greek it became *pneuma,* which is neuter. Saint Paul elevated *pneuma* to the Trinity as the Holy Ghost, which became the masculine *spiritus* in Latin.

Saint Augustine taught that Eve's original sins had condemned humanity to a state of corruption. Psychologically, the Fall describes the birth of *consciousness,* which implies the breaking of a state of original wholeness and unconscious unity with nature. But the Church took it literally. Original sin became its foundation stone, the necessary counterpart to Christ's redemption of humanity, despite the fact that he'd said nothing about it in the Gospels.

The only thing that might restore the lost innocence of (pre-Eve) Eden was *chastity*, wrote Augustine. Tertullian preached that woman was "the Devil's Gateway." Saint Aquinas wrote, "...woman is defective and misbegotten..." Later, the official textbook of the Inquisition instructed: "... *all witchcraft comes from carnal lust, which in women is insatiable.* "[76]

The church had split off more and more of human consciousness. First, long before, had come male from female, then Apollo from Dionysus. But Dionysus was too complicated and ambiguous to fit easily into its moralistic categories. He had remained in Rome for a while as "Jolly Bacchus," an easy rationale for a drinking party, a god of drunkenness but not of ecstasy. Eventually even Bacchus was outlawed. He returned in Renaissance art, but only as a cute and chubby child or a fat, old drunk.

Christians, however, desired the same bread and circuses that the Romans had. They found their vicarious intensity in the fascination with Christ's suffering, his *passion*. They flocked to the only theatrical presentations acceptable to the church, the passion plays. One of the most famous was *The Passion of Christ,* whose author lifted many lines directly from *The Bacchae*. Dionysus remained as the very shadow of Jesus.

Jesus was now the suffering god, but not the ecstatic, bisexual destroyer of boundaries, and no longer a Prince of Peace. Worshipers beheld his stern figure, the *Pantocrator* ("ruler of all"), glaring down from church ceilings, amid horrifying Last Judgment scenes. "Because a monotheistic psychology must be dedicated to unity," writes Hillman, "its psychopathology is intolerance of difference."[77] Catholicism never (and *has* never) renounced its claim to be humanity's exclusive means of redemption. For a thousand years, white men would rape and pillage to hasten the coming of the Prince of Peace.

But Dionysus, an archetypal image of the psyche, had to live somewhere, and it certainly couldn't be in Christ's mild and antiseptic heaven. He and the other Pagan deities went underground. Europe assigned those Dionysian traits that couldn't be grafted onto Jesus to the Devil.

In Hebrew myth, *Satan,* an adversary of humans and enforcer of Jehovah's will, originally served a holy purpose. The word's meaning gradually changed from "opponent" into a personality whose nature is to obstruct. As Persian dualism influenced Judaism, Satan became God's evil twin, a rebellious prince in eternal opposition to the divine will. The Septuagint used the Greek word *diabolikos* (accuser, slanderer), which became the English "devil." Hebrew myths of the fallen angel (*Lucifer,* or "light-bringer") added to the image of this eternal opposition: "How thou art fallen, oh day-star..." (Isaiah 14:12).

In the process, Judaism established the foundations for European racism. Light/white became synonymous with spirit/goodness, while dark/black represented the material world. The New Testament solidified the image; Barnabus described Satan as the "Black One." Saint Jerome linked blackness with sex; the Devil's strength was "in his loins." Augustine (himself a North African) claimed that everyone is black until he accepts Christ.

The choice was now clear and unambiguous. If one wasn't a Christian, he followed the dark prince. In this form, writes Needleman, the Devil becomes irredeemably evil: "All the truly terrifying images of the devil are in one way or another rooted in the *diabolical.*"[78] As early as the second century, Clement of Alexandria declared that the gods of *all other religions* were demons. Since their mere existence placed in doubt the belief in one true God, they could only be in league with Satan. The church now had an Other to justify its purpose: saving mankind from this devil who sent his legions to drag humans back toward their own corrupt bodies.

Scholars disagree as to how Satan received his popular image. Some claim that the earliest model was the lecherous goat-god Pan. Early Christians feared Pan because of his shameless sexuality and his association with the wilderness, where hostile spirits lay in wait. He caused *panic.* They depicted Satan with Pan's hooves, oversized phallus and horns, which Dionysus also had. The horns carry a potent ambiguity, writes historian Jeffrey Russell. They symbolize Satan's power and evoke the "mysterious, frightening otherness of animals...not only fertility but also night, darkness and death."[79] Some link Satan with the European Horned God, consort of many Goddesses, especially on Crete. These images evoked the ambiguous mix of fertility and death (*not* evil) that indigenous people still understand, but which the modern mind splits into two figures.

Others connected Satan with Hades, ruler of the underworld, but they missed the larger picture. Hades was also known as *Pluto,* or "wealth." Here is as sharp a divide as we can find between the tribal and monotheistic minds. Perceiving "wealth" in the underworld means two things. One is that death and decay are necessary components of life. Secondly, mythological thinking connects inner and outer, or the literal and symbolic. The underworld is also the world below conscious awareness, where both unacceptable carnal urges and unacknowledged gifts lie. There is no reason to assume that ideas such as this are foreign to the tribal mind, that Freud "discovered" the unconscious. Indeed, he said, "Everywhere I go I find a poet has been there before me." Though few claim that Dionysus was a direct model for the Devil, he was worshipped as *Melangius* ("of the Black Goatskin"), and Herakleitos said that Dionysus and Hades were one and the same.

The fifth-century Council of Toledo officially assigned Satan cloven hooves, horns, donkey ears, fiery eyes, a sulfurous smell and, like Priapus, an enormous penis. Artists depicted him as deformed, to indicate his inner defects, or as lame, from his fall from Heaven. He sometimes had bat-like wings, or an extra face on his belly, knees or buttocks. His blackness indicated the lack of goodness; later he was red, the color of sexuality, or blue, from Hell's cold. He was male, because a force so powerful couldn't be female. He disguised himself to undermine Christian values. The paranoid imagination filled the air with vast armies of diabolic accomplices, including the Antichrist, who was expected to lead the forces of evil at the end of history. Alternatively, medieval folklore, writes Russell, "tamed the terror by allowing humans to dupe the Prince of Darkness with native wit and guile," so it sometimes depicted him as an easily outwitted buffoon.[80]

It wasn't until the fourteenth century, however, that the most malignant images of Satan appeared. The Devil carried the shadow of the Western mind, both sadistic violence and insatiable sexuality. "Typically, the 'pure-itan' must remain in some sort of contact with the Devil," writes Kovel, "while keeping him sufficiently alien to sustain the regime of projection."[81]

Satan was *alluring,* sometimes through beauty and sometimes through a fascination with horror itself. Alan Watts wrote that artists painted Heaven as calm and boring, while depictions of Hell, from Bosch to Disney, are exuberant "riots of imagination."[82] In literature, Dante and Milton elaborated this picture of the Devil and his realm.

The paranoid imagination created enemies within to match those without. More dangerous than pagans were Satan's followers who took the form of heretics ("able to choose") and schismatics who divided the community with false doctrines. Here is the origin of the Puritan fascination with the inner and outer Others. Satan could attack both from without ("obsession") and from within ("possession.")

When Christians assigned him a realm to administer, they named it after *Hella,* Icelandic goddess of the underworld, sister of the wolf who threatens to emerge and wreck vengeance upon the gods of the upper world. Greece, however, retained indigenous associations. There, the lord of Hell is still *Charon*, the ferryman of the river Styx, and rural Greeks still place coins over a dead person's eyes to pay the ferryman. If Hades (as Pluto/wealth) is forgotten, his ferryman still makes a tidy profit.

In both Greek and Hebrew myth, the underworld was a gloomy but neutral warehouse for the dead. Only the worst sinners, such as Sysiphus and Tantalos, suffered eternal punishment. Everyone else, good and evil alike, led the same cheerless existence in its cold, dark, *boring* halls. Old ideas of retributive justice, however, offered a problem by holding men accountable for their ancestors' sins. Eventually this punishment seemed unjust; only the guilty should be punished. And bad men often died without suffering. Churchmen found a solution in Orphic doctrine, which claimed that souls were imprisoned in bodies subject to decay as well as to sin. They transferred appropriate punishment to the afterlife, but this shift required that the underworld be a place of universal, eternal torment.

Its Lord evolved from a featureless warden of the shades into a complex, ambivalent figure (his *Lady*, the goddess Persephone, said by some to be Dionysus' mother, was omitted). As Satan, he served the holy purpose, to punish sinners. Yet as Lucifer, the fallen angel, he worked *against* the grand design by sending his demons to tempt Christians into sin.

Some early paintings retained the old equation of evil with the feminine. Here, the underworld was a great yawning cavern, or a whale with open jaws, swallowing sinners into her bottomless belly. Christ battled the dragon-whale, in a tradition reaching back — again — to Tiamat.

With banishment of the feminine, demonizing of Dionysian aspects of the masculine, loss of initiation and literalization of the mythic imagination, all the factors were in place. The ultimate product was the authoritarian organization of society, the perpetual mass violence, the genocides, the ecological devastation and the struggle for control of the rest of the world that we euphemistically refer to as "European history."

For 1,500 years, however, there have been periodic resurgences of pagan values, including traditions such as Hermeticism, Alchemy, the Cathars, the age of Chivalry, Jewish Kabala, Islamic Sufism and especially the worship of the Virgin Mary, Europe's unrecognized mother goddess. Dozens of cathedrals were built at sites that had been sacred to earlier pagans. The French alone dedicated over eighty cathedrals to Mary during the twelfth and thirteenth centuries. Her name (from *mare*, "sea") retained associations with early goddesses who had emerged from the primordial womb of life. She became the sustainer of humankind and mediatrix between humans and god. Artists paired her with her son, ruling the universe as two complementary principles. Crusaders brought back dark-colored pagan figurines from the East. These "Black Madonnas" are still revered in some two hundred shrines from Spain to Poland.

The dim memory of Dionysus stayed alive in these cathedrals in hundreds of "Green Man" sculptures. He appeared during carnival as the King of Fools and as the hairy "wild man," who lived between town and wilderness. And until the thirteenth century, people *danced* in church.

One place in Europe, southern Spain, has kept alive a Dionysian consciousness as a shadow of its inquisitorial history. It is apparent in the thinly disguised goddess worship of the Holy Week processions, in the ritual ecstasy of Flamenco music, and in the bullfight, the roots of which can be traced back to the bull rituals of Minoan Crete. Historian Allen Josephs writes that Spaniards, "to satisfy their ... Dionysian need...created the *corrida* (bull fight) and turned the killing of the scape-bull into an art that is closer to the origin of art than any we know."[83]

The gylanic tradition asserted itself in Romantic literature, in the myths of the Holy Grail and the Arthurian romances, and in Ireland, where the witch-craze never truly materialized. In the Renaissance, Pagan appreciation of beauty and love of the body challenged Christianity's contempt for the flesh, and Pagan themes reasserted themselves in art. The twentieth century witnessed Latin American Liberation Theology and the revitalized African-American Christianity that empowered the Civil Rights movement. Each gylanic resurgence, however, has encountered overwhelming, reactionary backlash.

Western art, architecture, music, literature, philosophy and technology advanced. But the literalized myths that gave Europeans their desperate energy and propelled them to extremes of both production and destruction created a vast cultural shadow and an unceasing need for Others. "Woman" had been Europe's primary Other since prehistory. But the male unconscious required additional projection screens.

The culture that was eating millions of its own children accused Jews of sacrificing Christian children. Judaism was a unique case; since Christianity had emerged from it, Christians had to demonize Jews to define themselves in opposition, just as the Hebrews had previously done to the surrounding cultures. But long after Paganism had been crushed, Jewish resistance to assimilation implicitly questioned the triumph of the Christian revelation. For centuries, Jews came to expect annual orgies of violence prior to Easter. The followers of the God of Love annually recreated his passion and that of Dionysus before him by killing Satan's designated representatives.

The medieval paranoid imagination found temptation everywhere, even in music. The church identified a dissonant chordal sound — the "tritone," or "devil's interval" (later it was basic to Jazz and Blues), and forbade it in performance. The banishment of temptation even from music initiated yet another transformation over time. Music and dance had been inseparable up to the Renaissance. But gradually, this connection began to fade with the Baroque. By the nineteenth century, music was essentially non-participatory; one *sat* and *listened*.

The concepts of one emperor, one God and one religion led to the ultimate literalization: no legitimate society that wasn't Christian, and no salvation outside the Church. However, this required universal assent because even mild heresy not only threatened to corrupt society; it could bring God's wrath upon guilty and innocent alike.

With the inexplicable advance of Islam, however, Christianity confronted a new and immensely powerful Other that questioned its assumptions of superiority. The Church responded by distracting its nobles from killing each other and enlisting their energies into crusades of conquest and extermination against the infidels. A new figure emerged: the warrior-monk, pledged to both chastity and eternal warfare. It became glorious to die even in defeat because it would be a *martyr's* death.

The Crusades mark the first merger of the paranoid and predatory imaginations. Pope Urban offered the soldiers both remissions of sin (now, violence was a ticket to paradise) as well as an incentive to martyrdom. The result was a scale of atrocities that still puzzles historians, who, writes Bruce Chilton,

> ...have not factored in the sacrificial dimension of Urban's appeal. Self-sacrifice, more than self interest, is the hidden hand guiding this strange and relentless history...Crusading was a license, not only to kill, but also to...indulge other appetites, absolved in advance..."[84]

"Absolved in advance." A theological twist of words gave millions of men full permission to act out the most grotesque and sadistic fantasies, which they had previously allowed into consciousness only by projecting them upon the Other.

Joseph Campbell referred to the twelfth century, when Christians built cathedrals to the virgin and slaughtered thousands of infidels, as the beginning of the breakdown of European myth. The failure of the Crusades created thousands of rootless and unemployed veterans. The Church, desperate to enforce conformism, diverted their energy into conquest of Europeans opposed to its authority, especially the Cathars. When they conquered Beziers in southern France, the victors asked the papal legate how to distinguish between the heretics and the normal Catholics. His response has echoed down through the centuries, to be repeated in Viet Nam: *"Kill them all; God will know which are his."* Then, with southern France pacified, the crusaders turned their rage further south. Eventually, in expelling both Moslems and Jews from Spain, they destroyed the pluralistic, tolerant culture that had flourished there for centuries, the last place in Europe that had maintained respect for the Other. Even later, crusaders ruthlessly pacified large swaths of northern and eastern Europe that had remained essentially pagan.

The Inquisition began in the thirteenth century because it became necessary to establish identity, once again, by creating otherness. It crowded Jews into ghettos and required them to wear identifying marks. Whereas in the more stable early middle ages, heretics had usually been banned from the community, now *burning at the stake* became the universal penalty for unorthodox behavior. The ritual sacrifice of the scapegoat re-stabilized the community and guaranteed orthodoxy. If he actually confessed, his death provided a catharsis for all (and all were required to be present). And his sins condemned his *children:* after the execution, local churches displayed the sackcloth he'd worn for *ten generations* so as to denounce his descendants.

Here we can begin to perceive the true cost of the nationalism that was beginning to develop. For thousands of years, the individual had identified with a *clan* and had a totemic relationship to ancestors, spirits and animals in a community small enough for him to be personally acquainted with all of its members. There had been little need for otherness. Athens, though much larger than traditional villages, had organized its citizens into small-scale brotherhoods whose primary allegiance was to *place*. The individual had emerged from that place and would return to it; it was his mother. Then, for a few centuries, he had identified as a Christian, attached to a place-less, universal community of believers in a sky-father.

In the Early Modern period, however, he began to identify as a "Frenchman" or a "Spaniard," in highly regulated mass entities. Since church and state were effectively the same, to be French also meant to be Catholic. States banished regional languages and demonized people across the mountains who (though also Catholic) spoke different dialects and obeyed different kings. There would be no more pan-European cooperation to crusade against Muslims, because *other Europeans* were now the Other. Nationalism, however, meant a loss of individuality and further erosion of myth and initiation. The only forms of ritual that survived were ceremonies of inclusion and exclusion.

Standing just behind the warrior-Christ was *Kronos*. Renaissance art depicted him as grim Father Time, advancing across the centuries, sweeping all before him with his scythe. The fourteenth century saw the first public clocks (on churches) and the transformation of linear time into mechanical time. Zerzan writes, "…connection to the natural world or to the present was lost, subsumed to the tyranny of the machine and of production."[85]

Following the invention of printing and the spread of literacy,

Catholicism's contradictions finally exploded into Reformation and Counter-Reformation. At the same time, Europe faced the scientific revolution, increasing urbanism and emergent capitalism. The nobility fenced off the common fields for the first time, leading to new extremes of wealth and poverty. And as I have mentioned earlier, under Calvinism poverty became, for the first time, an indication of sin.

These massive social changes led to anxiety, isolation and epidemics of depression. Both Catholicism and Protestantism significantly restricted communal celebrations such as Carnival. Luther took the next step in the evolution of patriarchy by banning the feminine principle entirely from the church, declaring "Ye shall sing no more praises to Our Lady, only to our Lord." Protestants raised othering to new heights: heretics; Jews; Turks; Africans; Native Americans and Catholics. Even radical Protestants served the Devil. To Calvin, the Pope was the Antichrist himself. Consuming new forms of literature (such as the Faust legend), Europeans took the Devil *more* literally than they had in the Middle Ages.

Around 1500-1550, Christianity and Islam reached an impasse that more or less stabilized their borders. Spain expelled the Moors and Austria repulsed the Turks, who had conquered Constantinople. Spain attacked Mexico in the same year, 1517, that Luther began his insurrection against the Catholic Church. Colonialism and reformation began together.

Europe turned its rage both inwards (holy wars *within Europe* raged for a hundred years) and further outwards, against the New World. In 1648, the Peace of Westphalia finally announced that each prince would have the right to determine the religion of his own state (*"Whoever rules, his religion"*), the options being Lutheranism or Catholicism. Subsequent European wars were not about religion, but rather revolved around issues of state.

The discovery of the Americas, however, only added to the apprehension. Suddenly, there were vast lands inhabited by people who were inconceivably Other. Unashamed of their naked bodies, they thrived without technology or ceaseless striving, engaged in no holy wars and spent their time in ritual and dance. Had God created them? Were they humans or demons?

The extended religious wars and the attacks on faith itself increased the anxiety that led to the witch-craze of the fifteenth to seventeenth centuries (*not,* as commonly assumed, of the Middle Ages). The paranoid imagination found witches everywhere. It was said that they made pacts with the Devil, accepted eternal punishment in exchange for sensual gratification and (once again) ate children in a blasphemous parody of the Eucharist. Conservative estimates put those executed at 100,000. Most were poor, rural women who were accused, writes Eisler, "…of being sexual; for in the eyes of the Church, all the witches' power was ultimately derived from their 'sinful' female sexuality."[86]

Our lasting image of witches is of old women led by a demoness, flying broomsticks to their horrible Sabbath. The image endures because it expresses men's fear, going back at least as far as *The Bacchae,* of unrestrained, independent women. We recall Pentheus furious (yet curious) that the maenads were dancing freely in the mountains. The same fear and resulting search for a scapegoat would appear much later in Nazi claims that Jews were behind German feminism. Fear of the liberated woman and her desires is never far from awareness, because *those very desires themselves* are never far from consciousness.

Women were not the only people the Devil entranced. Some claim that the phrase "flaming faggot" derives from the practice of using the bodies of homosexual men as kindling to start the fires under the accused witches.

Such madness seems utterly distinct from the rational, secular outlook that was emerging. Science, however, grew out of the same polarizing of spirit/matter and superiority of male over female as did Christianity. Feminist Betty Roszak writes that both women and nature were objects of the male scientist's curiosity, and both had to be tamed and interrogated: "…men need not have any scruples in 'entering and penetrating into these holes and corners' because the 'inquisition of truth' is the scientist's purpose. He must put nature 'on the rack'…"[87] Indeed, Francis Bacon formulated the scientific method at the height of the witch craze. Searching for empirical truth that was separate from the body (a dried-out, Apollonian vision), he was the intellectual ancestor to the creators of nuclear weapons just as the Inquisition was the seed of McCarthyism and the Patriot Act.

The persecutions waned by the eighteenth century. But the stress inherent in the clash between the monolithic Christian universe and the steady encroachment of scientific materialism grew. "In the new era," writes Ehrenreich, "the sacralization of war would depend less on established religions...and more on the new 'religion' of nationalism."[88] While American Puritans were massacring the Pequots in Connecticut, the Thirty Years War killed a third of Germany's population.

Ultimately, the rage of uninitiated men in a desacralized world led to colonial destruction, the slave trade, environmental degradation, two *world* wars, several genocides and the nuclear age. White men had lost so much of their indigenous soul that they couldn't help fearing or hating those who had not. By 1900, they controlled eighty-five percent of the world's land mass, having destroyed hundreds of tribal cultures and tens of millions of people.

For some alternative meaning to these grim centuries, we can return to the search for and the voice of the Other. Martin Prechtel argues that the attitudes of both the missionary and the conquistador arose from "...having no true parents, no true initiations for the young...a culture that promoted an empty grandiosity that covered up a mass cultural depression."[89] Economic explanations of colonialism are not sufficient to explain its infinitely creative, massive violence. *Europe expanded across the globe to fill a spiritual hole,* but imperialism simply pushed that dimly remembered lost unity further away.

The ultimate expression of Europe's sickness, the separation of Christ and the Devil, played out on American soil, where whites encountered their dark projections in dark African bodies. Patterson writes that well into the twentieth century, "The cross — Christianity's central symbol of Christ's sacrificial death — became identified with the crucifixion of the Negro."[90]

We ask in our own innocence, *didn't they notice the irony?* Recall that *clergymen* presided over many lynchings. Photographs printed as postcards show well-dressed, Christian adults and children grinning at the camera while black men roast over bonfires. These images, like those of the Holocaust ("burnt offering"), always elicit disbelief. How can people become so fully dehumanized as to enjoy such horror? Who are the real victims?

But lynch mobs are merely the ugly cousins of our American hero. Willing "to die to set men free," he cuts swaths of carnage across history.

He stands at the end of five millennia of abstraction and literalization, *killing* men to set them free. Precisely at the height of the lynchings, he was decimating the population of the Philippines.

The Pagan Dionysus continually suffers, dies and is reborn, with his humor and lust intact. But when men excise the humor and the lust he becomes Jesus, who dies *once,* while nature devolves into a fallen world. By the nineteenth century he becomes the fully literalized American warrior-monk. Having accomplished his violent retribution, this secular Christ dies *to the community — by leaving.* Instead of being the willing victim (and consort) of the Goddess, he saves women from his evil twin. He still serves the Goddess, as literal woman, but he has all the power and she, on her pedestal, has none. Leaving her, he leaves his children impoverished.

I dwell on this history because tens of millions have responded to the dizzying pace of change by interpreting the images of a dying myth absolutely literally, just as Europeans did in the fourth, twelfth and sixteenth centuries. A third of Americans describe themselves as fundamentalists or Evangelicals. Half believe in Revelation and deny evolution. A third of us believe that *all other religions* serve Satan. They listen to 1,600 Christian radio stations and watch 250 Christian TV stations. Fundamentalists control the Republican Party. To ingratiate himself among them, *every* President from Carter to Bush II claimed to be reborn or fundamentalist. Even the religiously moderate Obama asked the anti-abortion extremist Rick Warren to give the invocation at his inauguration.

Without the vast influence of American fundamentalists, the world political landscape, from the population explosion, to global warming, to the wars on drugs and terror would look completely different. Their resistance to birth control has condemned millions to death by AIDS or poverty. For thirty years, their mad visions of apocalypse have utterly determined American policy in the Middle East. Frank Schaeffer, formerly a major televangelist, knows that for these people, "The 'purpose' of the Jews is to be there to be killed after the Second Coming. Christian Zionists love Israel the way oncologists love cancer."[91] *Muslim extremism might not exist as a major force at all without Christian-American support for Israel.* Three generations of anti-communist repression has ensured that the only organized, nationalist resistance to the American empire has been by fundamentalists, who were not politically active until the 1970s.

But Christianity is also our model for the *secular* duality of absolute good and evil. The twentieth century and its 100 million war dead could only have happened after two millennia of religious dogma. In culture, science and art we have long assumed relativity, but not in the realm of conflict. Since 1914, we have fought our wars with the goals of either unconditional surrender or near-total annihilation of the enemy. Auschwitz and Hiroshima sealed the agreement. The crusade in Viet Nam took the concept a step further. Americans barely distinguished between friend and foe, dropping the vast majority of their bombs on *South* Viet Nam. Decades later, the demonizing and vengeance continue unabated.

This is how we get our minimum daily requirement of Dionysus: splitting him into two irreconcilable figures of Christ (or Allah, or "the nation") and the Other. We either project Satan outwards onto the enemy or we introject him, despising our own corrupt selves. The search for Jesus' golden redemption is repeatedly blocked by his evil twin, who demands to be recognized and accepted as part of the Self. Satan lives within the modern soul, and his name is original sin. The phrase may have lost its potency, but it remains deeply embedded in its psychological equivalent: shame.

The culture that eats its children engenders massive rage, which, turned inward, becomes shame. Nearly every modern child makes what amounts to an early, non-verbal decision: *If adults don't care for me, they don't love me, and it must be my own fault.* This leads to the search to recover innocence through addiction, bigotry or conversion.

In exchange for belief, evangelical religion offers divine forgiveness and a return to innocence, the Garden before Eve. In Heaven, writes Vine Deloria, we receive "imperishable bodies in which (we) can do exactly the same things that were punishable offenses in the present life."[92] But anything other than *self*-forgiveness simply reinforces one's core beliefs. Ultimately, belief cannot deliver the innocence it promises, because it remains split. The "saved" person gives his corrupt nature to God without doing the long, hard work of grief and introspection, what D.H. Lawrence called, "...patience, and a certain difficult repentance." *He still refers to himself as a sinner.* Remaining convinced at heart of his unworthiness, he is desperate to stuff the truth back into unconsciousness. His legitimate spiritual longings calcify into religious fanaticism, which, as Jung wrote, "is always a sign of repressed doubt." But since the energy, the sense of sin, must go somewhere, he must project it onto others. Seeing his own darkness in another person, he is compelled to proselytize. If he can covert the other to believe as he does, then the enormous weight of shame is — briefly — lifted. In the extreme, if he cannot convert, then he must *eradicate* any expression of heresy. And we shouldn't feel superior. Since all modern people share this monotheistic consciousness to some degree, writes Hillman, we are all "psychologically Christian."[93]

All must "serve somebody," as Bob Dylan sang. Behind Jesus are our actual gods: progress, technology, production, consumption and competition, all aspects of the child-eater, Kronos.

I also dwell on this history for another reason. Despite the cruelties of mass religion and its collusion with the state, we cannot imagine a new way without a return to the ritual roots of spirituality. But renewal of the world will come through friendship with the "spirits," not with their literalized substitutes. And certainly there are countless exceptions, from the Civil Rights movement to Liberation Theology. But to the extent that it demonizes much of the psyche, religion banishes both soul and spirit. Mainstream faith simply serves the state, retaining the form without the content: convenient piety; Sunday church attendance; and ceremonies of the status quo. And fundamentalism is content without form: emotional catharsis and anti-intellectualism that twists the longing for *communitas* into misogyny and racism.

Mass religion, nationalism, consumerism and addiction are *all* results of the breakdown of the mythic imagination, examples of low-quality Dionysus and retreats from the terrifying ambiguity of existence. None can fill the great hunger in our souls. At best, they reinforce our sense of innocence while keeping us distracted from the madness that surrounds us.

FIVE: MENTAL ILLNESS

> *Men are so necessarily mad, that not to be mad would amount to another form of madness.* — *Blaise Pascal*

If Dionysus were to address Psychology, he might ask such questions as these: Are child molesters criminals, sinners or sick persons? Why are terrorists or tyrants *evil,* rather than sick? Why are convicted murderers *not* considered insane? Why does society punish criminals without rehabilitating them? Why are the mentally ill disproportionately female and poor? Do Americans hate children simply because their parents are poor? In a dysfunctional culture, what is a dysfunctional family? What is functional? Why do Americans take so many drugs, legal or not? Why, in these maddening times, isn't everyone running through the streets raving and grieving? Is willful innocence a form of madness?"

The god of madness lives in our asylums and halfway houses and among the homeless. And at home: one in four adult Americans suffer from a diagnosable mental disorder in a given year; six percent are seriously debilitated; and half of us will develop a mental disorder at some time in our lives.

Depression in particular has doubled since World War Two, with each generation showing higher rates than the last. It now impacts nineteen million American adults. Ten percent of us (six percent of boys and girls) take antidepressants. Forty-one percent of young adults experience major depression, and nearly a third of them exhibit alcohol dependence by age thirty-two. Eighteen percent of college students take prescription psychological medications, and suicide is their second leading cause of death. At least thirty thousand Americans commit suicide annually.

Although the percentage of people confined to mental hospitals has declined since the 1960s, the numbers of those seeking professional help has increased. Still, nearly three-quarters of those with serious psychiatric problems never see a psychiatrist at all, turning instead to alcohol and tranquilizers.

Statistics indicate that plenty of us are going crazy, but, asks Dionysus, *who defines sanity?* For decades, Benjamin Rush's definition prevailed: "Sanity — an aptitude to judge of things like other men, and regular habits, etc." Freud added the abilities to love and work. Thomas Szasz, however, insists that most mental illness is composed only of behaviors that psychiatrists (white, middle-class men) disapprove of, and this category describes all of society's Others. Behaviors such as masturbation and homosexuality no longer fit, but others are continually added.

"Female" behavior is the baseline for determining what is rational. Nineteenth century women were committed to asylums for flirting too much, refusing to marry men chosen by their fathers and excessive religious fervor. Asylums, writes Phyliss Chesler, functioned as "penalties for *being* 'female,' as well as desiring...*not* to be."[94] The gender imbalance remains, even if such behaviors are no longer valid excuses for institutionalizing women. As recently as 1984, a guideline published by an association of private hospitals suggested that sexual promiscuity was cause for immediate hospitalization for teenage girls. Now, it remains safer for women to express their dissatisfaction with depression than through violence (which is more typically male behavior). One in eight women will be diagnosed with depression during her lifetime, and she is twice as likely as a man to receive electroshock treatment.

Middle-class women utilize private therapy, but they enter mental hospitals in great numbers in midlife, when they are both overworked and beginning to feel sexually and maternally expendable. Chesler claims that most simply give in to the mixed expectations of their social condition, which provided them few options before 1970s feminism. *Single, divorced, and widowed women all have lower rates of mental illness than married women, and the reverse is true for men.* Poor women, however, are controlled more directly by the penal system and state mental hospitals, which are also the dumping grounds for older women.

Clearly, society uses definitions of sanity to scapegoat the Other. In 1851, a doctor proposed a psychiatric condition *(Drapetomania)* to explain the irrational tendency of black slaves to flee captivity. Rush diagnosed rebels against federal authority as having an "excess of the passion for liberty" that "constituted a form of insanity" and labeled this illness "anarchia."

What about the children? We are back to mythic questions. The dominant medical perspective, still reflecting Puritan prejudices, states that millions of children are born "neurologically defective" (a more acceptable term than "evil").

The pharmaceutical industry provides the answer to nature gone wrong (previously known as Satan, and cured by baptism at birth). Two and a half million children (one million of them under four years old) manage hyperactive and attention deficit behaviors with Ritalin. Peter Breggin, MD, writes that the ADD diagnosis was developed specifically to justify "the use of drugs to subdue the behaviors of children in the classroom."[95] The U.S. produces and consumes ninety percent of the world's Ritalin, most of which is given to our children, including ten percent (and in some areas, *twenty* percent) of *all* ten-year-old boys. Altogether, some eight million children have received prescriptions for mental conditions.

However, when we hear of epidemics of depression and anxiety, we need to ask whose interest that impression serves. Follow the numbers: between 1995 and 2002 the number of children and teens diagnosed with depression doubled. American doctors are *five times more likely* than British doctors to prescribe antidepressants to minors. Follow the myths. By minimizing the impact of poverty, irrelevant schooling and the culture of violence, the medical priesthood supports the notion of innocence among *adults*.

Back to the numbers: physicians who have received substantial payments from the pharmaceutical industry are five times more likely to prescribe drugs to children than those who have refused such payments. This industry annually spends *$25 billion* on marketing worldwide, and employs more Washington lobbyists than there are legislators.

Madness is big business under capitalism. Due to this pressure, each edition of the Diagnostic and Statistical Manual (DSM) has included more mental disorders than the last. The current 1994 edition lists 297.

One of those new "disorders" is "Premenstrual Dysphoric Disorder" (PMDD). Why would the DSM demonize a natural condition? Follow the money: shortly before, with the patent on Prozac about to expire in 1999, its manufacturer, Eli Lilly & Co., rebranded it as "Sarafem" and marketed it as the cure for this new condition. The DSM complied and recommended antidepressants as the only psychiatric therapy for PMDD. Both Lilly's patent on Prozac and its profits were extended for seven years.

Deinstitutionalization reduced the asylum population from 500,000 in 1955 (half of all hospital beds) to the current 60,000. But Reagan-era budget cuts decimated the community mental health systems that supported the released patients, making thousands homeless. Drastic overbuilding of hospitals in the 1970s left many institutions in serious financial trouble. Psychiatry provided the answer to this problem with new diagnoses like "oppositional defiant disorder." Marketing campaigns convinced some thirty thousand families that private hospitalization was the only thing that kept their children from suicide. The result: six times more adolescents (primarily white and middle-class) are confined to psychiatric wards than in 1980. Teens in *public* facilities have actually decreased, because minority kids go to *real* jails, where they receive no treatment.

Enforced hospitalization exemplifies the paradoxical loss of freedom in a society that claims personal liberty as its highest value. It also evokes the astonishingly brutal history of treatment of the mentally ill, in which all manor of torture was used well into the twentieth century, including mustard baths, application of hot irons, "punishment chairs," electro shock and "refrigeration therapy." This is the realm of the Grand Inquisitors. As C.S. Lewis wrote, "...those who torment us for our own good will torment us without end, for they do so with the approval of their own conscience..."[96]

In Szasz's view, the "therapeutic state" uses psychiatric justifications to strip individuals of their rights. It creates two classes: those who are stigmatized as mentally ill and subject to coercive intervention, and the majority, whose conventional behavior indicates their innocence. "Only in psychiatry are there 'patients' who don't want to be patients," he says. No one else, neither priest nor judge, has the psychiatrist's power to have someone committed, even if he came of his own free will. "If you're in a building that you can't get out of, that's not a hospital; it's a prison."[97]

Certainly, many of the involuntarily committed are considered dangerous to themselves or others. Yet too often, psychiatrists function as the Church once did, as agents of the state, as gatekeepers who determine who is or isn't the Other.

It is possible that poet Theodore Roethke romanticized suffering when he asked, "What is madness but nobility of soul at odds with circumstance?" Yet we can't consider mental illness outside of its social, cultural and political contexts. Psychologist Mary Watkins writes, "The symptom as it appears in the individual points us also toward the pathology of the world, of the culture."[98] Depression is not rare among non-Western people, but it increases when they move to America. Some claim that schizophrenia is more prevalent in cultures like ours that combine high rates of poverty with low senses of social belonging.

Our characteristic American expectation of positive emotions and life-experiences makes feelings of sadness and despair more pathological in this culture than elsewhere. Christina Kotchemidova writes, "Since 'cheerfulness' and 'depression' are bound by opposition, the more one is normalized, the more negative the other will appear."[99]

Ronald Laing argued that the modern family functions "… to repress Eros, to induce a false consciousness of security… to promote a respect for 'respectability.'"[100] To be respectable is to produce, and to *look cheerful*. American obsession with feeling good ("pursuing happiness") is enshrined as a fundamental principle of the consumer society. As Kotchemidova explains, "Our personal feelings are constantly encouraged or discouraged by the culture of emotions we have internalized, and any significant deviance from the societal emotional norms is perceived as emotional disorder that necessitates treatment."[101] The average American feels real pressure to present him/herself as cheerful in order to get a job. Once he/she is employed, putting on a ready-made smile is simply not enough. "Corporations expect their staff to *actually* feel good about the work they do in order to appear convincing to clients."[102]

She argues that twentieth century America took on cheerfulness as an identifying characteristic. The new consumer economy of the 1920s called for cheerful salespeople and an American etiquette that obliged "niceness" and excluded strong emotionality. Among the dozens of self-help cheerfulness manuals, Dale Carnegie's *How to Win Friends and Influence*

People (1936) sold more than fifteen million copies. In the 1950s, the media industry invented numerous ways, including the TV "laugh track," to *induce* cheerfulness. In the 1980s, politicians discovered cheerfulness; all Presidents since Reagan smile in their official photos (none had done so before). And of course we have the "smiley face," which sold over 50 million buttons at its peak in 1971.

Most advertising is in some sense selling happiness or the relief from unhappiness, rather than a product. Despite all the "stuff," however, our obsession with individualism subverts social networks, making it difficult for those in emotional or spiritual crises to find containment except through drugs, madhouses or religious literalism. The cultural pressure to appear upbeat invalidates sadness, a legitimate emotion, by pathologizing it into depression. Psychologist Lesley Hazleton argues that feeling good has become no longer simply a right, but "a social and personal duty."[103] When society won't accept normal depression, however, sad people become ashamed and alienated from themselves. They may feel that their suffering is their own fault, and that others, those who appear to be happy, are normal (in religious terms, among the elect).

Our medical gatekeepers colluded with these prejudices when they changed the definition of "normal bereavement" in the current DSM from one year to two months.[104] Most physicians take less than three minutes to diagnose depression. And psychiatrists administer drugs instead of psychotherapy in over seventy percent of patient visits.

Other gatekeepers at *Time* Magazine described 1950s left-wing comedians Mort Sahl and Lennie Bruce as "sicknicks." But simultaneously, hipsters used "crazy" in positive terms. The powerless attain some control by inverting language, as 1960s blacks used "bad" to replace "good" and teenagers used "sick" to indicate approval in the 1990s. Now, marginalized youth of the Hip-Hop generation say "down" to indicate agreement or approval.

Clearly, however, madness predates capitalism, and economics doesn't explain all of it. Enter Dionysus. Madness is fundamental, an *archetypal* aspect of the psyche. Plato spoke of the "divine madness" that comes as gifts from the gods: *poetic* madness was inspired by the Muses; Apollo was the patron god of *prophetic* madness; Aphrodite and Eros inspired *erotic* madness; and Dionysus was the patron of *ritual* madness. Recall Walter Otto: "A god who is mad! ... There can be a god who is mad only if there is a mad world which reveals itself through him."[105] Hillman, who sees pathology as existentially human, summarizes the old thinking: "...insanity is following the wrong god."[106]

Madness as "low-quality Dionysus" is another expression of the return of the repressed. Lopez-Pedraza writes, "Illness is essentially repression."[107] "Mad," after all, has other meanings: angry, rabid. What if we were to think of mental illness as an unconscious attempt by a socially powerless person to unite body and feeling (or if we were to substitute "uninitiated" for "psychotic")? Then madness becomes part of a natural (if painful and often unsuccessful) attempt to heal oneself, to restore balance. And this, according to Somé, is precisely the intention of ritual.

As Jung taught, the society that emphasizes extreme Apollonian values and represses the Dionysian sets up a dynamic in which the god can only return in the symptoms. This impacts many women who feel compelled to repress feminine values. In taking on the compulsively driven, cutthroat standards of the corporate world, they are like the women of Thebes who cry out unconsciously for Dionysus to release them. Marion Woodman writes that when *thinness at any price* becomes a god, the repressed gods take vengeance through somatic distortions like obesity or anorexia:

> The Dionysian "madness" inherent in compulsive eating
> may be a modern expression of what was earlier known as
> "possession" and in more recent years as "hysteria"... The
> symptom may be the cross on which thousands are forced
> to writhe because they are unaware of the androgynous god
> striving towards consciousness.[108]

Mythologically, the gods are returning from exile. In historical terms, many Americans experience the traumas of racism, poverty, childhood abuse, misogyny or delayed stress. But we *all* suffer from the long-term, collective emotional effects of the shift from paganism to monotheism. We all suffer from *dissociation.*

We are the net products of a process that has taken some two hundred generations to unfold, reaching its peak with our current political and corporate leaders. Psychiatrist Russel Lee writes, "The very qualities of egocentricity and megalomania characteristic of many psychoses are precisely those that lead men to aspire to high office." Bruce Bower describes psychopaths as "superficially charming, intelligent people who...lie about almost everything because they neither understand nor care about others," and argues that in the business world, "increased corporate rewards for risk taking and nonconformity can offer the psychopath faster career movement than before."[109]

Every American suffers from suppressed grief, which returns as anxiety, addiction, narcissism and depression. The mad culture, led by madmen, requires scapegoats whom we sacrifice to restore our innocence. Three million Viet Nam veterans carry the burden of delayed stress for us all. Movies that portray them as ticking time bombs allow Middle America to consider memory's immense power without confronting its universal application. But, says Dionysus, we are *all* ticking.

Who best displays our national shadow for us but our children? Look at their clothing: baggy pants drooping below the waste, butt-cracks showing, untied shoes, oversized, black, hooded sweatshirts. A style of presentation common among adolescents everywhere, regardless of ethnicity or social class that cries out, *Look at us, look at what we carry for you!*

They and all depressed people carry the shadow of our manic celebration of progress, extraversion, cheerfulness and grandiosity. They are the canaries in the mineshaft, showing us that the more politicians and celebrities emphasize these American characteristics, the more depression will spread. We who can channel the madness into consumerism feel welcomed into the community of the elect, while those who cannot do so prove *our* righteous standing — and our innocence.

At least since the beginning of the nuclear age, popular culture has hesitantly acknowledged this condition. Novels like *Catch-22, Slaughterhouse Five* and *One Flew Over The Cuckoo's Nest* encapsulate the notion that modern society, with its stressful pace of change and nearly constant fear and anxiety, is mad or maddening. Paul Shepard writes that we all experience an "epidemic of the psychopathic mutilation of ontogeny." In simple terms, we don't grow up the way nature intended anymore. We are, by indigenous standards, children.[110]

Clearly, any compassionate caregiver hopes to reduce suffering. "Successful treatment," writes E. Fuller Torrey, "means the control of symptoms."[111] But when psychotherapy merely attempts to recover a sense of "productive normalcy," that condition which is itself one of the *causes* of our unhappiness, it becomes yet another effort to recover lost innocence, as well as a condemnation of an archetype ruled by the mythic image of Dionysus. Banishing him, we welcome ourselves to the madhouse.

Zerzan takes this idea a step further: "To assert that we can be whole/ enlightened/healed within the present madness amounts to endorsing the madness."[112] It is partially a question of awareness, much of which is conditioned by the media. On the one hand, we collude in mass denial, blissfully unaware of both our complicity and our capacity to change. On the other, media obsession with crime and terrorism increases our anxiety. This decades-long, roiling, alternating sense of both paranoia *and* denial — intermittent conditioning — defines our peculiarly American form of collective madness.

From this perspective, a major function of the myth of innocence is to suppress our grief. Many men are well aware of this condition. One of the most common statements heard at mythopoetic men's retreats is: *I haven't cried in thirty years, and I won't allow myself to start. If I did, it would never stop.* This leads to a view of madness as the fine line between delusion and revelation, or between the return of the repressed and spontaneous initiation, the territory of *The Bacchae.*

The return of Dionysus can appear as emotional dismemberment. For centuries, however, such experiences have typically occurred outside of any ritual containers. Schizophrenics enter liminal space alone, without guides, and psychiatry now diagnoses them with bio-chemical imbalances or genetic defects that require lifelong drug treatment to repress the symptoms.

Jungians such as John Weir Perry see schizophrenia as a natural renewal process. Many of his patients described visions consistent with the ancient symbolism of kingship and initiation. Joseph Campbell wrote that such fantasy "perfectly matches that of the mythological hero journey."[113] From this perspective, madness becomes an inward and backward process, under the dubious guidance of the mad god himself.

In historical accounts of persons who went mad but also had religious experiences, most took their revelations literally. They experienced death, apocalypse, crucifixion, sexual inversion, fertility and rebirth. A mythologist would identify *all* these visions as images of initiation. Those who did recover saw past the literal to the metaphoric. In 1830 John Perceval wrote, "The spirit speaks poetically, but the lunatic takes the literal sense."[114] Hillman observes, "Only as Perceval becomes humorous, doubtful and ironic does he become sane."[115] Perceval moved from gravity to levity.

But he was an exception. Most get stuck in what Robert Moore calls "chronic liminality," as illustrated by the myth of Ariadne. Many heroes entered the underground labyrinth, only to be killed by the Minotaur. Theseus defeated it because he had kept in contact with the world above by means of Ariadne's thread. It enabled him to return to the light (normal consciousness) after completing his task. Those who have no thread of connection to community remain below in that "labyrinth of transformative space," but only partially transformed.[116] Thus, says Moore, many pathological states are nothing other than failed initiations. And again I note that approaching the symbolic brush with death can evoke literal death. One of Moore's clients was lucid enough to say, "I need to die, before I kill myself."[117] Seven centuries earlier, Rumi advised, "Die *before* you die."

Until the seventeenth century, Europeans believed that madmen were close to the unseen world and accepted them within the community. Traditional Africans still perceive mental distress as a call for help. Indeed, madness is a sign that *the community* (who know nothing of "family systems therapy") is sick. They perceive crazy people as undergoing crises resulting from the activity of spirit and protect them, hoping that their healing will benefit the community. To them, the spirits of a sick world speak through the most sensitive of us, those with the most fluid boundaries.

But can men transform themselves, by themselves, in a demythologized world that lacks real community? Shortly before his death, Ernest Hemingway wrote, "What do you think happens to a man going on 62 when he realizes that he can never write the books and stories he promised himself? ...If I can't exist on my terms, then existence is impossible."[118]

Suicide was his failed initiation, the heroic ego's *literal* response to the *symbolic* challenge of transformation. By contrast, James Joyce brought his daughter to Jung for treatment. Jung (who knew the descent to the underworld) could see that the girl was psychotic, but he was more interested in her father: "His 'psychological' style is definitely schizophrenic, but with the difference...the ordinary patient cannot help talking and thinking in such a way, while Joyce willed it and...developed it with all his creative forces."[119]

Joyce had both the will and the talent to move his madness into art. Some just get lucky. As Plato wrote, "...the greatest blessings come by way of madness, indeed of madness that is heaven-sent."[120] Chapter Eleven will describe how that process has begun in America.

PART THREE

WAKING UP FROM THE AMERICAN DREAM

INTRODUCTION

⁂

Does history have a purpose? The idea that it progresses from creation to second coming satisfies only fundamentalists (exemplars of the paranoid imagination), while capitalists (exemplars of the predatory imagination) assume no meaning whatsoever — except that the winners die with the most toys.

America has chased its Dionysian shadow into a cultural dead end. Having described the toxic mimic of a life that we might have lived, I search in the cracks of the dying empire for signs of new growth. If we imagine that history moves in great cycles, then perhaps we are merely stuck in a particularly noxious era characterized by innocent violence and violent innocence. And "noxious" and "innocent" come from the same root.

The new story can only be half-told and half-imagined since it is barely beginning, and changes at the mythic level happen with glacial slowness. Still, it is only in a dark time, as Roethke wrote, that the eye begins to see. To begin to tell a new tale, we'll take another look at the twentieth century, this time from a cultural perspective.

It is our job to make women unhappy with what they have.
B. E. PUCKETT, ALLIED STORES CORP.

———

If I could find a white man with a Negro sound I could make a billion dollars.
SAM PHILLIPS

———

Elvis Presley is the greatest cultural force in the twentieth century.
LEONARD BERNSTEIN

———

America when will you be angelic?
When will you take off your clothes?
When will you look at yourself through the grave?
ALLEN GINSBERG

———

One may judge of a king by the state of dancing during his reign.
ANCIENT CHINESE MAXIM

———

Bobo-malay, shushu maya
(Lord, make this body dance!)
DAGARA, WEST AFRICA

11

ALL SHOOK UP, OR THE WHITE DIONYSUS

OUR DISEASE — the Western divorce of consciousness from flesh — appears as consumerism, environmental degradation, fundamentalism, perpetual war, genocide and racism. Yet, strangely, it is possible that the terrible uprooting and enslavement of some fifty million black people (only a third of whom survived the passage) actually initiated a great healing process. Compounding this colossal irony, the individuals most responsible came from America's most bigoted region. Southern whites reacted with extraordinary violence (committing at least 5,000 lynchings between 1890 and 1930) when former slaves attempted to move into the mainstream of life. Shameful as this period was, however, it brought out both our most feared contradictions as well as the seeds of renewal.

For all its sorrows, the twentieth century saw several brief periods when Dionysian madness seized the Apollonian mind in its flight from the body and brought it back to Earth. African-American *music* fundamentally altered America and began the slow process of cleaning out the festering wounds underlying both Puritanism and materialism.

Throughout the Jim Crow era this spirit survived in the black church.

Even though many of its members absorbed the conservative social values of their former masters, there was never any mind-body split in the *practice* of their religion, which some white churches copied. Southerners, both white and black, have been in this bind for generations, writes Michael Ventura. "A doctrine that denied the body, preached by a practice that excited the body, would eventually drive the body into fulfilling itself elsewhere." The call-and-response chanting and rhythmic bodily movement typical of southern preachers absolutely contradict their moralistic sermons. This contributes to "the terrible tension that drives their unchecked paranoias."[1]

Music, sacred or secular, held rural communities together by providing a safety valve from the stifling pressure of rigid conformism. Those (again, both white and black) who most exemplified this paradox were the traveling singers who mediated between the community's sentimentalized idea of itself and the forbidden temptations of the outside world.

Were these men merely entertainers, or did they serve a profoundly valuable role as messengers from the unknown? David Abram observes that in tribal cultures, shamans rarely dwell *within* their communities. They live at the periphery, the boundary between the village and the "larger community of beings upon which the village depends for its...sustenance."[2] These intermediaries ensure an appropriate energy flow between humans on the one hand, and ancestors, spirits, plants and animals, or (to reduce things to psychology) unconscious aspects of the personality, on the other. Inhabitants of this world know that they live in contact with other worlds and are fed by them.

In 1920, the South was still a primarily rural society with a living folklore that extended back to Ireland, Scotland and Africa. For this reason, and despite all its feudal horrors, the people of the region retained a vestigial memory of the permeable boundaries between the worlds; and it was the singers, preachers and storytellers who mediated the edge. By contrast, the urban North was characterized by the crowded, dirty, noisy, mechanized life of factories and tenements (for the poor) and the intense drive for money and status powered by the Protestant Ethic (for the middle-class and rich). Both pressures for conformism and old community and family values were loosening considerably. However, these people paid a considerable price in alienation from the natural world. Modern life, writes Greil Marcus, "…had set men free by making them strangers."[3]

After World War I, the anxieties of the new century also threatened to overwhelm the small-town values of self-denial, strict moral conduct and racial exclusion in the South. Great political rifts were growing that would eventually explode in the 1960s. Northern social movements, often led by immigrants, were demanding reforms. Women were about to achieve the right to vote, just as city dwellers were becoming the majority of the population. Reactionary forces responded in the form of the Palmer Raids, the F.B.I. and the resurgent Ku Klux Klan. And, as the average age of the onset of puberty decreased while the age at marriage increased, adolescents began to find themselves in a prolonged period of dependence upon their parents, who first used the word "teenage" around 1920.

The pace of change led to drinking rates that have not been equaled since. In 1919, the government gave in to Protestant pressure and declared Prohibition. Until 1933, it was illegal to sell or transport intoxicating beverages. America, alone among industrialized nations, declared that the celebration of Dionysus in even this most literal form was unacceptable. But the repressed quickly returned; sixty percent of the public continuously violated the law. "Dionysus," writes Lopez-Pedraza, "took his revenge in bootlegging, gangsters and violence."[4] Curiously, "underworld" now implied organized crime, rather than the abode of ancestors. It still served as a mirror of the upper world, but now of its rapacious capitalism. Americans murdered each other at three times current rates. Instead of a revival of Protestant asceticism, America had the "roaring twenties."

As African-Americans agitated for inclusion in the American dream, technology in the form of radio and records brought their culture into the mainstream. Soon, everyone was dancing; indeed, the dance craze known as "the Charleston" (popularized by white musicians) was actually a West African ancestor dance. In another period of gylanic resurgence, people spoke openly about sex, gender and the body's demands for pleasure. The white ego was loosening up. Stephen Diggs writes that this "alchemical process" melded western individual consciousness with tribal orality: "Where the Northern soul, from shaman to Christian priest, operates dissociatively, leaving the body to travel the spirit world, the African priest, the Hoodoo conjurer, and the bluesman ask the *loa* to enter bodies and possess them."[5]

Still, the Klan claimed four million members. There were several urban riots in 1919 (all characterized by white-on-black violence), when servicemen returned from Europe. In 1921, whites destroyed the black section of Tulsa, killing up to 300 blacks. In 1923, they burnt down the black town of Rosewood, Florida, killing dozens. It was a particularly cruel irony. Even as whites were experimenting with tentative rejection of their ancient hatred of the body, they were savagely punishing people who seemed to exemplify natural comfort in the body. And at precisely the same time in Europe, the Nazis were blaming the breakdown of traditional sex roles on Jews. But Blacks were now in a uniquely influential position. Even as they suffered continued segregation and repression, their music (at least watered-down versions of it) was challenging the white majority's most fundamental beliefs.

Recall that Pentheus was both revolted by and attracted to his cousin Dionysus. Myth reminds us that fascination always lies just beneath hatred of the Other, because *the Other is an unrecognized part of the Self*. America played out much of its love-hate relationship with Dionysus throughout the century on the field of popular music.

This process has moved in a dialectical series of cultural statements. To simplify, blacks merge western techniques with indigenous African forms to create something brand-new. Whites copy it but dilute its intensity. Individual whites (such as Paul *Whiteman* and Benny *Goodman*) reap most of the profits. Then younger blacks emerge with a revitalized musical expression, but this time with the intention of restoring black identity, as a conscious choice to remain outside of acceptable boundaries. The message is, *"We are not you."* It is a statement about otherness, for once, *by the Other,* which prefers exclusion if the result is the survival of authentic art. Again, whites copy the new form, carefully removing its most Dionysian elements to make it more acceptable and marketable. But white youth reject the diluted forms in favor of those enjoyed by black youth. From Dixieland to Hip-Hop, the cycle has repeated for nearly a century. Recall how the Greek *xenos* can mean either stranger or guest. In this twisted dialogue, whites have consistently feared contamination by the stranger (black people), yet they often long for the emotional and bodily freedom offered by the guest (black *culture*). This is an essential aspect of whiteness itself. "The white itch to affect blackness," writes Kevin Phinney, "is an ineffable part of the American experience."[6]

In 1933, Congress acknowledged the failure of Prohibition, but tied legalization of alcohol to higher minimum legal drinking ages. The new scapegoats, teenagers, effectively distracted the public from the continuing epidemic of *adult* alcoholism.

The pendulum swung back during the Depression. Just as Prohibition was repealed, Hollywood submitted to Catholic pressure and agreed to censor itself, suppressing all suggestions of intimacy in and out of marriage. Walt Disney attained huge popularity with his sanitized, asexual cartoons. In his movies, write Jewett and Lawrence, "Sex had become sufficiently innocent, trivial... that every family knew it could trust itself to go to the movies."[7] In this compromise between the Puritan and the Opportunist, America traded away one manifestation of the Pagan sensibility (erotic images) to get another (alcohol) back.

But the Opportunist soon had the upper hand, because this period also marked the transition to the consumer culture. After World War Two, the bulk of industrial activity became the manufacture of "goods." Rather suddenly, youth, far from being a threat to society, became its ideal. Advertising suggested that things people bought would make and keep them young. Prior to this time, elders almost everywhere had enjoyed the highest respect, while adolescence was a brief period of intense preparation for adulthood. More paradox: a society that was slaughtering or neglecting its young determined that it was best, like Peter Pan, to never grow up. Perhaps this isn't so paradoxical, since maturity implies transcending innocence and recognizing memory. In 1930, survivors of slavery and of the massacre of Wounded Knee were still alive. There was much to remember and much to deny. Staying young is a way of "killing time" (*Kronos*). But by suspending its process, we never express our innate gifts, and we leave little of value to the next generation. We trade experience for innocence.

America overcame the Great Depression by making total war and became immensely rich and influential. But, writes psychologist Clarissa Pinkola-Estes, the war created "a culture turned back on itself... one that had become dry from much loss of blood."[8] One of its primary symbols was John Wayne, who modeled a powerful yet restrained and sexually detached masculinity. In addition, his cowboy movies were cold-war allegories with clear political overtones. Tim Riley writes, "It was if the cold-war curtain came down both across Europe and across some imaginary field in the American male psyche that held men in check..."[9]

In reaction, both resisting and longing to heal the mind-body split that Wayne represented, America dreamed up a vacancy for a moistening archetypal presence, the rising up of at least one soul to enact the needed mysteries. Jack Kerouac articulated the angst that some whites felt, "... wishing I were Negro, feeling that the best the white world had offered was not enough ecstasy for me, not enough life, joy, kicks, darkness, music, not enough night."[10]

Despite the low-grade residue of anxiety brought on by the nuclear age, peacetime unleashed a torrent of energy and new levels of affluence. Class tensions lessened and unions began to decline, as working people entered the middle class and voted accordingly. Their (white) children were the first in history to grow up in such affluence, the first to be raised under Dr. Spock's permissive ideas, and the first to expect an extended adolescence in college.

There had been a general loosening of inhibitions during the liminal insecurity of wartime. But afterwards, a backlash arose against women, millions of whom lost their jobs to the returning soldiers. Betty Friedan described a deep sense of depression, frustration and resentment among women. Magazines that had encouraged them to go to work before the war now praised "homemakers," with "a single purpose... to sell a vast array of new products..."[11]

While conservatives whipped up fear of communist "penetration" of government, television brought low-key sexualization of commodities into every home. Advertisers discovered that nothing sells so well as when it is subtly associated with the female body. The relatively new experience of owning mass-produced products created a placeless community of consumers. "Men who never saw or knew one another," wrote Daniel Boorstin, "were held together by their common use of objects so similar that they could not be distinguished even by their owners."[12] Never before had so many people determined their identity in such a thin and artificial way. Happy consumers tolerated or remained ignorant of the perpetual war economy that ensured foreign markets and unending supplies of raw materials.

Circumstances were preparing the ground for the emergence of the youth culture. The early1950s witnessed a convergence of unique factors, starting with what became known as the "baby boom." From 1947 until 1980, the population of thirteen to thirty-year-olds increased every year. Teenagers were more affluent as a group than any previous generation. By 1956, thirteen million teens were spending $7 billion/year. They had no memory of the Depression or the war and no instinct to save money, but they *were* aware that nuclear war might negate any future. At a deeper level, however, their bodies were about to explode in the universal, if inchoate, cry for initiation. By 1960, three-quarters of movie audiences would be teenagers, prompting a Hollywood executive to complain, "It's getting so show business is one big puberty rite."

Rural America's population declined steeply. Between 1945 and 1970, some twenty-five million people left the farms forever. Advertising and cheap mortgages (for white people) made possible by the G.I. Bill convinced them and everyone else that cars were a necessity. The new mobility contributed to the breakdown of urban, ethnic communities. In previous migrations, large, multi-generational groups had moved together, following two persistent themes of American myth; cities were no good, and one could always make a new start in life by settling the wilderness. Indeed, by the mid-1950s, city life in the popular imagination was encapsulated by Ralph Kramden's filthy, cramped apartment in *The Honeymooners* TV show. By contrast, *Father Knows Best, Ozzie And Harriet* and many other shows presented suburbia as the Promised Land.

But this escape from the inner cities had a different intention and a different result. Countless young couples left their crowded neighborhoods and the ethnic accents and recipes of their parents and moved to the suburbs. Many no longer identified as "hyphenated Americans" (as Woodrow Wilson had sneered), but simply Americans. As this happened, however, a generation of (white) children grew up missing the experience of knowing or living with their extended families. They lost connection to elders, who were being exiled to retirement communities or nursing homes. The nuclear family lacked historical continuity; it was essentially little more than an isolated consuming unit. And yet the new emphasis on individualism was negated by relentless advertising pressure that channeled most personal choices toward conformism. "Organization men" gave their allegiance to corporations and uprooted their families from one suburb to another whenever their jobs changed. William Whyte wrote that they "left home spiritually as well as physically, to take the vows of organization life."[13]

Something else was disappearing — the oral tradition. Previous generations had learned their myths (and their history, which was often the same thing) by listening repeatedly to storytellers. As recently as 1935, an actor named De Wolf Hopper died, having recited *Casey At The Bat* over 10,000 times to enraptured audiences across the country. And as the unmediated, oral transmission of culture was dying out, technology was making it easier for whites to encounter the cultural creations of the Other. By 1955, three-quarters of households had TV; by 1960, American companies sold ten million portable record players a year.

As for their parents, the images in their heads had been *delivered* in two main ways: over the radio, into their private living rooms (at least radio allowed them to imagine their own images); or from movies, the one experience that most Americans now had in common. Movies, writes Ventura, had "usurped the public's interest in the arts as a whole and in literature especially."[14] Whereas indigenous people had *participated* in their entertainment, Americans (except for dancing) were passive consumers of culture. The Western mind-body split comes to its extreme in the concept of an *audience*. It "... has no body... all attention, all in its heads, while something on a screen or a stage enacts its body."[15]

Television added a new dimension; it portrayed events far away *as they happened.* By showing how others lived, especially the contented middle class, it raised expectations among the poor and had an immediate impact on politics. Without television the civil rights movement may not have got started when it did. And it showed teenagers dancing. Ultimately, though, TV turned Americans into "couch potatoes." When they were not in their cars, enjoying the freedom of the open road, they were generally at home, glued to the tube.

Soon, the tube was on six to eight hours per day, as millions ritually asked, "What's on tonight?" Consuming their junk-food snacks along with the myths of post-war America, they witnessed the "togetherness" of the white, suburban family, with either the benevolent patriarch (Robert Young) or the irrelevant but lovable Dad (William Bendix). And they observed, over and over, the righteous hero's confrontation with the Other, who appeared as commie, gangster, redskin or space alien. But all dilemmas, comic or serious, resolved themselves just before the final commercial.

Commercials. Americans came to expect regular interruptions to hear that redemption was possible through owning the latest gadgets or consumable products. The 300-year-old Puritan heritage of delayed gratification was being pushed underground, like the pagan gods themselves, not to re-emerge for thirty years. Economist Victor Lebow announced this new world, without irony. The economy "…demands that we make consumption a way of life, that we convert the buying and use of goods into rituals…We need things consumed, burned up, replaced, and discarded at an ever-increasing rate."[16] Having endured a generation of depression and war, adults were claiming their reward.

But they also sacrificed something — the imagination. Instead of ancestors and spirits, they worshipped entertainers, athletes and name brands. Remnants of ancient clan competition still existed, but now it was between Ford and Chevy, Budweiser and Miller or Cheer and Tide. And few asked the old questions anymore: *What is my purpose in this life? Whom do I serve? What do I owe to those who came before me and those who come after me?*

One could certainly make a case against this last statement. Millions of parents who had experienced the Depression were proud to scrimp and save so that their children might have the educational and material advantages they had never had themselves. Yet, when the baby boomers articulated their rebellion, they commonly lamented the commercialized, dangerous, polluted, banal, meaningless world that their parents were leaving them. Due to war, divorce, life in the suburbs and careers, the fathers, especially, were simply not present. Psychologist Joseph Pleck notes that Freud and Jung had seen the father as critically important in the child's psychological development, but now he was "a dominating figure, not by his presence, but by his absence."[17]

Milton Viorst writes that the theme of the 1950s was "security: internal security (McCarthy), international security (massive retaliation), personal security (careerism). And yet no one felt secure."[18] Other factors came later: Civil Rights and Viet Nam, which provided the focus for dissent; and the birth control pill, which finally allowed women to independently manage their sex lives. A final factor had always existed, although Americans had never attended to it except in wartime: the need to identify as an initiatory *group*, to go through the rites of passage not as individuals but *together*. America was poised unstably between its Puritan heritage and the hedonism of the consumer lifestyles.

Imagine America entering the liminal period of 1953-1955. Imagine it as a time during which the empire reached its apogee (the current madness being merely a last gasp), when the seeds of its collapse first sprouted. The U.S. had a position of security that was unparalleled in human history, with absolute control over the Western Hemisphere and both oceans. Its economy and culture dominated the world. And yet anticommunist hysteria was running wild.

In April 1953, President Eisenhower barred gays from all federal jobs. In June, the government executed Julius and Ethel Rosenberg. The Korean War ended in stalemate in July, just as the Cuban revolution began. In August, the C.I.A. overthrew Iran's government. Kinsey's second volume, on female sexuality, appeared in the fall. *War of the Worlds* left viewers staring fearfully at the stars for signs of the next incursion by The Other, while *Shane* presented the lone Redemption Hero in his most classic form, literally riding off into the sunset. In December, the first issue of *Playboy* with nude pictures of Marilyn Monroe arrived.

In May, 1954 the French surrendered at Dien Bien Phu. Ten days later, the Supreme Court made its decision in *Brown vs Board of Education,* jumpstarting the Civil Rights Movement. In June, Congress added the words "under God" to the Pledge of Allegiance, and the C.I.A. overthrew another democracy in Guatemala. Three days later, Viet Nam was divided, marking the official beginning of America's involvement. In August, as the C.I.A. defeated the insurrection in the Philippines, Congress made membership in the Communist Party a felony.

Rebel Without A Cause opened in early 1955. In July, "In God We Trust" became mandatory on all currency. The Soviets detonated their first H-bomb in August, ending the U.S. monopoly on nuclear terror. Allen Ginsburg's October recitation of *Howl* announced the "Beat Generation" to America. In December, shortly after Emmett Till's murderers were acquitted, Rosa Parks refused to give up her bus seat to a white person. And one other thing: in July 1954, Elvis Presley released his first record.

America was entering a period of continuous change from which it has never recovered. The spark that set things off occurred when southern whites blended country music and blues, just as the civil rights movement was making its move and all Americans were scrambling to acquire televisions. Stephen Diggs calls this the blues revolution: "Dionysus is inciting the instinctual maenads to pull Pentheus from the treetop back down to earth and then tear his detached vision to bits."[19] To Ventura, this is "... one of the most important moments in modern history."[20]

Musicologists debate issues such as whites appropriating black music, fabricated consumer markets and the talent of individual musicians. But the critical point is Elvis's emergence (from the South, from beyond the pale). Soon, television allowed everyone to see white men performing like blacks, men who were comfortable in their bodies and defiantly, humorously, ambiguously sexual, men who challenged John Wayne's code of masculinity.

Eldridge Cleaver wrote, "... contact, however fleeting, had been made with the lost sovereignty — the Body had made contact with its mind —

and the shock...sent an electric current throughout this nation."[21] It was
another revival of the Dionysian mode in a culture that had long been
ruled by a poor version of the Apollonian. In contrast to "containment,"
the theme that dominated so much of public life, youth became *en-theos*,
taken over by the god of ecstasy. Quickly, the nature of western dance and
performance changed. And along with the released energies came much
that was unexpected.

The music was so intense and its performers so young that it sparked a
collective flame. None of the individual factors alone could have catalyzed
the change. Within only a few months the youth market exploded. More
important, a youth *movement* began shortly and spread across the world. For
perhaps the first time, an entire generation saw the world in fundamentally
different terms from its parents and chose to define itself as separate.
Unknown to the youth, the only models for this phenomenon in all of
history had been the groups of young men going into the liminal madness
of initiation together.

Recall the accounts of African boys dancing before the elders' huts,
demanding to be initiated. Now picture young white girls (who might
have been timid and obedient as individuals) forming mobs, breaking
through police lines to approach their Dionysian priests, and sometimes to
"dismember" them as the Maenads had done with Pentheus:

> I heard feet like a thundering herd, and the next thing I knew
> I heard this voice from the shower area... by the time we got
> there several hundred must have crawled in...Elvis was on top
> of one of the showers...his shirt was shredded and his coat
> was torn to pieces. Somebody had even gotten the belt and
> his socks...he was up there with nothing but his pants on and
> they were trying to pull at them up on the shower.[22]

Suddenly, the madness broke out as the return of both erotic excitement
as well as (in a few years) profound rage, signaling the opening of the gates
through which *all* of the culture's repressed energies would flow. But there
were few elders to guide and welcome them, because now *it was the elders*

themselves against whom the youth were rebelling. The result was — for two decades — an international community more or less in agreement about a broad number of issues, the most central of which was that they were inheriting a world of fathers who were killing their children.

In 1960, well before antiwar protests, 50,000 Americans demonstrated for civil rights with 3,600 arrests. For white students, this activism marked their first connection to the Other as well as the direct (if temporary) *experience* of otherness. Many felt more commonality with young minorities than with their parents.

It was a fearfully revolutionary event, children of the slaves mixing with children of the masters. That summer "the Twist" burst upon the scene, "a guided missile," wrote Cleaver, "launched from the ghetto into the very heart of suburbia," succeeding as politics couldn't do in helping whites reclaim their bodies.[23] Getting up and dancing individually or in groups broke down the traditional Western barrier between performer and immobile audience. It meant a revival of a participatory process rooted in ecstatic, Pagan religion that had been repressed and marginalized for centuries. And, since dancers soon stopped holding hands, it meant that *girls didn't have to follow anymore.*

The same collective urge that gave rise to the Twist also propelled John Kennedy into office and invited idealism and new possibilities. Consequently, youth took his death particularly hard. It is no coincidence that a new form of *maenadism* — "Beatlemania" — erupted only two months later. Ehrenreich writes, "At no time during their U.S. tours was the group audible above the shrieking."[24] Susan Douglas argues that the resonance between Kennedy and the Beatles allowed for "a powerful and collective transfer of hope."[25]

The ecstatic experience of dancing to rock music evoked a desire for other non-material ways of knowing. It helped to define this community of initiates, who shared a fascination with both the introspection offered by psychedelics and the easy, if fleeting, access drugs provided to *communitas.* For a few years, millions of young people commonly distinguished between those who opposed the war, got high, listened to rock, wore long hair and rejected the Puritan Ethic, and those who didn't. Or: between Dionysian ecstasy and Apollonian security. Or: between authentic and contrived innocence.

Many attempted to reclaim that innocence in rural communes. Whether it was in those pastoral images or in urban circuses like Haight-Ashbury, the rebellion drew its power from its negation of the bland conformism of suburbia. But the phrase, *"Don't trust anyone over the age of thirty!"* revealed a profound grief about the loss of elderhood. Adults could not initiate youth into a meaningful world, because that world had disappeared and because they had never been initiated themselves.

All the issues repressed by the culture for so long burst into the open. Millions marched against the war, not merely because it was a mistake (as apologists still contend), but because it was mad, imperialist genocide. Their parents, the generation that had survived the Depression, saved Europe from the Nazis and consumed the myth of innocent intentions could only respond with, *"My country — right or wrong!"* The youth, however, who always see the mythic issues quite clearly, responded: *"Hey, hey, LBJ! How many kids did you kill today?"*

Civil rights agitation sparked movements for the rights of women, Latinos, farm workers, Indians, gays, prisoners, the disabled, the environment and the inner soul. Countless people realized that psychedelics expanded awareness and hinted at spiritual realms that conventional religion could never understand and was staunchly opposed to. Eventually, millions investigated natural foods, aerobics, the human potential movement and Eastern religion. By the 1990s, hundreds of meditation centers were established in America.

But every gylanic resurgence provokes andocratic reaction. When the war ended, the central focus for activism disappeared. "The music died," as Don McLean sang. The tenuous connection between rebellion and pleasure began to open up. Perhaps, since rock (unlike its parent, the blues) is the musical expression of uninitiated young men, this was inevitable. The coalition broke up into its constituent parts: a few violent (and heavily publicized) revolutionaries on the one hand; apolitical mystics on another; and minorities and single-issue activists on a third. The space for another toxic mimic appeared, idealism collapsed into consumerism, and the youth movement receded back into the youth *market*. Critics now debate whether commercial youth culture is deliberately created in order to separate youth from their families, recreating them as vulnerable consumers, or whether, as Frith writes, their real needs "— to make sense of their situation, to overcome their isolation — are dissolved in a transitory emotional moment."[26]

From the pagan perspective, youth do have innate needs. They need to briefly separate out so as to go through the initiatory fires under the capable guidance of elders, to return, to be recognized and welcomed back, and then to re-imagine the world. But as they matured, American youth succumbed to narcissistic self-absorption, cynicism, fundamentalism, economic pressures or the temptations of scapegoating. And the youth market, now controlled almost completely by a few mega-corporations, exists only to exploit and channel the various forms of low-quality Dionysus. The counterculture ended, writes Ehrenreich, "by affirming the... materialistic culture it had set out to refute."[27] Rock and most of its descendents are now little more than the background music to new frenzies of consumerism and nationalism.

Musical preference still expresses identity. But now it distinguishes *between* youth populations, rather than defining a broad community separated from their parents by a generation gap. Ronald Reagan co-opted Bruce Springsteen's "Born in the USA;" beer and car companies sponsor tours by musicians; loudspeakers play *"We will rock you"* as the bombers take off; CIA torturers blast Heavy Metal into prisons to disorient prisoners; and Jimmie Hendrix's *Voodoo Child* is played at boot-camp initiations.[28] Skinheads sell racist rock over the Internet, while misogyny drives much Hip Hop. The volume increases as civic involvement declines.

However, the memory of that tentative healing of the mind-body split survives, and Americans now commonly acknowledge the desire for authenticity. Whether they search for it in rock or gospel music, meditation, hiking, gardening or cocaine is, to an extent, irrelevant. The genie is out of the bottle; despite the media barrage, even commercials hint that we are capable of so much more. Despite constant pressure to conform, we have assumed the primacy of this search. Many baby boomers and many of their children still carry an idealism that counters the prevailing cynicism and fear. And the *energy*, the desperate, if unconscious craving for initiation, felt by new (and often fatherless) generations, is as strong as ever. The creative imagination openly opposes the culture of innocent violence and violent innocence.

The madness is still at the gates. Ventura argues that, for better or for worse, successive generations of youth have spontaneously produced "... forms — music, fashions, behaviors — that prolong the initiatory moment."[29] A period that in the tribal world lasted only a few weeks has now been extended into decades. The pace of change has kept millions in a state of ongoing liminality throughout their entire lives. But if we reduce such phenomena to psychology and see only a population of eternal adolescents who are duped by consumer culture, we are missing the point. We have all become initiates, without being welcomed home, stuck in the middle of a great transition. In some parts of the Third World, literally half the population is composed of teenagers, crying out to be seen. This is tragic, but it is also our best hope for renewal. "Hence their demand — inchoate, unreasonable and irresistible — is that *history* initiate them."[30]

But what about Elvis? How do we understand that thirty-two years after his death, forty-four countries host 525 fan clubs, and an Elvis search engine has 330 sites with over 500 books, or that fans refer, humorously or not, to an "Elvis religion"? We cannot explain this away, because we are in the realm of mystery, where images are our only guides and questions are more important than answers. Would someone else have created the same reactions? Certainly, there were countless talented black performers, and later, many whites. All we can say is that America and the world needed someone like him *at that particular moment*, an "animus man," what Pinkola-Estes refers to as "one who acts out the unrealized soulfulness of others... (appearing) to be only that which others most desired."[31] The collective consciousness dreamed up his image to carry its projection of Dionysian energy.

His art had roots in Africa, where everything originates in ritual. As much as racial oppression had conspired to break down and denature those African forms, an energy and a wisdom that questioned (as Dionysus does) most of the assumptions of western culture still came through. It was the energy of the body, rather than of the head.

Segregationists rightly perceived in Elvis and his followers more than a simple threat to respectable codes of behavior. Blacks could enjoy this "Devil's music" amongst themselves, but it was a corrupting influence when it was exposed to white children. Again, *what were they so afraid of?* The simple answer is the threat of miscegenation. But on a deeper level, the Loosener was breaking away from the acceptable convention of the *black* "American Dionysus," first among southern whites, then in the cities, and then, via television, across the world.

Elvis delighted in expressing paradox. His images, writes Erika Doss, were "a tangled hybrid of fact and desire."[32] His voice dissolved racial boundaries, and his obvious bodily comfort offered the same possibility for gender. Men (at least *white* men) had never seemed so loose. He deliberately wore mascara and wild clothes in wilder colors to exaggerate this ambiguity; and he drove a *pink* Cadillac. Offstage he was exceedingly polite; onstage he was sullen, defiant and self-mocking. By singing both rock and gospel, he straddled the boundaries of sacred and profane music. He combined small-town values and an astonishing, urban energy. In a sense, he was both mortal and immortal, like Dionysus and the other suffering gods before him.

Compared with John Wayne's dominant image of masculinity, writes Tim Riley, Elvis was "...a completely different kind of man, more complex, more open to change, less fixed on a single idea or attitude."[33] He personified liberation and transgression. Teenagers adored him because his clear affront to the bourgeois world gave them permission to follow. Like Johnny Appleseed, wrote Cleaver, he "sow[ed] seeds...in the white souls of the white youth of America."[34] But he also embodied *transformation.* As such, from his position at the border between the worlds, he beckoned especially to women, inviting them into Dionysian ritual — the madness, the *pharmakon* — that is both cause and cure of itself (later, the publishers of a 1998 translation of *The Bacchae* would acknowledge the connection by putting a mug shot of Elvis in his army uniform on the cover).

What are the other mythic images here? Many commentators insisted that the source of the generation gap was the Oedipus complex. Certainly there was rage against authority. But if young people dreamed of patricide, it was directed against *Kronos'* insatiable appetite for his own children, and it was driven by a sense of betrayal. After all, hadn't oracles warned Ouranos, Kronos and even Zeus that their children would overthrow them? Isn't that fear at the root of the patriarch's reign of terror? Two myths intersected in the 1960s. The universal dream of the hero's journey collided with a nightmare, the refusal to anoint the new kings and queens of the world. Youths demanded initiation and meaning, while elders stiffened and offered the false choice of either stultifying conformity or literal sacrifice.

Americans were enacting other myths as well. Recall Hephaestus, venting his rage against Hera and imprisoning her in a golden chair. Hadn't he been confining women on the "pedestal" of patriarchy? Remember how only Dionysus could loosen him up, teaching the lame god to dance, after which he released Hera and married Aphrodite. The madness of Dionysus brought the cure. Pentheus, by contrast, retreated into a masculinity so brittle that Dionysus could effortlessly crack it and release the repressed feminine energies that eventually overwhelmed him.

This is Elvis' deepest mythic significance. A unique combination of talent, ambition and overdue cultural changes *waiting to be sparked* created an icon. He became both a gatekeeper and a role model who loosened the boundaries of the American ego. Perhaps it would be better to speak of "the" Elvis (like "the" Christ), since his personal life is far less important than the archetypal role he embodied.[35]

But archetypes demand to appear in their fullness, and all the more so when we (inheritors of the Judeo-Christian-Islamic tradition) refuse to look at their darker sides, except as the Other. I have argued that without Christ's advent as a pure god of love, there would have been little need to imagine Satan. Similarly, because millions projected only the image of the savior upon Elvis, he was forced to live out both sides of the old story. Within the Christian framework of American myth, many saw his death as a sacrifice *for* the world — but merely as entertainment — rather than as enacting renewal *of* the world. As with the Catholic saints, his devotees give ritual attention to his *death date,* not to his birthday.

Disillusionment with politics led in a different mythic direction by the 1980s. Elvis, writes Pinkola-Estes, became the focus of the *cultus* of the dying god, "a drama in which a dried out culture requires the blood sacrifice of the king in order to…rebuild itself."[36] In the symbolic world, he joined the eternal scapegoats Osiris, Dionysus and Jesus. Another book cover *(E: Reflections On The Elvis Faith)* shows a man wearing a tattoo with an image of Elvis and the words *He Died For Our Sins*. In this context, his suffering, his drug-addict death and his failure to find happiness despite wealth and fame made him (and later, Michael Jackson) even *more* attractive to his fans.

Many of his fellow "looseners" (Dean, Monroe, Hendrix, Morrison, Joplin, etc.) died before Elvis; yet the mold had been cast in *his* image in 1955. Since then, other entertainers who could not hold the archetypal fullness of Dionysus or Aphrodite have followed him to the underworld. Ginzburg, Timothy Leary and Ken Kesey played the loosener role with somewhat more balance. Still others (Jim Jones, Charles Manson and David Koresh) enacted the darkest of Dionysus's masked roles, leading crazed maenads on murderous rampages. Nevertheless, Elvis has achieved immortality; in 2007 his estate earned $40 million. He remains as popular in death as in life because he served in a very real sense as America's initiator. Ventura concludes, "It is not too much to say that, for a short time, Elvis was our 'Teacher' in the most profound, Eastern sense of that word."[37]

Humorous "Elvis churches" thinly mask the inarticulate but broad conviction that some god descended and resided briefly among us. Doss argues that Americans "mix and match" their beliefs and practices, and that his veneration is a "strong historical form of American religiosity."[38] Consider the vast array of relics at and the pilgrimages to his sacred shrine. After the White House, Graceland is *the most popular house tour in the country,* drawing over 750,000 visitors per year. In 1997, on the twentieth anniversary of his death, 60,000 fans came there, and over 10,000 participated in an all-night vigil at his grave. Consider the many Elvis "sightings," as if he never died or has already returned. Finally, consider the thousands of impersonators who, as in the *Imitatio Christi,* devote their lives to him every night in nightclubs (his ritual containers) in almost every country.

Recall that Dionysus descended to Hades and raised Semele to Heaven.

Similarly, while the spirit of feminism was veiled in America's collective unconscious, young Elvis descended to America's underworld, Memphis's black ghetto. The blues had power (and danger) because it tapped into the soul's depth, where extremes of joy and grief meet each other. Having become a conduit for that dark and terrible beauty, he emerged into the light (the national spotlight of show business) precisely at America's initiatory moment. And in some profound yet inarticulate way, he brought guests with him. He brought both the Goddess and the beginning of the long memory. His eroticism, writes Doss, encouraged girls "to cross the line from voyeur to participant...from gazing at a body they desired to *being* that body."[39] *Abandoning control* — screaming and fainting, and eventually *choosing* to be sexual on their own terms, to desire their own orgasms — was the beginning of their revolution. One woman writes that Elvis "made it OK for women of my generation to be sexual beings."[40]

It became apparent that millions of girls had deep longings and deep pockets. Quickly, the music industry responded with "girl groups." By the early sixties, this music was the one area in popular culture that gave voice to their contradictory experiences of oppression and possibility. It encouraged girls to become active agents in their own love lives. By allying themselves romantically and morally with rebel heroes, they could proclaim their independence from society's expectations about their inevitable domestication. And even when the lyrics spoke of heartbreak and victimization, the beat and euphoria of the music contradicted them.

And the music was made by *groups* of girls. It was, writes Susan Douglas, "a pop culture harbinger in which girl groups, however innocent and commercial, anticipate women's groups, and girl talk anticipates a future kind of women's talk."[41] If young women could define their own sexual sensibility through popular music, couldn't they define themselves in other areas of life? Another woman claims, "Rock provided...women with a channel for saying 'want'...that was a useful step for liberation."[42] Eventually, their desires crystallized as the quest for the authentic in all areas. Decades later, Douglas argues that "...singing certain songs with a group of friends at the top of your lungs sometimes helps you say things, later, at the top of your heart."[43]

Hepheastus released Hera from the golden chair. One might argue that in the 1970s men released women from the pedestal of ideal womanhood. In fact, women destroyed that golden prison themselves. Clearly, feminist demands for autonomy, equality, safety and choice were long overdue. But American women were also the first to elucidate the new (or remember the old) thinking that may inspire fundamental change at the mythic level. The women's spirituality, pagan and even the men's movements were all outgrowths of secular feminism. Cynthia Eller writes that feminism began by asking why little girls had to wear pink and big girls had to wear high heels, but it "...segued naturally into one that asked why God was a man and women's religious experiences went unnoticed."[44]

Did Elvis lead us to the re-awakening that may re-animate and re-sacralize the world? Perhaps that is a bit grandiose. But Dionysus demands that we ask just how much reasonable, dispassionate discourse has achieved. "You have tried prudent planning for long enough," says Rumi. "This is *not* the age of information," writes poet David Whyte,

> *This is the age of loaves and fishes,*
> *People are hungry,*
> *And one good word is bread*
> *For a thousand.*

Problems cannot be solved at the same level of awareness that created them.
ALBERT EINSTEIN

———

What is now proved was once imagined.
WILLIAM BLAKE

———

Anything dead coming back to life hurts.
TONI MORRISON

———

Breakdown is breakthrough.
MARSHAL MCLUHAN

———

The situation is so dire that we can't afford the luxury of realism.
CAROLINE CASEY

———

The visionary is the only true realist.
FEDERICO FELLINI

———

Be joyful even though you've considered all the facts.
WENDELL BERRY

12

INTO THE MYSTERY

HERE IS OUR SITUATION. Martin Luther King said, "...the arc of the moral universe is long, but it bends toward justice." May it be so. Bertolt Brecht, however, began a poem with, "He who laughs has not yet heard the terrible tidings." Who was more accurate? Brecht knew that it is critical to break through the walls of denial, to comprehend how dreadful our plight actually is, *to feel* how much we have lost. Yet pessimism can create its own reality. Expecting the worst, we are very likely to find it; then hope quickly turns into despair. Or we can descend into a polarizing anger that replicates conventional demonization of the Other. Brecht knew this, too. In the same poem, he wrote:

> *Even the hatred of squalor*
> *Makes the brow grow stern.*
> *Even anger against injustice*
> *Makes the voice grow harsh.*[1]

Optimistic denial or pessimistic realism — the two poles of the dilemma cry out for a third position. We need a creative imagination that will allow us to both acknowledge the truth and also to picture what we want to regain. Perhaps, as Roethke wrote, it is *only* in a dark time that the eye begins to see with a new kind of innocence. So, I invite you to plunge on with a characteristically American, foolish optimism tempered by an unveiled knowledge of the hideous darkness in our national soul.

What does it mean to be at the end of an age? We are living in the last phases of the Judeo-Christian-Islamic mythic universe. For a thousand years, these stories nourished the Western individual and connected him/her to the community. Over a second thousand years, they have gradually lost their hold on us, and we have been left with *isms:* nationalism, patriotism, fundamentalism and alcoholism. And the factory jobs that sustained the strongest *ism*, consumerism, are gone, never to return. Even if they still existed, the age of unbounded industrial growth, fueled by the myth of infinite resources, is also concluding. So is the "American Century." Where has any empire in history gone but down once it reached its peak? If we use criteria other than military power — dread of the future, decreased participation in the affairs of the *polis,* unprecedented gaps between rich and poor, the desperate retreat into innocence, and now, the threat of complete economic collapse — we can sense the fragility of Pentheus' seemingly permanent towers.

Great fear lies just below our default mode of cheerfulness. I don't simply mean the fear of the Other that elites have manipulated for centuries. Many live as if there will be no future. Millions of others are obsessed with Biblical apocalypse or with secular endings ranging from terrorist catastrophe to global warming. We can hardly minimize the actual dangers we confront. Yet to examine the fear, or, if we were honest, the *anticipation* that many obviously display is to approach the psychic energy that drives us: the archetypal cry for initiation. At the root, the image and energy of apocalypse is a metaphor for the death and rebirth of the ego in the process of transformation.

This is one of those rare moments in world history when dominant values are in a wild state of transition that actually mirrors the initiatory liminality experienced — or longed for — by adolescents everywhere. And yet, our demythologized world has reduced our ability to think metaphorically. When we can no longer imagine *inner* renewal, we project *literal* images onto the natural world. This bizarre mix of deep pessimism and religious longing has indeed created its own reality.

But we can find deeper meanings to "the end of days" in worldwide ritual traditions. Tribal people celebrated winter solstice by extinguishing and rekindling fires, welcoming the temporary return of the dead, acknowledging the community's sins and retelling creation stories. They re-enacted primordial chaos and liminality in order to revive a world in decline. In the turning of the larger cycles, storytellers told of deteriorating values, darkness, floods and conflagrations — even humanity's disappearance — before the birth of the new world. This much older, indigenous expectation of cyclic renewal predates the Christian end-times by millennia.

There is yet another meaning to "endings." Seen from the detached perspective of the mystic, from the inspired eye of the poet or from the cyclic movements of our lungs, *each moment* expresses both birth and death, each of which is an essential aspect of life.

This is not to deny this huge and painful transition. What do we *do* when we face the facts of great endings, which we experience emotionally as fear of death and ideologically as apocalypse? The proper response is to fully engage in the universal experience of extended mourning; indeed this will be the central focus of this last chapter. But once again recall the meaning of apocalypse. At the end of an age we have the opportunity to see truths that have been veiled behind outdated myths. When an entire civilization ignores the invitation, then, in Yeats' words, it is a "rough beast," instead of a divine child, that "slouches towards Bethlehem to be born." In mourning and letting go of what is dying, however, we can discover new (or much older) truths. Remembering the Celtic proverb — "Death is the middle of a long life" — we can see more clearly for a while and gain the strength and courage to support what is struggling to be born.

I suggest an order of priorities of concern. The most primary is immediate human suffering: war, poverty, disease and hopelessness. Without question, everyone deserves at least minimal comfort, health and stability. No child deserves to suffer because its parents can't find work.

The second level is long-term environmental degradation: overpopulation, global warming, auto-immune diseases, species extinction, polluted water and air, and lost topsoil. The good news is that theoretically we can address *all* these issues politically. Most of these problems could be greatly and quickly ameliorated if nations simply stopped fighting, taxed the rich appropriately and diverted the *two trillion dollars* annually spent on war to peaceful use. A simplistic, naïve vision, but true. *If only...*

Similarly, humanity can contain and eventually reverse the environmental crisis by giving up our car addictions, shifting to a sustainable economy and reducing the birth rate (poor people voluntarily reduce the size of their families when they feel economically secure). All of this requires great psychological change, but we can easily imagine it. If only... And millions of activists are currently working to achieve these changes.

But each level of resolution can invite either further denial (*"A little fixing — electing Democrats"*) or deeper mystery (*"What does the Earth, what do our ancestors, want?"*) There is a vast, practical literature detailing how to address our political and environmental decline. We don't need another how-to book. What we do need is a third, deeper level of assessment that acknowledges the mythic sources of our dilemma. After all, isn't the literal loss of species an expression of the more fundamental, symbolic collapse of the creative imagination? And hasn't that breakdown invited the paranoid and predatory imaginations to fill the gap?

For all our fear and despair, I don't think we've realized *how bad things are,* how much of our innate capacity for loving community we have lost. Providing everyone with a middle-class income would *not* fulfill the soul's needs, especially the cry for initiation. The myth of material progress is both a toxic mimic of proper relationship with the *mater* as well as a primary cause of our crises.

When we acknowledge this level, it becomes clear that long-term sustainability requires changes in consciousness as fundamental as those that occurred in the long transition from the indigenous world to the modern. This is both bad news and good. Such changes took millennia in the First World to be completed, but only a few generations in the Third World. Perhaps these more recent transitions can be altered in a relatively short time. The challenge is for Americans to take the initiative and create a sustainable world in this generation, before two billion Chinese and Indians become as hopelessly addicted to materialism as we have been. We cannot ask the Third World to slow down its growth if we will not reverse ours.

America's most recent "Great Awakening" began in the 1950s with the Civil Rights movement, but it remains under the radar. Elite opinion keeps terms such as "Pagan" and "Goddess" confined to the periphery, where it also dismisses radical political analysis as conspiracy theory. But the revival of indigenous spirituality grows in the darkness, away from the light of innocence.

The rule of uninitiated men underlies *all* of modernity's ills, but this story is slowly changing. The elders say that there is still time. Native Americans speak of making all decisions with the next seven generations in mind, and this kind of thinking must be our guide. In this chapter I re-imagine the story that we have told ourselves about ourselves and suggest some of the indigenous wisdom that we must re-learn to facilitate renewal. We are called to attend the funeral of patriarchy, to mourn the dying King before we can celebrate his rebirth in equal consort with his Queen.

THE POLYTHEISTIC IMAGINATION

The predatory and paranoid imaginations each take their energy from the loss of the soul's innately creative imagination. Robert Bly writes, "Religious right-wingers don't realize that their literalism is the spiritual twin to the... shallowness and hedonism that they rail against."[2] For three generations, American public education produced compliant workers and mindless consumers. For three *more* generations, children's brains have been flooded with pre-digested TV images just when they should have been learning how to create images from within. Failure to *make* imagery means having no imagination of the possible.[3] This is our post-modern condition. Ironically, TV helped facilitate change as well, beginning with its coverage of the Civil Rights movement. We now have *worldwide* environmental and peace movements, and feminism has emerged as a permanent political — and religious — force.

At another level, whether through the calm attention of Yoga, natural foods and body therapies or through the ecstatic release of popular music and the discipline of fitness programs, Americans have begun the long pilgrimage back into the body. It is no coincidence that these revolutions have occurred simultaneously with the emergence of blacks and gays out of the national underworld. Slowly, painfully and generously, people of color and unconventional sexuality have offered white America the opportunity to pull back its projections from the Other. Remembering the erotic demands of the body, we encounter the needs of the soul.

Now we are called to remember things we have never personally known, to remember what the land itself knows, that which has been concealed from us by our own mythologies. We have the opportunity to *remember who we are,* and how our ancestors remembered, through art and ritual. Their most profound myths arose in the inconceivably distant past, as the communal dreams of their cultures. Our task is unique: inviting something new, yet strangely familiar, to re-enter the soul of the world. We can do this invocation in two ways. The first is to restore memory and imagination. To Federico García Lorca, imagination was "synonymous with discovery… (it) fixes and gives clear life to fragments of the invisible reality where man is stirring."[4] We can replicate the original process of myth making and dreaming, by telling as many alternative stories, as often as possible, for as long as necessary, until they coalesce into the world's story.

The second thing is to engage in the rituals — and *do* the arts — that bypass the predatory and paranoid imaginations and stimulate the creativity that makes new myths. "Hope is reborn each time someone awakens to the genuine imagination of their own heart," says Michael Meade. By convincing the spirits of the Other World to aid rather than thwart the soul, imagination builds a bridge between fate and destiny.[5] We need to use sacred language, in the subjunctive mode: *let's pretend, perhaps, suppose, maybe, make believe, may it be so, what if* — and *play.* This "willing suspension of disbelief" is what Coleridge called "poetic faith." Then, says Lorca, the artist stops dreaming and begins to desire. Love moves from imagination, which "creates a poetic atmosphere," to *inspiration,* which invents the "poetic fact."[6] Thus the imagination, engaged by the restoration of memory, moves toward inspiration, where new life comes not from us but *through* us.

One example is dance as active imagination. Psychologist Antonella Adorisio writes of movement exercises intended to bridge the artificial gap between psyche and body. There are times when the images "seem to want to be embodied. When this occurs the experience shifts from *dancing with* a particular image to allowing oneself to *be danced* by it."[7] This is precisely the experience of a contemporary practitioner of Voudoun, or of a Greek *Bacchant.*

Now, all creative acts have political implications. Poet Dianne Di Prima writes, *"The only war that matters is the war against the imagination."* Another poet, Frances Ponge, says that genuine hope lies in "...a poetry through which the world so invades the spirit of man that he becomes almost speechless and later reinvents a language."[8] We are required to collapse so deeply into the mournful realization of how much we have lost that we become speechless. Only from that position can new forms of art and language arise that might break the spell of our amnesia. Then it is possible for us to speak and act without being throttled by belief systems riddled with unconscious forms of violence.

For at least fifteen years, the best new American poetry has been disseminated *orally.* Print—for the first time in 500 years—has lost its primacy in communication.[9] It is as if the smothering blandness of TV that birthed "couch potatoes" who no longer read also brought forth a compensating expression in the *spoken* word. Poets and storytellers counteract the flood of images being pounded into the brain by our electronic initiators. In a noisy time, the mouth begins to speak. It is no coincidence that the most vibrant language is coming not from the academy at the center of the culture, but from the periphery, from the streets, in Hip-Hop, in poetry "slams," and from the young and disenfranchised who refused to be silenced. Lalo Delgado spoke from that place:

> *stupid america,*
> *see that chicano*
> *with a big knife*
> *in his steady hand*
> *he doesn't want to knife you*

he wants to sit on a bench
and carve christ figures
but you won't let him.
stupid america, hear that chicano
shouting curses on the street
he is a poet
without paper and pencil
and since he cannot write
he will explode.
stupid america, remember that chicanito
flunking math and english
he is the picasso
of your western states
but he will die
with one thousand masterpieces
hanging only from his mind.[10]

Can we imagine a society like Bali where people practice dance, music, painting or sculpture so universally that they have no word for "art?" Similarly, the Dagara term closest to "art" is one that translates as "sacred," and people perceive little difference between artists and healers.[11]

In the tribal world, art (as ritual) serves to balance the worlds of the living and the unseen. Healing comes through memory, both in purging grief and guilt and in creatively re-framing one's story, what Hillman calls "healing fictions." Mythology tells of art's ancient connection to memory: it was Memory herself, *Mnemosyne,* who mated with Zeus and birthed the Muses. Perhaps all art is remembering something that *already exists.* Artful reconnection to memory reverses the work of Kronos, countering Time's linear progress with the cyclic imagination of Memory, who knows both past and future. Myth, which provides the basic pattern, connects to story or memoir, which provides the details. Jung said that myth offers us two gifts: a story to live by, and the opportunity to disengage or "dis-identify" from an outmoded pattern and thus re-engage in a different way with the archetypal energies from which our stories arise.

Freeing oneself from old ways of seeing requires the creative imagination. Susan Griffin argues that this is "...a collective activity...What one is willing to see is dependent on what others see...A change in public perception will change the public."[12] Eventually, the unthinkable becomes thinkable. Ultimately, both individuals and cultures heal by *re-membering* what we came here to do. Recall *The Bacchae's* ambiguous ending: do Agave and Cadmus simply reassemble Pentheus, or do they re-member him as an initiated man? Creative re-membering can result in a similar ending, but with a different meaning closer to the essence of the story. If we choose the initiatory ending, then we choose to welcome the Other back into our bodies, souls and nation. The Stranger becomes the Guest, and his darkness becomes our blessing. It is said that Memory's daughters, the Muses, collected the scattered limbs of dismembered bodies; it was they — art — who reassemble what the madness of the world rips apart.

EMERGING MYTHS OF THE 21ST CENTURY

Joseph Campbell said, "You can't predict what a myth is going to be any more than you can predict what you're going to dream tonight."[13] We can imagine, however, what the new myths *won't* be. If we survive, our stories will not fit into any of the three dominant patterns. First, they will not be stories of original sin, patriarchy, tribalism, disconnection from the Earth, or any other simplistic fundamentalism. Secondly, they will not consist of the movement of dead matter from the Big Bang through billions of arbitrary combinations of elements into a life that lacks any sense of purpose. And they will not express the third alternative, the cynical view that "it's always been like this." They will reject capitalism's origin myths of individualism, ruthless competition and social Darwinism.

Campbell did predict that the only myth worth talking about would express the metamorphoses of the Earth and all living beings. It would construct a mesocosm that connects *all* individuals to each other and to the universal macrocosm of spirit, which will be living, interdependent Nature. We can take this idea as a jumping-off point and imagine that it would characterize human beings more through their relations with others and less as separate entities. It would speak of fluid boundaries rather than the rigid walls of the ego or the nation-state. It would emphasize diversity rather than uniformity. Power would necessarily exist in this story, but it would bring people together and actualize their essential gifts, rather than create hierarchies of domination. The macrocosm would exist in dynamic tension with a decentralized sense of place.

Like the Hindu deities, the actors in the new myths will be aware of existing within a story. They will ask not for belief, but to be *entertained*. Knowing their own darkness, they will be motivated not by self-restraint, but by what they *love*. Aesthetics — knowing something because we love it — will become important once again. "Aesthetic passion restrains war," writes Hillman.[14] Heroes (of both genders) will emerge from community, find a blessing in the darkness and return with it, rather than restoring innocence to Eden and disappearing into the sunset. Our concepts of gender will change when storytellers teach that male and female exist in everyone in varying degrees. Stories will still contain conflict, but listeners will know that it reflects the inner dynamics of the psyche. Tellers will learn that the most important stories will be best told in certain places and at certain times.

For thirty years, images of the *Whole Earth* have begun to focus this story. Scientific ideas such as the Gaia Hypothesis explain that the planet's natural systems reveal long-term self-regulation, like "the behavior of a single organism, even a living creature," as biologist James Lovelock writes.[15] Another image, the *Web of Life*, implies the interconnectedness of any living ecosystem. When one strand is broken, the web starts to unravel. What affects one part of an ecosystem affects the whole in some way. Such thinking brings us back to old notions like the *anima mundi* — the soul of the world — that speaks to us through the unconscious images of dreams and art.

Remembering requires the re-emergence of cultural forms to counter our amnesia ("against Mnemosyne"), our *forgetting that we have forgotten so much*. Once these forms have arisen to create the containers — the sense that it is finally safe enough to *feel* what has been lost — then all the marginalized and split-off aspects of psyche and society may well return. Perhaps most prominent among them will be modern images of the archetypal energy that the Greeks once imagined as Dionysus. *Welcomed back* rather than merely tolerated, the old gods may be more helpful than vengeful. As chronological time recedes back into cyclic time, remembering offers visions of the future as well as the past. It offers the possibility of resolution ("finding solutions again"). We may perceive that our crises as well as our solutions have a periodic, cyclic nature. We may find that we have faced disaster ("against the stars") before and survived.

We will discover that the meanings of many of our religious symbols (such as the cross, the snake and the tree of life) have shifted radically over the centuries, from symbols of life and rebirth to symbols of death, and that they can change back again. The new stories, seemingly fresh and original, will actually be a return to origins. We may then pay more attention to the words of our remaining indigenous elders, and look backwards in order to see forward. We will see the return of the Goddess, along with her son/consort.

Many origin myths begin in images of perfection and typically fall into a few basic scenarios. One is the decline from a pure, golden race to an era of strife and ignorance (the Greek version). A second is Paradise Lost, the fall from innocence into knowledge and sin (the Hebrew myth). Christianity extends the second to apocalyptic finality. Modernity has contributed myths of progress, from lower to higher (the technological utopia), from sin to salvation (the religious solution) or to the Marxist paradise of equality.

There are other traditions, however, such as Astrology and Hindu cosmology. They speak of vast cosmic cycles and offer the possibility of a (re-) emerging story, the myth of matricentric (*not* matriarchal) origin. This story is already approaching mythic proportions not simply because millions already entertain its images of female empowerment, but because it takes us out of a linear sense of history and back into the processes of the natural world. This *story* of times when all genders lived in partnership allows us to imagine our own myth of return (and the return of myth). Subjunctive mode: "If it happened once, why can't it happen again?" Skeptics might suggest that this story simply mirrors Biblical myth (with the onset of patriarchy — women's fall from grace — substituting for the departure from Eden). But the Goddess is not a mirror image of the omnipotent, omniscient Heavenly

Father. She is the inherent spiritual capacity in every individual, our most ancient image of the soul. She exists in all beings that paradoxically emerge from and return to her. In a non-linear story, remembering leads to the possibility of re-experiencing the past, both as pleasure and as suffering, and this can lead to releasing the binds that prevent people — and peoples — from approaching the next phase of the cycle.

With both the remaining indigenous wisdom as well as the new tools of archetypal psychology available to us, we can imagine a return to a world where we can reconstruct the original power dynamic between male and female. If we imagined a full psychic life in which good and bad, dark and light exist within everyone, the Other would become oneself. Then other distinctions — race, class and nation — might wither away as well.

We intuitively understand the bumper sticker: "She's back, and she's pissed!" But will She return raging and inconsolable, or will She accept our welcome? We can imagine the answer. It is still within the power of the human community to influence the nature of Her return, and the method is ritual.

THE RETURN OF RITUAL

Americans have been participating in all kinds of rituals, generally quite unconsciously, for a long time. These include: rituals that confirm our status as gendered adults; rituals that exclude the Other from the *polis*; and rituals that reaffirm our competitive values, our consumer appetites and the means by which we appear to select our leaders. Most importantly, we participate in rituals that seal our complicity in the great secret — that we periodically need to sacrifice large numbers of our own children so that a system that satisfies fewer and fewer of us may survive. But we can no longer afford the luxury of unconsciously colluding in our own innocence. We must choose to deliberately involve ourselves in the sacred technologies that indigenous people still offer us.

Participation in the evolving forms of ritual will facilitate emergence of the new myths. The purpose of authentic ritual is to re-establish balance, clarify intention and recover the memory in our bones. The old knowledge has never completely left us, but the spirits need to know that we are interested. Engaging in "radical" ritual with the intention of aligning one's purpose with spirit is to *conjure* ("with the law"), or to invoke aid from the other world. This invites us into unpredictable, chaotic, creative space, into *communitas*. Here is where new images, insights and metaphors are born, just as adults are born in initiation. Liminality, wrote Victor Turner, is "pure potency, where anything can happen..."[16] The sequence is: ritual → liminality → imagination/creativity/insight → new mythic structures.

To some extent, this happened in the 1960s. Millions of young people were attracted to psychedelics precisely because they found conventional religion boring and irrelevant. The drug/music scene was (generally) non-violent, non-hierarchical, inclusive, mystical and playful. *Communitas* was more valuable than either personal heroics or individual dissociation from the body. But the experience dissipated, partially because the youth movement was age-specific and not a true community. Although the times themselves remained chaotic, most participants moved on ("grew up") to more stable, conventional identities, even though (or perhaps because) their initiations were incomplete. "The sixties," writes Paglia, "never completed its search for new structures of social affiliation...'do your own thing' encouraged individualism but produced fragmentation."[17]

But the forms — the group ecstasy of rock music, the environmental, gay and feminist movements, the image of the Whole Earth, and the revival of Goddess-oriented paganism — remain. In addition to the thousands of practicing Buddhists in America, there are now considerable populations of neo-pagans in all urban areas, especially New York, San Francisco and New Orleans, where large influxes of immigrants from Latin America and Asia have brought their own polytheistic forms. By one estimate, the wider population of "cultural creatives" in Europe and America has grown to a quarter of the population.[18]

We can quickly distinguish radical ritual from the civic religion's ceremonies of the status quo, which at best are highly predictable events that comfort the lonely. At worst they legitimize existing power relations, re-affirm privilege and demonize the Other.

By contrast, radical ritual has the familiar three-part, *un*predictable logic of the Hero's Journey: separation, liminality and re-incorporation.

The community creates a relatively safe container through music, rhythm and invocation. Once the spirits enter, however, *they* are in control, not humans. Their presence is indicated by spontaneous emotional expression. These rituals proceed on the assumption that problems in this world reflect imbalances in the other, and their intention is to restore that lost harmony. Somé writes that such reciprocity "cancels out the whole sense of hierarchy."[19] Successful ritual both requires *and* leads to a sense of community where diversity is respected, and exploitative or violent acts are seen for what they are: the behavior of uninitiated people who never felt welcomed into the world.

RITUALS OF WELCOME

It all begins with a sense of being welcome in the world. In parts of Africa, people count their birthdays not from the date of birth but from the first time a child enters its mother's mind. Before conception, or once she knows she's pregnant, she goes into the wilderness with friends to pray until she intuits the unique song of the child to be born. She teaches it to the father-to-be, and they sing it while conceiving the child, inviting it to come from the other world and join them. Later, she sings it to the child in her womb *and teaches it to the entire village.*

During the birth the entire village gathers to sing the song and welcome the new spirit. At such times, Somé heard women singing other statements (oddly reversing those sung to a recently dead person in Tibet) such as *"You have come to a crossroads. The light you see in front of you is the light of the village that awaits you. "*[20] The village sings the person's unique song to him or her at every major transition — entry into school, initiation, marriage, and death — with the constant intention of reminding the person of his or her unique purpose and value to the community.

There is one other occasion when they may sing it. If he commits a crime, they call him to the center of the village, surround him and sing of love and forgiveness, not punishment. They know that only one who has *forgotten his song* — his purpose — would intentionally harm others. And when someone is reminded of who he is, that he is welcome in the world, he never succumbs to violence or alcoholism. Thus, a friend is someone who knows your song and can sing it to you when you have forgotten it.

I am not concerned here with proof from ethnological data, or with arguments about child socialization. Whether or not this actually happens, it is *a story that could be true.* It has mythic quality. It touches the heartstrings: "*If only...*" And it serves as an example. Already, Americans have begun to welcome the newborn in the natural childbirth movement. For two generations, children have arrived with their mothers alert and their fathers present, determined not to be as distant as their own fathers. This may seem insignificant, but it marks the beginning of the end of the reign of *Ouranos,* the original distant father. And in another context, activists are already applying these ideas to finally welcoming recent war veterans home to community.

RITUALS OF INITIATION

Start from the cliché: It takes a village to raise a child. Add that the village *needs* to raise that child, because each new generation's task is to revitalize the community. In other words, it takes initiated youth to raise a village. Finally, add a pun: without initiation, youth will *raze* the village. Untransformed masculinity inevitably turns antisocial, the village dies and culture collapses. Initiation involves rituals of welcome, from one state of being to another. Tribal people understand that the reincorporation phase, *confirmation by the community,* is as important as the changes experienced in liminality. Transformation is incomplete, *wasted,* until it has been witnessed.

The greatest impediment to the creation of formal initiation rituals in America is the lack of real community, not the capacity for mythic thinking, which youth have in abundance. Prechtel writes, "...true initiations would be impossible until the modern world surrenders to the grief of its origins and seeks a true comprehension of the sacred."[21] We must, however, start somewhere, acknowledging our clumsiness and honorable intentions. Everywhere, small but committed groups are coming together over this issue, taking tentative steps toward making some form of initiation available, and contributing to a growing literature.[22] They take groups of adolescents into extended isolation in nature, often confronting them with a serious ordeal. The elders use poetry, storytelling and drumming to place their project within a broader context. Meade writes:

> There are two things I try to achieve in teaching myth to
> youth. First of all, I hope their imagination gets caught,
> and they have an experience of mythological thinking...
> awakening to the world of meaning, which young people are
> seeking. Secondly, I hope they connect to something symbolic
> and meaningful in themselves and get a sense that...they
> are carrying a story, and if they live that story out they will be
> connected to the culture and the cosmos.[23]

Ideally, the youths discover original images of beauty and a sense of purpose. At present, the ritual forms come from worldwide indigenous traditions, but eventually they will spring out of American soil and speak of the ancestors, literal and spiritual, of these youth. The elders make it clear that something must be *sacrificed and mourned* in order for new life to enter. Finally, the youth (perhaps carrying on their bodies symbols of their changes, like the tattoos they already favor) return home, where friends and family welcome them, acknowledging their new status.

But this story is only beginning, because *all* communities are in crisis now. This mystery lies at the core of the transition to a new age: how — and why — do we initiate the young into a culture of death? Which comes first? Initiated adults or a stable community capable of welcoming them? The effort will take many generations. But what other choices do we have?

RITUALS OF MARRIAGE

Why do we cry at weddings? Some may identify with the happy newlyweds, who evoke joyful memories or wishes for the future. At a more fundamental level, however, weddings (like births) proclaim a *new start*, a second chance, a new world, permission to turn our backs on past mistakes. In many tribal cultures, elders recited the society's creation myths of cosmos emerging out of chaos at such ceremonies, in the attempt to restore wholeness and promote fertility, in both the newlyweds and their farmlands.

It is the *hieros gamos* — the *sacred* marriage — that we cry for. We watch the enactment of life's hidden unity: sun and moon, Heaven and Earth, King and Queen, and good and evil within each person present. Maya weddings in Guatemala acknowledged that a young man had *already* been initiated into the mysteries of the feminine, writes Prechtel: "...a man had to marry his own soul, his Spirit Bride, before he could truly love a flesh-and-blood woman."[24]

In a culture so permeated by fear of the Other, we also unconsciously celebrate the union of Stranger and Guest, of America's innocent lightness and its racial shadow. On the social level we celebrate the blending of two families who might otherwise conflict with each other. West African *families*, rather than the bride and groom, recite collective vows, and only after elaborate rituals in which they humorously test each other's worthiness.[25]

And some of our tears are of grief, reminders — as in all ritual — that something must be sacrificed for new life to be born. We mourn the death of the bride's (and our own) identity as adolescent, regardless of her actual age. Mythologically speaking, she is moving from the first phase of the Triple Goddess, the Maiden, into the second, the Mother. Eventually she will die as mother to become the Crone. This initiation is reflected in traditional Greek weddings, where the symbolisms of wedding and funeral remain very close. When the groom's friends "kidnap" the bride, they are re-enacting Hades' abduction of Persephone, who must die as innocent maiden before she can become Queen of the Underworld.

Myth provides many images of sacred marriage: Zeus and Hera (union of equals); Ares and Aphrodite (war and love); Hephaestus and Aphrodite (beauty and artist); Orpheus and Eurydice (artist and muse); and Ariadne and Dionysus (originally, Goddess and consort). Twelfth-century Christian art re-created that union in the "coronation of the virgin:" young adults Jesus and Mary (clearly *not* mother and son) enthroned together.

Plato wrote of humanity's original wholeness. There were three races: males, females and hermaphrodites. Each being had two faces, four arms and four legs, until Zeus for some reason ordered that they be cut in half. This left each half with a desperate yearning for the other. Feeling sorry for them, Zeus moved their genitals around to the front, so that they might have some satisfaction. Ever since, all humans have wandered, searching for re-integration. Those who descended from the all-male ancestors search for the other half-male that will complete them, the women do the same with other half-women, and the descendents of the hermaphrodites search for the opposite-sexed beings who will return them to their original wholeness. "And now," writes Plato, "when we are…following after that primeval wholeness, we say we are in love."[26]

Twenty-first century weddings will take these diverse images into account, consciously honoring the *hieros gamos*. Instead of sparing no financial expense, participants will spend the maximum of *imagination*. Elders will speak of ecstasies, responsibilities and conflicts. Bride and groom will acknowledge the paradox of being complete in him-or-herself, while simultaneously needing the other "half." The community will pledge to help the new couple *remember their purposes*. By doing so, everyone will be reminded to continually re-animate their own relationships. And as a necessary component of the festivities, people will mourn — consciously — the death of the maiden in everyone.

The presence of initiated men and women will result in far fewer unwanted pregnancies, and those children who *are* born will be highly valued. Everyone, however, will acknowledge a communal responsibility: if the couple's erotic bond doesn't survive, both families will still remain committed to the wellbeing of the children. Such ceremonies will lay the foundation for making even divorce into sacred ritual in which participants can look past animosity toward sorrow, and suffer together. Divorce will aspire to full closure, so that new life can arise from its ashes. Weddings will take on the social and spiritual importance they have in tribal culture, because people will acknowledge that the re-creation of the *world* is taking place.

RITUALS OF CONFLICT

Consider three characteristics of modernity: first, polarization into extreme positions of right and wrong; second, the lack of true, initiated warriors and the elevation of the Hero to high status; and third, the loss of effective rituals of conflict. The paranoid imagination sees conflict as necessary to defend against, convert or eliminate the Other. To the predatory imagination, conflict is a fact of a life: kill or be killed; take what you can; and no apologies. Both accept any level of violence necessary to attain their goals, including genocide.

What if conflict had a completely different function? Tribal people once believed that it existed neither to eliminate alternative voices nor as a tool for rape and plunder, but *to bring people together.* We see vestiges of this in the Gaelic language. One cannot say, "I am angry at you," but only, "There is anger *between* us." This wisdom is present in the word *competition* (communally petitioning the gods). *Engagement* can refer either to martial or to marital affairs. *Animosity,* with its connections to *animal, animate, animation* and *anima,* derives from the Latin for "breath of life." If we follow animosity to its archetypal source, we find the one breath we all share.

Although Greek myth is full of horrific violence, it provides a surprising image in the war god, *Ares.* He is called "killer of men," a stereotyped murder machine who desires only blood. Zeus calls him, "most hateful to me..."[27] But beyond the *Iliad,* he appears in few fully elaborated myths. Instead, writes Hillman, "He presents himself in action rather than in telling...The god does not stand above or behind the scene directing what happens. He *is* what happens."[28]

Like all inhabitants of the polytheistic imagination, Ares is more complicated than he seems. An immortal, he is an image of the divine, and thus of the psyche. This tells us first that Greek culture understood that martial values are fundamentally human, not to be demonized and certainly not to be ignored. Second, some say that Ares was taught to *dance* before he was taught the arts of war. Third, he was Aphrodite's lover. This most masculine god and this most feminine goddess birthed *Harmonia,* grandmother of both Dionysus and Pentheus. Thus, in pagan thinking, the war god had a "harmonious" relationship with the feminine that balanced his destructiveness. There is sublime beauty in war, and there is conflict in love. Harmonia is the product of the Warrior in a balanced relationship with its complementary archetype, the Lover. Love and war beget harmony, as Psyche and Eros beget voluptuousness.

Soldiers entering battle invoked Ares, asking for strength and courage.

But they also called upon him to *prevent* conflict from degenerating into uncontrollable violence, as in this seventh-century B.C.E. hymn:

> *Hear me, helper of mankind, dispenser of youth's sweet courage,*
> *beam down...your gentle light on our lives... diminish that*
> *deceptive rush of my spirit, and restrain that shrill voice in my*
> *heart that provokes me to enter the chilling din of battle...let me*
> *linger in the safe laws of peace...*[29]

This poetry invites us to imagine a consciousness that loves conflict as a form of relationship, seeking restoration of harmony rather than domination. "Who would have imagined," writes Hillman, "that restraint is what Ares offers?"[30]

An initiated warrior exhausts non-violent forms of persuasion (the realms of Athena and Hermes) before resorting to the most minimal level of violence. This is standard hero ideology, of course. But here is the difference: this warrior sees violence as the *failure* of symbolic conflict. If he is forced into combat, he goes sadly. If he survives and returns, he grieves for *all* the dead, because he knows that his enemy was a part of himself.

Even so, he may require deep and protracted immersion in the feminine waters of atonement before returning to normal life. Much of the post-war ritual activity in primitive societies was intended to expiate guilt, including various kinds of ritual penance after killing. Often the returning warrior was considered sacredly polluted and had to undergo additional purification rituals. A Pima warrior withdrew from battle the moment he killed his opponent to begin his rites of purification. Any Papago man who had killed an enemy underwent a difficult, sixteen-day ordeal of purification before being readmitted to society. Mythic Irish warriors had to be purified of their battle frenzy. After a great battle *Cuchulain* was still red-hot with war fury and remained extremely dangerous to his own people. The women solved the crisis by marching out naked to greet him. When the sight momentarily stunned Cuchulain, men grabbed him and plunged him into a vat of icy water. His heat caused it and a second vat to evaporate and explode into steam. Only on the third dunking did he cool down enough; the city was saved.

The archetypal warrior stands vigilant, aware of his own dark potential and watching for external danger. In serving the Divine King of the psyche, he is charged with protecting boundaries. This doesn't imply rigid armoring. He determines which outside elements to welcome and which are dangerous.

An example from biology is the immune system. The skin and lining of the small intestine are semi-permeable membranes that *know* what to allow inside (air and nutrients) and what to keep out (microbes and toxins). When intruders cross the boundaries, certain white blood cells sound the alarm, others neutralize the invaders and still others curtail the immune response when the danger is over. Then the body creates *antibodies* to remember (memorialize) the event and protect against future ones. The system discriminates between the two aspects of *xenos*: stranger and guest. Similarly, in Irish myth the *Fianna* warriors guarded the borders of the realm and questioned all strangers, *"Would you like a poem or a sword?"*

Ares loves conflict, but he is first and foremost a protector. No monk, he retains his amorous relationship to Aphrodite. But Christianity, despite its historic dynamism and belligerence, cast him out. Like Dionysus, he finds expression only in images of the Other. So from the pagan perspective, just as Aphrodite's exile leads to pornography, the *absence* of the war god causes literal violence that might otherwise be expressed symbolically.

Why, in the most competitive society in history, do "proper" middle-class people avoid actual confrontation, restricting it to spectator sports? Perhaps we intuitively know that normal social interactions cannot contain conflict and prevent it from turning into literal violence; it simply isn't safe. Our myth of redemption through violence polarizes us into one of the two most easily assumed stances: the path of denial and/or retreat, or the path of extermination. We inevitably resort to either fight or flight.

Ritual provides a third alternative: staying in relationship without being violent. It requires, however, that participants acknowledge the reality of the Other. Traditional Dagara married couples engage in conflict rituals *every five days*. Certain that there will be no physical violence, each person simultaneously vents all accumulated emotions. If necessary, the entire village witnesses and affirms this ritual. Long experience has shown them that conflict causes damage to the entire community if it is removed from a bounded ritual container and brought out into the profane openness of daily life.

A second example is the *kecak* dance performances of Bali that convert aggression into art. The entire male population of a village (including boys) may enact battle scenes from the Hindu epics, with neither physical harm nor easy resolution of light over dark. Another is the *bertsolariak*, the Basque poetry competitions, in which each participant improvises in accordance with a given meter, taking his cue from his rival's poem.

Urban African-American culture abounds in the ritualized conversion of aggression into creativity. Examples include break dancing, poetry slams and "the dozens," verbal jousting in which antagonists poetically insult each other's mothers. Mythologist Lewis Hyde writes that the *loser* is "the player who breaks the form and starts a physical fight...who chooses a single side of the contradiction" between attachment and non-attachment to mother. The winner artfully holds the tension of the opposites.[31]

Aphrodite's sensual fury is hardly different from that of Aries. Their union is one of sames rather than of opposites, and thus *passionate aesthetic engagement* can restrain violence. Long-term discipline of an art — any art — tames hasty emotional expression and the urge for vengeance but *not* its passion. Violence is beyond reason; what counters it must be equally unreasonable. "Imagine a civilization," muses Hillman, "whose first line of defense is each citizen's aesthetic investment in some cultural form."[32]

Mythopoetic men's conferences have evolved effective conflict rituals that allow men to engage with each other on subjects as frightening as race and sex without either leaving or getting violent. In this context, safety means feeling secure enough within the ritual container to take risks. If men remain in this heat of confrontation long enough, they may get past anger to the underlying grief, to *suffer together* and to cleanse their souls.

The same principle holds for both individuals and large groups. Tragic Drama could be the model for future conflict rituals, which might enact our greatest moral conflicts before the citizens and challenge them to hold the tension of the opposites without succumbing to the temptation of quick resolution. Such rituals could lead to a long-term reframing of the meaning of the hero. We might learn to value this archetype's protective and healing capacity, including the power of non-violence. Questioning the myth of violent redemption would lead to considering that initiated masculinity has a great variety of expressions. Women might acknowledge that patriarchy is caused not by men but by the lack of *initiated* men. The roles of the military and the police could shift from controlling the Other to — artfully — protecting the borders of the realm. The entire military could become the *Coast Guard,* real Homeland Security. Pentheus would invite Dionysus into the city for a competition of dance and poetry.

RITUALS OF GRIEF

We must ask seriously, *what would an America that invited Dionysus back actually look like?* The easy answer is a replay of the 1960s: sex, drugs & rock 'n roll, long hair, rebellion, spontaneity and chaos. However, celebration and release without the compensating expression of grief reduces to mere spectacle. A more insightful response is to realize that the culture would have to relax its boundaries — of gender, race, self and other — *without knowing what will come in,* because opening to one extreme means opening to others as well. It is to invite the madness back, in hopes that it might save us from our own culturally induced, hyper-rational, violence-at-a-distance, disembodied madness. America will have to dwell in the territory of grief. For the return of Dionysus means the cracking open of innocence, and through the gaps (as William Stafford wrote) will come "... the horrible errors of childhood..."

Why do we weep at scenes of firemen on 9/11 searching for the dead, especially *their own dead,* or of relatives of the victims requesting anything, even bone fragments, from a relative's body? What of soldiers in Viet Nam who risked their lives (often losing them) attempting to recover dead bodies? Why, thirty-five years later, does the search for bodies continue? Why is the Viet Nam Veteran's Memorial America's most popular shrine?

What is the value in "paying our last respects" (respect = "to look again")? Why indeed must we *pay?* Why hope that a deceased soul be "at rest?" How do we define that state? Is there any consensus on the meaning of "closure?" Why do we universally agree on the importance of proper burial — and why do we so rarely achieve it?

Recall that "underworld" can mean transformation, the second of three stages of the Hero's journey. When the psyche hears of "death," it dreams of a temporary return to liminality prior to rebirth into some new state. But completion of the transformation, as in all initiations, requires intervention by those who can facilitate proper burial of the old form and welcome of the new.

Proper burial is a fundamental theme in Greek myth. *The Iliad* includes many scenes of warriors fighting and dying to reclaim corpses. Patroklos' ghost comes to Achilles in a dream, asking him to complete his cremation and burial, because Hades has forced him to wander until the rites are completed. Zeus, unable to change his mortal son Sarpedon's fate, whisks the corpse back home to receive the proper rites.

Toni Morrison's phrase "disremembered past" describes that which is neither remembered nor forgotten but haunts the living like a ghost. The path to closure, for the soul and for the soul of the culture, must go directly through the recovery of memory and mourning rather than through forgetting. Only then can the "corpses" of our lives receive proper burial. Authentic grief rituals can align one's conscious wish for closure with the deeper intentions of the unconscious. This is depicted mythically when King Priam, escorted by Hermes — the Guide of Souls — begs Achilles for Hector's body. Priam must confront both the corpse and the cause of its death. The remarkable scene concludes with the two implacable enemies grieving together. Acceptance of the truth at this level leads to real closure and unites people like nothing else. Surprisingly, the epic ends not with the account of the Trojan Horse, but with Hector's funeral.

The Odyssey has many scenes of mourning. Before Odysseus visits the underworld, Circe instructs him to feed its ghosts sacrificial blood (a metaphor, I think, for grieving) that will enable them to speak. Afterwards, he cannot proceed homeward without first returning to her island and burying one of his dead crewmen. Later, after slaying the suitors who had ruined his palace, he refuses to allow his maids to celebrate, telling them, "It is not piety to glory... over slain men."

Proper burial is one of tragic drama's most common themes. Of thirty-three surviving, complete works, at least nine deal directly with it. These plays reflect the old belief that the dead need action *by the living* to complete their transition to the other world. The living need this as well, because souls who wander between the worlds inevitably cause suffering on Earth. In many traditions, the unburied dead haunt those who should have performed the appropriate rites. In ritual terms, such souls are stuck in liminality, not having accomplished the third phase of the transition, incorporation into the other world. Like vampires, they are "undead," "betwixt and between."

We see this pattern in indigenous funeral customs: death is a *process* that requires deep commitment on the part of the survivors. In parts of Africa, the nearest equivalent to "hell" is to be cut off from the ancestors. In many places, the period of liminality only begins with the funeral. Funeral rites in Japan and Tibet culminate on the forty-ninth day after death. Jewish tradition has extensively timed rites of mourning. The Irish wake is intended to "keep the dead awake" as they journey to the other side. Wild reversals of normal social relations confuse the ghosts and prevent them from returning to this world as revenants. Such cultures understand the critical importance for health and stability — in both worlds — of complete *closure.*

The idea of ritual closure implies the goal and intention of unambiguous completion. It requires communal actions to ensure that a major transition, once begun, concludes with no residue of unfinished business, that is, *unexpressed emotion.* Closure is important in all transitions, but after a death, these are rites of passage for the survivors as well as for the deceased. Completion of their ritual responsibilities, during which time they too have been in liminality, moves the living into a new phase of life. When survivors aren't allowed sufficient time to grieve, however, the wounds close too soon, remain infected and never heal.

Across the world, we find many examples of the curious yet psychologically sophisticated practice of "secondary treatment," in which the condition of the corpse becomes a model for the condition of the soul. The community inspects the decomposing remains for signs that the soul has moved on. In rural Greece, ancient traditions remain intact behind a thin Christian veneer. Following a death, all participate in Greek Orthodox memorial services, especially if the deceased has committed crimes and cannot enter Paradise without having his sins forgiven. Long after the funeral, women sing daily laments at the grave that are strikingly similar to wedding songs, a reminder of the mythic "marriage with death." Three to five years later, relatives exhume and inspect the bones. If the bones aren't completely free of flesh, everyone assumes that the soul continues to wander, causing potential harm to the village. So the bones are re-buried for another two years and then re-exhumed. Clean, white bones indicate that the soul has finally entered Paradise. The people then place them in the ossuary, or bone-house, making the empty grave available for another — temporary — resident. The period of liminality for both the soul and its relatives ends, and everyone can move on, free of the weights of both grief and responsibility.

Forms of secondary burial occur in Borneo, Madagascar, Spain, South China, Taiwan and Bali, where the bones of the dead are dug up and cremated in elaborate ceremonies. The Balinese believe the recently deceased are dangerous, even demonic. But *after* the rituals of closure, they venerate them as ancestral gods. Medieval Europeans believed that the living could affect the death process. In Catholicism, souls that are not sufficiently sinless to enter heaven must first be purified in Purgatory. The prayers of the living decrease the time the dead must spend there. Both the requiem mass and the Jewish Kaddish were originally intended to aid the dead in these transitions.

Only when they complete their journey to the other world are they able to aid the living. In exchange, claim the Maya, the ancestors ask to be fed through two actions: full emotional life, especially mourning, and regular expression in art, ritual and language of *beauty*. The Maya feed their ancestors through *aesthetic* responses to the world. They believe, writes Prechtel,

> ... that the dead rowed themselves to the other world in "a
> canoe made of our tears, with oars made of delicious old
> songs." Our grief energized the soul of the deceased so that
> it could arrive intact onto the Beach of Stars... our dead were
> well received by the "last happy ancestor" and then initiated
> further into the next layer of life.[33]

But if truly felt grief was absent, or if the deceased had not been fully initiated, the soul could not complete the journey and was forced to turn back. It would then take up residence in the body of a young person. The ghost would "eat the life of that person" and others through violence, accidents and alcoholism until the community completed the appropriate rites. Only when humans do not feed the spirit world by embodying their authentic selves — when they do not live in alignment with their purpose — do the spirits come and take literal death as a poor substitute.

Traditional Vietnamese believe that the souls of the dead linger near their families for four generations. Without proper burial rites, however, they cannot continue to the spirit world. Because 250,000 people are missing from the "American War," many believe that Viet Nam is full of "wandering souls" *(co hon)*. Once people finally accept — often after extensive searches — that a relative's body will never be found, they build an empty, "windy tomb" *(ma gio)* in the family plot. On their national holiday, the "Day of Wandering Souls" *(Tet Trung Nguyen),* they tend these tombs, praying that all souls might return home.

In this imagination, a fully grieved soul is "born" into the other world. This is why women (who know birthing as men cannot) traditionally play major roles in funeral rites. In parts of Africa, the full transition takes even longer: one becomes an ancestor only when all surviving relatives have also died, and there is no one left to remember him or her.

Freud and Becker explained that these customs resolve the opposition of life and death by denying death's finality through belief in the afterlife. But by reducing ritual to psychology, they did more than patronize tribal people; they missed profound insights. Extended emotional catharsis and completion of ritual obligation give closure, to a degree almost inconceivable to the modern mind. Even without secondary treatment, death is so common in any Third World village that regular, authentic rituals ensure that the emotional load of suppressed grief rarely builds up to toxic levels. In our culture of denial and tearless, controlled funerals, however, we completely overlook this indigenous insight. Properly conducted funerals give everyone who attends (in West Africa, the entire village as well as any visitors) the opportunity, indeed the responsibility, to regularly attend to unfinished business with their own dead, or with anyone else.

Without carrying this *daily, lifelong* burden, it is possible to live in the present. This explains the curious but common observation by Western travelers that Third World peasants, despite their grinding poverty, are *happy*. Somé's people alternate between deep mourning and celebration of life in all its abundance: "People who cannot weep together are people who cannot laugh together...The other side of real grief is real joy."[34] Regular descent into the emotional extremes of such rituals can create the space for new community identity without recourse to projecting the unacknowledged parts of that identity upon on a scapegoat.

Inability to achieve closure haunts our modern American souls. Looking back at the charred ruins of history's most violent century, we see that certain factors become clear. One is the resolution of disputes through violence — *Apollonian, high-tech violence at a distance* — that insulates us from the consequences of our actions. The second is the Anglo-Saxon cult of masculinity that prevents men from shedding tears. As so many war veterans have admitted, if they were to let only a little out, the floodgates would burst and they would be overwhelmed. The third is the massive, *karmic* (there is no other word for it) weight of our ungrieved histories of genocide and slavery.

Finally, the myth of innocence justifies America's crimes with God-inspired goodness and purpose: we had to destroy the village (country, world) in order to save it. Separated from both Europe and Asia by great oceans and insulated from the human consequences of our imperial policies by a compliant media, we rarely hear the cries or see the bodies. Even if we do, our moral intelligence is polarized so fully into distinctions of absolute good and evil that we assume the victims deserved their fate.

How else would the shameful images from Abu Ghraib and Guantanamo (where one suspect was "waterboarded" *183 times*) fade so quickly from public memory? Is it any wonder that (white) Americans cry so sparingly at funerals?

Denial of death meets the cult of celebrity. We *do* mourn for dead movie stars (in 2007, CNN covered Anna Nicole Smith's funeral for ninety minutes uninterrupted by any commercials). Public attendance at their funerals and shrines allows thousands to vent their feelings. Having projected so much upon entertainers, who have certainly replaced the pagan gods, many grieve as if they personally knew them, or if part of themselves had died. As with Elvis and the Catholic saints, we honor their memory on their death dates, not their birth dates. Dying young, they remain frozen in time, immortal, never having to grow old like those who innocently deify them.

In recent decades, however, the American heart has begun to crack open. Our best example, the Viet Nam Veterans' Memorial, serves three primary purposes. First, it offers a place for people who have no common political or cultural language to share public sorrow. Second, as a receptacle for thousands of photographs, poems and memorabilia, it invites us to conduct emotions from one world to the other, to enter an active, ritual *conversation* with the dead. Third, its actual design reveals deeper purpose. Sinking gradually, like blood on soil, it subtly reminds us of our collective responsibility to the dead and of the knowledge that can be found in the dark earth. It "… coaxes everyone into the same ritual of descent," writes Ventura, "a ritual that the psyche can't help but recognize."[35] The polished black marble surface reflects our faces behind the inscribed names, as if we were among them, looking back into our own eyes. The veil between the worlds is very thin there.

The Wall and those who tend to veterans remind us that we all — simply by being Americans — suffer from post-traumatic stress. PTSD occurs within a wider syndrome: our endemic numbing, denial of death and addiction to innocence.

Actual war veterans are partially transformed survivors who have experienced a terrible, three-part initiation without completing it. With this insight in mind, psychologist Ed Tick has instituted a three-part healing process: purification, storytelling and restitution.[36] Without remembering and grieving, writes psychiatrist Jonathan Shay, veterans continually re-enact their traumas. But telling one's story within a trusted community can "rebuild the ruins of character." For such healing to occur, however, listeners must be willing "to experience some of the terror, grief and rage that the victim did. This is one meaning, after all, of... *compassion.*"[37]

The wound leads to the gift; the need to make meaningful narrative out of trauma leads to the search for authentic community. Veterans and the greater public for whom, in more ways than one, they have suffered, should meet together, "face to face in daylight, and listen, and watch, and weep, just as citizen-soldiers of ancient Athens did...We need a modern equivalent of Athenian tragedy."[38]

A second phenomenon, The AIDS Memorial Quilt, is the world's largest community art project, now encompassing 44,000 panels. Over 14 million people have visited it at thousands of displays worldwide, including five times on the National Mall. The process of panel making has built a community of concern and greatly facilitated public mourning.

A third factor in the cracking open of the American heart is the revival on American soil of indigenous mourning rites. Two aspects of Latin culture are profoundly influencing white attitudes toward death. One is the tradition of erecting roadside shrines *(descansos)* at the sights of car accidents. These spontaneous, temporary creations reduce the enormity of the event to a "more manageable human scale," writes anthropologist Sylvia Grider. Typically lasting through the liminal period between death and burial, they are metaphoric thresholds that represent the "end of numbness and the beginning of the ability to take action."[39]

The custom has spread to the inner city, where young people are intuiting — or remembering — old rituals, including African and Celtic traditions of pouring alcohol libations at gravesites. Now they are poured where deaths actually occur. An Oakland policeman observes, "...every time there's a murder, you see one."[40] In addition to stationary shrines, *moveable* shrines have appeared. By wearing "R.I.P." t-shirts emblazoned with pictures of murdered young people, family and friends protest against the anonymity of urban violence.[41]

This revival reflects both innate moral intelligence — the voice of the indigenous soul — as well as a sense of permissiveness. People of color are offering whites the insight that it isn't shameful to mourn in public. Latino and black peace activists have taken it to the next level, with processions that cross the boundaries of gang territories and stop to grieve at death sites, announcing the commonality of tragedy on both sides.

Another Latino influence is the *Day of the Dead, or Dia de los Muertos*. Its toxic mimic, Halloween, is a festival of innocent consumption, with dozens of theme parks and annual spending of $5 billion. Along with horror movies (and their common theme of the return of the dead), writes David Skal, Halloween gives us a space "where death reigns triumphant but no one ever has to grieve."[42] But behind Halloween lie the Catholic holidays of All-Saint's Day and All-Soul's Day, and behind *them* lies the far older Celtic New Year, *Samhain,* the point at which the light half of the year changes into the dark half on November 1st. These events reflect very common indigenous beliefs that at certain times, the veil between the worlds briefly becomes thin, and the spirits of the dead return, to be fed by the living. The Greeks held their All Souls' Days in February, the Germanic tribes at Yule time, the Japanese and Aztecs in August. Like the Celts, the Egyptians celebrated theirs on November 1st. In Rome, the Festival of Isis ran from October 28th to November 1st, followed by the lamentation for the dying god Osiris. The Medieval Church, acknowledging that it could never stamp out these pagan traditions, established November 1st as All Saints' Day in the eighth century and November 2nd as All Soul's Day in the tenth.

Spanish conquerors brought the tradition to Mexico, where it fused with local customs. Mexican-Americans in turn brought their home altars and "dinners for the dead" (better to feed them with food they love than to feed them with more death) to San Francisco, which has had a large annual procession for over twenty years, as well as many pagan grief rituals.

African spirituality sees nature as the dwelling place of ancestral spirits who have registered every harmful thing done to the Earth, as, writes Somé, "a vast field of grief."[43] So healing and balancing of the dark and light aspects of the world takes place in natural settings. Many indigenous grief rituals (and contemporary re-creations) involve vocalization and symbolic expulsion of emotions and memories that are considered toxic if held inside too long. But such poisons, like the end products of digestion, are considered to be nutritious to the Earth-goddess, who gladly absorbs and recycles them.

When *communal* grief is impossible, the Internet provides venues to create spontaneous shrines. Dozens of "cybershrines" containing photographs and opportunities to light "virtual candles" appeared after the deaths of Princess Diana, Pope John Paul II and Michael Jackson and after 9/11 and the Asian tsunami. In addition, many sites exist that allow living people to compose "last messages to loved ones" that will be delivered after they die, while another catalogues the deaths of MySpace members. Some critics argue that its interactive nature subtly panders to our denial of death by implying that the dead are still with us. This leads to the question of the Iraq and Afghanistan wars and virtual grieving. President Bush refused to appear at soldiers' funerals, and TV networks refused to show their coffins until he was out of office. In response, private citizens have created many websites to memorialize the dead. They include portraits and encourage visitors to add their own memorial statements; thus they serve as a kind of electronic "wall."

However, these flag-bedecked websites typically emphasize the theme of sacrifice for freedom. This is unfortunate, and not simply for political reasons. Justifying death in terms of *any* ideology is a subtle form of denial that may prevent real closure. They subvert the primacy of grief, diluting it with reassurances of American innocence. In the process, many of them reveal our underlying myths by referring to the original willing sacrifices of Abraham/Isaac and God/Christ. But they gather their energy from the shadow version of those stories, which is more fundamental to patriarchy: the killing of the children. The divine Christ re-enacts the annual death of the world, like Dionysus and Osiris before him. But the *human* Jesus, like Isaac before him, asks why his father has forsaken him and whether there is any meaning in these murders. The military cybershrines agree that our war victims have died to perpetuate the state.

But the "real" thing continues to bubble up from the margins where the indigenous soul still thrives. The African imagination of ritual closure has long taken root in New Orleans' Jazz funeral parades, which have two sections. The "first line" consists of marshals, musicians, the family of the deceased and pallbearers, followed by a "second line" of local people. The band plays slow hymns and dirges as the procession moves from church to cemetery in the first stage of the familiar three-part ritual format.

The second stage is interment at the cemetery, where both the dead and the living briefly share liminal space. In the third stage, the procession home, the second line takes over and the tone changes from melancholy to celebration. The band (now in the rear, separating the living and the dead) shifts into high-spirited tunes, and the mourners' slow cadence becomes wild dancing, or "second lining." The return to the neighborhood becomes a celebration of life which re-integrates mourners into their community.

If we were to combine two concepts, Greek tragedy and New Orleans funerals, the implications for America's healing would be enormous. Imagine mass public rituals in which warriors and civilians, rich and poor, women and men, white and black, gay and straight, and mad and "normal" confront the impossible paradoxes and crimes of our history and *suffer together*. Imagine a president standing in this container, begging forgiveness from a descendent of a slave and a Native American. Imagine everyone grieving for all those who died as soldiers, victims and activists, for the extinct species and even for the forests that once covered the continent. Imagine the relief at having finally shed tears together as a mosaic of uncommon peoples, and the gratitude bordering on ecstasy with which an entire nation would dance the "second line" on its way back home.

Ultimately, transforming our American denial of death will require individuals who feel a calling for this work, who could reframe the meaning of the scapegoat. The new scapegoat would commit to a life of continual awareness and mourning of life's irresolvable, tragic side. But rather than leaving the world like a monk or dying for it like a Christ, he would live all the more fully for it like a Bodhisattva by facilitating the emergence of large-scale, public grief rituals. By bearing his own shadow, he'd help to liberate the collective and heed the call to become "a man of sorrows... acquainted with grief" (Isaiah 53:3).

Rituals of Reconciliation

Joshua Chamberlain was a general in the Union Army who recorded the awesome spectacle of Robert E. Lee's surrender on April 9, 1865:

> Before us in proud humiliation stood... men whom neither toils and sufferings, nor the fact of death, nor disaster, nor hopelessness could bend from their resolve...thin, worn, and famished, but erect, and with eyes looking level into ours, waking memories that bound us together as no other bond... On our part not a sound of trumpet more, nor roll of drum; not a cheer...but an awed stillness rather, and breath-holding, as if it were the passing of the dead! ...How could we help falling on our knees, all of us together, and praying God to pity and forgive us all![44]

He knew as few could know that the two armies, ground down by four years of carnage, had *suffered together.* Despite the hatred — or perhaps because of it — they had erased some of that sense of otherness that drives men to violence. The surrender, of course, didn't heal the nation's wounds, but Chamberlain's vision invites us into the imagination of reconciliation.

Mythology provides other openings. Refusing to pass on the family curse to future children, Orestes chooses a terrible initiation and ends the curse. Dionysus helps Hephaestus achieve reconciliation with Hera by loosening his masculine ego. Odysseus returns home to Penelope only after his own heroic ego has been polished clean by several Goddess figures. The reconciliation of male and female invites the return of the King and the Queen and the rejuvenation of the realm. Parsifal's healing begins when the Christian hero meets the Other, a Muslim knight, who is revealed as his half-brother.

In Celtic tales, corpses are immersed in boiling cauldrons and emerge alive and whole. Cauldrons of abundance feed multitudes and never empty. The Holy Grail is such a container, an inexhaustible source of nourishment. In another tale, a hairy man emerges from a lake of the Other World, carrying a cauldron that brings healing to the realm. These stories indicate similar routes toward reconciliation and renewal: loosening of the ego; the balancing influence of the feminine; the cathartic impact of water and the tears of grief. Baptism originated as such a ritual of immersion. Pre-Christian African purification rituals included immersion in rivers and healing by the spirits of the water, after which participants were reborn.

True reconciliation ("to make friendly again") requires two parties: the veteran and his community; or one person or group with the Other. It acknowledges that everyone involved has suffered. It assumes a sense of interconnectedness and sees generosity and compassion, not competition, as the highest values (although *rituals* of competition may bring people together).

In southern Africa, this quality is known as *ubuntu*. Archbishop Desmond Tutu writes, "When we want to give high praise to someone, we say... 'so-and-so has *ubuntu*.'... 'My humanity is caught up, is inextricably bound up, in yours.'... 'I am human because I belong, I participate, I share.'"[45] Knowing they are part of a greater whole, people who have *ubuntu* are not threatened by others' good luck; indeed, they feel diminished when others suffer. Their values survive despite the dehumanizing effects of oppression. In short, they behave like initiated individuals. It was in this spirit of *ubuntu* that South Africa began its Truth and Reconciliation Commission, with the intention of achieving *restorative justice.*

Tribal communities prefer healing to punishment. The Acholi people of Uganda resolve conflicts through compensation and the *Mataput* ritual ("drinking of the bitter root from a common cup.") There are reconciliation traditions among the Maori of New Zealand, in Hawaii *(ho'oponopono)* and throughout Native America. The Winnebago traditionally elected two chiefs. The war chief reacted to threats by preparing for violence. But the *peace chief* responded in precisely the opposite fashion, making determined gestures of peace. He offered protection to the accused and sanctuary even to the guilty. But this arrangement was not meant to create a balance of equal forces. The peace chief had a very slight superiority, because he represented the higher function of forgiveness over vengeance.

In American retributive or punitive justice, since the victim has suffered, so must the criminal. Offenders, however, are accountable to the *state*, not to the victim. In restorative justice, crime is rooted in human error (forgetting one's purpose), rather than in sin or innate evil, and offenders are accountable to those they have harmed. The first priority of the rebalancing process is healing the victim physically, emotionally and spiritually. But when everyone is interconnected, a *relationship* — or several — must be repaired. So the perpetrator (and sometimes his family) apologizes, asks for forgiveness and demonstrates his intention to make restitution with the victim, the community and the spirits. To ritually cleanse his soul, he must *face* his victim, his ancestors and himself. Since his healing is as important as that of the victim, he is expected to remain an integral part of the community.

There are over 300 victim/offender mediation programs in the U.S. and more than 900 in Europe. But the world's greatest example (since copied in several other countries, most notably Rwanda) is South Africa. Tutu freely admits that it was a highly flawed process, and many of the worst military offenders wouldn't cooperate. However, given the extent of destruction, inequality and hatred in that tortured land, he believes that the nation achieved an astounding degree of healing.

The formula was simple: full disclosure of the truth in exchange for amnesty and freedom for all perpetrators, along with symbolic acts of restitution (the nation couldn't afford real compensation) for the thousands of victims. The commission's intention was to prevent denial, forgetting and the festering bitterness that inevitably leads to further reprisals. It met for three years in highly publicized assemblies that led to both emotional catharses for victims and public shaming for offenders. Its motto was "The truth hurts, but silence kills." Eventually receiving over twenty thousand statements, it dealt with the grossest violations in public hearings. Many people asked for little compensation; often having their stories heard was all they wanted. They were satisfied simply knowing that their suffering would not be forgotten.

With *ubuntu* as the guiding philosophy, the commission assumed that white perpetrators were also victims. By dehumanizing blacks they had cut the web of interconnectedness with the Other and dehumanized themselves. Although many chose denial or feigned ignorance, others applied for amnesty, told *their* stories, expressed remorse and publicly asked forgiveness of those whom they had offended, or of their survivors.

The process revealed that people could choose to not dwell in bitterness, but to forgive and reconcile. *Often, victims were eager to meet perpetrators so they could forgive them.* The fact that some couldn't forgive was itself a valuable lesson; their refusal indicated that the power of forgiveness lies in the fact that it cannot be taken for granted. But when one abandoned desire for revenge and risked forgiving, the act liberated both persons.

Ultimately, forgiveness became critical to a new beginning. This brings us back to proper burial. Over two hundred persons had "disappeared," and the commission took extraordinary steps to find their bodies. As one survivor (like many 9/11 families) asked, "Can't you find...just a bone, that I could give his remains a decent burial?"[46] Amazingly, since the police had frequently buried identity papers with their victims, they exhumed, identified and re-interred fifty bodies. Survivors found some peace. *Disclosure led to closure.*

Creativity springs not from the center, but from the margins. During this same period, long efforts by Native Americans and Hawaiians culminated in a law that encouraged the repatriation of ancestral bones from museum shelves for final burial.[47]

South-Central Los Angeles has suffered from generations of gang wars, with over fifteen thousand fatalities. One day in 1989, several members of one gang, heartsick at the meaningless carnage, donned the neutral color of black and marched unarmed into their rival's territory, singing peace songs. Their risk resulted in a truce that lasted several years and spread to forty cities. The gangs created rituals of reconciliation (such as tying their red and blue bandannas together) that signified the intention to cooperate for the greater goal of social justice.

Luis Rodriguez favors authentic *rehabilitation*. Rather than giving youthful offenders more jail time, he suggests *enough* time: "Enough... ritualized and sacred time," well monitored and instructive, as in monasteries.[48] The guiding principle vitalizes the cliché, *No child left behind*; every child has value, and his survival depends on the survival of all. He suggests reviving the idea of *sanctuary*. One who is about to enter the initiation of prison could be held temporarily in a healing circle that would briefly suspend the laws of the land and engage the laws of spirit. Incarceration could become a sacred space where offenders could work through the traumas of childhood and prepare to bring their gifts back to the community. In this spirit, Latino groups have brought both Native American sweat lodges and Buddhist meditation into the prisons.

In Buddhism, forgiveness is larger than rage, because it includes it. Millions acknowledge this when they enter twelve-step groups. After making "fearless moral inventories" of their lives, they make "direct amends" to those they have harmed. The alcoholic cannot heal without healing his relationships. Until he makes amends, he cannot forgive himself. Many Viet Nam veterans have perceived that closure requires concrete acts of atonement. Some mentor their own homeless; others organize tours of Viet Nam, where they reconcile directly with old foes and build schools. The ritual act of atonement may involve leaving requests for forgiveness at the Wall, such as this one:

> Dear Sir:
> For twenty-two years I have carried your picture in my wallet.
> I was only 18 years old that day that we faced one another...
> Why you didn't take my life I'll never know. You stared at
> me for so long...yet you did not fire. Forgive me for taking
> your life...many times over the years I have stared at your
> picture and your daughter, I suspect. Each time my heart and
> guts would burn with the pain of guilt. I have two daughters
> myself now...I perceive you as a brave soldier defending his
> homeland. Above all else, I can now respect the importance
> that life held for you...It is time for me to continue the life
> process and release my pain and guilt. Forgive me, sir.[49]

Others *offer* forgiveness, but only after the lengthy struggle to acknowledge that vengeance can't bring loved ones back, and that forgiveness offered too soon can be another form of denial. Some families of murder victims have met and befriended the killers. Others have created lobbying groups to abolish the death penalty. Perhaps the ultimate form of reconciliation is with the ancestors and the spirits of the land. For many — such as descendants of slaves and slave owners — "soul work" includes imaginatively healing relationships that go back generations, in which most of those who profit from slavery's legacy have neither admitted their responsibility nor asked for forgiveness.

But the literal always points to the symbolic. Traditional Africans see the violence and trauma of modernity as a consequence of a broken relationship between the worlds. Spirits who haven't been fed with grief and beauty feed on the bodies of the living. How else do we explain our fascination with the "undead" in horror movies? In this imagination, many ancestors who had helped perpetuate colonialism long ago desire forgiveness. They want their living descendants to take responsibility (not blame) for their crimes and atone for them. In America, this is complicated by the fact that most ancestors are buried very far away, and that countless people live far from their birthplaces. But, it is said, those spirits who witnessed our birth continue to watch, and attending to them can unleash vast forces of healing. Somé writes, "They know…what needs to be done. It's up to us to tell them we're open to receiving that knowledge so we can take the proper action, because we're still caught in a human body…So, one way to heal the ancestors is to grieve them."[50]

Sometimes the situation requires intervention by a third party. On March 22, 1624, a large war party of Brazilian Aricoure Indians stopped at a Yao village, on their way to attack their Carib enemies. The Yao, who were common friends of both tribes, secured a peace. They scripted a ceremony in which the Caribs obliged the Aricoures to wait on the seashore with their weapons. As the Caribs fitted their arrows to their bows, ready to let fly, the Aricoures took water and poured it on their heads. This done, the Caribs, throwing down their arms, rushed into the canoes of the others and embraced them. Then the Yaos entertained the two groups, who had never known peace between them before, for eight days. The stranger had become the guest.

ANOTHER LOOK AT AMERICAN DIONYSUS

As part the American origin story, European settlers demonized the natives
and identified themselves as "not the Other." This decision ultimately led to
genocide, memories of which we have repressed into the underworld of the
disremembered. Its legacy has played out in four centuries of scapegoating
and the sacrifice of generations of young men in the false initiation of war.

Too complex to be held in a single image, Dionysus took up temporary
residence among the Indians, and then in a long series of immigrants,
from Irish and Chinese to Latino and Muslim. When these images proved
insufficient, the white psyche split Dionysus further, into the black internal
Other and the red communist external Other, which served the purposes of
empire for generations before evolving into the Terrorist. Always Dionysus
was willing to offer America images of its own dark soul, so it could see
what it so longed to reconcile with. Yet America responded by lashing out,
trying to force those images back outside the walls of the city, back onto
the shoulders of the Other. And still, we might imagine (to use Christian
terminology) that the god loved us so much that he always returned to show
us the path to suffering — and eventually to laughing — together.

When fear of communism was at its height, Dionysus rose again as
the sexually ambivalent Rock Star: Elvis; Little Richard; Mick Jagger;
Jim Morrison; James Brown; Prince and many others. This uninitiated
priesthood presided clumsily and unsuccessfully over the rituals in which
youth re-inhabited their bodies and women reclaimed their sovereignty. But
the darker side of the archetype also appeared as disturbed but charismatic
figures — Charles Manson, Jim Jones and David Koresh — who led crazed
maenads on lethal rampages.

In order to imagine a future, we must look back for the images that
will sustain us. Dionysus existed on *this* soil long before whites arrived. One
of the most widely distributed prehistoric images, found throughout the
Southwest as far as Peru, is the flute-player *Kokopelli*. In countless examples
ranging from petroglyphs and kachina dolls to t-shirts and coffee mugs, he
either suffers a painful hunchback or carries a backpack bulging with seeds.
He may be dancing, lying on his back or making love to a woman.

He heralds the coming of spring, bringing warmth, seeds and new life along with his music. The sun comes out, the snow melts, grass emerges, birds begin to sing, animals gather around him and the people sing and dance all night. The Hopis say he spends most of his time, like Johnny Appleseed, sowing seeds and teaching agriculture, or — like Dionysus at the *Anthesteria* — seducing the women. In the morning, he is gone, but crops are plentiful and women are pregnant. Like Orpheus, he charms all nature with his music, making the earth ready to receive his seeds. Some say his pack is filled not with seeds but with *songs*, which he trades for new ones as he travels. Like Dionysus, he has a foot in each world. His flute carries prayers to the unseen world, and his pack of seeds is the response; ritual, as music, connects the microcosm and the macrocosm. Anyone who listens, anyone who does not ignore the strange messages from the Other, finds luck and prosperity.

Kokopelli is the original American Dionysus for several reasons. His hunchback indicates that he suffers; like Dionysus, he is close to humans. Daniel Deardorff writes, "...the gifts, dreams, seeds, songs, messages are stored and camouflaged within the deformity...the mark of exclusion, the wound, becomes the fount of creative generosity, healing and innovation."[51] Both wounded gods fertilize the world, leaving their seeds to grow among women, who appreciate them more than men do. Each brings something else: *joy*, but only when welcomed as guest rather than as stranger. Finally, like Dionysus, the patron of drama, Kokopelli arrives from outside the *polis* on the sound of music, in the human imagination.

So it is no surprise that, like images of *Pele* in Hawaii, the Horned God in northern Europe and Raven in the Pacific Northwest, images of Kokopelli are so common in commercial and kitsch art. The pagan gods are returning whether we invoke them or not. *Consciously* invoked, they offer themselves as images of our own potential, as stimulants to the imagination in a time when consumerism threatens to crush it. As we plunge further into the mystery, we have another image of American Dionysus to consider, now that Elvis has given us permission to dance.

The new American Dionysus will be a non-violent citizen/warrior who defends women, children and nature. He will value Apollo's insights while remaining rooted in his body. He will love women (or men) without requiring them to carry his own feminine nature. He will be uncontainable, a breaker of boundaries, because imagination comes from the margins. He will hold many truths and paradoxes together without dividing those within the gates from those without. He will bring fertility through his love for music, dance and poetry. He will be present for initiating the youth. Since he will know death very well, he won't need to literalize it. Equal parts man of sorrow and man of joy, he will proudly carry his own wounds, knowing that they made him what he is. And when he fails at these impossible tasks, he will forgive himself, because he will know his own song.

That song has not been lost. Like the Hindu prince Gautama (who lived at about the same time as the Classical Greeks), we have experienced Eden within a fortified palace and assumed that it would last forever. The walls of privilege, ignorance and innocence insulated him from the knowledge of suffering, old age, complicity and death. These walls also kept him, however, from becoming a man. When Gautama finally wandered outside and was shocked to discover the truth, he found himself catapulted into a journey of the soul that eventually resulted in his new name: The Buddha, or "the one who has awoken."

REFRAMING

Our task is to do more than simply deconstruct outmoded belief systems. They hold us not merely because of generations of indoctrination, but because of their mythic content. They grab us, as all myths do, because they refer to profound truths at the core of things. If those truths have been corrupted to serve a culture of death, they still remain truths, and they remain accessible through the creative imagination. We cannot simply drop myths by virtue of realizing that they are myths; we must go further *into* them. The methods for doing so are ritual, art and seeing through — *de-literalizing* — the predatory and paranoid imaginations back to their source in the creative imagination. It means telling the same stories, but reframing them until we discover their essence. In Native American terms, we will need to search for our original medicine.

Americans have some advantages in our worship of change and our assumption that newer is better. Our fascination with the new masks our anxiety about the present, our grief at how diminished our lives have become and our fear of being erased in a demythologized future. But it also awakens the archetypal drive to slough off old skin and be reborn into a deeper (*not* higher) identity. We can cook down the cliché, "We want a better future for our children" to: "We want to be remembered as ancestors by those who come after us." We can use this fascination with change to escape the myth of progress. As ceremonies of the status quo evolve into authentic ritual, change can become *transformation.*

New myths are attempting to manifest. The other world is offering help, but indigenous wisdom insists upon our full participation. We will develop that capacity as we build our willingness to imagine. This is why the renewal of the oral tradition is so important; it enables us to go beyond the literal and think metaphorically.

We can start by reframing capitalism's basic — and bizarre — superstition that if each person pursues his own narrow interests, then the common good is advanced. Instead, we must imagine a society in which individuals enhance both their own wellbeing and the greater good only when they *give* fully of themselves. This implies an indigenous concept of abundance in which the role of money is to facilitate the transition of *value* from its source in the Other World to its recipients in this world, and back. Wealth is a warehouse in transit, temporary storage. As in a potlatch, one accumulates it in order to give it away.

Our precious individualism is quite literally killing us. According to research cited by Robert Putnam in *Bowling Alone,* if you do not belong to any group at present, joining a club or a society of any kind cuts in half the risk that you will die in the next year. When researchers dropped samples of a cold virus directly into subjects' nostrils, those with rich social networks were four times less likely to get sick.

Appreciation of *interconnectedness* makes us both held by and accountable to the larger communities of nature and spirit that surround us. "Dominion" can become "stewardship" or "husbandry," which can free us from our mad obsession with growth. Why not replace the GDP with the "Gross National Happiness" index, a concept that the nation of Bhutan is actually attempting to put into practice?

We could re-imagine progress within a broad conception of cyclic time. We would move backward, not toward racist and misogynist "traditional values," but toward a gylanic balance of masculine and feminine. Faith in progress might evolve into the deep hope that rises only when we have lost our innocence and known true despair. We might reframe mobility, that safety valve of escape from responsibility, into a love of *place*. As Gary Snyder has suggested, we might act as if we were going to live in the same place for the rest of our lives.

We can replace "development" with "liberation" (from *Liber*, Dionysus) in both its Buddhist and political senses. Then the obsession with growth will be revealed as a *spell* that monotheistic thinking has cast over the indigenous soul. Liberation, as spell-breaking and veil-lifting, allows resolution to arise out of older wisdom. The Third World does not need to replicate the "developed" world's mistakes. In America, the shadow of growth (both economic and spiritual) is depression, and here is a clue: in previous depressions, we have learned to *stop buying things we did not need*. And we can do it again, this time by choice. This is the simple, concrete solution to consumerism, pollution and exploitation. With other options commonly available — authentic initiation and education, true community, fulfilling work, participatory culture, *loving our own bodies* — we would happily drop our desperate quest for "stuff." We would reframe consumption as an indicator of happiness. We would realize that the opposite of consumption is neither thrift nor poverty but generosity.

Below the pressure to compete and accumulate lies an older assumption, *scarcity*. As Regina Schwartz has shown, the mythic image of the vindictive, Old Testament God implies parental hostility, limited quantities of love and sibling rivalry. "When there is only room for one at the top, sons cannot grow up to be their fathers, man cannot become God."[52] The creative imagination can reframe scarcity and the struggle for survival into original blessing and infinite fecundity. The meaning of competition could revert back to its origins: "petitioning the gods together."

Scarcity assumptions (if there is little to go around, then only the "elect" will have it) led to the creation of Puritanism. We must reframe the compulsion to work unceasingly into the drive to remember and deliver our unique gifts. Finding a sense of belonging from what we give rather than from what we accumulate will free us from blaming capitalism's victims for their own suffering. With less energy invested in success, we'd find less shame in failure. "Unemployment" and "idleness" would transform into the opportunity to have sacred time, to do more important things than make money. "Self-improvement" could become a non-dogmatic, *communal* spiritual quest. Addictions stemming from our misguided search for meaning and a true home in the world might simply melt away. Then "self-interest" would shift eventually to the needs of the soul and "prosperity" would not be measured in numbers.

We would reframe Puritanical contempt for the body into an inclusive, protective, expressive, humorous eroticism. Heterosexuals would appreciate gays as gatekeepers and whites would recover the natural "rhythm" that they have required blacks to carry for them. We could shamelessly entertain images of lust and loss of control without needing to project them upon others. Antonin Scalia could go ahead and enjoy his images of 60,000 naked people. The paranoid imagination would lose its suffocating grip on our emotions, as we reframe anxiety itself into the natural curiosity and hospitality of people who know who they are — people who have nothing to fear from encountering "Other" values.

If we perceived abundance in spiritual terms, we could also reframe the predatory imagination. Entertaining the possibility that we are held in concentric spheres of care by non-human powers, we would lose interest in exploiting others. Feeling welcome in the world, we would laugh at primitive ideas like "dog eat dog" and "every man for himself." Then we could detach ourselves from the constant flip-flop between fear and denial that we have been subjected to for so long.

As compassion and stewardship replace competition and domination, we will re-appraise another basic myth: the hero. Heroes certainly won't disappear; the earth needs *real* heroes like never before, but we will prefer "peace heroes" to "war heroes." As we support ritual containers for initiation and welcome youths back into the community, we will feel the hero's journey within ourselves. We will no longer be fascinated by men who risk their lives crushing the Other to restore the peace of denial. We will applaud those who commit to the hard work of relationship with the feminine, men who *don't* ride off into the sunset.[53]

Rebirth will hinge upon replacing Rambo with Odysseus, who leaves home a hero but returns transformed by his initiations at the feet (and in the beds) of goddesses. Having encountered many small deaths, he returns as the saved rather than the savior. As they say in Africa, when the big death finds him, it will find him alive.

Reframing the concept of the hero will enable us to take back what we have projected onto entertainers. We will still admire those who excel in athletics, public service and the arts as models for everyone to pursue their own destinies. But as the images of the pagan divinities return, as we understand them as aspects of our own souls, the cult of celebrity will wither away.

We could drop the patronizing moral superiority that justifies interventions and invasions (both international and interpersonal), transforming them into the desire to encourage (give heart to) the best in people, to see others find their own voices. As patriotism shrivels back into love of the earth — "matriotism" — we would re-establish our primary allegiance to *specific* places. Whites and blacks might finally feel welcome on this land. Racism and witch-hunting would transform into appreciation of diversity. And our primary statement of identity could shift from the negative, "We are not them" to the neutral, "We are us," and eventually into the positive Mayan greeting, *"You are the other me."*

Both crusades and charities would transform into invitations to share privilege equally, and Americans would re-appraise government. Equality would once again be as important as freedom, and *justice* would mediate between them. Instead of meaning personal fulfillment unimpeded by government, freedom would imply public commitment made possible *by* government. We would replace the white-bread *melting pot* with a new metaphor reflecting the diversity of soul and world: a polychromatic *mosaic* of shining ethnic facets, each reflecting all the others. In such a world, white would have no privilege over black, nor male over female. "Liberty" might lose some of its exclusively masculine tone.

We would no longer need to demonize anyone, nor would we require anyone to suffer for us, because we would carry the marks of our own initiations. Authentic indigenous communities (even if they rarely exist any more) were composed primarily of initiated individuals who were well aware of their own dark potentials. Such communities were able to consciously ritualize their conflict without literalizing it or searching for sacrificial victims, and they can exist again.

The world would still be a "vale of soul-making," as Keats wrote, but we would no longer believe that is *fallen*. Indeed, we wouldn't believe anything, in the religious sense of something being unalterably true, or in the scientific sense of something being demonstrably provable. Imagine millions of Americans no longer needing to interpret Biblical poetry as literal fact. "Belief" would return to its German roots where it is connected to love and cherish, something closer to "entertaining possibilities." Christ himself could join those suffering gods who preceded him. Without the model of and belief in a god who sacrifices himself to redeem others, we would begin to redeem ourselves. Imagine shifting our distrust of the Other to the environmental crisis, a stance in which everyone would be "we," united in the defense of the Earth. We would reframe "Red, White and Black" by adding "Green," and national borders would dissolve. A Graffiti on the Mexican side of the U.S. border wall says, "Turn this wall on its side and it becomes a bridge!"

The word "sacrifice" (to make sacred) would revert to its original meaning: *voluntary* approach to the underworld for the renewal of self and community. It would acknowledge the intimate connection between death and rebirth that constitutes initiation. What is "made sacred" would once again be the person who endures the terrifying ego death that precedes new identity. Sacrifice would become renunciation of our claim to control, permanence and superiority. Jung writes, "What I sacrifice is my own selfish claim, and by doing this I give up myself."[54] The sacrifice of Isaac — our most fundamental mythic narrative — would once again symbolize the offering up of *Abraham's own innocence*. Now we could sacrifice whatever interferes with communal and personal harmony. The ancestors don't require human or even animal bodies, but *grief and beauty: lives lived in fully emotional, creative authenticity. As* Miguel de Unamuno wrote, "The chiefest sanctity of a temple is that is a place to which men go to weep in common."[55] Thus, sacrifice points us toward Dionysus, who invites us to live *in this moment*, dying into the next, constantly aware that something new waits to be born.

Happy to sacrifice what we don't need, we would reassess consumerism. We would shift from *consuming* culture (both accumulating stuff and passively ingesting electronic media) to *making* culture. We would no longer settle for sitting passively while the burdens of our unfulfilled lives get resolved electronically. We would value ourselves too much for that.

Making culture would allow us to drop the need for *divertissement* (being diverted), *performance* (to provide completely) and *amusement* (related to the *Muses*). We'd create real *entertainment* (holding together). Entertaining possibilities, we would ritually renew ourselves through shared suffering and shared ecstasy. In return, the art we would make (the new mesocosm) would hold *us* all together.

Shared ecstasy: a few tastes of our real potential and the potential of real community would make us realize how little we have been willing to settle for. We would reframe the "pursuit of happiness" — a deeply constrained vision typical of our narrow emotional range, which is itself the expression of the refusal to grieve — into the pursuit of joy and ecstasy.

Those who can grieve together can laugh together. Re-acquainting ourselves with the old rituals of grief, closure and initiation, we would reframe our characteristic denial of death. We would perceive death as the final initiatory transition endured by people who have lived the lives they were intended to live. Death — as a necessary, periodic restructuring of identity — would become our friend, sitting (as Carlos Castaneda wrote) on our right shoulder, reminding us to pay attention to the fleeting beauty of the world. And we could change the old question of the death-fathers, *"What are you willing to die for?"* into the initiatory challenge, *"What are you willing to fully live for?"*

RE-IMAGINING AMERICA'S PURPOSE: THE WOUNDED HEALER

Myths, even deceitful political myths, stick with us for good reason. They *grab* us because their potency rests on a core of truth. America provides a unique challenge in the study of myth because, except for Native stories, our myths do not arise from this ground, nor do they show us the archetypal soul. Still, they have no less a hold on us because they are only ten or fifteen generations old. Understanding their contradictions will not make them go away. But if we assume *telos* — purpose — we must imagine that even the myths of American innocence and violent redemption can lead us to the universal archetypes. If we can hold the tension of these opposites (the myths and the realities) perhaps we can begin to re-articulate meaning in a world that is descending alternately into chaos and fascism. *If we cannot disengage from our myths, then we need to look deeper into them.*

To speculate on the deeper meaning of our civil religion is to risk falling into a morass of cliché. For 400 years, apologists, from preachers and novelists to Radio Free Europe and Rush Limbaugh, have presented an America divinely ordained to defend freedom (military coups), nurture democracy (repress self-determination), spread prosperity (steal resources) and inspire opportunity (enforce racial oppression). But this mythic language tugs at our emotions. Even when we know better, we want America to be what it claims to be — *we want to believe* — or disappointed, we become cynical and disengaged. Indeed, cynicism is a self-fulfilling prophecy; as fewer vote, the rest are more easily manipulated.

But *what if* America were born so that freedom could spread everywhere? What if the uniquely good fortune of white Americans has been the container for a story that has not yet been told?

Many people in the helping professions such as doctors, ministers and psychotherapists were "caretakers" as children in their own families. One study found that twenty-three percent of both students and faculty in a nursing school were children of alcoholics. If, as adults, they project their suffering onto their patients and replicate their family roles, therapeutic relationships can become polarized, subtle agreements of collusion. The patient is "sick," the therapist is "well," and each holds the other's shadow. But who can heal the traumas of another's soul without first knowing his or her own wounds? In another case of the search for the Other, many people who become helpers are unconsciously searching for their own healing.

Personal psychology expresses social myth, which is enacted in history. Even liberals still commonly support government policies that promise to "cure" underdevelopment and tyranny — elsewhere. Few perceive how America projects her unrecognized wounds of genocide and intolerance upon other nations, the "patients" who require "intervention," so that the "healer" may repress her national traumas, where they fester in the dark stream of forgetfulness.

But in this story that we tell ourselves about ourselves we no longer have the luxury of easy judgment. We can and must choose to emphasize wholeness rather than dysfunction; we have to ask what may be struggling to be born. Those who consciously suffer their wounds, enter the fires of initiation, acknowledge their betrayals and atone for their transgressions may become wounded healers in a deeper sense. Such people (and nations) no longer need to locate illness in the Other. They can truly *see* the Other. In this imagination, America's "mission" isn't merely a smug excuse for adolescent posturing and imperial conquest, but a search for its own soul. An America that lifts the veils and cleans out its wounds could become the healer who could actually help others.

Let us proceed, aware of the emotional tugs, wondering if they grab us for reasons we haven't discovered yet. Within the word "believe" is the German *liebe* — "to love." Ultimately, the basic questions of Archetypal Psychology (What does the symptom point to? What does it *want* from us?) are the same as the African villager's: *Has this soul (or nation) forgotten its song?* If we were speaking of an alcoholic we would ask not simply what family traumas generated his addiction, but what makes him seek the *spirits* only in a bottle. Our national addictions — the Opportunist's consumer paradise and the anxieties of the Paranoid Imagination — never could nourish us for long. What universal themes live beneath the clichés?

Our American cosmogony begins, as all do, with the original "deities" (the Pilgrims and founding fathers) who created a world out of "nothing." If we take a radical perspective, we acknowledge that from the start, their new world functioned to concentrate and perpetuate wealth. American history becomes a series of conquests, painful expansions of freedom and counter-measures to protect privilege, culminating in today's bleak realities. *The rich vs. the poor, or the predatory and paranoid imaginations vs. the return of the repressed.*

Alternatively, we can take a philosophical approach. Jacob Needleman insists that the founding fathers were *spiritual* men, adherents of a timeless wisdom, who created a system to "allow men and women to seek their own higher principles within themselves."[56] The nation was formed of unique ideals and potentials, not from ethnicity; and this explains its universal appeal, even if those ideals have been perverted into their opposites by men far less mature than those founding fathers. *The American Dream vs. the nightmare of dreams deferred.*

Or we can muse poetically about what is approaching, if we could only recognize its song. *Time/Kronos vs. Memory/Mnemosyne.* From this perspective, we could read our history as a baffling, painful, contraction- and contradiction-filled birth passage in which the literal has always hinted at the symbolic.

If America remembered its song as *"This Land Is Your Land"* rather than *"bombs bursting in air,"* we would understand "freedom" as willing submission to the soul's purpose. We would understand liberty as the social conditions that allow that inner, spiritual listening to happen. Diversity and multiculturalism would reflect the vast spaces of the polytheistic soul, and conflict would be about holding the tension of the opposites to create a third thing, something entirely new. We would remember that the purpose of "self-improvement" is service to the communal good, and that individualism points us toward our unique *individuality.*

Remembering its true song, America would remember its body, Mother Earth, and this would mean the end of both Puritanism and its predatory shadow, those twin beasts that have ravaged the bodies of actual women. Connecting in this sacred manner to the land would naturally lead to rituals of atonement for the way we have treated her, and to a revival of the festivals that celebrate the decline of the old and birth of the new. New Year's Day could become a national day of atonement (a *Yom Kippur*) to acknowledge our transgressions and our willingness to start anew. On Independence Day (now *Inter*dependence Day), we would reaffirm that such a start requires the support of the larger community of spirits and ancestors.

Remembering America's song would allow us to overcome our shameful contempt for our own children and to see them for who they are, rather than as projection screens for adult fantasies of innocence. Our national narratives with their deadly subtexts of child sacrifice would become stories of initiation, renewal and reunion with the Other. Then, unlike Pentheus, America would have no need to taunt the immense force of repressed otherness by bellowing, *"Bring it on!"*

And now the Other, in all its colors and genders, will have emerged from the darkness and responded, asking us to join the rest of humanity as a "nation of suffering." If we saw ourselves in this light — not the direct sunshine of innocence, but the dim glow of an old campfire — we would understand our addiction to violence as a projection of that initiatory death (that we secretly desire) onto the world, and onto our children. We would withdraw those projections, putting them back where they belong, into the ritual containers of the community and the self. There we would meet the Stranger who has been inviting white America to dance; and we would know him as our self. This would open our imagination further; we would define ourselves in terms of what we are and not by what we aren't.

It would be *obvious* that democracy is meaningless when restricted to a small elite who force scapegoats to suffer. *Shared* suffering is the great gift otherness offers us. We would realize that if we suffered together in a ritual container, democracy would invite a higher (in Christian terms, the Holy Spirit) or deeper (in pagan terms, *the spirit of the land*) intelligence that could resolve conflict. We would realize that an appropriate metaphor has already arisen out of this land: the spirit of Jazz improvisation. Here is Wynton Marsalis:

> ... to play Jazz, you've got to listen (to each other). The music forces you at all times to address what other people are thinking, and for you to interact with them with empathy ... it gives us a glimpse into what America is going to be when it becomes itself.[57]

Comfortable with nuance, complexity and the vast gradations between black and white, we would realize that we had already dropped our fascination with evil. As in the Aramaic, we would view destructive behavior as *unripe*, as a cry for help, and we would know compassion.

Finally, as an initiated nation, we could cook *innocence* down. Our own light would no longer blind us. We would drop our grandiosity and arrogance. We would no longer wonder, *"Why do they hate us so?"* Innocence would signify the most basic of all mythic ideas: the new start. Then America could offer the song that the world has always seen in us: not that of a consumer paradise, a destructive adolescent or a wrathful father, but of the ancient story about what makes us human, the rare and lucky *opportunity* to accomplish what we came here to do.

Richard West, Director of the National Museum of the American Indian, proclaimed at its dedication ceremony, *"Welcome to Native America!...* The Great Mystery...walks beside your work and touches all the good you attempt."[58] Dionysus invites us to drop our outdated identities, emerge from the initiatory fires, announce our purpose and dance our way home, welcomed by people who have never forgotten our song. It's a hell of a story. As Rumi says, *"Out beyond ideas of wrongdoing and rightdoing, there is a field. I'll meet you there."*

NOTES

Notes to Part One Introduction

1. Lehmann-Haupt, Christopher, "Stanley Kunitz, Poet Laureate, Dies at 100," *New York Times,* 5/16/06
2. *Loose Ends,* p. 3
3. *Harvard University Gazette Online,* 6/5/08 (www.news.harvard.edu/gazette/2008/06.12/99-rowling.html)
4. *New York Times Magazine,* 2/8/2004

Notes to Chapter One

1. *Gods In Our Midst,* p. 23
2. *The Healing Wisdom Of Africa,* p. 3
3. *Men and the Water of Life,* p. 392
4. *Projection and Recollection in Jungian Psychology,* p. 106
5. *Beyond Belief: The Secret Gospel of Thomas*
6. Warren, Rick, *The Purpose-Driven Life* (Zondervan Publishing, 2002). This book has sold twenty-five million copies. *Time* has called it the best-selling hardback in U.S. history.
7. *The Myth Of Analysis,* p. 264
8. *The Lessons Of History,* p. 46
9. *Paris Review, Spring 1994*
10. *The World Behind The World,* p. 65
11. *The New Polytheism,* p. 129
12. *The Spell of the Sensuous,* p. 265
13. *Memories, Dreams, Reflections,* p. 3
14. *The Big Bang, the Buddha and the Baby Boom,* p. 39
15. *Transgressing The Modern,* p. 134
16. *Mythography — The Study of Myths and Rituals*
17. *The Myth Of Analysis,* p. 122
18. *The King & The Corpse,* p. 2-5

Notes to Chapter Two

1. *Masks Of Dionysus*, p. 33
2. Kerenyi, *Dionysus*, p. 115
3. *The Two Hands of God*, p. 48
4. *Sex, Art and American Culture*, p. 105
5. *A Terrible Love Of War*, p. 175
6. 92% of small-scale societies surveyed in the early 1960s encouraged ecstatic group ritual. Goodman, Felicitas, *Speaking In Tongues: A Cross-Cultural Study of Glossolalia* (Univ. of Chicago Press, 1972, p. 36)
7. Otto, *Dionysus*, pp.108, 95, 121
8. Freud, *New Introductory Lectures On Psychoanalysis*, p. 73
9. Otto, *Dionysus*, p. 136-48
10. Ibid
11. *The Light Inside The Dark: Zen, Soul and the Spiritual Life*, p. 19
12. *The Greeks And The Irrational*, p. 76-7

Notes to Chapter Three

1. Ortega Y Gasset, Jose, *Meditaciones del Quijote* (Madrid, 1957), p. 191
2. *Nothing To Do With Dionuysos?* Ch. 2, "The Ephebe's Song," p. 20-62
3. *A Commentary on the Complete Greek Tragedies of Aeschylus*, p. 12
4. *Kartharsis* also means that which clarifies understanding, or "the pleasure of seeing clearly after being in the dark" (Golden, Leon, "Aristotle on Tragic and Comic Mimesis," *American Classical Studies*, 29, 1992).
5. Aristotle, *Poetics*, 1449b, 27-28; *Greek Tragedy and the Emotions*, p. 24
6. *Aeschylus — The Oresteia*, p. 17-18
7. *Inconsistencies In Greek And Roman Religion I*, p. 96

Notes to Chapter Four

1. Jung, *Collected Works*, 9i, 50
2. Kerenyi, *Dionysus*, p. 70, 193
3. *The Other Within*, p. 127
4. *The Curse of Cain*, p. 5-6
5. *Running On Emptiness*, p. 33-35
6. *Gunfighter Nation*, p. 617
7. *The Denial of Death*, p. 160
8. *Dancing In The Streets*, p. 9
9. www.commondreams.org/headlines03/1016-01.htm
10. *The Masks of God: Vol. III, Occidental Mythology*, p. 21
11. *The Second Sex*, p. 163

12. Deuteronomy 22:21
13. Ezek. 16:7-34, 37-41
14. Exodus 23:19, 34:26, Deuteronomy 14:21
15. Kerenyi, *Dionysus,* p. 250-261
16. *Vamps and Tramps,* p. 79
17. *The Myth of Analysis,* p. 250
18. *Civilization and its Discontents,* pp. 74, 92, 142-3
19. *The Pursuit of Loneliness,* Chapter 4
20. *Homo Necans,* p. 229

Notes to Chapter Five

1. *Men and the Water of Life,* p. 233-4
2. *Long Life, Honey in the Heart,* p. 87
3. Ibid
4. *The Healing Wisdom of Africa,* p. 110
5. *Rites and Symbols of Initiation,* p. xii-xiii
6. Ibid, p. 88-91
7. *The Hero With A Thousand Faces,* p. 12
8. *Those Women,* p. 37
9. *Long Life, Honey in the Heart,* p. 116
10. www.malidoma.com
11. *The Healing Wisdom of Africa,* p. 276
12. *Long Life, Honey in the Heart,* p. 240
13. *Sex, Art and American Culture,* p. 62
14. *The Hero With A Thousand Faces,* p. 138
15. Bernstein, Jerome, "The Decline of Masculine Rites of Passage in Our Culture," *Betwixt & Between, p.* 143
16. *Men And The Water Of Life,* p. 129-30
17. *The Power of Myth,* p. 31
18. Chernus, Ira, "American Jews and the Myth of Israel," (http://spot.colorado.edu/~chernus/)
19. *Blood Rites,* p. 128
20. *The Birth of Pleasure,* p. 72, 224
21. Chomsky, in lecture
22. *A Rumor of War,* p. 10
23. *King, Warrior, Magician, Lover,* p. 5
24. Whitlock, Janis, "Self-injurious Behaviors in a College Population," *Pediatrics,* Vol. 117, June, 2006. Schildkrout, Enid, "Body Art As Visual Language," *Anthro Notes,* Winter, 2001. Beaudoin, Tom, *Virtual Faith: The Irreverent Spiritual Quest of Generation X* (Jossey-Bass, 2000).
25. *Rites and Symbols of Initiation,* p. xx-xxii
26. *Hearts And Hands,* p. 129

27.   Gatto, "Against School: How Public Education Cripples Our Kids, and Why," *Harper's*, 9/03, p. 33-8

28.   Ibid

29.   National Adult Literacy Survey and National Assessment of Educational Progress, in *Everything You Know Is Wrong*, p. 278

30.   *American Myth American Reality*, p. 149-50

31.   *In Midlife — A Jungian Perspective*, p. 47

32.   Tacey, "Spirituality and the Prevention of Suicide"

33.   Ratner, Lizzy, "Could Silicone Boob Jobs be Back?" *NY Times*, 9/10/06. Altogether, cosmetic surgery has increased five-fold in the past decade.

34.   Ryan, Joan, *San Francisco Chronicle*, 12/02/03, p. A21

35.   CBS interview by Leslie Stahl, 5/11/96. The sanctions continued for another seven years, bringing children's deaths to over a million.

36.   *The Bacchae*, p. 215, l. 1330. *The Passion of Christ (Christos Paschon)* was a twelfth-century text that reconfigured *The Bacchae* so as to tell the Christ story, mostly by quoting the Greek out of context. Scholars, assuming that its author plagiarized Euripides, have worked backwards from its text to fill in the missing lines of the play.

37.   *Dionysian Poetics*, p. 160-169, 354

Notes to Chapter Six

1.   *Joseph Campbell — An Introduction*, p. 124-5, 176

2.   *The Denial Of Death*, p. 50

3.   A long-time scholarly confusion has existed regarding both the meaning and the spelling of *Kronos*, whom some called *Cronus*. Beginning in the Hellenistic period, some confused *Kronos/Cronus* with *Chronos*, the personification of Time. To complicate things further, *Kronos'* Roman equivalent *Saturn* was originally a positive figure, the god of agriculture who presided over the Golden Age. But the Renaissance identified Saturn with devouring time, and he often appeared in images with his sickle or as devouring a child.

4.   Genesis 9:20-27, 10:6-20. Do Biblical sons bear the sins of their fathers? Yes they do, in three passages (Exodus 20:5 and 34:6-7 and Deuteronomy 5:9), and always "to the third and the fourth generations." In two other places, however (Deuteronomy 24:16 and Ezekiel 18:20), they do not.

5.   Ezek. 16:19-21

6.   Ps. 106:38

7.   Num. 25:11

8.   Gen. 19:8

9.   *Abraham's Curse*, p. 2

10.   Mathew 2:16

11.   *Those Women*, p. 31

12.   *Abraham's Curse*, p. 44

13.   *The Slaughter of the Innocents*, p. 59

14. *The History of Childhood*, p. 1
15. Ibid, p. 10
16. DeMause, Lloyd, "The Childhood Origins of the Holocaust" (www.geocities.com/kidhistory/cooth.htm)
17. Hillman, in lecture
18. Broyles, William Jr., "Why Men Love War," *Esquire,* November, 1984
19. Ibid
20. *The Archetype of Initiation*, p. 87
21. www.peacefulsocieties.org/index.html
22. *The Origins of War*
23. *Iliad*, Book 7, lines 357-9
24. Exodus 15:3, Joshua 6:21

Notes to Part Two Introduction

1. *The Healing Wisdom of Africa*, p. 183
2. Segal writes, "...equilibrium is not restored; we are left with...suffering meted out far beyond the offense" (*Dionysiac Poetics*, p. 213).

Notes to Chapter Seven

1. *The Fatal Environment*, p. 16-30
2. *American Holocaust*, p. 146
3. Psalm 58: 10
4. *Dancing In The Streets*, p. 145
5. Galatians 5:24
6. *The Protestant Ethic and the Spirit of Capitalism*, p. 104
7. Increase Mather, "The Wicked Man's Portion," in Sacvan Bercovitch, ed., *Execution Sermons* (New York: AMS Press, 1994)
8. Diggs, Stephen, "Alchemy of the Blues," *Spring 61*
9. *The Protestant Ethic and the Spirit of Capitalism*, p. 169
10. *Religion and the Rise of Capitalism* (www.monbiot.com/archives/2004/11/09/religion-of-the-rich/)
11. Lapham, Lewis, *Harper's*, May, 2003, p. 8
12. *Shadow Dancing in the U.S.A.*, p. 88-9
13. *White Racism*, p. 89
14. *Regeneration Through Violence*, p. 14-24
15. *The American Adam*, p. 5
16. *The American Soul*, p. 39
17. *Democracy In America*, p. 403
18. *From Slavery To Freedom — A History of Negro Americans*, p. 31
19. *Anti-Intellectualism In American Life*, p. 272-3

20. *Power And Innocence,* p. 57

21. http://hnn.us/roundup/entries/59787.html

22. *Mystery Train,* p. 20

23. *Soul On Ice,* p. 84

24. *Anti-Intellectualism In American Life,* p. 208

25. *The American Soul,* p. 13, 145

26. www.quotationspage.com/quotes/Malcolm_X/

27. *Democracy In America,* p.12

28. *The Myth of the West,* p. 124-5

29. *Virgin Land,* p. 55

30. Ibid, p. 101

31. Rich, Norman, *Hitler's War Aims: Ideology, the National State, and the Course of Expansion* (New York: Norton, 1973), p. 8

32. *The Terror Dream,* p. 276

33. *Stiffed,* p. 413-421

34. Weinman, Jaime, "The Searchers: the Most Flattered Movie of All Time," *Maclean's,* 6/05/06

35. *A Little Matter of Genocide,* p. 180-184

36. *The Invention of the White Race,* p. 214-5

37. Ibid, p. 251

38. Ibid, p. 243

39. *Between Barack And A Hard Place,* p. 116

40. *A People's History of the United States,* p. 29. Of that number, perhaps ten million were delivered alive to the New World, in ships that held two to three hundred persons. Do the math.

41. Fredrickson, George M., "America's Original Sin," *New York Review of Books,* 3/25/2004

42. *Understanding Power,* p. 255-7

43. *Democracy in America,* Vol. I, p. 373

44. *Blues People,* p. 84

45. *Shadow Dancing in the U.S.A.,* p. 146-7

46. Commager, Henry Steele and Samuel Eliot Morison, *The Growth of the American Republic* (1930, Oxford University Press, USA, 1980), p. 415- 418

47. *Race-ing Justice, En-Gendering Power,* p. 179-80

Notes to Chapter Eight

1. Moyers, Bill, "This Is Your Story," (www.commondreams.org/views03/0610-11.htm)

2. Diggs, Stephen, "Alchemy of the Blues," *Spring Journal 61,* p. 26-28

3. Helfand, Judy, "Constructing Whiteness" (www.academic.udayton.edu/race/01race)

4. *The Earth Shall Weep,* p. 228

5. Wilson, Woodrow, *History of the American People* (William H. Wise, 1930)

6. Black, Edwin, *War Against The Weak: America's Campaign To Create A Master Race* (Four

Walls Eight Windows, 2004). Bruinius, Harry, *Better For All The World: The Secret History Of America's Quest For Racial Purity* (Knopf, 2006).

7. Tom Hayden interview, *The Sun,* Jan. 2006, p. 8

8. *People's History,* p. 184

9. Melish, Joanne, *Disowning Slavery: Gradual Emancipation and Race in New England, 1780-1860* (Cornell University Press, 2000)

10. Handlin, Oscar, "Science And Technology In Popular Culture," *Daedalus* (1965), p. 160

11. *Society Without The Father,* Chapter VII

12. *American Myth, American Reality,* p. 233. Employees joke that "I.B.M." means "I've been moved."

13. *The Fatal Environment,* p. 25

14. Lears, Jackson, "The Belief in Regenerative War: Why So Many American Intellectuals Supported the Iraq War" (http://hnn.us/articles/1054oo.html)

15. *People's History,* p. 298. A second researcher (www.zmag.org/CrisesCurEvts/interventions. htm) lists 134 interventions between 1890 and 2001. A third lists 166 interventions between 1798 and 1945. Blum, William, *The C.I.A.: A Forgotten History* (London: Zed, 1986), appendix.

16. *People's History,* p. 362

17. *Habits Of Empire,* p. 236

18. Bellah, "Civil Religion in America," *Daedalus,* Winter, 1967, Vol. 96, p. 1-21

19. *Blood Sacrifice and the Nation,* p. 2-25

20. Bellah, lecture, Isla Vista, Ca, 2/21/86

21. *The American Dream,* p. 5-6

22. *Understanding Power,* p. 6-7

23. Blum, William, *Killing Hope: U.S. Military Interventions since WW II* (Common Courage, 1986), Introduction.

24. *Better Dead Than Red,* p. 8

25. www.killinghope.com

26. *Understanding Power,* p. 47-48

27. Adelman, Larry, "The Houses that Racism Built," *San Francisco Chronicle,* 7/03/03. Branch, Taylor, "Justice For Warriors, *New York Review of Books,* 4/12/07.

28. *The Fog of War: Eleven Lessons From The Life of Robert S. McNamara,* film by Errol Morris

29. Stinnett, Robert, *Day of Deceit* (Free Press, 1999)

30. "Ike on Ike," *Newsweek,* 11/11/63

31. "How Bush's Grandfather Helped Hitler's Rise to Power," *The Guardian,* 9/25/04. "FDR's Auschwitz Secret," *Newsweek,* 10/14/02).

32. *Chomsky's Politics,* p. 76

33. http://en.wikipedia.org/wiki/Cold_War

34. *Faces of the Enemy,* p. 25

35. *The Fifties, A Women's Oral History,* p. 201

36. *Red Hunting in the Promised Land,* p. 188

37. " Paper Clip" brought over 700 former Nazis into government service (Alvarez, Maria,

"CIA Admits Long Relationship With WWII German Gen. Reinhard Gehlen" *N.Y. Post*, 9/24/2000). "Northwoods" was a 1962 Pentagon contingency plan to blow up American planes and justify an attack on Cuba (Bamford, James, *Body of Secrets: Anatomy of the Ultra-Secret National Security Agency*, Anchor, 2002). MK Ultra involved multiple, secret exposures of large numbers of American citizens to potential toxins and carcinogens *(Between Barack And A Hard Place*, p. 137-139).

38. *Habits Of Empire*, p. 310

39. Linda Czuba Brigance, "For One Brief Shining Moment: Choosing to Remember Camelot," *Studies In Popular Culture*, April 2003/25.3. She concludes, "For forty years, the Camelot myth has organized our understanding of the public sphere and our role in it in a way that justifies the turn toward civic disengagement and cynicism. It tells us that our involvement is unnecessary: we did not create Camelot, we did not cause its demise, and we cannot facilitate its return... Freed from this daunting civic responsibility, post-Camelot Americans began an inevitable course toward disengagement from the political system and each other."

40. *Understanding Power*, p. 41, 91

41. *The Pursuit of Loneliness*, p. 33-4

42. *Fire In The Streets*, p. 311-321

43. Ibid, p. 542

44. *Understanding Power*, p. 199

45. *The Eagle's Shadow*, p. 183

46. Ibid, p. 196-200. Disney's annual sales exceed $20 billion.

47. Department of Defense publication, "Active Duty Military Personnel Strengths by Regional Area and by Country." As Chalmers Johnson has documented, the official figure of 761 foreign military installations is too low, for it does not include installations in Afghanistan, Iraq (over 100), Israel, Kosovo, Kuwait, Kyrgyzstan, Qatar, and Uzbekistan. Johnson estimates that an honest count would be closer to 1,000 (Johnson, Chalmers, *The Sorrows of Empire: Militarism, Secrecy, and the End of the Republic* (Metropolitan Books, 2004).

48. *The Culture of Make Believe*, p. 577

49. Doppelt, Jack, *Nonvoters: America's No-Shows*, Sage Publications, 2005

50. *Shadow Dancing in the U.S.A.*, p. 97

51. *The Culture of Fear*, p. XIX

52. *Junk Politics*, p. 116

53. Journalist William Rivers Pitt documents at least five occasions when damaging reports of administration malfeasance emerged in the media, only to be forgotten when the government quickly raised the terror alert(www.truthout.org/docs_2006/071307J.shtml). Also see Tim Dickinson, "Truth or Terrorism? The Real Story Behind Five Years of High Alerts" (www.rollingstone.com/politics/story/18056504/truth).

54. Bellah, "Individualism and the Crisis of Civic Membership," *Christian Century*, 3/20/96

55. Rev. 13:1, 20:1-3. Alternatively, Both Aphrodite and Dionysus also arise out of the sea.

56. Wills, Garry, *Reagan's America: Innocents At Home* (Doubleday, 1987), p. 4

57. *The Culture Struggle*, p. 115

58. *People's History*, p. 582

59. Lapham, "Tentacles of Rage," p. 41

60. *Understanding Power,* p. 5

61. *Warrior Dreams,* p. 71

62. Corcoran, Farrel, "The Bear in the Backyard: Myth, Ideology and Victimage in Soviet Funerals," *Communication Monographs 50* (12/1983)

63. *The European Dream,* p. 155

64. The Center For Defense Information estimates that, from 1948 through 1991, the U.S. alone spent over $13 trillion on the Cold War and the nuclear arms race (www.cdi.org/issues/milspend.html).

65. Corbett, Lionel, "War: Psychological and Spiritual Underpinnings," *Spring 81,* p. 95

66. *Warrior Dreams,* p. 291

67. *People's History,* p. 625; *New York Times,* 3/2/91

68. Johnson, Chalmers, "America's Empire of Bases" (www.TomDispatch.com), 1/15/2004.

69. 20% of all Democrats, 12% of all self-identified liberals, 39% of all women voters, one-third of all voters earning under $20,000 per year, 42% of those earning $20-30,000 annually, and 31% of all voting union members cast their ballots for Bush (Smith, Sam, "Still Smearing Ralph Nader for 2000," *Counterpunch,* 12/21/06).

70. *Rebuilding America's Defenses,* Project for a New American Century, 9/2000

71. Between Oct. 4 and Dec. 4, 2001, 389 stories appeared in the *New York Times* with "anthrax" in the headline. The anthrax was mailed to Democratic Senators Tom Daschle and Patrick Leahy, *leaders of the opposition to the Patriot Act,* on October 9. Chairman of the Judiciary Committee, Leahy managed the debate on the bill. After receiving the anthrax letter, Senate Majority Leader Daschle switched from supporting a 2-year limit on the Bill. *No Republican received an anthrax letter.* The House and Senate buildings were closed and not reopened until after the Patriot Act was passed. It became law on October 26.

72. *Democracy Matters,* p. 20

73. A study found that Bush and top officials publicly issued 935 false statements about the threat from Iraq between 9/11/2001 and the beginning of the invasion (www.huffingtonpost.com/2008/01/22/study-false-statements-p_n_82764.html).

74. www.wanttoknow.info/zogby911

75. Three million more people claimed they had voted than the official total.

76. Abate, Tom, "$1 Trillion Missing: Military Waste Under Fire," *San Francisco Chronicle,* 5/18/05

77. Berman, Morris, *Coming To Our Senses* (Harper Collins, 1990), p. 341-42

78. Shepard, *Nature and Madness* (in *Ecopsychology,* p. 35-7)

79. Studies indicate that many corporate CEOs are actual psychopaths, who "...have a profound lack of empathy...use other people callously and remorselessly for their own ends... pathological liars, master con artists, and heartless manipulators. Easily bored, they crave constant stimulation, so they seek thrills from real-life "games" they can win — and take pleasure from their power over other people (Alan Deutschman, "Is Your Boss a Psychopath?" *Fast Company,* July, 2005).

80. *The Earth Shall Weep,* p. 35-6

81.   Sharlet, Jeff, *The Family: The Secret Fundamentalism at the Heart of American Power* (Harper Perennial, 2009), p. 37

82.   Hedges, Chris, "Buying Brand Obama" (www.commondreams.org/view/2009/05/04)

83.   Palast, Greg, "The Day the President Turned Black (But Has He Turned Back?)" *Huffington Post*, 7/29/09

84.   *Between Barack And A Hard Place*, p. 9-11, 23-29, 86

85.   Ventura, Michael, "Paradox Obama 08" (*Austin Chronicle*, 11/21/2008)

Notes to Chapter Nine

1.   *Running On Emptiness*, p. 18-28

2.   *Ritual: Power, Healing and Community*, p. 32

3.   *The Chalice and the Blade*, p. 160

4.   Quoted in Hooper, John, *The New Spaniards* (Penguin, 1986), p. 152

5.   *Myths To Live By*, p. 179-181

6.   Hillman, James, "Look Out: Three Occasions of Public Excitation," *Depth Psychology: Meditations In The Field, p.* 173

7.   *The Curse of Cain*, p. 8

8.   Hillman, James, "Myths of the Family" (Audio Cassette, Sound Horizons Presents)

9.   *The Pursuit of Loneliness*, p. 20-30

10.   *The Healing Wisdom of Africa*, p. 91-92

11.   *History of the Idea of Progress*, p. 204

12.   Ibid, p. 238

13.   *Transgressing the Modern*, p. 66

14.   Almost all developed countries originally got rich not through free markets but through tariff protection and military conquest. nineteenth and early twentieth century U.S. tariffs of 40 to 50 percent were the highest in the world. Later, the U.S. government paid for 50 to 70 percent of the country's total expenditures on research and development from the 1950s through the mid-1990s, usually under the cover of defense spending (Ha-Joon Chang, *Bad Samaritan*, Bloomsbury, 2007).

15.   Quoted in Hollis, James, *Tracking the Gods: The Place of Myth in Modern Life, Studies In Jungian Psychology By Jungian Analysts,* 1995 (Toronto: Inner City), p. 26

16.   Hazleton, Lesley, *The Right to Feel Bad* (Doubleday, 1984)

17.   Lee, Richard, "What Hunters Do for a Living, or, How to Make Out on Scarce Resources," in R. Lee and I. DeVore (eds.), *Man the Hunter* (Chicago: Aldine, 1968)

18.   *The Curse of Cain*, p. 36

19.   Sahlins, Marshall, "The Original Affluent Society" (www.Primitivism.com/original-affluent. htm). Also see his *Stone Age Economics* (Aldine Transaction, 1972).

20.   *The Hero With a Thousand Faces*, p. 40-44

21.   www.sobonfu.com

22.   *The Pursuit of Loneliness*, p. 88-9

23.   *Mythography*, p. 417

24. *American Exceptionalism,* p. 154 (My italics).

25. *People's History,* p. 23

26. Wise, Tim, "Coloring Crime: Violence, Deviance and Media Manipulation" (www.timwise.org)

27. *Between Barack And A Hard Place,* p. 31

28. Title 36 USC 10,PL 344

29. *European Dream,* p. 41. This statistic implies that large numbers of the poor themselves agree with such an assessment; they have internalized the Puritan ideology.

30. *People's History,* p. 634

31. *Understanding Power,* p. 70

32. Ibid, p. 13-16

33. www.truthdig.com/report/item/200601017_reflecting_on_rumsfeld

34. www.kpfa.org/archives/index.php?arch=17237

35. *Democracy Matters,* p. 41

36. Hochschild, Arlie, "The Chauffer's Dilemma," *The American Prospect,* July, 2005

37. Glen Slater, "A Mythology of Bullets," *Spring 81*

38. *European Dream,* p. 32

39. *The Scapegoat Generation,* p. 127

40. *A Terrible Love of War,* p. 133

41. To arrive at these figures, subtract Social Security (raised and spent separately) from the federal budget. Then add veterans' benefits, Homeland Security, military expenditures within the Departments of Energy and NASA, 80% of interest on the national debt (caused by past wars) and supplemental expenses for Iraq and Afghanistan to the formal Defense Department budget. (War Resister's League: "Where Your Income Tax Money Really Goes." http://warresisters.org/piechart.htm)

42. The Pursuit of Loneliness, p. 42

43. Richard Hofstadter, "Reflections on Violence in the United States," in Richard Hofstadter and Michael Wallace, eds., *Violence In America* Sage, 1979)

44. *The Denial of Death,* p. 282

45. Ibid, p. 60-66

46. *The American Way of Death Revisited,* p. 51

47. *God Is Red,* p. 174-183

48. *Ritual,* p. 96

49. *On Death And Dying,* p. 15

50. *Shadow Dancing,* p. 94

51. *The American Soul,* p. 11

52. Hadas, Moses, ed., *Complete Plays of Sophocles,* (New York: Bantam, 1967), p. xi-xii

53. *Masks of Dionysus,* p. 92

54. *The Hero With A Thousand Faces,* p. 35-9

55. Ibid, p. 342

56. Hillman, "An Appreciation of Joseph Campbell," address to Mythic Journeys Conference, 6/6/2004

57. *Demon Lover,* p. 57

58. *The Image*, p. 57

59. Reagan himself, with rare candor, once admitted, "The camera doesn't lie. Eventually you are what you are." *Red Hunting in the Promised Land*, p. 190-197

60. *Blood Rites*, p. 228

61. *Demon Lover*, p. 165

62. *Warrior Dreams*, p. 114

63. *Gunfighter Nation*, p. 470

64. "The Great Mother, Her Son, Her Hero, and the Puer" in *Fathers and Mothers*, p. 197

65. *The American Monomyth*, p. 196

66. *American Myth, American Reality*, p. 164

67. *Regeneration Through Violence*, p. 563

68. Quoted by Lapham, Lewis, in *Harper's Magazine*, 9/03, p. 9 (my italics). This is a regular theme in cinema: in 1931 alone, Hollywood produced over fifty gangster movies in which the bad guys get away without being punished.

69. *Media Unlimited*, p. 201

70. *Warrior Dreams*, p. 80

71. *King Warrior Magician Lover*, p. 13

72. Ibid, p. 85

73. *Odyssey*, Book XI, lines 579-81

74. Knipe, Rita, *The Water of Life, A Jungian Journey Through Hawaiian Myth* (Honolulu, Univ. of Hawaii Press, 1989), p. 118-122

75. Sontag, Susan, "The Imagination of Disaster," in *Against Interpretation* (New York: Picador, 1966)

76. Haider, Asad, "Cinema and the Tsunami," *Politics and Culture* (http://aspen.conncoll.edu/politicsandculture/page.cfm?key=391)

77. Lecture, Pacifica Graduate Institute, April, 2002

78. Slouka, "A Year Later"

79. Lecture, Pacifica, April, 2002

80. Feder, Shanti, "The Tower", in *Parabola*, Spring, 2002, p. 58-60

81. Hillman, James, "Ground Zero: A Reading," in *Jungian Reflections On September 11*, p. 181-193

82. CNN, 9/11/2001

83. Feder, "The Tower"

84. *Transgressing The Modern*, p. 125

85. *Sex, Art and American Culture*, p. 24

Notes to Chapter Ten

1. *Ecstasy*, p. 18

2. *Dionysus In Exile*, p. 28

3. *Pagan Grace*, p. 21-22

4. Kipnis, Laura, "School For Scandal: The Larger Meaning of the Sordid Little Tale," *Harper's*, March 2009

5.   *A Terrible Love Of War,* pp. 123, 147, 167

6.   *Shadow Dancing In The U.S.A.,* p. 85-86

7.   Kotchemidova, Christina, "From Good Cheer to 'Drive-By Smiling': A Social History of Cheerfulness," *Journal of Social History,* Fall, 2005

8.   Wilmington, Michael, review of the film "Mystic River," *Chicago Tribune,* 12/07/03

9.   Solnit, Rebecca, "The Uses of Disaster," *Harper's,* October 2005, p. 31-37

10. Lears, Jackson, "The Belief in Regenerative War: Why So Many American Intellectuals Supported the Iraq War" (http://hnn.us/articles/1054oo.html)

11. Jung, *CW,* 18: 627

12. *American Monomyth,* p. 211

13. Ibid

14. *Tangled Memories,* p. 138

15. *Rituals of Blood,* p. 182-3

16. *Violence and the Sacred,* p. 79

17. *The Scapegoat Generation,* p. 122

18. Ruiz, Teofilo, *The Terror of History* (audiotape lecture series, The Teaching Company, 1998)

19. *Sex And Racism in America,* p. 116

20. Sellers, James, *The South and Christian Ethics* (New York: Association Press, 1962), p. 118-119

21. *Rituals of Blood,* p. 173-223

22. Ibid

23. *Newsweek,* 6/6/88

24. *Rituals of Blood,* p. 243

25. Ten percent of black men in their twenties are incarcerated, and 25% can expect prison time in their lifetimes. In their early thirties, they are imprisoned at seven times the rate of whites in the same age group. By their mid-thirties, 60% of black high school dropouts are now prisoners or ex-cons. SOURCES: "Study shows racial disparities in prison"(*AP,* 7/18/07); Jason DePearle, "The American Prison Nightmare," *New York Review of Books,* 4/12/07; Glenn C. Loury, "Why Are So Many Americans in Prison?" *Boston Review,* July/August 2007; N. C. Aizenman, "New High In U.S. Prison Numbers" *Washington Post,* 2/29/08; "Incarceration and Race" (Human Rights Watch, www.hrw.org/reports/2000/usa/Rcedrg00-01.htm). A related issue is *racial profiling.* Black or Hispanic subway riders are far more likely to get stopped and questioned by New York Police. Ninety percent of citizens stopped and questioned are either black or Hispanic, despite comprising only 49%of subway riders. Eighty-five percent of New Yorkers arrested for marijuana are either black or Hispanic. Throughout the city, 86% of those stopped and frisked by the NYPD were black or Latino. (*Progressive Review,* 2/20/08). Another issue is the calculation of poverty statistics. The government omits prisoners when calculating unemployment and poverty rates. Add them in, and joblessness swells — for young black men by more than a third. For young black dropouts, the jobless rate leaps from 41% to 65%. Only when counting prisoners do we realize that two out of three young black male dropouts were unemployed at the height of the 1990s economic expansion. Count inmates and you also erase three quarters of the apparent

progress in closing the wage gap between blacks and whites. The prison expansion created inequality and hid it from view.

26. *Hearts And Hands*, p. 168-172; *The Culture Struggle*, p. 106

27. Palast, Greg, "Economic Hit Men and the Next Drowning of New Orleans" (http://dissidentvoice.org/2009/08/economic-hit-men-and-the-next-drowning-of-new-orleans/)

28. *Between Barack And A Hard Place*, p. 69-72

29. Ellison, Ralph, *Shadow and Act* (New York: Vintage, 1953), p. 28

30. *Between Barack And A Hard Place*, p. 95

31. *Rituals Of Blood*, p. 250-5

32. Ibid. p. 272-6

33. Schor, Juliet, *Born to Buy: The Commercialized Child and the New Consumer Culture* (Scribner, 2004)

34. *Media Unlimited*, p. 69

35. Early, Gerald, *One Nation Under A Groove: Motown And American Culture* (Hopewell, NJ: Ecco, 1995), p. 134

36. Ryan, Lizza, "Return of the Nativist," *New Yorker*, 12/17/07

37. Smith-Lovin, Lynn, "Social Isolation in America: Changes in Core Discussion Networks Over Two Decades," *American Sociological Review*, 6/06/06

38. *Backlash*, p. 401-2

39. www.prisoncommission.org/public_hearing_2_witness_grassian.asp

40. DePerle, Jason, "The American Prison Nightmare," *New York Review of Books*, 4/12/07; Amy Goodman, "Felony Disenfranchisement Aids Republicans" (www.truthout.org/article/amygoodman-felony-disenfranchisement-aids-republicans)

41. Chomsky, in lecture

42. *Drugs, Addiction and Initiation*, p. 53

43. Minneapolis Anti-Pornography Ordinance, 1983, drafted by Catharine MacKinnon and Andrea Dworkin, quoted by McElroy, Wendy, "Pornography," in *Everything You Know is Wrong*, p. 151-154

44. *Pornography And Silence*, p. 111-112

45. McElroy, "Pornography"

46. Radway, J., *Reading The Romance* (Verso, 1987), pp. 75, 141-4

47. Hillman, *Pink Madness — Or Why Does Aphrodite Drive Us Crazy with Pornography?* (Audiotape lecture, Oral Traditions Archives, 1994); *Mythic Figures*, Vol. 6.1, Ch. 8

48. *Hellfire Nation*, p. 231

49. *Pink Madness*

50. *Transgressing The Modern*, p. 161

51. www.law.umkc.edu/faculty/projects/ftrials/conlaw/barnes.html

52. Quoted in *Mother Jones*, Jan-Feb, 2005, p. 16

53. www.cnn.com/2003/ALLPOLITICS/04/22/santorum.gays/

54. "Is Pornography Really Harmful?" (www.alternet.org/sex/67144/); "The Great Porn Misunderstanding: Pornography Is Mostly About Fantasy, Not Reality" (www.alternet.org/

sex/104863/the_great_porn_misunderstanding%3A_pornography_is_mostly_about_
fantasy%2C_not_reality_/)

55. www.rawstory.com/news/2006/Poll_Christians_addicted_to_pornography_0814.html; www.
newscientist.com/article/dn16680-porn-in-the-usaconservatives-are-biggest-consumers.
html?DCMP=OTC-rss

56. *Pink Madness*

57. *Between Barack And A Hard Place*, p. 57

58. *Myths and Mysteries of Same-Sex Love*, p. 163

59. Wise, Tim, "School shootings and White Denial" (http://academic.udayton.edu/
race/01race/white08.htm); Cheryl Fryar, et al, "Drug Use and Sexual Behaviors Reported
byAdults: United States, 1999ñ2002" (www.cdc.gov/nchs/data/ad/ad384.pdf); Drug Reform
Coordination Network (www.stopthedrugwar.org); *Progressive Review*, 2/28/06; Wise, Tim,
"Racial Profiling and its Apologists" (www.zmag.org/zmag//articles/march02wise.htm);
"Debunking the Hemp Conspiracy Theory"(www.alternet.org/drugreporter/77339/?page=en
tire);

60. "Daybreak for Marijuana: Most Americans Support Legalization," 12/10/09 (www.alternet.
org/blogs/DrugReporter/144496/daybreak_for_marijuana%3A_most_americans_support_
legalization)

61. National Household Survey on Drug Abuse, 6/15/03. Illicit drug use costs the U.S. almost
$200 billion a year, according to the National Institute on Drug Abuse. (www.nida.nih.
gov/Infofacts/index.html). Include alcohol and tobacco-related costs along with health
care, criminal justice and lost productivity and the figure exceeds $500 billion annually;
"Drug War's Collateral Damage" (http://cannabisnews.com/news/23/thread23159.
shtml); "NORMAL Releases Most Comprehensive Analysis of US Marijuana Arrest Data To
Date," (www.normal.org/index.cfm?Group_ID=6476); Substance Abuse and Mental Health
Services Administration (www.samhsa.gov/); www.stopthedrugwar.org/chronicle/365/
aflop.shtml; Worldwatch Institute, "Illegal Drug Harvests Remain High," 7/24/03 (www.
worldwatch.org). A 2006 study called cannabis the "top cash crop in the nation." ("Marijuana
Could Be a Gusher of Cash If We Treated It Like a Crop, Not a Crime"; www.alternet.org/
drugreporter/98317/).

62. *The Scapegoat Generation*, p. 160

63. Sieff, Daniela, "Confronting the Death Mother: An Interview with Marion Woodman," *Spring 81*

64. *The Hearts of Men*, p. 113

65. *The Botany of Desire*, p. 79

66. *Cleansing the Doors of Perception*, p. 27

67. *The God of Ecstasy*, p. 148-172

68. *The Soul's Code*, p. 8-11

69. *The Greeks and the Irrational*, p.149-156

70. *Nature And Madness*, p. 80

71. *The God of Ecstasy*, p. 167

72. *The Jesus Mysteries*, p. 207

73. *The Rise of Christianity*, p. 214

74. Karcher, Steven, "Which Way I Fly is Hell," *Spring 55*, p. 83-87

75. *The Alphabet and the Goddess*, p. 253

76. *Malleus Maleficarum* ("Hammer of Witches," 1487)

77. *A Terrible Love Of War*, p. 183

78. *The American Soul*, p. 261

79. *The Prince of Darkness*, p. 11-12

80. Ibid, p.11-12

81. *Red Hunting In The Promised Land*, p. 74

82. *The Two Hands of God*, p. 34-37

83. *White Wall Of Spain*, p. 151

84. *Abraham's Curse*, p. 173-5

85. *Running On Emptiness*, p. 76

86. *The Chalice & The Blade*, p. 140

87. Roszak, Betty, "The Spirit of the Goddess," in *Ecopsychology*, p. 293

88. *Blood Rites*, p. 176

89. *Long Life, Honey In The Heart*, p. 53

90. *Rituals of Blood*, p. 217

91. http://rawstory.com/2009/10/former-right-wing-leader-warns-of-religious-right-violenceanyone-can-be-killed/

92. *God Is Red*, p. 154

93. *A Terrible Love Of War*, p. 190

94. *Women And Madness*, p. 16

95. Breggin, Peter, MD, "Psychiatric Drugging of Children for Behavioral Control," in *Everything You Know Is Wrong*, p. 110-114

96. *Influencing Minds*, p. 156-167.

97. Szasz interview (www.psychotherapistresources.com)

98. Watkins, Mary. "Seeding Liberation," in *Depth Psychology: Meditations In The Field*

99. Kotchemidova, Christina, "From Good Cheer to 'Drive-By Smiling': A Social History of Cheerfulness," *Journal of Social History*, Fall, 2005

100. *The Politics of Experience* (1967), quoted in *Going Crazy*, p. 91

101. "From Good Cheer to 'Drive-By Smiling': A Social History Of Cheerfulness"

102. Ibid

103. Depression has been defined as "disturbance of affect." But "affect" is culturally determined. Positive expectations and assumptions of the right to the "pursuit of happiness" make feelings of sadness and despair more pathological in America than anywhere else. Hazleton, Lesley, *The Right to Feel Bad* (New York: Ballantine, 1984)

104. Steven Bezruchka, M.D., lecture, KPFA radio, 2/16/08: "Is America Making You Crazy?"

105. Otto, *Dionysus*, p. 136-40

106. *We've Had a Hundred Years of Therapy*, p. 169

107. *Cultural Anxiety*, p. 58

108. *The Owl Was a Baker's Daughter: Obesity, Anorexia Nervosa and the Repressed Feminine*, pp. 9-10, 103-4

109. *Going Crazy*, p. 213; Bower, Bruce, "The Predator's Gaze — Scientists Explore the Frightening World of Psychopaths" (www.sciencenews.org/articles/20061209/bob9.asp)

110. *Nature And Madness*, p. 124

111. Torrey, E. Fuller, *Surviving Schizophrenia: A Family Manual* (HarperCollins, 1988, quoted in Jay Neugeboren, "Infiltrating the Enemy of the Mind," *New York Review of Books*, 4/17/2008)

112. *Running On Emptiness*, p. 158-9

113. *Myths To Live By*, p. 208

114. Bateson, Gregory (ed.), *Perceval's Narrative* (Stanford University Press, 1961)

115. Hillman in lecture, Pacifica Graduate Institute, March, 2004

116. *The Archetype of Initiation*, p. 21

117. Ibid, p. 48

118. Hotchner, A.E., *Papa Hemingway* (1966), quoted in *Going Crazy*, p. 108

119. *Transgressing the Modern*, p. 93

120. Plato, *Phaedrus*, 244b

Notes to Chapter Eleven

1. *Shadow Dancing In The U.S.A.*, p. 132-4

2. *The Spell of the Sensuous*, p. 6-7

3. *Mystery Train*, p. 129

4. *Dionysus In Exile*, p. 77

5. "Alchemy of the Blues," p. 33-4

6. *Souled American*, p. 308

7. *American Monomyth*, p. 125-8

8. Pinkola-Estes, Clarissa, "Elvis Presley: Fama, and the *Cultus* of the Dying God," *The Soul of Popular Culture*, p. 36-9

9. *Fever*, p. 5

10. *On The Road* (NY: Viking, 1959, originally written in 1951)

11. *The Fifties*, p. 592-8

12. Boorstin, Daniel, *The Democratic Experience* (Random House, 1973), p. 90

13. *The Organization Man*, p. 3.

14. *Shadow Dancing In The U.S.A.*, p. 165-6

15. Ibid, p. 173

16. *The Journal of Retailing*, Spring 1955, p. 7

17. Pleck, Joseph H., "The Theory of Male Sex-role Identity: Its Rise and Fall, 1936 to the Present," in *The Making of Masculinities: The New Men's Studies*, Harry Brod, ed. (NY: Routledge, 1987), p. 34-5

18. *Fire In The Streets*, p. 60

19. "Alchemy of the Blues," p. 41

20. *Shadow Dancing In The U.S.A.*, p. 152

21. *Soul On Ice*, p. 196

22. *Careless Love: The Unmaking of Elvis Presley*, p. 190

23. *Soul On Ice,* p. 197-200

24. *Dancing In The Streets,* p. 210

25. *Where The Girls Are,* p. 113

26. *Sound Effects,* p. 42-45

27. *The Hearts of Men,* p. 114

28. Tietz, Jeff, "The Killing Factory," *Rolling Stone,* 4/20/06; Worthington, Andy, "Hit Me Baby One More Time, A History of Music Torture in the War on Terror" (www.counterpunch.org/worthington12152008.html).

29. *"The Age of Endarkenment, "* p. 47

30. Ibid

31. "Elvis Presley: Fama, and the *Cultus* of the Dying God," p. 42

32. *Elvis Culture,* p. 10

33. *Fever,* p. 16

34. *Soul On Ice,* p. 194

35. Delia Morgan, in "Cult of the Lizard King" (home.earthlink.net/~delia5/pagan/jmlk/cult-lizardking.htm), argues that Jim Morrison was a conscious, thus more appropriate, carrier of the Dionysian role in America. But he appeared ten years after Elvis had already broken down the walls.

36. "Elvis Presley: Fama, and the *Cultus* of the Dying God," p. 22

37. *Shadow Dancing In The U.S.A.,* p. 153

38. *Elvis Culture,* p. 75

39. Ibid, p. 136

40. Ibid, p. 144

41. *Where The Girls Are,* p. 97

42. *Sound Effects,* p. 239

43. *Where The Girls Are,* p. 304

44. *New Age Journal,* May/June, 1997, p. 66

Notes to Chapter Twelve

1. Brecht, Bertolt, "To Posterity"

2. *The Sibling Society,* p. 195-6

3. Pearce, Joseph Chilton, *Evolution's End: Claiming The Potential Of Our Intelligence* (Harper San Francisco, 1992), p. 165-7

4. Garcia-Lorca, Federico, "Imagination, Inspiration, Evasion," *Jubilat,* Issue 7

5. *The World Behind the World,* p. 63; Meade, Michael, *Initiation And The Soul* (audio CD, www.mosaicvoices.org)

6. Lorca, "Imagination, Inspiration, Evasion."

7. Adorisio, Antonella, "Belleza Orsini and Creativity: Images of Body and Soul from a 16th-Century Prison," *Spring 72,* p. 292

8. Meade, Michael, "The Silent Land is Our Homeland," (www.mosaicvoices.org)

9. Gioia, Dana, "Notes Toward a New Bohemia," (www.danagioia.net); Gioia, Dana, "Disappearing Ink: Poetry At The End Of Print Culture," *Hudson Review,* Spring 2003

10. Delgado, Aberlardo, "Chicano: 25 pieces of a Chicano Mind," (Barrio Publications (1972)

11. *The Healing Wisdom of Africa,* p. 96

12. Griffin, Susan, "To Love the Marigold: The Politics of Imagination," *Whole Earth Review,* Spring, 1996, p. 60-67

13. *The Power of Myth,* p. 32

14. *A Terrible Love of War,* p. 212

15. Lovelock, James, *Gaia: A New Look At Life On Earth* (Oxford Univ. Press, 1979)

16. *Mythography,* p. 361

17. "Cults and Cosmic Consciousness"

18. Ray, Paul H., and Anderson, Sherry Ruth, *The Cultural Creatives: How Fifty Million People Are Changing The World* (New York: Harmony Books, 2000)

19. *The Healing Wisdom of Africa,* p. 62

20. Ibid, p. 92

21. *Long Life, Honey In The Heart,* p. 356

22. Raphael, *The Men From The Boys;* Rodriguez, *Hearts And Hands.* Also see: Mahdi, L.C., Foster, Steven and Little, Meredith (eds.), *Betwixt And Between: Patterns of Masculine and Feminine Initiation* (Chicago: Open Court, 1987); Mahdi, L.C., Christopher, N.G, and Meade, Michael (eds.), *Crossroads: The Quest for Contemporary Rites of Passage* (Chicago: Open Court, 1996); Campanelli, Pauline, *Pagan Rites of Passage* (Llewelyn, 1998); and Weiner, Bernard, *Boy Into Man: A Father's Guide To Initiation Of Teenage Sons* (Transformation Press, 1992)

23. www.mosaicvoices.com.

24. *Long Life, Honey In The Heart,* p. 360

25. *Healing Wisdom of Africa,* p. 143-144

26. Plato, *Symposium,* 189-193

27. *Iliad,* trans. Robert Fitzgerald, Book V, lines 1015-16

28. *A Terrible Love Of War,* p. 83-4

29. *The Homeric Hymns,* p. 60-61

30. *A Terrible Love Of War,* p. 207

31. *Trickster Makes This World,* p. 272-275

32. *A Terrible Love of War,* p. 211-213

33. *Long Life, Honey In The Heart,* p. 7

34. *Ritual,* p. 96-126

35. *Letters At 3 AM,* p. 169

36. *War And The Soul,* p. 189-283

37. *Achilles In Vietnam,* p. 189

38. Ibid, p. 194

39. www.temple.edu/english/isllc/newfolk/shrines.html

40. St. John, Kelly, "Sidewalk Shrines of Teddy Bears, Liquor," *San Francisco Chronicle,* 8/5/03

41. May, Meredith, "R.I.P. Shirts Become an Urban Tradition," *San Francisco Chronicle,* 10/24/04

42. *Death Makes A Holiday,* p. 185

43. *The Healing Wisdom of Africa*, p. 54-5

44. *The Passing of the Armies*, p. 260-61

45. *No Future Without Forgiveness*, p. 31-2

46. Ibid, p. 189

47. Native American Graves Protection and Repatriation Act, 11/23/1990

48. *Hearts And Hands*, p. 141

49. *Offerings At The Wall: Artifacts From The Vietnam Veterans Memorial Collection*, p. 52

50. wwww.banyen.com/infocus/malidoma.htm

51. *The Other Within*, p. 55

52. *The Curse of Cain*, p. 115-119

53. Dirk Dunbar argues that American films of the last twenty years have been offering many countercultural heroes who question traditional cultural assumptions and support the emergence of new values. "Hollywood's Transformed Hero: A Countercultural Journey," *Journal of Religion and Popular Culture*, Volume VI: Spring 2004 (www.usask.ca/relst/jrpc/art6-hollywoodtrans-print.html).

54. Jung, "Psychology And Religion," *CW* 11, par. 397

55. de Unamuno, Miguel, "The Tragic Sense of Life" (www.listentogenius.com/author.php/157).

56. *The American Soul*, p. 9

57. Burns, Ken, *Jazz*, Episode 10 (Burbank: Warner Home Video)

58. "This Time, It's Native Americans Who Stake a Claim to Prime Land" (*Los Angeles Times*, 9/22/04)

BIBLIOGRAPHY

Abram, David, *The Spell of the Sensuous — Perception and Language in a More-Than-Human World* (New York: Pantheon, 1996).

Adams, Michael V., "Desegregating the White Ego," *Spring Journal*, # 62, 1997.

Adelman, Larry, "The Houses that Racism Built," *San Francisco Chronicle*, 7/03/03.

Aeschylus, *Aeschylus –The Oresteia*, Ed. Simon Goldhill (Cambridge University Press, 1992).

Aeschylus, *Aeschylus I, Oresteia — Agamemnon*, trans. Richmond Lattimore (University of Chicago Press, 1953).

Allen, Theodore, *The Invention of the White Race, Vol. II* (Verso, 1994).

Allport, Gordon, *The Nature of Prejudice* (Perseus Books, 1979).

Altschuler, Glenn C., *All Shook Up: How Rock'N'Roll Changed America*, (Oxford University Press, 2003).

Anderson, William, *Green Man — The Archetype of our Oneness with the Earth* (San Francsco: Harper Collins, 1990).

Andrist, Ralph, *The Long Death: The Last Days Of The Plains Indians* (New York: Collier, 1964).

Anzaldua, Gloria, "Chicana Artists: Exploring Nepantla, El Lugar De La Frontera," *NACLA Report On The Americas*, July-Aug., 1993.

Aries, Phillipe, *The Hour of Our Death* (New York: Vintage, 1982).

Aristotle, *Poetics* (Penguin Classics, 1997).

Asher, IJ, Thesis abstract, "What are the perceptions of five gay and lesbian youth as to the factors that caused them to attempt suicide?" *DAI*, Vol. 58-03A, p.784 (www.Virtualcity.com).

Axell, Albert, and Kase, Hideaki, *Kamikaze* (Longman, 2001).

Bakan, David, *Slaughter Of The Innocents: A Study of the Battered Child Phenomenon* (Boston: Beacon Press, 1971).

Banner, Stuart, *The Death Penalty: An American History* (Harvard University Press, 2002).

Baring, Anne and Jules Cashford, *The Myth of the Goddess, Evolution of an Image* (Penguin, 1993).

Barrett, William, *Irrational Man — A Study in Existential Philosophy* (New York: Doubleday, 1962).

Barson, Michael, *Better Dead Than Red!* (New York: Hyperion, 1992).

Bateson, Gregory (ed.), *Perceval's Narrative* (Stanford University Press, 1961).

Beaudoin, Tom, *Virtual Faith: The Irreverent Spiritual Quest of Generation X* (San Francisco: Jossey-Bass, 1998).

Becker, Ernest, *The Denial of Death* (New York: Simon & Schuster, 1973).

Begg, Ean, *The Cult of the Black Virgin* (Penguin, 1985).

Bellah, Robert N., "Civil Religion in America," in *Daedalus, Journal of the American Academy Of Arts & Sciences*, Winter, 1967, Vol. 96, # 1.

Bellah, Robert N., "Civil Religion in America," in Hudson, W.S., ed. *Nationalism And Religion In America* (New York: Harper, 1970).

Bellah, Robert N., "Individualism and the Crisis of Civic Membership," *The Christian Century*, 3/20/96

Bellah, Robert N., Richard Madsen, W.M. Sullivan, Ann Swidler, Steven Tipton, *Habits of the Heart: Individualism and Commitment in American Life* (University of California Press, 1985).

Bellesiles, Michael, *Arming America: The Origins of a National Gun Culture* (Soft Skull Press, 2000).

Benfer, Amy, "Nuclear Family Takes a Hit" (www.salon.com), 6/7/01.

Bercovitch, Sacvan, *The Puritan Origins of the American Self* (Yale University Press, 1975).

Berger, John, *Ways Of Seeing* (Penguin, 1973).

Bernstein, Jerome, "The Decline of Masculine Rites of Passage in Our Culture," in *Betwixt & Between, Patterns of Masculine and Feminine Initiation*, Mahdi, Foster and Little, eds. (La Salle: Open Court, 1993).

Berry, Patricia, ed. *Fathers And Mothers* (Dallas: Spring Publications, 1990).

Bettleheim, Bruno, *Symbolic Wounds* (The Free Press, 1954).

Biale, David, "The Hummer and the Prius," *San Francisco Chronicle*, 7/13/2003.

Blum, William, *Killing Hope: U.S. Military Interventions since WW II* (Common Courage Press, 1995).

Bly, Robert, *Iron John, A Book About Men* (Menlo Park: Addison-Wesley, 1990).

Bly, Robert, *The Sibling Society* (New York: Addison-Wesley, 1996).

Boas, George, *The Cult of Childhood* (Dallas: Spring Publications, 1966).

Boer, Charles, trans., *The Homeric Hymns* (Dallas: Spring Publications, 1970).

Bolen, Jean Shinoda, *Gods In Everyman — A New Psychology of Men's Lives And Loves* (New York: Harper & Row, 1990).

Bollas, Christopher, *Cracking Up: The World of Unconscious Experience* (New York: Taylor & Francis, 2004).

Boorstin, Daniel, *The Democratic Experience* (New York: Random House, 1973).

Boorstin, Daniel, *The Image: A Guide To Pseudo-Events In America* (Vintage, 1987).

Bradsher, Keith, *High and Mighty* (Public Affairs, 2003), quoted in *In These Times*, 3/17/2003.

Breggin, Peter, MD, "Psychiatric Drugging of Children for Behavioral Control," in Kick, Russ (Ed.), *Everything You Know Is Wrong: The Disinformation Guide to Secrets and Lies* (The Disinformation Company, 2002).

Broyles, William Jr., "Why Men Love War," *Esquire*, November, 1984.

Burkert, Walter, *Greek Religion* (Harvard University Press, 1985).

Burkert, Walter, *Homo Necans: The Anthropology Of Ancient Greek Sacrificial Ritual And Myth* (University of California Press, 1983).

Cahill, Thomas, *Sailing the Wine-Dark Sea: Why the Greeks Matter* (New York: Doubleday, 2003).

Calasso, Roberto, *The Marriage of Cadmus and Harmony* (New York: Knopf, 1993).

Campanelli, Pauline, *Pagan Rites of Passage* (Llewelyn, 1998).

Campbell, Joseph, *The Hero With A Thousand Faces* (New York: Bollingen Foundation, 1949).

Campbell, Joseph, *The Masks of God — Vol. III, Occidental Mythology* (Penguin, 1995).

Campbell, Joseph, *Myths of Light: Eastern Metaphors of the Eternal* (New World Library, 2003).

Campbell, Joseph, *Myths to Live By* (New York: Bantam, 1988).

Campbell, Joseph, *Pathways to Bliss: Mythology and Personal Transformation* (Novato, CA: New World Library, 2004).

Campbell, Joseph, *The Power of Myth* (New York: Doubleday, 1988).

Cantril, Hadley, *The Invasion From Mars* (New York: Harper & Row, 1966).

Capps, W. H., *The Unfinished War: Vietnam and the American Conscience* (Boston: Beacon Press, 1990).

Caputo, Philip, *A Rumor of War* (New York: Ballantine, 1977).

Carpenter, T.H. and C. A. Faraone (eds.), *Masks Of Dionysus* (Cornell University Press, 1993).

Carroll, Peter N., *It Seemed Like Nothing Happened — The Tragedy and Promise of America in the 1970s* (New York: Holt, Rinehart, 1982).

Casey, Caroline, *Making the Gods Work For You — The Astrological Language of the Psyche* (New York: Harmony Books, 1998).

Cassingham, Randy, *Losing My Tolerance for "Zero Tolerance"* (www.thisistrue.com).

Chamberlain, Joshua, *The Passing of the Armies* (Stan Clark Military Books, 1994).

Cheetham, Tom, "Quicksilver, Sulfur, and the Work of the World," *Spring Journal* # 69.

Chesler, Phyliss, *Women And Madness* (New York: Avon Books, 1972).

Children's Defense Fund, "Number of Black Children in Extreme Poverty Hits Record High" (www.children'sdefence.org), 4/30/03.

Chilton, Bruce, *Abraham's Curse: The Roots of Violence in Judaism, Christianity and Islam* (New York: Doubleday, 2008).

Chomsky, Noam, "Reasons to Fear U. S.," *Toronto Star*, 9/12/03.

Chomsky, Noam, *Understanding Power — The Indispensable Chomsky*, Ed. Mitchell, Peter R. and John Schoeffel (New York: The New Press, 2002).

Churchill, Ward, *A Little Matter of Genocide* (City Light, 2001).

Claremont de Castillejo, Irene, *Knowing Woman, A Feminine Psychology* (New York: Harper, 1973).

Clarke, Richard, *Against All Enemies* (Free Press, 2004).

Cleaver, Eldridge, *Soul On Ice* (New York: Ramparts Books, 1968).

Cohn, Norman, *The Pursuit of the Millennium: Revolutionary Millenarians and Mystical Anarchists of the Middle Ages* (Oxford University Press, 1970).

Coleman, Penny, *Flashback — Posttraumatic Stress Disorder, Suicide, and the Lessons of War* (Boston: Beacon Press, 2006).

Commager, H. S., *The American Mind: An Interpretation of American Thought and Character Since the 1880s* (Yale University Press, 1950).

Cooney, Robert and Michalowski, Helen, (eds.), *The Power Of The People: Active Nonviolence In The United States* (Peace Press, 1977).

Corelis, Jon, "Kent State Reconsidered as Nightmare," *Journal of Psychohistory*, Fall, 1980.

Corcoran, Farrel, "The Bear in the Backyard: Myth, Ideology and Victimage in Soviet Funerals," *Communication Monographs* 50, (12/1983).

Cowan, Lyn, "False Memories, True Memory, and Maybes," in *The Soul Of Popular Culture*, Ed. Mary Lynn Kittelson (Chicago, Open Court, 1998).

Cox, Harvey, "Sex And Secularization," in *The Sense of the Sixties*, Ed. Quinn, Edward and Paul Dolan (New York: The Free Press, 1968).

Crenshaw, Kimberly, "Whose Story Is That, Anyway?" in Morrison, Tony (ed.), *Race-ing Justice, En-Gendering Power: Essays on Anita Hill, Clarence Thomas, and the Construction of Social reality* (New York: Pantheon, 1992).

Cross, Gary, *An All-Consuming Century: Why Commercialism Won In Modern America* (Columbia University Press, 2000).

Cullen, Jim, *The American Dream, A Short History of an Idea that Shaped a Nation* (Oxford University Press, 2003).

Danforth, L. M., *The Death Rituals of Rural Greece* (Princeton University Press, 1982).

Daniélou, Alain, *Shiva and Dionysus* (New York: Inner Traditions, 1979).

Davies, Nigel, *Human Sacrifice in History and Today* (New York: Dorsett Press, 1981).

Davis, D.B., "Catching the Conquerors," *New York Review of Books*, 5/29 03.

Deardorff, Daniel, *The Other Within: The Genius of Deformity in Myth, Culture & Psyche* (Berkeley: North Atlantic Books, 2004).

de Beauvoir, Simone, *The Second Sex* (Cape, 1972).

Deloria, Vine, *God Is Red* (Golden, Colorado: Fulcrum Publishing, 1994).

de Mause, Lloyd (ed.), *The History of Childhood — The Evolution of Parent-child Relationships as a Factor in History* (London: Condor, 1976).

D'Emilio, John and Estelle Freedman, *Intimate Matters — A History of Sexuality in America* (University of Chicago Press, 1997).

Demos, John, *The Enemy Within: 2,000 Years of Witch-hunting in the Western World*, (Viking, 2008).

Demos, John, *The Unredeemed Captive: A Family Story From Early America* (Vintage Books, 1995).

DeMott, Benjamin, *Junk Politics* (Nation Books, 2003).

Derounian-Stodola, Kathryn (ed.), *Women's Indian Captivity Narratives* (Penguin Classics, 1998).

De Tocqueville, Alexis, *Democracy In America*, Ed. Richard D. Hefner (New American Library, 1955).

Deveroux, Paul, John Steele and David Kubrin, *Earthmind* (New York: Harper & Row, 1989).

Diggs, Stephen, "Alchemy of the Blues," *Spring Journal* # 61.

Digney, Marita, "Holy Madness at Heaven's Gate," in *The Soul Of Popular Culture*, Ed. Mary Lynn Kittelson (Chicago, Open Court, 1998).

Diller, Hans, "Euripides' Final Phase: The Bacchae," in Segal, Eric (ed.), *Greek Tragedy — Modern Essays in Criticism* (New York: Harper & Row, 1983).

Dodds, E.R., *The Greeks And The Irrational* (University of California Press, 1951).

Dorfman, Ariel, *The Empire's Old Clothes: What The Lone Ranger, Babar, And Other Innocent Heroes Do To Our Minds* (Penguin, 1983).

Doss, Erika, *Elvis Culture: Fans, Faith & Image* (University Press of Kansas, 1999).

Douglas, Susan J., *Where The Girls Are: Growing Up Female With The Mass Media* (New York: Three Rivers Press, 1995).

Downing, Christine, *The Goddess: Mythological Images of the Feminine* (New York: Crossroad, 1990).

Downing, Christine, *Gods In Our Midst* (New York: Crossroad, 1993).

Downing, Christine, "Looking Back At Orpheus," *Spring Journal* # 71.

Downing, Christine, *Myths and Mysteries of Same-Sex Love* (New York: Continuum, 1996).

Doty, William, G., "Originary Mythos," *Spring Journal* # 68.

Doty, William, G., *Mythography — The Study of Myths and Rituals* (University of Alabama Press, 2000).

Driver, Tom, *The Magic of Ritual* (San Francisco: Harper, 1991).

Dunkel, Greg, "Haiti's Impact on the U.S." (www.iaccenter.org).

Durant, Will and Ariel, *The Lessons Of History* (New York: Simon & Schuster, 1968).

Early, Gerald, *One Nation Under A Groove: Motown And American Culture* (Hopewell, New Jersey: Ecco, 1995).

Edinger, Edward, *Ego and Archetype* (New York: Penguin, 1973).

Ehrenreich, Barbara, *Blood Rites — Origins and History of the Passions of War* (New York: Henry Holt, 1997).

Ehrenreich, Barbara, *Dancing in the Streets — A History of Collective Joy* (New York: Henry Holt, 2006).

Ehrenreich, Barbara, *The Hearts of Men — American Dreams and the Flight From Commitment* (Doubleday/Anchor Books, 1983).

Ehrenreich, Barbara, "The Mystery of Misogyny," *The Progressive*, 12/2001.

Eisler, Riane, *Sacred Pleasure* (San Francisco: Harper, 1995).

Eisler, Riane, *The Chalice And The Blade* (San Francisco: Harper & Row, 1987).

Eisner, Robert, *The Road To Daulis: Psychoanalysis, Psychology And Classical Mythology* (Syracuse University Press, 1987).

Eliade, Mircea, *Cosmos and History: The Myth of the Eternal Return* (New York: Harper & Row, 1954).

Eliade, Mircea, *Rites and Symbols of Initiation* (Spring Publications, 1995).

Eller, Cynthia, *The Myth of Patriarchal Prehistory* (Boston: Beacon Press, 2000).

Ellison, Ralph, *Shadow and Act* (New York: Vintage, 1953).

Ellwood, Robert S., *The Sixties Spiritual Awakening: American Religion Moving From Modern To Postmodern* (Rutgers University Press, 1994).

Encyclopedia of Death and Dying (www.deathreference.com).

Euripides, *The Bacchae*, in *Euripides V*, Ed. Grene, David & Richmond Lattimore. Trans. William Arrowsmith (University of Chicago Press, 1968).

Euripides, *Euripides' Bacchae, Greek text and Commentary*, Ed. E. R. Dodds (Oxford: Clarendon Press, 1960).

Euripides, *Euripides: Bacchae*, trans. Paul Woodruff (Indianapolis: Hackett, 1998).

Evans, Arthur, *The God of Ecstasy — Sex Roles and the Madness of Dionysus* (New York: St. Martin's Press, 1988).

Faludi, Susan, *Backlash: The Undeclared War Against American Women* (New York: Crown, 1991).

Faludi, Susan, *Stiffed: The Betrayal of the American Man* (Perennial/Harper Collins, 1999).

Faludi, Susan, *The Terror Dream: Fear And Fantasy In Post-9/11 America* (New York: Henry Holt, 2007).

Farrow, Anne, Joel Lang and Jennifer Frank, *Complicity: How the North Promoted And Profited From Slavery* (Ballantine, 2005).

Feder, Shanti, "The Tower," *Parabola*, Spring, 2002.

Fermor, Patrick L., *Mani — Travels in the Southern Peloponnesus* (Harper, 1960).

Fimrite, Peter, "State Law Threatened by Public's Revulsion to Sex Offenders," *San Francisco Chronicle,* 3/8/04.

Finley, M.I., *The World of Odysseus* (New York: Viking Press, 1967).

Fox, Mathew, *Original Blessing — A primer in Creation Spirituality* (Santa Fe: Bear & Co., 1983).

Frank, Justin A., *Bush On the Couch* (Regan Books, 2004).

Frank, Leonard, *Influencing Minds: A Reader in Quotations* (Feral House, 1995).

Frank, Thomas, *What's the Matter With Kansas? How Conservatives Won the Heart of America* (Metropolitan Books, 2004).

Franklin, H. Bruce, *M.I.A. or Mythmaking In America* (Rutgers University Press, 1993).

Franklin, John Hope, *From Slavery To Freedom — A History of Negro Americans* (New York: Knopf, 1974).

Frazer, James G., *The Golden Bough* (Crown Publications, 1981).

Fredrickson, George M., "America's Original Sin," *New York Review of Books,* 3/25/2004.

Freke, Timothy, and Peter Gandy, *The Jesus Mysteries: Was the "Original Jesus" a Pagan God?* (New York: Three Rivers Press, 1999).

Freud, Sigmund, *Civilization and its Discontents* (London, Hogarth, 1953).

Freud, Sigmund, *New Introductory Lectures On Psychoanalysis* (New York: 1965).

Friedrich, Otto, *Going Crazy — An Inquiry Into Madness In Our Time* (New York: Avon Books, 1975).

Frith, Simon, *Sound Effects — Youth, Leisure, and the Politics of Rock'n'Roll* (New York: Pantheon, 1981).

Galeota, Julia, "Cultural Imperialism: An American Tradition," *The Humanist,* May, 2004).

Gantz, Timothy, *Early Greek Myth: A Guide To Literary And Artistic Sources* (Johns Hopkins University Press, 1993).

Gambino, Richard, *Blood of My Blood: The Dilemma of the Italian-Americans* (Doubleday, 1974).

Garcia-Lorca, Federico, "Imagination, Inspiration, Evasion," *Jubilat,* Issue 7.

Garland, Robert, *The Greek Way Of Death* (Cornell University Press, 1985).

Gatenby, Gavin, "Ninety-three years of bombing the Arabs" (www.brushtail.com.au/july_04_on/bombing_arabs_history.html).

Gatto, John Taylor, "Against School: How Public Education Cripples our Kids, and Why," *Harper's Magazine,* September, 2003.

Gatto, John Taylor, *Dumbing Us Down: The Hidden Curriculum of Compulsory Schooling* (New Society Publications, 1992).

Gatto, John Taylor, "Some Lessons From the Underground History of American Education," in *Everything You Know Is Wrong,* Ed. Russ Kick (New York: Disinformation Company, 2002).

Gellert, Michael, *The Fate of America: An Inquiry Into National Character* (Washington: Brassey's, 2001).

Gernet, Louis, *The Anthropology of Ancient Greece* (1981, London).

Gibson, James W., *Warrior Dreams: Violence And Manhood In Post-Vietnam America* (New York: Hill and Wang, 1994).

Gilligan, Carol, *The Birth of Pleasure* (New York: Knopf, 2002).

Gilmore, David D., *Manhood In The Making: Cultural Concepts Of Masculinity* (Yale University Press, 1990).

Gimbutas, Marija, *The Goddesses and Gods of Old Europe* (University of California Press, 1982).

Gioia, Dana, "Notes Toward a New Bohemia" (www.danagioia.net), 1994.

Gioia, Dana, "Disappearing Ink: Poetry At The End Of Print Culture," *Hudson Review,* Spring, 2003.

Giraud, Rene, *Violence and the Sacred* (Johns Hopkins University Press, 1972).

Gitlin, Todd, *Media Unlimited: How The Torrent Of Images And Sounds Overwhelms Our Lives* (New York: Holt, 2002).

Gladwell, Malcolm, "Big And Bad — How the S.U.V. Ran Over Automotive Safety," *The New Yorker,* 1/12/2004.

Glassner, Barry, *The Culture of Fear* (Basic Books, 1999).

Gorer, Geoffrey, *Death, Grief and Mourning* (Doubleday, 1965).

Gottner-Abendroth, Heide, *The Dancing Goddess: Principles of a Matriarchal Aesthetic* (Boston: Beacon Press, 1991).

Graves, Robert, *The Greek Myths* (London: Folio Society, 1996).

Grene, David and Richmond Lattimore (eds.) *Euripides V– The Complete Greek Tragedies,* trans. William Arrowsmith (University of Chicago Press, 1959).

Greven, Philip, *The Protestant Temperament* (New York: Knopf, 1977).

Grider, Sylvia, "Spontaneous Shrines: A Modern Response To Tragedy And Disaster," *New Directions In Folklore 5,* October, 2001.

Griffin, Susan, *Pornography And Silence* (New York: Harper, 1981).

Griffin, Susan, "To Love the Marigold: The Politics of Imagination," *Whole Earth Review,* Spring, 1996.

Grossman, David, "Evolution of Weaponry" and "Aggression and Violence" (www.killology.com).

Guralnuck, Peter, *Careless Love: The Unmaking of Elvis Presley* (Back Bay Books, 2000).

Guthrie, W. K. C., *The Greeks And Their Gods* (Boston: Beacon Press, 1950).

Gwin, Lucy, "Postcards From the Planet of the Freaks," in Kick, Russ (Ed.), *Everything You Know Is Wrong: The Disinformation Guide to Secrets and Lies* (The Disinformation Company, 2002).

Halberstam, David, *The Fifties* (New York: Villard Books, 1993).

Hall, Nor, "Channel A Muse," *Spring Journal* # 70.

Hall, Nor, *Those Women* (Dallas: Spring Publications, 1988).

Hampden-Turner, Charles, *Maps of the Mind* (New York: Collier, 1981).

Handlin, Oscar, "Science And Technology In Popular Culture," *Daedalus* (1965).

Harrod, James, "Dionysos and the Muses: A Deep Love Libido Myth," *Spring Journal* # 70.

Harrington, Michael, "The Statues of Daedalus," in Quinn, Edward G. and Paul Dolan, (eds.), *The Sense of the Sixties* (The Free Press, 1968).

Harrington, Michael, *The Other America* (MacMillan, 1962).

Harrison, Jane E., *Epilegomena to the Study of Greek Religion* and *Themis* (New York: University Books, 1962).

Harrison, Jane E., *Prolegomena To the Study of Greek Religion* (Princeton University Press, 1992).

Harrison, Robert P., *The Dominion of the Dead* (University of Chicago Press, 2003).

Harrod, James, "Dionysos and the Muses," *Spring Journal* # 70.

Hart, Mickey, *Drumming At The Edge Of Magic* (Harper San Francisco, 1990).

Harvey, Brett, *The Fifties: A Women's Oral History* (IUniverse, 2002).

Hedges, Chris, *War Is A Force That Gives Us Meaning* (New York: Public Affairs, 2002).

Helfand, Judy, "Constructing Whiteness" (www.academic.udayton.edu/race/01race/white11).

Hernton, Calvin, *Sex And Racism in America* (Doubleday/Evergreen, 1966).

Hertsgaard, Mark, *The Eagle's Shadow, Why America Fascinates and Infuriates the World* (New York: Farrar, Straus and Giroux, 2002).

Hesiod, *Theogony*, trans. Dorothea Wender (Penguin, 1973).

Hillman, James, *A Blue Fire, Selected Writings of James Hillman*, ed. Thomas Moore (New York: Harper, 1989).

Hillman, James, *Archetypal Psychology, A Brief Account* (Dallas: Spring Publications, 1983).

Hillman, James, *A Terrible Love Of War* (New York: Penguin, 2004).

Hillman, James, *Dionysos In Jung's Writing*, in *Facing The Gods*, ed. James Hillman (Dallas, Spring Publications, 1980).

Hillman, James, "Ground Zero: A Reading," in Zoja, Luigi and Donald Williams (eds.), *Jungian Reflections On September 11 — A Global Nightmare* (Daimon Verlag, 2002).

Hillman, James, *Healing Fictions* (Dallas: Spring Publication, 1983).

Hillman, James, "Look Out: Three Occasions of Public Excitation," in Slattery, D. P. and L. Corbett, (eds.), *Depth Psychology: Meditations in the Field* (Daimon Verlag, 2000).

Hillman, James, *Loose Ends– Primary Papers in Archetypal Psychology* (Dallas: Spring Publications, 1991).

Hillman, James, *The Myth Of Analysis* (New York: Harper, 1978).

Hillman, James, *The Myth of the Family* (audio tape, Sounds True, 1994).

Hillman, James, *Pink Madness — Or Why Does Aphrodite Drive Us Crazy with Pornography?* (audio tape, Oral Traditions Archives, 1994).

Hillman, James, "The Seduction of Black," *Spring Journal* # 61.

Hillman, James, *The Soul's Code* (New York: Random House, 1996).

Hillman, James, *Suicide And The Soul* (New York: Harper And Row, 1964).

Hillman, James, *The Thought of the Heart and The Soul of the World* (Spring Publications, 1997).

Hillman, James, *Uniform Edition of the Writings of James Hillman* (Spring Publications, 2007).

Hillman, James and Michael Ventura, *We've Had A Hundred Years of Psychotherapy and the World's Getting Worse* (Harper San Francisco, 1992).

Hofstadter, Richard, *Anti-Intellectualism In American Life* (Vintage, 1962).

Hodges, Karen, "Women, Depression and the Soul Image," *Spring Journal* # 65.

Hoffman, Michael, A., *They Were White and They Were Slaves, The Untold History of the Enslavement of Whites in Early America* (Dresden, New York: Wiswell Ruffin House, 1991).

Hogan, James C., *A Commentary on the Complete Greek Tragedies of Aeschylus* (University of Chicago Press, 1984).

Hollis, James, *Tracking the Gods: The Place of Myth in Modern Life* (Toronto: Inner City, 1995).

Homer, *The Iliad*, trans. Robert Fitzgerald (Anchor Doubleday, 1974).

Homer, *The Odyssey*, trans. Robert Fitzgerald (Vintage Classics Edition, 1990).

Hood, Robert E., *Begrimed And Black: Christian Traditions on Blacks and Blackness* (Minneapolis: Fortress Press, 1994).

Hort, Barbara, "The Sacred Story and the Divine Hush," *Spring Journal* # 70.

Hotchner, A.E., *Papa Hemingway* (1966).

Houston, Jean, *A Mythic Life* (San Francisco, Harper 1996).

Houston, Jean, *The Hero And The Goddess* (New York: Ballantine, 1992).

Hughes, Richard T., *Myths America Lives By* (University of Illinois Press, 2003).

Huntington, Richard and Peter Metcalf, *Celebrations of Death — The Anthropology of Mortuary Ritual* (Cambridge University Press, 1985).

Hyde, Lewis, *Trickster Makes This World* (New York: Farrar, Straus and Giroux, 1998).

Jensen, Derrick, *The Culture Of Make Believe* (New York: Context Books, 2002).

Jervis, John, *Transgressing The Modern* (Oxford: Blackwell, 1999).

Jewett, Robert, and John S. Lawrence, *The American Monomyth* (New York: University Press of America, 1988).

Jewett, Robert, and John S. Lawrence, *The Myth of the American Superhero* (Grand Rapids: Eerdmans Publishing, 2002).

Jewett, Robert, and John S. Lawrence, *Captain America and the Crusade Against Evil* (Grand Rapids: Eerdmans Publishing, 2003).

Jezer, Marty, *The Dark Ages — Life In the United States 1945-1960* (Boston: South End Press, 1982).

Johnson, Chalmers, "America's Empire of Bases" (www.TomDispatch.com), 1/15/2004.

Johnson, Robert, *Balancing Heaven and Earth* (Harper Collins, 1998).

Johnson, Robert, *Ecstasy: Understanding The Psychology of Joy* (San Francisco: Harper & Row, 1987).

Jones, Leroi (Amiri Baraka), *Blues People* (New York: William Morrow, 1963).

Jones, Prudence and Nigel Pennick, *A History Of Pagan Europe* (Barnes & Noble, 1995).

Josephs, Allen, *White Wall Of Spain* (University of West Florida Press, 1990).

Josephson, Eric and Mary Josephson (eds.), *Man Alone: Alienation In Modern Society* (Dell, 1962).

Jung, Carl, G., *Collected Works* (Princeton University Press, 1981).

Jung, Carl, *Memories, Dreams, Reflections* (New York: Vintage, 1965).

Kabbani, R., *Europe's Myths of the Orient* (Macmillan, 1986).

Karcher, Steven, "Which Way I Fly is Hell," *Spring Journal # 55*.

Karp, Walter, *The Politics of War* (Moyer Bell), 2003.

Katznelson, Ira, *When Affirmative Action Was White: An Untold History of Racial Inequality in Twentieth-Century America* (Norton, 2005).

Keen, Sam, *Faces of the Enemy* (Harper & Row, 1986).

Kerenyi, Carl, *Dionysus, Archetypal Image of Indestructible Life* (Princeton University Press, 1976).

Kerenyi, Carl, *The Gods Of The Greeks* (New York: Thames & Hudson, 1998).

Kerenyi, Carl, *The Religion of the Greeks and Romans* (New York: Dutton, 1962).

Kick, Russ (ed.), *Everything You Know Is Wrong: The Disinformation Guide to Secrets and Lies* (The Disinformation Company, 2002).

Kinsey, Alfred, et al, *Sexual Behavior in the Human Male* (Philadelphia: Saunders, 1948).

Kipnis, Aaron, "Prisoners of Our Imagination: The Boys Inside the American Gulag," in Slattery, D. P. and L. Corbett, (eds.), *Depth Psychology: Meditations in the Field* (Daimon Verlag, 2000).

Kirsch, Jonathan, *God Against The Gods: The History of the War Between Monotheism and Polytheism* (Viking Compass, 2004).

Kittelson, Mary Lynn (ed.), *The Soul of Popular Culture: Looking at Contemporary Heroes, Myths and Monsters* (Chicago: Open Court, 1987).

Knee, Jonathan A., "Is That Really Legal?" *New York Times*, 5/2/2004.

Knipe, Rita, *The Water of Life, A Jungian Journey Through Hawaiian Myth* (University of Hawaii Press, 1989).

Kornfield, Jack, *A Path With Heart: A Guide Through the Perils of Spiritual Life* (Bantam, 1996).

Kotchemidova, Christina, "From Good Cheer to 'Drive-By Smiling': A Social History of Cheerfulness," *Journal of Social History*, Fall, 2005.

Kovel, Joel, *Red Hunting in the Promised Land: Anticommunism and the Making of America* (Basic Books, 1994).

Kovel, Joel, *White Racism* (New York: Columbia University Press, 1984).

Kramer, Allen and Mary Gomes, "The All-Consuming Self," in Roszack, Theodore, Mary Gomes, Allen Kanner (eds.), *Ecopsychology: Restoring the Earth, Healing the Mind* (San Francisco: Sierra Club Books, 1995).

Kubler-Ross, Elizabeth, *On Death And Dying* (New York: MacMillan, 1969).

Kwon, Heonik, *Ghosts of War in Vietnam* (Cambridge University Press, 2008).

Laing, R.D., *The Politics of Experience* (Pantheon Books, 1967).

Lakoff, George, "Metaphor, Morality, and Politics, Or, Why Conservatives Have Left Liberals in the Dust," *Social Research* (Vol. 62, Summer, 1995).

Lapham, Lewis, "Tentacles of Rage," *Harper's Magazine*, September, 2004.

Larsen, Steven, *The Mythic Imagination* (New York: Bantam, 1990).

Lattimore, Richmond, *The Poetry of Greek Tragedy* (New York: Harper, 1958).

Lembcke, Jerry, *The Spitting Image: Myth, Memory and the Legacy of Vietnam* (New York University Press, 1998).

LeShan, Lawrence, *The Psychology of War* (New York: Helios, 2002).

Lerner, Gerda, *The Creation of Patriarchy* (Oxford University Press, 1986).

Levi, Antonia, "The New American Hero: Made In Japan," in Kittelson, Mary Lynn (ed.), *The Soul of Popular Culture: Looking at Contemporary Heroes, Myths and Monsters* (Chicago: Open Court, 1987).

Lewis, R.W. B., *The American Adam* (University of Chicago Press, 1959).

Lipset, Seymour Martin, *American Exceptionalism* (New York: Norton, 1996).

Lopez-Pedraza, Raphael, *Cultural Anxiety* (Daimon Verlag, 1990).

Lopez-Pedraza, Raphael, *Dionysus In Exile* (Chiron Publications, 2000).

Lorenz, Konrad, *On Aggression* (Bantam, 1966).

Lovelock, James, *Gaia: A New Look At Life On Earth* (Oxford University Press, 1979).

Lubiano, Wahneema, "Black Ladies, Welfare Queens and State Minstrels," in Morrison, Tony, ed, *Race-ing Justice, En-gendering Power: Essays On Anita Hill, Clarence Thomas, and the Construction of Social Reality* (New York: Pantheon, 1992).

Maas, Peter, *Love Thy Neighbor: A Story Of War* (New York: Knopf, 1996).

Macary, Maggie, *Mother Love* (www.headlinemuse.com), May 2002.

MacDonald, J. F., *Television and the Red Menace: The Video Road to Vietnam* (New York: Praeger, 1985).

Mahdi, L. C., N. G. Christopher and Michael Meade (eds.), *Crossroads: The Quest for Contemporary Rites of Passage* (Chicago: Open Court, 1996).

Mahdi, L.C., Steven Foster and Meredith Little, (eds.), *Betwixt And Between: Patterns of Masculine and Feminine Initiation* (Chicago: Open Court, 1987).

Males, Mike, *The Scapegoat Generation* (Common Courage Press, 1996).

Males, Mike, and Kenneth Chew, "The Ages of Fathers in California Adolescent Births, 1993," *American Journal of Public Health,* Vol. 86, # 4, April, 1996.

Mander, Jerry, *Four Arguments For The Elimination Of Television* (New York: Quill, 1978).

Mann, Charles, *1491: New Revelations of the Americas Before Columbus* (Knopf, 2005).

Manning, Richard, "The Oil We Eat," *Harper's Magazine,* Feb. 2004.

March, Jennifer, "Euripides the Misogynist?" in Anton Powell, ed., *Euripides, Women and Sexuality* (RNY: Routledge, 1990).

Marcus, Greil, *Mystery Train, Images of America in Rock'n'Roll Music* (New York: Plume/Penguin, 1997).

Markale, Jean, *The Pagan Mysteries of Halloween* (Inner Traditions, 2000).

Marshall, S. L. A., *Men Against Fire: The Problem of Battle Command* (University of Oklahoma Press, 1978).

May, Rollo, *The Cry For Myth* (New York: Delta Books, 1991).

May, Rollo, *Power And Innocence* (New York: Norton, 1972).

McCoy, Alfred W., *The Politics of Heroin in Southeast Asia* (New York: Harper, 1972).

McElroy, Wendy, "Pornography," in Kick, Russ (Ed.), *Everything You Know Is Wrong: The Disinformation Guide to Secrets and Lies* (The Disinformation Company, 2002).

Meade, Michael, *Holding the Thread of Life* (Mosaic, audio cassette, 2003).

Meade, Michael, *The Water Of Life* (Greenfire Press, 2006).

Meade, Michael, *The World Behind The World: Living At The Ends Of Time* (Greenfire Press, 2008).

Mealer, Bryan, "In the Valley of the Gun," *Harper's Magazine,* May, 2004.

Melton, Ada Pecos, "Indigenous Justice Systems and Tribal Society," *Judicature,* Vol. 79, # 3 (Nov-Dec, 1995).

Metzger, Deena, *Entering The Ghost River: Meditation On The Theory and Practice of Healing* (Hand To Hand, 2002).

Miller, Alice, *The Drama of the Gifted Child* (New York: Basic Books, 1981).

Miller, David L., *The New Polytheism* (Dallas: Spring Publications, 1981).

Miller, Kirby, *Emigrants and Exiles: Ireland and the Irish Exodus to North America* (Oxford University Press, 1985).

Mitford, Jessica, *The American Way of Death Revisited* (New York: Vintage, 1998).

Monbiot, George, "Puritanism of the Rich," *The Guardian,* 11/9/2004.

Moore, Robert, *The Archetype of Initiation,* ed. Max Havlick (Xlibris, 2001).

Moore, Robert, and Douglas Gillette, *King Warrior Magician Lover* (Harper San Francisco, 1990).

Morgan, Robin, *Demon Lover — The Roots of Terrorism* (New York: Washington Square Press, 2001).

Morone, James A., *Hellfire Nation: The Politics of Sin in American History* (Yale University Press, 2003).

Morrison, Tony (ed.), *Race-ing Justice, En-Gendering Power: Essays on Anita Hill, Clarence Thomas, and the Construction of Social reality* (New York: Pantheon, 1992).

Morton, H.V., *A Stranger In Spain* (New York: Dodd, Mead & Co., 1955).

Murdock, Maureen, "Telling Our Stories: Making Meaning from Myth and Memoir," in Slattery, Dennis (ed.), *Depth Psychology: Meditations in the Field* (Daimon, 2001).

Muwakkil, Salim, "Reparations Suit Leaves Opening," *In These Times*, 3/1/04, p. 13.

Nash, Gary B., *Red, White & Black: The Peoples of Early North America* (Prentice Hall, 2000).

Needleman, Jacob, *The American Soul* (New York: Jeremy Tarcher, 2002).

Needleman, Jacob, "Two Dreams of America" (Fetzer Institute, *Essays on Deepening the American Dream, #1,* Winter, 2003).

Nef, John U., *War and Human Progress, an Essay on the Rise of Industrial Civilization* (New York: Norton, 1963).

Nelson, Jack, Carter Center Lecture, 9/23/98, (www.emory.edu).

Nilsson, Martin, *Greek Folk Religion* (University of Pennsylvania Press, 1972).

Nisbet, Robert, *History of the Idea of Progress* (New York: Basic Books, 1980).

Nisker, Wes, *The Big Bang, the Buddha and the Baby Boom* (San Francisco: Harper, 2003).

Nixon, Greg, "American Education: Horror of Experience," *Spring Journal* # 62.

Nixon, Greg, "Education as Mythic Image," *Spring Journal* # 69.

Noble, David, *Beyond The Promised Land: The Movement And The Myth* (Toronto: Between The Lines, 2005).

Noble, Vickie, *Motherpeace — A Way to the Goddess through Myth, Art, and Tarot* (New York: Harper & Roe, 1983).

Orloff, Alexander, *Carnival: Myth and Cult* (Worgl, Austria, Perlinger, 1981).

Ortega Y Gasset, Jose, *Meditaciones del Quijote* (Madrid, 1957).

Osherson, Samuel, *Finding Our Fathers* (New York: Fawcett Columbine, 1987).

Otto, Walter, *Dionysus — Myth and Cult* (University of Indiana Press, 1965).

Pagels, Elaine, *Beyond Belief: The Secret Gospel of Thomas* (New York: Random House, 2003).

Paglia, Camille, "Cults and Cosmic Consciousness: Religious Vision in the American 1960s," (www.bu.edu/arion/paglia_cults).

Paglia, Camille, *Sex, Art and American Culture* (New York: Vintage, 1992).

Paglia, Camille, *Vamps And Tramps: New Essays* (New York: Vintage, 1994).

Palast, Greg, *The Best Democracy Money Can Buy* (New York: Penguin, 2003).

Paris, Ginette, *Pagan Grace: Dionysos, Hermes, and Goddess Memory in Daily Life* (Dallas: Spring Publications, 1990).

Parke, H. W., *Festivals of the Athenians* (Cornell University Press, 1977).

Patterson, Orlando, *Rituals of Blood: Consequences of Slavery in Two American Centuries* (Washington: Civitas Counterpoint, 1998).

Pausanias, *Guide To Greece*, ed. Peter Levi (Penguin, 1984).

Pearce, Diana, "The Feminization of Poverty: Women, Work and Welfare," *Urban and Social Change Review*, 2/78.

Pearce, Joseph Chilton, *Evolution's End: Claiming The Potential Of Our Intelligence* (Harper San Francisco, 1992).

Perera, Sylvia B., *The Scapegoat Complex: Toward A Mythology Of Shadow And Guilt* (Inner City Books, 1986).

Perry, John W., *The Far Side of Madness* (Prentice-Hall, 1974).

Perry, John W., *Lord of the Four Quarters* (New York: Paulist Press, 1991).

Persico, Joseph, *Eleventh Month, Eleventh Day, Eleventh Hour — Armistice Day, 1918* (New York: Random House, 2004).

Persig, Robert, *Zen and the Art of Motorcycle Maintenance* (New York: Bantam, 1977).

Peters, Edward, *Inquisition* (University of California Press, 1989).

Phinney, Kevin, *Souled America: How Black Music Transformed White Culture* (New York: Billboard Books, 2005).

Pinkola-Estes, Clarissa, "Elvis Presley: Fama, and the *Cultus* of the Dying God," in Mary Lynn Kittelson, ed., *The Soul Of Popular Culture* (Chicago, Open Court, 1998).

Pinkola-Estes, Clarissa, *Women Who Run With The Wolves* (New York: Ballantine, 1992).

Plato, *The Collected Dialogues*, ed. Hamilton & Cairns (Bollingen, 1961).

Pollan, Michael, *The Botany of Desire* (New York: Random House, 2001).

Prechtel, Martin, *Long Life, Honey in the Heart* (New York: Tarcher/Putnam, 1999).

Project for a New American Century, *Rebuilding America's Defenses*, 9/2000.

Prose, Francine, "Voting Democracy Off The Island," *Harper's Magazine,* March, 2004.

Quinn, Edward G. and Paul Dolan, (eds.), *The Sense of the Sixties* (The Free Press, 1968).

Rabinowitz, N. S. and A. Richlin, (eds.), *Feminist Theory and the Classics* (New York: Routledge, 1993).

Radway, J., *Reading The Romance* (Verso, 1987).

Rai, Milan, *Chomsky's Politics* (London: Verso, 1995).

Raphael, Ray, *The Men From the Boys — Rites of Passage in Male America* (University of Nebraska Press, 1988).

Rawls, Walton (ed.), *Offerings At The Wall: Artifacts From The Vietnam Veterans Memorial Collection* (Atlanta: Turner Publishing, 1995).

Ray, Paul H., and Sherry Ruth Anderson, *The Cultural Creatives: How Fifty Million People Are Changing The World* (New York: Harmony Books, 2000).

Rehm, Rush, *Marriage to Death: The Conflation of Wedding and Funeral Rituals in Greek Tragedy* (Princeton University Press, 1994).

Reis, Patricia, "Mnemosyne's Well of Remembrance," *Spring Journal* # 70.

Rekers, George, M.D., "Impact of Father Absence on Children's Sexual Development," *In Focus,* (Family Research Council), 1993.

Rich, Norman, *Hitler's War Aims: Ideology, the National State, and the Course of Expansion* (New York: Norton, 1973).

Richlin, Amy, "The Ethnographer's Dilemma," in Rabinowitz, N. S. and A. Richlin, (eds.), *Feminist Theory and the Classics* (New York: Routledge, 1993).

Rifkin, Jeremy, *The European Dream* (Penguin, 2004).

Rigoglioso, Marguerite, "Awakening to the Goddess," *New Age Journal,* May/June, 1997.

Riley, Tim, *Fever: How Rock 'n' Roll Transformed Gender In America* (New York: St. Martin's Press, 2004).

Robbins, Alexandra, *Secrets of the Tomb: Skull & Bones, The Ivy League and the Hidden Paths of Power* (Boston: Back Bay Books, 2002).

Robertson, James O., *American Myth American Reality* (New York: Hill & Wang, 1980).

Robinson, Daniel, "The City and Civic Life," Part 11 of *Greek Legacy: Classical Origins of the Modern Word* (audio tape, The Teaching Company, 1998).

Rodriguez, Luis, *Hearts And Hands: Creating Community In Violent Times* (New York: Seven Stories Press, 2001).

Rosenfeld, Richard N., "What Democracy?" *Harper's Magazine,* May 2004.

Rosenmeyer, Thomas, *Tragedy and Religion: The Bacchae,* in Segal, Erich (ed.), *Greek Tragedy: Modern Essays in Criticism* (New York: Harper & Row, 1983).

Roszack, Theodore, Mary Gomes, Allen Kanner (eds.), *Ecopsychology: Restoring the Earth, Healing the Mind* (San Francisco: Sierra Club Books, 1995).

Rouget, Gilbert, *Music And Trance* (University of Chicago Press, 1985).

Romanyshyn, Robert, "The Orphic Roots of Jung's Psychology," *Spring Journal* # 71.

Rowlandson, Mary. *The Sovereignty and Goodness of God...a Narrative of the Captivity and Restauration* (1682).

Ruiz, Teofilo, *The Terror of History* (audiotape, The Teaching Company, 1998).

Rushkoff, Douglas, *The Merchants of Cool,* PBS TV documentary, transcript excerpted in *Whole Earth Review* (Summer, 2002).

Russell, J.B., *The Prince of Darkness* (Cornell University Press, 1992).

Samuels, Andrew, *The Plural Psyche: Personality, Morality and the Father* (London: Routledge, 1989).

Sardar, Ziauddin and Merryl Wyn Davies, *Why Do People Hate America?* (New York: Disinformation Press, 2002).

Savage, Judith, "Ain't No Angel: AIDS and the Abandoned Soul," in Kittelson, Mary Lynn (ed.), *The Soul of Popular Culture: Looking at Contemporary Heroes, Myths and Monsters* (Chicago: Open Court, 1987).

Scheuer, Jeffrey, *The Sound Bite Society: How Television Helps The Right And Hurts The Left* (New York: Routledge, 2001).

Schlesier, Renate, "Maenads As Tragic Models," in Carpenter, T.H. and C. A. Faraone (eds.), *Masks Of Dionysus* (Cornell University Press, 1993).

Schulte Nordholt, Jan Willem, *The Myth of the West: America as the Last Empire* (Grand Rapids: Eerdmans Publishing, 1995).

Schwartz, Regina, *The Curse of Cain: The Violent Legacy of Monotheism* (University of Chicago Press, 1997).

Seaford, Richard, "Dionysus as Destroyer of the Household," in Carpenter, T.H. and C. A. Faraone (eds.), *Masks Of Dionysus* (Cornell University Press, 1993).

Segal, Charles, *Dionysiac Poetics and Euripides' Bacchae* (Princeton University Press, 1997).

Segal, Charles, *Interpreting Greek Tragedy* (Cornell University Press, 1986).

Segal, Erich (ed.), *Greek Tragedy: Modern Essays in Criticism* (New York: Harper & Row, 1983).

Segal, Robert A., *Joseph Campbell — An Introduction* (New York: Penguin, 1990).

Sellers, James, *The South and Christian Ethics* (New York: Association Press, 1962).

Simpson, Colin, *The Lusitania* (Little, Brown, 1973).

Sharman-Burke, Juliet, and Liz Greene, *The Mythic Tarot* (New York: Simon &Shuster, 1986).

Shepard, Paul, *Nature And Madness* (San Francisco: Sierra Club Books, 1982).

Shay, Jonathan, *Achilles In Vietnam* (New York: Simon & Shuster, 1995).

Shay, Jonathan, *Odysseus In America* (New York: Scribner, 2002).

Shlain, Leonard, *The Alphabet Versus The Goddess* (Penguin, 1998).

Shohat, Ella, "Gender and the Culture of Empire: Towards a Feminist Ethnography of the Cinema," *Quarterly Review of Film and Video* (1991), 13.

Simon, Bennett, *Tragic Drama And The Family* (Yale University Press, 1988).

Skal, David, *Death Makes A Holiday* (New York: Bloomsbury, 2002).

Slater, Phillip, *The Glory of Hera* (Boston: Beacon Press, 1968).

Slater, Phillip, "The Greek Family in History and Myth," *Arethusa*, Vol. 7, 1974.

Slater, Phillip, *The Pursuit of Loneliness: American Culture At The Breaking Point* (Boston: Beacon Press 1972).

Slattery, Dennis (Ed.), *Depth Psychology: Meditations in the Field* (Daimon, 2001).

Slifer, Dennis and James Duffield, *Kokopelli: Fluteplayer Images in Rock Art* (Santa Fe: Ancient City Press, 1994).

Slotkin, Richard, *Gunfighter Nation: The Myth of the Frontier in 20ʰ-Century America* (Harper, 1992).

Slotkin, Richard, *Regeneration Through Violence: The Mythology of the American Frontier,1600-1860* (Wesleyan University Press, 1973).

Slotkin, Richard, *The Fatal Environment: The Myth Of The Frontier In The Age Of Industrialization, 1800-1890* (University of Oklahoma Press, 1985).

Slouka, Mark, "A Year Later," *Harper's Magazine*, September, 2002.

Smith, Dinitia, "Demonizing Fat in the War on Weight," *New York Times*, 5/1/2004.

Smith, Henry Nash, *Virgin Land: The American West as Symbol and Myth* (New York: Random House, 1950).

Smith, Huston, *Cleansing The Doors Of Perception* (New York: Tarcher/Putnam, 2000).

Smith, Page, quoted by Bill Moyers, 6/04/03, "This is your story" (www.commondreams.org).

Smith, Sam, "Why do we have a war on drugs, anyway?" (www.progressivereview.com).

Solomon, Alisa, "War At The Door," *Village Voice*, 2/21/02.

Somé, Malidoma, *The Healing Wisdom Of Africa* (New York: Tarcher/Putnam, 1998).

Somé, Malidoma, "Rites of Passage," *In Context* (Winter, 1993).

Somé, Malidoma, *Ritual: Power, Healing and Community* (Portland: Swan Raven & Co., 1993).

Somé, Sobonfu, (www.sononfu.com).

Sontag, Susan, "The Imagination of Disaster," in *Against Interpretation* (New York: Picador, 1966).

Sontag, Susan, *Illness as Metaphor and AIDS and its Metaphors* (New York: Doubleday, 1989).

Sophocles, *The Complete Plays of Sophocles*, ed. Moses Hadad (Bantam, 1967).

Spitzer, Anais, "In the Mirror of Myth," *Spring Journal # 67*.

Stanford, W.B., *Greek Tragedy and the Emotions* (London: Routledge, 1983).

Stannard, David, *American Holocaust* (Oxford University Press, 1992).

Stark, Rodney, *The Rise of Christianity* (Harper San Francisco, 1997).

Stein, Murray, *Feminine Spirit and Dionysus* (audiotape, Jung Center, San Francisco).

Stein, Murray, *In Midlife, A Jungian Perspective* (Dallas: Spring Publications, 1983).

Stephenson, Carl, *Mediaeval Feudalism* (Cornell University Press, 1942).

Stephenson, John S., *Death, Grief, and Mourning* (New York: The Free Press, 1985).

Stevens, Anthony, *On Jung*, (London: Penguin, 1990).

Stillman, Peter, *Introduction To Myth* (Boynton/Cook Publications, 1985).

Stinnett, Robert, *Day of Deceit* (Free Press, 1999).

Stirnimann, Victor-Pierre, "The Terror and the Temple," in Zoja, Luigi and Donald Williams (eds.), *Jungian Reflections On September 11 — A Global Nightmare* (Daimon Verlag, 2002).

Stone, I. F., *The Hidden History of the Korean War* (Little, Brown, 1988).

Storace, Patricia, *Dinner With Persephone, Travels In Greece* (New York: Vintage, 1996).

Strausbaugh, John, *E: Reflections on the Birth of the Elvis Faith* (New York: Blast Books, 1999).

Stroud, Joanne H., ed., *The Olympians — Ancient Deities as Archetypes* (New York: Continuum, 1996).

Sturken, Marita: *Tangled Memories: The Vietnam War, The AIDS Epidemic, And The Politics Of Remembering* (University of California Press, 1997).

Tacey, David, "Spirituality and the Prevention of Suicide," paper presented at 10th Annual Suicide Prevention Australia national conference, Brisbane, June, 2003.

Tarnas, Richard, *The Passion of the Western Mind: Understanding the Ideas That Have Shaped Our World View* (New York: Ballantine Books, 1991).

Tarrant, John, *The Light Inside The Dark: Zen, Soul and the Spiritual Life* (Harper, 1998).

Tate, Greg, *Everything But The Burden: What White People Are Taking From Black Culture* (New York: Harlem Moon, 2003).

Tawney, R. H., *Religion and the Rise of Capitalism* (Transaction Publishers, 1998).

Thayer, E. L., *Casey At The Bat, a Centennial Edition*, Afterword by Donald Hall (Boston: Godine, 1988).

Thomson, George, *Aeschylus And Athens* (New York: Grosset & Dunlap, 1968).

Tick, Edward, *War And The Soul: Healing Our Nation's Veterans From Post-Traumatic Stress Disorder* (Quest Books, 2005).

Tiger, Lionel, *Men In Groups* (New York: Vintage, 1970).

Toews, Gene, "Multiple Personality Disorder: Pathologies of the Soul" (www.headlinemuse.com).

Toth, Jennifer, *The Mole People, Life In the Tunnels beneath New York City* (Chicago Review Press, 1995).

Turner, Fred, *Echoes of Combat: Trauma, Memory and the Vietnam War* (University of Minnesota Press, 1996).

Turner, Victor, *The Ritual Process* (Cornell University Press, 1969).

Turse, Nick, "A My Lai a Month," *The Nation*, 12/01/08.

Tutu, Desmond, *No Future Without Forgiveness* (New York: Doubleday, 1999).

Tuveson, Ernest Lee, *Redeemer Nation: The Idea of America's Millennial Role* (University of Chicago Press, 1980).

Ulanov, Ann Belford, "Religion's Role in the Psychology of Terrorism," in Zoja, Luigi and Donald Williams (eds.), *Jungian Reflections On September 11 — A Global Nightmare* (Daimon Verlag, 2002).

U.S. Commission on Child and Family Welfare, Report, 1996.

van der Dannen, Johan, *The Origin of War: The Evolution of a Male-coalitional Reproductive Strategy* (http://rint.rechten.rug.nl/rth/dennen/dennen6.htm).

Ventura, Michael, "The Age of Endarkenment," *Whole Earth Review*, Winter, 1989.

Ventura, Michael, *Letters at Three A.M.: Reports On Endarkenment* (Dallas: Spring Publications, 1993).

Ventura, Michael, *Shadow Dancing In The USA,* (New York: Tarcher, 1985).

Vernant, Jean-Pierre, *Mortals And Immortals* (Princeton University Press, 1991).

Vernant, Jean-Pierre, *The Universe, The Gods, And Men* (Harper Collins, 2002).

Versnel, H. S., *Inconsistencies In Greek And Roman Religion I: Ter Unus* (Leiden, 1990).

"Village of Reconciliation," (audiotape, Oral Traditions Archives, 1996).

Viorst, Milton, *Fire in the Streets — America in the 1960s* (New York: Simon & Schuster, 1979).

von Franz, Marie-Louise, *Projection and Recollection in Jungian Psychology* (Chicago: Open Court, 1987).

von Franz, Marie-Louise, *The Psychological Meaning of Redemption Motifs in Fairy Tales* (Toronto: Inner City Books, 1980).

Wade, W.C., *The Fiery Cross: The Ku Klux Klan in America* (New York: Simon & Schuster, 1987).

Waite, Arthur E., *The Pictorial Key To The Tarot,* (Blauvelt, NY: Rudolf Steiner Publications, 1971).

Wald, Johanna, *The Failure of Zero Tolerance* (www.salon.com), 8/29/2001.

Waller, George (ed.), *Puritanism In Early America* (London: Heath & Co., 1973).

Walzer, Michael L., *Revolution of the Saints* (Harvard University Press, 1965).

Wasson, R. Gordon, Carl Ruck and Albert Hofmann, *The Road to Eleusis* (New York: Harcourt Brace Jovanovich, 1978).

Wasson, R. Gordon, *SOMA, Divine Mushroom of Immortality* (New York: Harcourt Brace Jovanovich, 1968).

Watkins, Mary, "Seeding Liberation," in Slattery, Dennis (Ed.), *Depth Psychology: Meditations in the Field* (Daimon, 2001).

Watts, Alan, *The Two Hands of God* (Collier Books, 1969).

Weber, Max, *The Protestant Ethic and the Spirit of Capitalism* (New York: Charles Scribner, 1958).

Weiner, Bernard, *Boy Into Man: A Father's Guide To Initiation Of Teenage Sons* (Transformation Press, 1992).

Weintraub, Stanley, *Silent Night — The Story of the World War I Christmas Truce* (New York: Penguin, 2001).

Weisenburger, Steven, *Modern Media* (New York: Hill and Wang, 1998).

West, Cornell, *Democracy Matters* (Penguin, 2004).

West, Cornell, "Progressive Politics in these times: From Visions to Actions" (audio CD, KPFA Radio, Berkeley, 11/15/2001).

Whyte, William H., *The Organization Man* (Anchor, 1957).

Wigglesworth, Michael, "God's Controversy with New England," *Proceedings of the Massachusetts Historical Society,* XII (1871-1873).

Willis, Ellen, *Beginning to See the Light: Sex, Hope And Rock-And-Roll* (University Press of New England, 1992).

Wills, Garry, *Reagan's America: Innocents At Home* (Garden City: Doubleday, 1987).

Wilmington, Michael, review of the film "Mystic River," *Chicago Tribune,* 12/07/03.

Wilson, James, *The Earth Shall Weep: A History of Native America* (Atlantic Monthly Press, 1998).

Winkler, John J. and Froma Zeitlin (eds.), *Nothing To Do With Dionysos? Athenian Drama In Its Social Context* (Princeton University Press, 1990).

Winkler, John J., "The Ephebe's Song," in Winkler, John J. and Froma Zeitlin (eds.), *Nothing To Do With Dionysos? Athenian Drama In Its Social Context* (Princeton University Press, 1990).

Wise, Tim, *Between Barack And A Hard Place: Racism And White Denial In The Age Of Obama* (San Francisco: City Lights Books, 2009).

Wise, Tim, *White Like Me: Reflections on Race from a Privileged Son* (Soft Skull Press, 2005).

Woodman, Marion, *The Owl Was a Baker's Daughter: Obesity, Anorexia Nervosa and the Repressed Feminine* (Toronto: Inner City Books, 1980).

Worldwatch Institute, "Illegal Drug Harvests Remain High," 7/24/03 (www.worldwatch.org).

Yarnell, Judith, *Transformations of Circe, The History of an Enchantress* (University of Chicago Press, 1994).

Yates, Brock, *Outlaw Machine* (Boston: Little, Brown, 1999).

Zeitlin, Froma, "Playing the Other," in Winkler, John J. and Froma Zeitlin (eds.), *Nothing To Do With Dionysos? Athenian Drama In Its Social Context* (Princeton University Press, 1990).

Zeitlin, Froma, "Staging Dionysus between Thebes and Athens," in Carpenter, T.H. and C. A. Faraone (eds.), *Masks Of Dionysus* (Cornell University Press, 1993).

Zerzan, John, *Running On Emptiness — The Pathology of Civilization* (Los Angeles: Feral House, 2002).

Zigler, E.F., and M. Frank (eds.), *The Parental Leave Crisis* (Yale University Press, 1988).

Zimmer, Heinrich, *The King & The Corpse* (Princeton: Bollingen, 1948).

Zinn, Howard, *A People's History of the United States* (New York: Harper, 2003).

Zoja, Luigi, *Drugs, Addiction and Initiation — The Modern Search For Ritual* (Daimon Verlag, 2000).

Zoja, Luigi and Donald Williams (eds.), *Jungian Reflections On September 11 — A Global Nightmare* (Daimon Verlag, 2002).

Zoja, Luigi, "September 11th: Transatlantic Reflections," in Zoja, Luigi and Donald Williams (eds.), *Jungian Reflections On September 11 — A Global Nightmare* (Daimon Verlag, 2002).

Zweig, Bella, "The Primal Mind: Using Native American Models for the Study of Women in Ancient Greece," in Rabinowitz, N. S. and A. Richlin, (eds.), *Feminist Theory and the Classics* (New York: Routledge, 1993).

INDEX

Barry Spector writes about American history and politics from the perspectives of myth, indigenous traditions and archetypal psychology. He is a regular contributor to *Jung Journal: Culture & Psyche* and the online journal *Mythic Passages* (www.mythicjourneys.org/guest_spector.html). Many of his essays can be found on his website: www.barryandmayaspector.com

CPSIA information can be obtained at www.ICGtesting.com
Printed in the USA
LVOW041659101111

254414LV00001B/147/P